Privacy and Data Protection Law in Italy

Privacy and Data Protection Law in Italy

Paolo Balboni

This book was originally published as a monograph in the International Encyclopaedia of Laws/Privacy and Technology Law.

Founding Editor: Roger Blanpain
General Editor: Frank Hendrickx
Volume Editors: Jos Dumortier, Pieter Gryffroy, Ruben Roex & Yung Shin Van Der Sype

Wolters Kluwer

Published by:
Kluwer Law International B.V.
PO Box 316
2400 AH Alphen aan den Rijn
The Netherlands
E-mail: lrs-sales@wolterskluwer.com
Website: www.wolterskluwer.com/en/solutions/kluwerlawinternational

Sold and distributed by:
Wolters Kluwer Legal & Regulatory U.S.
920 Links Avenue
Landisville, PA 17538
United States of America
E-mail: customer.service@wolterskluwer.com

ISBN 978-94-035-0249-6

e-Book: ISBN 978-94-035-0259-5
web-PDF: ISBN 978-94-035-0269-4

The Author

Paolo Balboni (PhD) is Professor of Privacy, Cybersecurity, and IT Contract Law at the European Centre on Privacy and Cybersecurity (ECPC) within the Maastricht University Faculty of Law. His main research focuses are artificial intelligence, cybersecurity, data management/sharing, ESG, and data protection as a corporate social responsibility, which together can be used to help organizations responsibly further their economic targets and, at the same time, positively contribute to the development of a fair data-centric society.

He is a qualified lawyer specialized in ICT, Privacy & Cybersecurity and admitted to the Milan Bar and registered with the Amsterdam Bar. He is a founding partner of ICT Legal Consulting (ICTLC), an international law firm, and ICT Cyber Consulting, a company specialized in information/data security. Prof. Dr Balboni is a recommended lawyer ranked by *The Legal 500* EMEA 2023 in the areas of Data Privacy and Data Protection and Industry Focus: TMT. He is the Chairman of the European Patent Office (EPO) Data Protection Board, Member of the EUMETSAT Data Protection Supervisory Authority, Member of the Europrivacy Board of Experts, Member of the European Commission's Expert Group on B2B data sharing and cloud computing contracts, and Member of the Cloud Security Alliance's AI Safety Expert Group. Prof. Dr Balboni furthermore advises governments on national matters concerning cybersecurity and privacy, and in 2018, he drafted the national Surinamese Privacy and Data Protection Law.

He is the author of the books *Trustmarks in E-Commerce: The Value of Web Seals and the Liability of their Providers* and *Data Protection as a Corporate Social Responsibility* and numerous publications on data protection by design, cloud computing, big data and smart analytics, internet of things, Law Enforcement Agencies' access to data, intellectual property, contractual and data protection aspects of blockchain technology, and the relationship between privacy/data protection and the use of information in order to fight online-terrorist propaganda, recruitment, and radicalization.

The Author

Table of Contents

Table of Contents

List of Abbreviations

AgCM	*Autorità garante per la Concorrenza e del Mercato* (Italian Competition Authority)
AgCom	*Autorità per le Garanzie nelle Comunicazioni* (Italian Authority for Telecommunications)
AgID	*Agenzia per l'Italia Digitale* (Agency for Digital Italy)
CAD	*Codice dell'Amministrazione Digitale* (Digital Administration Code)
CJEU	Court of Justice of the European Union
D.L.	*Decreto Legge* (Law Decree)
D.Lgs.	*Decreto Legislativo* (Legislative Decree)
D.M.	*Decreto Ministeriale* (Ministerial Decree)
D.P.C.M.	*Decreto del Presidente del Consiglio dei Ministri* (Decree of the President of the Council of Ministers)
D.P.R.	*Decreto del Presidente della Repubblica* (Decree of the President of the Republic)
ECHR	European Convention on Human Rights
ECtHR	European Court of Human Rights
GdF	*Guardia di Finanza* (Financial Police)
GDPR	General Data Protection Regulation
GPDP	*Garante per la Protezione dei dati personali* (Italian Data Protection Authority)
ICT	Information Communication Technology
MiSE	*Ministero dello Sviluppo Economico* (Ministry of Economic Development)
R.D.	*Regio Decreto* (Royal Decree)

List of Abbreviations

Preface

As the editor and coordinator of this encyclopaedia, it is my purview to provide an overview of the Italian data protection landscape so as to set the stage for the remainder of this work.

The Italian Data Protection Authority (‘*Garante per la Protezione dei dati personali*’, hereinafter ‘GPDP’) is one of Europe’s most active authorities. More precisely, Italy is collocated within the top five enforcers of the General Data Protection Regulation (GDPR) both in terms of the economic impact of the sanctions issued as well as with respect to the *number* of sanctions issued as of October 2023. In descending order, the countries with the highest EUR amount of sanctions under the GDPR are: Ireland (over EUR 2.85 billion – twenty-seven fines), Luxembourg (over EUR 746 million – thirty-one fines), France (over EUR 338 million – thirty-seven fines), Italy (over EUR 134 million – three hundred fines), and the United Kingdom (over EUR 75 million – thirteen fines).[1] It is interesting to note that the number of sanctions issued by an authority does not necessarily correspond to such sanctions being particularly impactful in terms of economic (EUR) amounts, yet both figures examined together provide relevant information for understanding the enforcement landscape. In terms of the number of sanctions issued, Spain is the most active supervisory authority, having issued over 740 fines; the GPDP is the second most active authority, having issued at least 300 fines to date; Germany is the third most active country in data protection enforcement with its authorities having issued 163 fines; Romania is in fourth place with 153 fines; and Hungary is the fifth most active supervisory authority with 68 fines having been issued.

The message derived from the aforementioned numbers is clear: the GPDP is an extremely active authority in terms of issuing sanctions, making it increasingly prominent as a ‘high-risk’ country when it comes to data protection compliance and the risk of a sanction being imposed, which may be issued for a relatively high amount. Additionally, Spain, Germany, Romania, and Hungary are high-risk countries when it comes to regular data processing activities, given the propensity of the authorities to issue sanctions for infringements of data protection law. In contrast, Ireland and Luxembourg issue few sanctions but of extremely high amounts, also suggesting that they are high-risk due to the economic amount of the sanctions issued to date.

---

1. The ICT Legal Consulting Research Team keeps track of all European enforcement actions with respect to the GDPR.

In addition to being a leader in GDPR enforcement in general terms, the GPDP is taking a strong stance on new technologies such as generative Artificial Intelligence (AI), the protection of children, and transparency, being one of the first authorities to sanction the use of dark patterns.[2] This encyclopaedia takes into account not only Italian law on the matter but also relevant decisions issued by the GPDP for completeness.

It must not be taken for granted that the GPDP's actions on specific matters – such as enforcement with respect to AI – demonstrate that it is truly setting the stage for actions with respect to other authorities. For example, in spring 2023, the GPDP imposed an immediate temporary limitation on ChatGPT, forbidding OpenAI from processing the data of Italian users. The ban came about due to several relevant GDPR violations. Namely, the GPDP identified a lack of information provided to users and those whose data were collected for the training of the AI system, a lack of a legal basis for the collection and processing of training data, and the fact that answers provided by ChatGPT in relation to natural persons often do not correspond to the truth (hence violating the principle of accuracy).

The ChatGPT case also highlights the GPDP's attention to data processing in relation to children. Indeed, the authority also raised concerns with respect to age verification. More precisely, the GPDP questioned if the output of the platform led to children being served responses which are inappropriate for their age and level of awareness, even if the service is allegedly targeted to users above the age of thirteen, according to OpenAI's very own terms of service.

Similarly, the GPDP led the call for a strong coordinated action with respect to TikTok with the aim of improving the protection of children. The GPDP had found issues with respect to age verification, transparency, and default data protection settings, an action which pushed the social media giant to improve its data protection posture, especially with respect to children.[3]

It should also be noted that in recent years, the GPDP has demonstrated what may be seen as a highly collaborative approach with market operators. Indeed, it has promoted, e.g., the 'State of Privacy' conference, in which it actively promotes dialogue with relevant public and private sector stakeholders with the aim of engaging and discussing issues related to data processing and new technologies.

The GPDP has also recently made attempts to popularize the notion of privacy and make it fun. This is demonstrated in the example of 'Easy privacy information via icons? Yes, you can!'[4] contest organized by the authority – I am honoured to share the icons developed by myself, Kate Francis, and the other members of the Icon Working Group within the Maastricht University Data Protection as a Corporate Social Responsibility research project carried out at the European Centre on

2. *See* Cristiana Santos and Arianna Rossi, *The emergence of dark patterns as a legal concept in case law*, Internet Policy Review, 31.7.2023, https://policyreview.info/articles/news/emergence-of-dark-patterns-as-a-legal-concept.
3. *See* Paolo Balboni, 'Safer Internet Day: The Tale of TikTok under the Spotlight of the Italian DPA' [Personal Blog], (9.2.2021), https://www.paolobalboni.eu/index.php/2021/02/09/safer-internet-day-the-tale-of-tiktok-under-the-spotlight-of-the-italian-dpa/.
4. *See* Maastricht European Centre on Privacy and Cybersecurity – ECPC Data Protection Icons, https://www.garanteprivacy.it/web/guest/home/docweb/-/docweb-display/docweb/9727446.

Privacy, and Cybersecurity was among the winners of the contest and our icons can be used freely by any organization under a CC-BY licence – *see* Figure 1.

Figure 1 Privacy Icons

Source – Maastricht European Centre on Privacy and Cybersecurity.

A member of the GPDP, Mr Guido Scorza, has furthermore demonstrated a strong willingness to make 'Privacy Pop' – to genuinely make privacy something fun, popular, and accessible to the general public. His participation in the 2023 Privacy Symposium in Venice plays a testament to this celebratory ascertain.

This editorial project concerning Privacy and Data Protection: Italy was edited with the contributions of several scholars and professionals, as well as the editing, overview and specific contributions of Professor Paolo Balboni. In particular:

Davide Baldini not only drafted a significant number of chapters but also played a fundamental role in assisting me in the relevant editing of the contributions made by other authors. Davide drafted Chapter 3, 'The Information and Communications Technology Market', ('The Italian ICT Market in General', 'The Level of Digitalization of Italian Enterprises', and 'Investments in ICTs'); Chapter 4, 'E-Government' ('The Digital Administration Code and Other Relevant Legislative Acts', 'Digital Citizenship, Identity and Online Public Services', and 'The Telematic Civil Process ("PCT")'; Part I: Privacy protection in Italy, Chapter 1, 'Privacy protection in the Constitution', ('The Italian Constitution: A Brief Overview', 'The Right to Privacy and Personal Data Protection within the Italian Constitution'; Chapter 3, 'Privacy in electronic communications (national transposition of the e-Privacy Directive)', ('Systematic Collocation within the Personal Data Protection Code', 'Scope of Application and Relevant Definitions', 'Cookie Law', 'Processing of Traffic Data', 'Unsolicited Communications and Processing of Personal Data within Public Directories (referral)', 'Itemised Billing', 'Calling Line Identification Requirements and Exceptions for Nuisance and Emergency Calls', 'Location Data Other than Traffic Data', and 'Automatic Call Forwarding'); Part III on General Principles, Chapter 2, 'Legal grounds' ('Introduction', 'Consent for Marketing Activities', 'Consent for the Use of Cookies and Other Tracking Technologies', 'Validity of Consent in Relation to the Offer of Information Society Services Directly to a Child', and 'Processing for Compliance with a Legal Obligation or for the Performance of a Task Carried Out in the Public Interest or in the Exercise of Official Authority'); Part VII, Chapter 4, 'Transfers for reasons of public interest'. Together with Isabella Oldani, Davide Baldini drafted Part IX on Specific processing situations, Chapter 1, 'Processing for journalistic purposes and academic, artistic or literary expression', ('The Constitutional Protection of Journalistic, Academic, Artistic and Literary Activities', 'Derogations to some Provisions of the Personal Data Protection Code', 'Other Italian Law Provisions which are Relevant to Processing Operations Carried Out for Journalistic Purposes', 'Deontological Rules Relating to the Processing of Personal Data in the Exercise of the Journalistic Activity', 'GPDP Decisions on Processing Operations Carried Out in the Context of Journalistic Activities', 'GPDP Decisions on the Dissemination of Personal Data on Social Networks', 'GPDP Decisions and Recommendations on the Dissemination of Personal Data in relation to the Covid-19 Outbreak', and 'GPDP Jurisprudence on Request of De-listing from Search Engine Results').

Kate Elizabeth Francis, who also revised the contributions from the English language perspective, drafted Chapter 1, 'General Background of the Country', ('Premise', 'Roman Law', 'After the Middle Ages', 'Unification of Italy', 'Geography, Demographic and Cultural Composition', 'Political System', and 'The Legislative Process'); Chapter 2, 'National application of European and international conventions (incl. national jurisprudence regarding ECHR Art. 8', ('Introduction', 'The Italian Constitution and the European Convention on Human Rights', 'Italy and the European Convention on Human Rights', and 'Violations of Article 8 ECHR by the Italian Republic'); Part VIII on Enforcement, Chapter 2, 'Composition', Chapter 6, 'Penalties', ('Criteria for the Application of Administrative Fines', 'Procedural Rules for the Adoption and Quantification of Administrative Fines and Other Corrective Measures', and 'Appeal Against GPDP Decisions').

Francesca Tugnoli drafted Chapter 4, 'Personal data relating to criminal convictions and offences, 'Other relevant national legal provisions regarding the protection of privacy', ('Obligations of Professional Secrecy [Including Equivalent Obligations of Secrecy]', 'Churches and religious associations', 'Law Enforcement Agencies', 'National security services', and 'Other specific regimes'); Part VIII 'Chapter 4. Remedies', ('Introduction', 'Remedies in front of the GPDP', and 'Judicial Remedies'); Chapter 5, 'Liability of controllers and processors', ('Criminal Liability', and 'Civil Liability'; Part IX, Chapter 2, 'Processing of personal information versus public access to official documents', ('Introduction: The Various Rights of Access in the Italian Legal Systems', 'Safeguards and Limitation to the Rights of Civic Access and Documental Access', 'GPDP Decisions', and 'Other specific cases'); Part X on Specific data protection regimes, Chapter 1, 'Obligations of professional secrecy (incl. equivalent obligations of secrecy)', ('Introduction', 'Overview of the Main Types of Secrecy'; Part X, Chapter 3, 'Law enforcement agencies (National transposition of Directive 2018/680)', ('Introduction: Italian Law Enforcement Agencies', and 'Overview of the National Transposition of Directive 2018/680: Legislative Decree 51/2018'; Chapter 5, 'Other specific regimes (e.g., civil protection, etc.)', ('Criminal Provisions as Safeguards of Confidentiality', 'The Italian Regulation of Whistleblowing', 'The Italian Regulation of Wiretapping', and 'Cyberbullying').

Luciana Di Vito drafted Part II on National data protection law, Chapter 1, 'Background: general description of the national data protection law (+ short presentation of other relevant national legislation)'; Part VIII on Enforcement, Chapter 1, 'Supervisory authorities', ('The GPDP at a Glance' and 'The Relationship with other Authorities'; together with Francesca Tugnoli, Luciana Di Vito drafted Part VIII, Chapter 3, 'Competence, tasks and powers', ('Competence', 'Tasks', and 'Powers').

Camilla Serraiotto, together with Davide Baldini, drafted Chapter 2, 'Scope of the national law (material, personal, territorial)', ('Introduction', 'Personal and Material Scope of Application', and 'Territorial Scope of Application'). In Part V, Camilla Serraiotto drafted Chapter 3, 'National rules with regard to processors', ('The Data Processor in General', 'Some Specific Qualifications Decided by the GPDP: Labour Consultants and Members of Companies' Supervisory Bodies', and 'The Duty of Supervision of the Data Controller Towards the Data Processors: Culpa in eligendo and culpa in vigilando').

Raffaella Cesareo drafted Chapter 3, 'Concepts (national jurisprudence – also previous to the GDPR -, DPA opinions + divergent and additional definitions)', ('The Concepts of "Communication" and "Dissemination" of Personal Data', 'The Person Authorised to Process Personal Data', and 'The "Internal Data Processor"; Part III, Chapter 3, 'Special categories of data', ('The notion and protection of 'data relating to health' under the jurisprudence of the Supreme Court of Cassation', 'Processing of special categories of personal data for objectives of relevant public interest', 'Further conditions, including limitations, with regard to the processing of genetic data, biometric data or data concerning health', and 'General GPDP authorizations concerning the processing of special categories of personal data').

Angela Pisani and Enza Cirone drafted Chapter 4, 'Minors' ('Provisions of the Italian Data Protection Code Relating to Minors', 'Child's Consent in Relation to Information Society Service', 'GPDP Decisions on Children's Consent in Relation to Information Society Services: The Case of TikTok', and 'GPDP Decisions on the Dissemination of Children's Personal Data on Social Networks'); Chapter 8, 'Restrictions (national implementation of Art. 23 of the GDPR)', ('Provisions of the Personal Data Protection Code Relating to Restrictions on the Rights of Data Subjects', 'GPDP Decisions on Processing Operations Carried Out in the Context of Restrictions to the Rights of Data Subjects'); Part V, Chapter 4, 'Data protection impact assessment and prior consultation', ('Introduction', 'List of Types of Processing, to Be Subjected to a DPIA under Article 35, paragraph 4, GDPR (so-called Blacklist)', and 'GPDP Decisions on DPIAs'); Part VII, Chapter 3, 'Transfers from public registers'.

Federico Gatta drafted Part III on General principles, Chapter 1, 'Data quality principles'. Together with Isabella Oldani, Federico Gatta also drafted Part VI on 'Codes of conduct and certification (left open attending future developments)', ('Rules of Conduct', 'Codes of Conduct in Force under Italian Law', 'Certification Schemes under Italian Law', and 'Other Instruments and Sets of Rules Relevant within the Italian Legal Framework'; together with Laura Senatore and Luciana Di Vito, Federico Gatta drafted Part IX, Chapter 4, 'Processing in the context of employment', ('General Rules for Processing in the Context of Employment', 'Management of E-mails in the Context of Employment: the GPDP Guidelines

Applying to the Use of E-mail (and Internet) and the Relevant GPDP's Decision', 'GPS Systems', 'Video surveillance', and 'Biometric Data as a Means of Physical or Logical Access to the Workplace'); Part X, Chapter 2, 'Churches and religious associations', ('Introduction', 'The General Authorisation Issued by the GPDP', 'The Catholic Church: CEI General Decree no. 389/2018', and 'Relevant GPDP Decisions').

Alessandra Poggio drafted Part IV on Data subject rights, Chapter 1, 'Right to be informed' ('Right to be informed in the healthcare sector', 'Right to be informed in the context of further processing for scientific research or statistical purposes', and 'Right to be informed: information regarding received CVs'); Chapter 5, 'Right to restriction; and Part IX, Chapter 3, 'Processing of the national identification number'.

Laura Senatore and Giovanni Cortese drafted Part IV on Data subject rights, Chapter 2, 'Right of access' ('Educational Materia from the GPDP on the Right of Access', 'Access to Data Concerning Deceased Persons', 'Access to Banking Data', 'Access to Personal Data and Access to Administrative Documents (referral)', and 'Relevant Decisions of the GPDP on the Right of Access'); Chapter 6, 'Profiling', ('Introduction', 'Relevant Decisions from the GPDP on Profiling', 'Period of storage of data for profiling purposes: useful decisions from the GPDP', and 'Classification under the Code of Conduct for telemarketing and teleselling'). Part V Chapter 5, 'Data Protection Officer', was drafted by Laura Senatore and Camilla Serraiotto ('Guidance from the GPDP Regarding the Appointment and Role of the DPO', 'Appointment of a DPO in connection with processing carried out by judicial authorities acting in their capacity as such', 'The Liability of the DPO', and 'Decisions from the GPDP and from Italian Courts concerning DPOs').

Nicola Franchetto, Andrea Strippoli, and Isabella Oldani drafted Part VII on International transfers, Chapter 1, 'General principles (refer to the GDPR provisions + add national DPA opinions, etc.)', ('Data Transfers in General', 'Decisions Adopted by the GPDP Concerning Data Transfers', 'Transfers Carried out by Competent Authorities in the Context of the Prevention, Investigation, Detection and Prosecution of Criminal Offences or the Execution of Criminal Penalties' and Chapter 2 on 'Transfers in the context of international agreements (e.g., mutual legal assistance treaties)', ('Transfer in the Context of Mutual Legal Assistance Treaties', 'Transfer in the Context of the EU-PNR Directive', 'Transfers in the Context of Automated Processing under the Convention 108 and the Convention 108+', and 'Transfers Between Financial Supervisory Authorities for the Purpose of Suppressing Unlawful Conducts in the Financial Markets').

Davide Fioravanti drafted Part IV on Data subject rights, Chapter 3, 'Rights of rectification', ('The limits of the right of rectification: objectively ascertainable elements', and 'Right of rectification in the field of medical, biomedical and epidemiological studies and research'); Chapter 4, 'Right to erasure', ('The Right to Erasure in the Italian Legal System' and 'The Right to Erasure vis-à-vis the Freedom of the Press'); Chapter 7, 'Right to object'. Davide Fioravanti and Laura Senatore also drafted Part V on Duties of controllers and processors, Chapter 1, 'National rules regarding duties of controllers', ('Introduction', 'Transfer of Personal Data to Third

Parties for their Autonomous Direct Marketing Purposes', and 'Lead Acquisition'). Also in Part V, Davide drafted Chapter 2, 'National rules regarding joint controllers'.

Isabella Oldani drafted Part IX, Chapter 5, 'Processing for scientific research, public archiving and statistical purposes', ('Applicable Normative Framework', 'Processing for Archiving Purposes in the Public Interest or for Historical Research Purposes', 'Processing for Statistical Purposes or Scientific Research Purposes', and 'GPDP decision of 5 June 2019 adopted pursuant to Article 21, paragraph 1, of D.Lgs. 101/2018, pertaining to the processing of special categories of personal data carried out for purposes of scientific research'); Part X, Chapter 4, 'National security services', ('The Italian Security Intelligence System', and 'National Data Protection Rules Applicable to the Italian Security Intelligence System'). Wendy Kuyoh and Marie-Claire Najjar furthermore assisted Davide Baldini and Kate Francis.

Prof. Dr Paolo Balboni

Chapter 1. General Background of the Country

§1. Premise

1. In order to adequately comprehend the Italian legal framework, it is necessary to have a basic understanding of the country's history and past and present political milieus. As suggested by Livingston et. al., 'the history of Italian law can best be understood in relation to the cultural, political, social, and economic histories of Italy'.[5] Indeed, Italy boasts a great cultural and legal history.

This history commences in classical antiquity with the Greek colonies of Southern Italy, the rich Etruscan culture, and the influence of both on the rising Roman civilization. In particular, the Roman Republic (which lasted until the end of the first century BC) gave crucial importance to the law. Some of the legal concepts and proceedings elaborated during the Roman civilization, collectively known as 'Roman Law', continued to be studied and transmitted for centuries after the fall of Rome and laid the foundations for many Western legal systems. After the fall of the Western Roman Empire (traditionally set in AD 476), the Italian peninsula continued to play an important role in European culture and economy through the Middle Ages, the Renaissance, and modernity.

2. This Chapter will briefly explore the pre-unification of the Italian state and will go on to discuss post-unification so as to set the stage for the following chapters in a historically contextualized manner.

§2. Roman Law

3. Roman Law, as the legal system of ancient Rome, came to be known, was slowly elaborated during the many centuries of the Roman civilization, which lasted from the foundation of the city – set in 753 BCE in the traditional, largely mythical account – through the Roman Republic and the following Roman Empire, which expanded to much of Western Europe, the Middle East, and the North African Mediterranean coast before collapsing under pressure from the outside, internal struggles, and economical problems. Together, those factors, indeed, led to the fall of the so-called Western Empire in the fifth century CE.[6]

As suggested in the preceding section, Roman law is considered to be the basis for the majority of European legal systems.[7] Its system continued to be used in the Eastern Empire until its downfall in AD 1453.[8] For these reasons, a brief presentation in the context of this Volume is merited.

5. *See* Michael A. Livingston, Pier Giuseppe Monateri & Francesco Parisi, *The Italian Legal System: An Introduction* 2, (2nd ed. Stanford Law Books 2015).
6. Peter G. Stein, *Roman law,* Encyclopaedia Britannica (10.11.2020), https://www.britannica.com/topic/Roman-law.
7. *Roman law*, Bodleian Libraries University of Oxford (26.09.2022), https://libguides.bodleian.ox.ac.uk/law-roman.
8. *Ibid.*

4. Sources of Roman law are divided into *leges* and *iura*.[9] *Leges* were composed of 'all general enactments of the emperors, particularly in public law', and today's rough equivalent of case was found in *iura*, or the 'opinions of those jurisconsults endowed with *ius respondendi ex auctoritate principis*'.[10]

However, during the middle of the third century CE, this conception of law lost steam, and there was a need for reform.[11] Justinian became the ruler of the Eastern Empire in AD 529 and published his *Novus Justinianus Codex*; after its publication, he oversaw the 'compilation' of the *iura*, publishing fifty books known as the *Digesta* or *Pandectae*, which entered into effect on 30 December 533 CE and which 'made necessary a second edition of the Code in order to unify and harmonize the parts of the legislative system and to add the enactments of Justinian made after 529'.[12] Justinian thus developed the twelve books of his *Codex repetitae praelectionis*, replacing the former legislation.[13]

5. All Justinian legislation was extended to the Italian peninsula after the Eastern Roman Empire under Justinian reconquered the territory from the Ostrogoths.[14] Roman law furthermore played a fundamental role in the development of not only the modern Italian legal system but also the Western world and modern legal systems.[15]

§3. After the Middle Ages

6. With the fall of the Western Roman Empire, Italy entered a long historical phase during which territorial unity was lost for many centuries – notably, this lasted until the Kingdom of Piedmont and Sardinia was able to unify most of the country and proclaim the Kingdom of Italy in 1861. A single 'Italian' history, therefore, does not exist for the Middle Ages and most of the modern era, at least from a political perspective, as the Italian Peninsula witnessed numerous foreign invasions and long phases of internal struggles, what we now refer to as the Italian state being divided up into many different political entities. However, from an economic perspective, due to its strategic position in the Mediterranean sea and the long-lasting effect of being the centre of Roman civilization, the Italian peninsula as a whole continued to be the richest part of Europe until the Renaissance period.[16]

7. People coming from outside Italy also had a deep influence on the legal framework during the centuries. In AD 568, a Germanic tribe known as the

9. *See* Livingston et al., *supra* n. 5.
10. *Ibid.*, at 4.
11. *Ibid.*
12. *Ibid.*, at 6.
13. *Ibid.*
14. *Ibid.*, at 7.
15. Hessel E. Yntema, *Roman Law and Its Influence on Western Civilization,* 35 Cornell Law Review 77, 88 n. 1 (1949). Available at https://scholarship.law.cornell.edu/cgi/viewcontent.cgi?referer=&httpsredir=1&article=1570&context=clr.
16. *See* Emanuele Felice, *Ascesa e declino: Storia economica d'Italia* 36 (Il Mulino 2015).

Langobards or Lombards invaded a vast swath of the Italian peninsula.[17] The Lombards 'introduced into Italy the principle of the personality of law, the norm among the Germanic peoples'.[18] Having no written law themselves, it was only in AD 643 that the *Edictum*, comprised of 388 chapters and considered to be the 'most complete statement of the customary law of any of the Germanic tribe' was published and subsequently added to by the successors of Lombard King Rothari, now known as the *Edictum regum Langobardorum*.[19]

Langobard private law continued to apply even after the Frankish conquest in AD 774.[20] Livingston points out that multiple sources of law were present in early Medieval Italy, including Roman law, Langobard law, Frankish law, and other Germanic laws.[21]

In order to deal with this legislative fragmentation, multiple *capitula* were promulgated; the *Capitulare Italicum* was added to the Langobard Edict in the early eleventh century, also because the Frankish legislation was perceived as a continuation of the Langobard one.[22]

8. Charlemagne invaded Northern and Central Italy in AD 774 and founded the Kingdom of Italy (soon to become part of the Holy Roman Empire), which was able to assert power in those areas until the end of the tenth century but gradually lost its ability to effectively govern the country. In the twelfth-fourteenth centuries, many cities in Northern Italy organized themselves in self-ruling statelets, becoming largely autonomous from the increasingly nominal sovereignty of the Holy Roman Empire.

9. Later, some of those cities became the centre of powerful regional entities, usually under the rule of a family that established hereditary dynasties and came to govern the state as de facto monarchs. Among them are some of the most famous principalities during the Late Medieval and Renaissance periods, such as the Visconti and the Sforza in Milan, the Este in Modena, Reggio Emilia and Ferrara, the Medici in Florence, and the Gonzaga in Mantua.

A notable exception to this dynastical evolution was Venice, that started as a scattered group of villages in the islands outside the coast of Northeast Italy around the tenth century CE and grew to become one of the leading commercial and military power of the entire Eastern Mediterranean Sea in the thirteenth-sixteenth centuries, all while maintaining its independence and developing a remarkably stable form of government (a peculiar kind of oligarchy) until its final demise in 1797.

10. Meanwhile, in Central Italy, a new force gradually increased its power and territorial reach: that of the Pope, the spiritual leader of the Catholic Church. The

17. *Lombards and Byzantines*, Encyclopaedia Britannica, https://www.britannica.com/place/Italy/Lombards-and-Byzantines.
18. *See* Livingston et al., *supra* n. 5, at 8.
19. *Ibid.*
20. *Ibid.*
21. *Ibid.*, at 9.
22. *Ibid.*

importance of Rome as the seat of the Papacy slowly rose from the early beginnings of Christianity, even if, for many centuries, it lacked a proper territorial domain and was effectively part of the successive Byzantine, Langobard, and Frankish dominations. Sovereignty was finally attained in AD 756 with the so-called donation of Pippin, granted by the Frankish ruler Pippin III (known as 'the Short').

Papal States, as the territories ruled by the Holy See came to be known, ultimately ended up covering most of Central Italy (Tuscany excluded) and part of Northern Italy at the height of their power in the early sixteenth century and lasted until the Capture of Rome by Italian troops in 1870.

11. From a legal perspective, Papal States saw the development of a peculiar kind of law that blended some principles of the Roman tradition with concepts rooted in religious Christian law. Indeed, the law of the Roman Catholic Church, known as 'canon law', has a two-way relationship with Italian law: Rome was the centre of Christianity, and the Catholic Church heavily influenced Italian culture.[23] The two categories of law delimited by the Church are human and divine law; divine law supposedly has divine origins, as the name suggests.[24] It 'is further divided into divine positive law (as revealed in the Bible and in tradition) and natural law (rules taught by nature, discovered by human reason, and applicable equally to all men). Human law is divided into canon law, consisting of the canons and decretals, and civil law'.[25]

12. The oldest 'canonical collections' date back to the fifth century and were later updated and transmitted to Charlemagne in AD 774; they were then adopted as the general code of the Frankish Church at the Diet of Aachen of AD 802 when the collection became known as the '*Dionysio-Hadriana*'.[26] The Donation of Constantine, also known as the '*Donatio Constantini*', also played an important role in terms of European politics and religion. The *Donatio Constantini* allegedly bestowed both land and power to Pope Sylvester I, but in the fifteenth century, Lorenzo Valla discovered that the *Donatio Constantini* was forged.[27]

13. In this period, however, Roman legal thought was increasingly relied upon.[28] More specifically, the '*Lex romana canonice compta'*, dating back to the early ninth century, contained 'the *capitula romanae legis ad canones pertinentia*, the Roman law applicable and adapted to the ecclesiastical legal system. The materials were selected from the Institutes, the Code, and to a greater extent from the Novels of Justinian.'[29] Furthermore, the '*Collectio Anselmo dedicata*', representing 'the first collection to contain the canonical and Roman texts of Justinian's era arranged in systematic form', are said to clearly delineate the mutual influences that

23. *Ibid.*
24. *Ibid.*, at 10.
25. *Ibid.*
26. *Ibid.*
27. The Editors of Encyclopaedia, *Donation of Constantine*, (8.11.2016), https://www.britannica.com/topic/Donation-of-Constantine.
28. *See* Livingston et al., *supra* n. 5, at 10.
29. *Ibid.*, at 11.

Roman and canon law had on each other.[30] Indeed, Livingston et al. note that 'This interrelationship may be characterized as a true reception, through which Roman norms formally came to be part of the legal system of the Church.'[31]

14. Southern Italy followed yet another historical path, where strong local differences can be observed. Sicily, for example, fell under Byzantine rule shortly after the fall of the Western Roman Empire and was later invaded by the Arabs (965) and the Normans (1060). The island was alternatively separated or reunited with the southern part of the Italian Peninsula following the dynastic struggles of the Angevins, rulers of the mainland of French origin, and the Aragonese from Spain.

In 1442, Alfonso V of Aragon was able to conquer Naples and its dominions, moving the capital to Naples itself and establishing the so-called Kingdom of the Two Sicilies. After decades of struggle with the French Kingdom, Southern Italy and Sicily fell under Spanish rule again in 1504 and were governed by Spanish viceroys for the following two centuries, a period largely considered of economic decline. Another dynasty of Spanish origin, the Bourbons, conquered the Kingdom of the Two Sicilies (or Kingdom of Naples) in 1734 and established an autonomous and strongly centralized state. It became part of Italy after Giuseppe Garibaldi's invasion of 1860.

§4. Unification of Italy

15. Foreign invasions were by no means a prerogative of the southern part of the Peninsula. Starting in 1494 with the invasion of Charles VIII of France, the North too became the theatre of decades of conflict between the major European powers of that time, namely the French Kingdom, the Spanish Kingdom, and the Holy Roman Empire. Partly following the complex dynastic struggles at the European level and partly following the lack of strong unitary states such as the ones establishing themselves in other countries such as France or Spain, the many territorial entities in Northern Italy went through a long succession of short-lived alliances, wars, and changes of hands, while foreign (as well as Italian) mercenary troops took a heavy toll on the local economy and social fabric.

For example, Milan – until then a duchy under the Sforza – changed hands between the French and the Sforza at least six times in 1499–1529, only to fall under Habsburg rule (i.e., the ruling family of the Holy Roman Empire) in 1535.

Philip II, son of the emperor Charles V, began Spanish rule in 1540, which was to last until 1706. That year, Milan passed from Spanish to Austrian rule.

16. Napoleonic troops swept through Northern Italy and established nominally republican governments under French influence in 1796–1797, which were later united under the (French-controlled) Kingdom of Italy in 1805. As a result, Bonaparte's Civil Code was instituted in different areas of Italy over a number of

---

30. *Ibid.*
31. *Ibid.*

years.[32] Indeed, the *Codice di Napoleone: Il Grande pel Regno d'Italia* had an important impact throughout the peninsula, providing essential uniformity in the Italian legal system[33] which was previously largely fragmented for the reasons illustrated above. Following the unification of Italy discussed briefly below, the Napoleonic Code, in fact, inspired the 1865 *Codice Civile*, or Italian Civil Code, closely mirroring it.[34]

17. After the fall of Napoleon, Austrian rule came back to Italy with the Kingdom of Lombardy-Venetia, tightly controlled by ministers in Vienna and a number of satellite states under local monarchs tied to the Habsburg family.

18. The so-called Restoration – a decision shared by the major European powers to go back to the status quo ante the Napoleonic years – marked the deepening of Austrian influence in all of northern Italy as well as Tuscany.

Starting with the beginning of the nineteenth century, a wide cultural movement pushed the idea of a unified Italian state, leading to uprisings and conspiracies in various parts of Italy with the common aim of doing away with foreign domination. Some were suppressed by the local authorities; others gave way to concessions from local rulers, and some to revolutions and short-lived republics.

In 1848, for example, a popular insurrection broke out in Palermo, Sicily, leading to new constitutions granted in the Kingdom of the Two Sicilies, Piedmont, Tuscany and the Papal States. Vienna chose to turn to repression instead: the Kingdom of Piedmont and Sardinia, until then a relatively minor force in the Italian landscape, decided to wage an unfortunate and short-lived war against the Austro-Hungarian Empire.

19. A few decades later, it was ultimately the Kingdom of Piedmont and Sardinia itself, ruled by the Savoy dynasty, that was able to carry out the unification of Italy through a series of three wars known in Italy as the 'Wars of Independence'. One of the crucial military endeavours in those conflicts was the rapid invasion in 1860 of the Kingdom of Naples by an initially small contingent of volunteers led by Giuseppe Garibaldi. In 1861, the process of unification of the country, known as the *Risorgimento* (literally 'Resurgence'), came to a symbolic conclusion with the proclamation of the Kingdom of Italy, even if Rome was conquered only in 1870 when Italian troops entered the city, which became capital the following year.

32. *Il Codice Civile: The First Translation of Napoléon's Code civil: Introduction*, The Law Library of Louisiana (19.5.2021), https://lasc.libguides.com/Il-Codice-Civile.

33. *Ibid.*

34. *Ibid.* Also note that interestingly, in 1859 during the Second War of Independence, Giuseppe Montanelli, Italian politician and author, wrote 'I am in favor of adopting the Napoleonic civil code for the Kingdom of Italy. What is a gratification to France is a benefit to us … The Emperor of France will be able to show that the arms of France pave the way for progressive ideas. The sacred words of the pronouncement will be: Long Live the Kingdom of Italy; Long Live Vittorio Emanuele the king of Italy; Long Live the Napoleonic Code.'

20. Italy was heavily involved in the First World War and fought at the north-eastern border with the Austro-Hungarian Empire. Its final victory led to the gain of the last territories forming present-day Italy, i.e., the areas around Trento and Trieste, as well as Southern Tyrol.

21. A few years after the end of the war, the country saw the rise of the first Fascist regime in Europe with Benito Mussolini, who forged an alliance with Nazi Germany and followed its racist policies towards Jews and other minorities. After the disastrous defeat in the Second World War and the fall of fascism, the House of Savoy – which was seen as an accomplice of the fascist regime – came to an end with a referendum that chose the republican form of government in 1946.

22. The years soon after the Second World War saw a fast growth of the Italian economy, the so-called Italian economic miracle or Italian economic boom, lasting until the end of the 1960s (with peak years in 1958–1963). The 'boom' established the country as one of the most industrialized nations in the world.

In foreign policy, Italy became part of NATO and was one of the founding countries of what ultimately became the European Union.

Even in the presence of one of the strongest Communist Parties in Western Europe, the Italian political landscape was dominated by the Christian Democracy ('*Democrazia Cristiana*') as a relative majority party that usually ruled in various coalition governments with smaller parties until the 1990s. Major outbreaks of political violence from left- and right-wings terrorist groups, as well as a bombing campaign and extensive meddling from foreign intelligence services and internal actors linked to some parts of the Italian security services, occurred between 1969 and the early 1980s in what are collectively known as the 'Lead Years' ('*Anni di piombo*').

23. A political upheaval followed the end of the Soviet Union and a huge judicial investigation into political corruption in the early 1990s ('*Mani Pulite*', literally translated as 'Clean Hands'), leading to an abrupt end of almost all of the major parties active until then and the incrimination of thousands of political figures at the national and local level. The following years were dominated by the rise of 'new' political forces – such as the *Forza Italia* party founded by the magnate Silvio Berlusconi in 1994, the independentist Northern League, and later the Five Star Movement – and increased instability of the political landscape.

§5. Geography

24. Italy is located in Southern Europe and is commonly described as a 'boot' protruding into the Mediterranean Sea accompanied by two sizable islands, Sardinia and Sicily (as well as a number of smaller islands). Italy shares land borders with France, Switzerland, Austria, and Slovenia.

25. The country boasts a varied landscape comprising various mountain ranges, including the Alps and the Ligurian Alps in the northwest, respectively, the tectonically unstable Apennine range running down the peninsula, as well as valleys, hills and plains. Italy is 302,073 square kilometres, 41.6% of which is hilly, 35% mountainous and 23.2% plains.[35]

26. The first level of administrative divisions in Italy are the regions, of which there are twenty (five have various degrees of special autonomy), the second are provinces (there are two self-governing provinces, namely Bolzano/Bozen and Trento), and the third are municipalities.

The geographic borders of the regions largely follow historical territorial divisions.[36] There are over 7,900 municipalities in Italy, the majority of which are small or very small.[37] The majority of the population (68.5%) live in medium-sized municipalities.[38] In 2019, nearly half of the population lived in the plains (49.1%), and 38.8% lived in hilly areas.[39] It can be said that the Italian 'territorial system is characterized by a small number of metropolitan areas and a huge number of medium, small and very small urban settlements'.[40]

Cities or densely populated areas account for only 3.2% of municipalities but contained 35.3% of the population in 2019. Along these lines, over half (55.6%) of the population lives in functional urban areas.[41]

27. In terms of geographical distribution of the population, Northern Italy is the most densely populated area of the peninsula. In 2022, an estimated 15,848,100 individuals resided in the Northwest, 11,561,676 in the Northeast, 11,740,836 in the centre, 6,380,649 in the islands, and 13,451,861 in the south.[42] Rome, Milan, Naples, Turin, and Palermo were the five largest cities in Italy in terms of population in 2021.

---

35. Principali Dimensioni Geostatistiche e Grado di Urbanizzazione del Paese, ISTAT (1.09.2014), https://www.istat.it/it/archivio/137001.
36. *Regional and local government*, Encyclopaedia Britannica, https://www.britannica.com/place/Italy/Regional-and-local-government.
37. *See Annuario Statistico Italiano 2020*, ISTAT, https://www.istat.it/it/files//2020/12/C01.pdf, at 2.
38. *Ibid.*
39. *Ibid.*
40. *Italy*, https://urbact.eu/italia.
41. Note that 'The OECD, in cooperation with the EU, has developed a harmonised definition of functional urban areas (FUAs). Being composed of a city (or core) and its commuting zone, FUAs encompass the economic and functional extent of cities based on daily people's movements (OECD, 2012); (Dijkstra, Poelman, & Veneri, 2019). The definition of FUA aims at providing a functional/economic definition of cities and their area of influence, by maximising international comparability and overcoming the limitation of using purely administrative approaches. At the same time, the concept of FUA, unlike other approaches, ensures a minimum link to the government level of the city or metropolitan area.' *See Italy: Functional Urban Areas,* OECD (July 2022), https://www.oecd.org/cfe/regionaldevelopment/Italy.pdf. *See also* ISTAT, *supra* n. 37 (*Annuario Statistico Italiano 2020,* ISTAT, https://www.istat.it/it/files//2020/12/C01.pdf), at 2.
42. *Popolazione residente al 1 gennaio,* ISTAT (2.10.2022), http://dati.istat.it/Index.aspx?DataSetCode=DCIS_POPRES1&Lang=it.

28. The economy is largely divided along regional lines in terms of the north, centre and south/islands, with the north having the highest employment rates and investment-to-GDP ratios and the lowest share of households being in relative poverty.[43] Instead, the south and islands perform the worst in these three areas.[44]

§6. Demographic and Cultural Composition

29. Since 2014, when Italy's population registered at 60.3 million, the population has been in steady decline.[45] According to provisional data from ISTAT (*'L'Istituto nazionale di statistica'* or Italian National Institute of Statistics), as of January 2022, the population has decreased to 58,983,000.[46] The number of foreigners located in Italian territory, accounting for 8.7% of census participants in 2020, was 5,171,894.[47] As of January 2022, the total number of foreign residents was 5,193,669.[48]

30. It is clear that the country is coming very close to experiencing a population crisis, with ISTAT projecting the population to decrease to 57.9 million by 2030, 54.2 million in 2050, and 47.7 million in 2070.[49] At the same time, there is an expected 'demographic crisis of the territories' where four out of five municipalities are expected to shrink in terms of population in the next ten years; this is expected to take place in an overwhelming nine out of ten rural municipalities.[50]

In 2021, the total fertility rate or number of children that a woman would give birth to was 1.25.[51] In fact, some experts have claimed that the COVID-19 pandemic has further played a role in Italy's declining birth rate with '399,431 births registered in 2021 against 404,892 in 2020 – the 13th consecutive yearly fall and the lowest number since the unification of Italy in 1861'.[52]

---

43. 2021 OECD Economic Survey of Italy: Laying the foundations for a stronger recovery, OECD (6.9.2021).
44. *Ibid.*
45. *See Demographic Indicators: Year 2021*, ISTAT (8.4.2022), https://www.istat.it/it/files//2022/04/Demographic-indicators_year_2021.pdf, at 3.
46. *Ibid.*
47. Censimento della Popolazione e Dinamica Demografica – Anno 2020, *ISTAT* (9.12.2021) https://www.istat.it/it/archivio/264511#:~:text=Al%2031%20dicembre%202020%2C%20data,al%202019%20(%2D405.275%20individui).
48. *Popolazione straniera residente al 1 Gennaio 2022 per età e sesso – dati provvisori*, ISTAT (26.9.2022), https://demo.istat.it/strasa2022/index.html.
49. *Households and Population Projections – Base 1/1/2021*, ISTAT (22.11.2022), https://www.istat.it/en/archivio/274900.
50. *Ibid.*
51. *See* ISTAT, *supra* n. 37 (*Annuario Statistico Italiano 2020*, ISTAT, https://www.istat.it/it/files//2020/12/C01.pdf), at 4.
52. *Births in Italy hit record low in 2021, population shrinks*, Reuters (14.3.2022, 4:29 PM GMT+1), https://www.reuters.com/world/europe/births-italy-hit-record-low-2021-population-shrinks-2022-03-14/.

31. Life expectancy at birth in 2021, without gender distinction, is 82.4 years.[53] The median age in Italy as of January 2022 was 46.2 years.[54]

32. In terms of the economy, the GDP per capita in Italy in 2021 was USD 35,551.3,[55] 26% less than OECD best performers.[56] Productivity in Italy is 17% lower than the OECD's best performers.[57] According to the OECD, inequality in Italy is higher than it is in other advanced economies, with the poorest 20% of households earning 6.6% of total income.[58]

§7. Political System

33. Italy is a parliamentary republic with a President of the Republic acting as Head of State, established by the Constitution of 1948.[59] The President is elected by the Parliament, is considered a *super partes* figure whose overarching aim is to guarantee compliance of Italian politics with the Constitution, and represents the unity of the nation.

In line with the above, the President's most important powers are arguably the possibility to dissolve the Parliament, the power to veto the passing of legislation approved by the Parliament (although the President is bound to pass the legislation, if the Parliament approves it again despite the veto), and naming the President of the Council.

The President of the Republic is also the commander-in-chief of the Italian Armed Forces and presides over the Superior Council of the Judiciary ('*Consiglio Superiore della Magistratura*'). The President's term of office lasts for seven years and can be re-elected.

34. The Prime Minister of Italy, also known as the President of the Council of Ministers ('*Presidente del Consiglio dei Ministri*' and, informally, '*Presidente del Consiglio*' 'Premier' or '*Primo Ministro*'), is appointed by the Head of State, the President of the Italian Republic, on the basis of the results of the election and the political composition of the Parliament.

The Prime Minister is in charge of general government policy, ensuring political and administrative consistency, coordinating the work of ministers, maintaining relations with the President of the Republic, and carrying out any other relevant

53. *See* ISTAT, *supra* n. 37 (*Annuario Statistico Italiano 2020*, ISTAT, https://www.istat.it/it/files//2020/12/C01.pdf), at 3.
54. *Ibid.*, at 1.
55. *GDP per capita (current US$) – Italy*, World Bank (2021), https://data.worldbank.org/indicator/NY.GDP.PCAP.CD?locations=IT.
56. *Italy Economic Snapshot: Economic Forecast Summary* (June 2022), OECD, https://www.oecd.org/economy/italy-economic-snapshot/.
57. *Ibid.*
58. *Ibid.*
59. *See infra* Part. I, Ch. 1, §1, for a brief overview of the Italian Constitution of 1948.

duties as conferred to the figure by law. The Prime Minister also informs the Parliament of the composition of the government and, importantly, presents the government's programme to the Italian Parliament to obtain a vote of confidence.[60] The Prime Minister moreover acts as the Vice President of Italy's Supreme Council of Defence; the same figure presides over the Interministerial Committee for the Security of the Italian Republic and coordinates governmental activities with respect to EU policies and the government's relative positions.[61]

35. The Italian Parliament, under the so-called perfect bicameralism principle established in Article 55 of the Constitution, is comprised of the Chamber of Deputies ('*Camera dei Deputati*') and the Senate of the Republic ('*Senato della Repubblica*'), each performing the same functions, which consist of:

(i) developing legislation (Article 70 and following of the Constitution);
(ii) the constitution review function (Article 138 of the Constitution);
(iii) the 'political policy function', understood as the possibility to grant or revoke confidence in the government (Article 94 of the Constitution);[62]
(iv) exercising control over the executive.

36. Pursuant to Article 82 of the Constitution, each Chamber has the power to investigate 'public interest, appointing for this purpose from among its members special commissions – including bicameral commissions – endowed with the same powers and limits as the judicial authority'.[63]

The Italian Constitution also requires that the two Chambers meet in a 'Common session' chaired by the speaker of the Chamber of Deputies to carry out some specific functions which include the election of the President of the Republic, in which regional delegates participate pursuant to Article 83 of the Italian Constitution, in case of vote over impeachment of the President of the Republic, and to attend the oath of allegiance of the latter,[64] as well as for the election of a third of the constitutional judges[65] and a third of the Superior Council of the Judiciary.[66]

37. The members of the Chamber of Deputies and the Senate of the Republic are 'elected by universal, direct and secret suffrage'.[67] In theory, parliamentary elections are held every five years. However, due to political instability, elections often take place more frequently. The President of the Republic also has the power to dissolve the Chambers.

---

60. *See The President of the Council of Ministers*, Italian Government Presidency of the Council of Ministers, https://www.governo.it/en/prime-minister/11813.
61. *Ibid. See also* Art. 95 of the Italian Constitution and Art. 5 of L. 400/1988.
62. *See Il Senato nel sistema bicamerale: Il Parlamento*, Senato della Repubblica, https://www.senato.it/istituzione/il-senato-nel-sistema-bicamerale/il-parlamento.
63. *Ibid.*
64. *See* Art. 91 of the Italian Constitution.
65. *See* Art. 135 of the Italian Constitution.
66. *See* Senato della Repubblica, *supra* n. 62. *See also* Art. 104 of the Italian Constitution.
67. *Ibid.*

38. The Chamber of Deputies was originally comprised of 630 deputies of no less than 25 years of age and was elected by all Italians above 18 years of age. Instead, the Senate was composed of 315 senators who could be no younger than 40 years old and could only be elected by Italians of at least 25 years of age.[68] However, in September 2020, a constitutional referendum was held in which 69.96% of voters elected to reduce the number of members of the Chamber of Deputies to 400 and the number of senators to 200, amending Articles 56 and 57 of the Italian Constitution.[69] This change took effect in the next general election which took place on 25 September 2022.

Following the aforementioned referendum, Article 56 of the Constitution was amended; pursuant to this amendment, 8 of the 400 deputies are elected by the overseas constituency, and the seats are distributed among the constituencies by 'dividing the number of the inhabitants of the Republic, as resulting from the last general census of the population, by three hundred ninety-two and distributing the seats in proportion to the population of each constituency'.[70] Article 57 of the Italian Constitution was also amended to foresee that of the two hundred elected senators, four are elected by the overseas constituency. The Article reads that:

39. No region or autonomous province may have a number of senators less than three; Molise has two and Valle d'Aosta one. The distribution of seats among the Regions or Autonomous Provinces, after application of the provisions of the preceding paragraph, shall be made in proportion to their population as shown by the last general census, on the basis of whole quotients and the highest remainders.

40. It is also relevant to note that in addition to the elected members, the Senate of the Republic also includes 'former Presidents of the Republic as ex officio and life senators, as well as senators for life, appointed by the President of the Republic from among citizens who have distinguished the country for high merits in the social, scientific, artistic or literary fields'.[71]

§8. The Legislative Process

41. In Italy, as suggested above, the legislative function of the State is carried out by both Chambers of the Italian Parliament pursuant to Article 70 of the Italian Constitution.[72] This means that in order for a proposed bill to become a law, it is necessary for both the Chamber of Deputies and the Senate to approve the exact same text.[73]

---

68. *Ibid.*
69. Il referendum sul taglio dei parlamentari si terrà il 29 marzo, la Repubblica (272020).
70. *See* Art. 56 of the Italian Constitution, available at https://www.quirinale.it/allegati_statici/costituzione/costituzione.pdf. Author's translation.
71. *See* Senato della Repubblica, *supra* n. 62. Author's translation.
72. *See* Camera dei Deputati, *Il cammino di una legge*, http://legislature.camera.it/cost_reg_funz/671/672/documentotesto.asp.
73. Camera dei Deputati, *The Passage of a Law Through Parliament,* https://en.camera.it/4?scheda_informazioni=15.

The Italian procedure for law-making, the so-called *iter legislativo,* consists of a number of stages. These stages are illustrated below:

(i) the legislative initiative commences with the introduction of a bill;
(ii) as a second step, the legislative initiative is presented and approved by the Chamber in which the bill was first presented;
(iii) as a third step, the bill is sent to the other house for the approval of its wording or amendments; if it is amended, it goes back and forth between the Chamber until it is approved in the same form by both Chambers;
(iv) the text is then promulgated by the President of the Republic; the President then has the power to either send the bill back to the Parliament for it to be reconsidered;
(v) as a final step, the bill is published in the Official Gazette and normally enters into force after fifteen days from its publication.

42. The ordinary procedure for approval by the Chamber of Deputies consists of two stages. First, the bill (consisting of at least one article and an explanatory memorandum) is introduced. It can be introduced by the Government, each member of the Parliament, the population, the Regional Councils, or the National Council for Economy and Labour ('CNEL'). In Italian, bills put forth by the government are called '*disegni di legge*', while all others are referred to as '*proposte di legge*'.[74] The bill is then assigned to a parliamentary committee which is in charge of carrying out an initial assessment and consideration of the bill. The committee is also charged with preparing a specific text which is discussed on the Chamber floor and is 'known as Committee acting in a reporting capacity for this reason'.[75]

The Committee has the possibility to deal with two or more bills and develop a single report to be discussed on the Chamber floor. It may also select only one bill to be discussed and appoint a sub-committee to merge multiple bills. Committees may also interact with each other; for example, a committee can provide advice and suggestions and make their opinions known with respect to specific parts of bills under their competency. It is also possible for the Committee to make and discuss proposed amendments to bills. Expert hearings may also be held where necessary. More specifically, '[a]ny opinions and information deemed necessary are acquired also by means of hearings of experts and officials and the government participates in the preliminary study and drafting of the bill'.[76]

Upon completion of the aforementioned process, the Committee's rapporteur presents a report to the Chamber floor which contains the text prepared by the Committee. Minority reports written by members of Parliament in disagreement with the draft text may be attached to the report. A debate in the Chamber then pursues with the so-called Committee of Nine. The Committee of Nine is composed of:

74. *Ibid.*
75. *Ibid.*
76. *Ibid.*

43. The rapporteur and representatives of the Parliamentary Groups. On the Floor of the House, during the consideration of the bill, the members of the Committee of Nine sit at a semi-circular table in front of the Deputies' benches. Situated at the base of the plenary hall, the Committee of Nine is an important point of reference in the work of the House.[77]

44. With respect to the ensuing debate, the rapporteur provides a presentation, addresses are provided by the government representative, and members of Parliament express the positions of diverse groups. The articles of the relevant bill are examined, and amendments are presented and voted upon. Finally, if there are any motions, they are considered, and following the delivery of the explanations of the vote, the next step is the approval of the bill.[78]

45. The ordinary procedure must be followed, pursuant to the Italian Constitution and the Rules of Procedure of the Chamber, for specific types of laws.[79]

However, two shorter procedures are also possible in certain circumstances, these include:

(i) 'The consideration and approval of a bill by a Committee acting in a legislative capacity'.[80] In this case, the committee acting in such capacity is tasked with both the consideration and the definite approval of a bill. In this case, however, the bill is to be 'resubmitted to the Floor of the House if a demand to this effect is made by the Government, one tenth of the Deputies or one fifth of the members of the Committee.'[81]

(ii) 'The consideration of a bill by a Committee acting in a drafting capacity.'[82] In this case, the committee is tasked with preparing the bill's text on behalf of the House floor. The House in this case cannot amend the text of the bill and only has the power to vote on the bill's articles and the motion for final approval.[83]

46. The same procedure is followed for any bills adopted by the Italian Senate. Importantly, however, 'in the case of a bill already approved by the Chamber and that has returned to the Chamber because the Senate has made some amendments, the Chamber will examine only the amended parts'.[84]

47. After both Chambers of the Italian Parliament approve the same wording of the bill, it must be promulgated by the President of the Italian Republic. In cases where the President returns the bill to the Parliament, the President is required to voice the reasons for requiring re-examination. The Parliament is, however, not

77. Camera dei Deputati, *Standing Committees*, https://en.camera.it/4?scheda_informazioni=11.
78. Camera dei Deputati, *supra* n. 73.
79. *Ibid.*
80. *Ibid.*
81. *Ibid.*
82. *Ibid.*
83. *Ibid.*
84. *Ibid.*

bound to follow the President's indications, so this possibility of veto is usually considered, de facto, as expressing a power of mere moral suasion. Following promulgation, laws are made public.[85]

48. The Italian Ministry of Justice is tasked with publishing the law, which consists of publishing it in the Official Journal of the Italian Republic. The law then comes into effect on the fifteenth day following its publication, save alternative cases which are specified in the law. The law is dated with the date of its promulgation; instead, the number assigned to it represents its inclusion in the official collection of laws of the Italian Republic.[86]

85. *Ibid.*
86. *Ibid.*

Chapter 2. Telecommunications Infrastructure

§1. Connectivity and the Digital Divide

49. As stated by the Italian Presidency of the Council of Ministers, 'Telecommunication networks have become the nervous system of any modern nation.'[87] At the same time, investments in Information Communication Technologies (ICTs) 'are key drivers of social welfare and economic development'.[88] With this background, this Chapter will explore the state of telecommunications infrastructure within the Italian Republic by looking at connectivity, responsible authorities, and relevant national initiatives to improve ICT infrastructure and close the digital divide.

Italy is a latecomer in terms of ICT infrastructure and digitalization; more than half of Italians still do not have basic digital skills.[89] In 2021, 90.5% of Italian households had internet access, and the Italian fixed-broadband penetration rate was 31.1%.[90] However, the number of households which now have access to Very High-Capacity Network (VHCN) technology is only at 44% (the EU average is 70%), and while Fiber To The Premises (FTTP) is increasing, only 44% of all households and 17% of households in rural areas have coverage.[91]

At the start of the COVID-19 pandemic, when education and learning were moved online in early 2020, 65.8% of Italian students experienced some difficulty – mainly related to the quality of their connection.[92] The vast majority of students – three quarters – who followed classes online experienced connectivity issues, reaching nearly 80% in the country's south.[93]

The long-term digital divide in Italy exacerbates sociocultural and economic inequalities, and education level has been associated with 'differences in the availability of and access to ICT technologies and equipment'.[94] In 2021, three out of ten Italian families did not have a computer and internet connection at home.[95]

50. The COVID-19 pandemic expedited the use of ICT; in both 2020 and 2021, regular Internet use grew across age groups, more businesses started selling their goods via the web, and the public administration started to offer more services

87. *See* Presidenza del Consiglio dei Ministri *The Italian strategy for next generation access network*, https://www.agid.gov.it/sites/default/files/repository_files/documentazione/next_generation_access_network_-_english_version.pdf, at 4.
88. *See* Rapporto *BES 2021: Il Benessere Equo e Sostenibile in Italia*, Istituto Nazionale di Statistica (21 Apr. 2022), https://www.istat.it/it/archivio/269316, at 209. Author's translation.
89. *See* European Commission, *Digital Economy and Society Index (DESI) 2022: Italy*, https://digital-strategy.ec.europa.eu/en/policies/desi-italy, at 5.
90. *Ibid. See* Freedom House, *Freedom on the Net 2022, Italy,* https://freedomhouse.org/country/italy/freedom-net/2022#footnote2_7jztgpw.
91. *See* European Commission, *Digital Economy and Society Index (DESI) 2022: Italy*, https://digital-strategy.ec.europa.eu/en/policies/desi-italy.
92. *See* ISTAT, Rapporto *BES 2021: Il Benessere Equo e Sostenibile in Italia*, Istituto Nazionale di Statistica, 21.4.2022, https://www.istat.it/it/archivio/269316. Author's translation.
93. *Ibid.*, at 65–66.
94. *Ibid.*, at 219.
95. *Ibid.*

online.[96] As confirmed by ISTAT (the '*Istituto Nazionale di Statistica*', i.e., the 'National Institute of Statistics'), however, 'the digital divide remains large'.[97]

Despite the figures presented above, more recently, the country has started to catch up with its European Union counterparts in terms of high-speed networks and the offering of digital services. Italy is even said to be 'catching up' and doing so 'at a remarkable pace'.[98] In the World Economic Forum's 2016 Global Information Technology Report, Italy 'climbed' ten places to obtain a Networked Readiness Index (NRI) rank of forty-five, meaning that it is the 45th of 139 economies covered by the report.[99] More recently, in the European Commission's Digital Economy and Society Index (DESI) 2022, Italy ranked 18th of twenty-seven EU Member States included in the report.[100] Boasting an over-DESI connectivity score of 61.2, Italy is 7th in the EU in terms of connectivity.[101] 5G coverage in populated areas, including coverage provided by spectrum-sharing technology, is at 99.7%,[102] and Next Generation Access (NGA) was at 97% in 2021.[103]

§2. Responsible Authorities

51. The Telecommunications (*'Comunicazioni'*) department of the Italian Ministry of Economic Development (also known as 'MiSE' or '*Ministero dello Sviluppo Economico*') is the body in Italy which is primarily responsible for the implementation and planning of the national plan for broadband.[104] More specifically, MiSE is in charge of adopting measures as they are defined in the Italian Government's 2015 plan for the expansion of ultrafast broadband in the country known

96. *Ibid.*, at 209.
97. *Ibid.*
98. European Commission, *Digital Economy and Society Index (DESI) 2022: Italy*, https://digital-strategy.ec.europa.eu/en/policies/desi-italy.
99. *See* World Economic Forum, *The Global Information Technology Report 2016*. The 2016 country profile for Italy is available at the following link: https://reports.weforum.org/global-information-technology-report-2016/economies/#economy=ITA. For information on how to interpret the data presented, *see* https://reports.weforum.org/global-information-technology-report-2016/how-to-read-the-countryeconomy-profiles/.
100. European Commission, *Digital Economy and Society Index (DESI) 2022: Italy*, https://digital-strategy.ec.europa.eu/en/policies/desi-italy.
101. *Ibid.*, at 10.
102. 'The increase can also be attributed to the coverage and spectrum usage obligations attached to the rights of use of the 5G pioneer bands awarded in 2018, according to the regulation set by AGCOM (Decision No 231/18/CONS), the Italian National Regulatory Authority in the field of Electronic Communications. In this context, all Italian provinces are now starting to benefit from commercial 5G services. Further progress is expected towards the achievement of the target for uninterrupted 5G wireless broadband coverage in all urban areas, major roads and railways by 2025 because of the coverage obligations attached to the rights of use of the 700 MHz band, which will be available for use to the operators (already holding the rights of use) from 1 Jul. 2022.' *See* European Commission, *Digital Economy and Society Index (DESI) 2022: Italy*, at 10.
103. *Ibid.*
104. European Commission, *Broadband in Italy*, 7.6.2022, https://digital-strategy.ec.europa.eu/en/policies/broadband-italy. Also note that thanks to 'Law Decree 16 May 2008, n. 85 ('Urgent Provisions Regarding the Modification of Government Structures'), the functions of the former Ministry of Communications, and its inherent financial, material and human resources, were transferred to the

as '*La Strategia nazionale per la Banda Ultra Larga*' or 'SNUBL'.[105] SNUBL aims to 'bring connectivity to 1 Gbps throughout the country by 2026 and foster the development of fixed and mobile telecommunications infrastructure, as outlined in the National Recovery and Resilience Plan (NRP) and ahead of European targets set at 2030'.[106]

MiSE furthermore is in charge of managing the Italian National Registry of the infrastructures ('*Sistema informativo nazionale federato delle infrastrutture*' also known as 'SINFI').[107] MiSE and the Italian Authority for Telecommunications ('*Autorità per le Garanzie nelle Comunicazioni*' or 'AgCom') share the responsibility of managing access to frequencies and numbers for electronic communications network services (ECNS).[108]

AgCom is in independent administrative body established by Law 31 July 1997, no. 249. It is in charge of regulating and supervising electronic communications, publishing, and broadcasting sectors. It ensures competition between market operators and aims to protect the fundamental freedoms of individuals by way of inspections, investigations, and the issuance of sanctions. The Authority is accountable to the Italian Parliament, which elects its members, defines its statutes, and establishes its powers.[109] AgCom also regulates Next Generation Access (NGA), technical standards, and prices.[110]

Ministry of Economic Development' as reported by Giovanni Ziccardi, *IEL Privacy and Technology Law – Italy*, (Jos Dumortier, Pieter Gryffroy, Ruben Roex, Yung Shin Van Der Sype eds, Kluwer Law International BV, Netherlands 2019).

105. *See* Ministro per l'innovazione tecnologica e la transizione digitale, *Banda Ultra Larga: La Strategia Italiana per la Banda Ultra Larga*, https://innovazione.gov.it/progetti/banda-ultra-larga/.
106. *Ibid.*
107. European Commission, *Broadband in Italy*, European Commission, 7.6.2022, https://digital-strategy.ec.europa.eu/en/policies/broadband-italy.
108. *See* AGCom, *Spectrum Management and Policy Issues in the EU and Italian framework*, 7.10.2011, https://www.agcom.it/documents/10179/539715/Studio-Ricerca+07-12-2011+1/be38c9cd-ea70-4294-99b2-fdd210d6d6f1?version=1.0. Note that, as explained at 3, 'The Ministry of Economic Development is in charge of Spectrum Allocation matters (Frequency Allocation Table):

    - The National Regulatory Authority is in charge of Spectrum Assignment plans (both in the telecommunications and broadcasting sectors).
    - Authorisations (and rights of use for scarce resources) are issued by the Ministry (until 2001 by the Authority).
    - AGCOM is in charge for setting up the rules for spectrum access (number of rights of use, bandwidth per right, geographical limitation, tender procedure, awarding criteria, criteria for setting the fees, coverage obligations, asymmetrical conditions) and for access to numbers with significant value.
    - AGCom also gives the Ministry an official opinion (not binding) on the Frequency Allocation Plans.
    - Tender procedures are carried out by the Ministry. In case of procedure of national relevance the responsibility can be given to a specific Committee of Ministries, upon AGCom proposal.'

109. AGCom, *Che cos'è l'Autorità*, https://www.agcom.it/che-cos-e-l-autorita.
110. *See* Presidenza del Consiglio dei Ministri, *The Italian strategy for next generation access network*, https://www.agid.gov.it/sites/default/files/repository_files/documentazione/next_generation_access_network_-_english_version.pdf). *See also* European Commission, *Broadband in Italy*, European Commission, 7.6.2022.

The Italian Agency for Digital Italy (*'Agenzia per l'Italia Digitale'* or 'AgID') of the Presidency of the Council of Ministers is charged with meeting the objectives of the Italian digital agenda and contributing to the promotion of ICT to foster economic growth and innovation in the country.[111] To this end, AgID coordinated the implementation of a three-year plan for ICT and digitalization in public administration.[112]

The Italian Presidency of the Council of Ministers coordinates, by way of the Committee for the spread of high-speed broadband known as 'COBUL' (comprised of the Presidency of the Council of Ministers, MiSE, AgID, and Infratel Italia SpA), national ultra-broadband policy.[113]

§3. Primary Market Players

52. In Italy, Internet Service Providers (ISPs), the entities which provide users Internet services, including e-mail and connectivity, providing fixed lines, include TIM with 43.9% of market shares, Vodafone with 16%, Fastweb with 14.7%, WindTre with 13.8%, Linkem with 3.2%, Eolo with 2.9%, and others accounting for 5.5%.[114] In terms of fixed network broadband and ultra-broadband lines, TIM had 42.4% of the market, Vodafone 16.5%, Fastweb 14.9%, WindTre 14.1%, Linkem 3.5%, Eolo 3.1%, Tiscali 2.2% and others, 3.4%.[115] All ISPs must be authorized by MiSE to carry out such activities.

As of September 2021, in terms of fixed network broadband and ultra-broadband total lines, for Digital Subscriber Line(s) (DSL), there were 4.43 million accesses, for Fixed Wireless Access (FWA) 1.68 million accesses, Fiber to the Cabinet (FTTC) 9.95 million accesses, and FTTH 2.44 million accesses.[116]

Major mobile operators include WindTre, TIM, Vodafone, Iliad, and Poste Mobile, and the vast majority of mobile network subscribers have prepaid SIM cards.[117]

Italian Legislative Decree 8 November 2021, no. 207, on the Implementation of Directive (EU) 2018/1972 of the European Parliament and of the Council of 11 December 2018 Establishing the European Electronic Communications Code was published in the Italian Official Gazette on 8 December 2021 and entered into force on 24 December 2021. The D.Lgs. 207/2021 updated the regulation of telecommunications services, creating a new simplified procedure for obtaining general authorizations for network and electronic communication services offered to the public,

111. AgID, *About us*, https://www.agid.gov.it/en/agency/about-us.
112. AgID, *2019–2021 Three-Year Plan for IT in the Public Administration,* https://www.agid.gov.it/sites/default/files/repository_files/three_year_plan_for_it_in_public_administration_2019-2021.pdf.
113. European Commission, *Broadband in Italy,* European Commission, 7.6.2022, https://digital-strategy.ec.europa.eu/en/policies/broadband-italy.
114. *See* AgID Communication Markets Monitoring System no. 4/2021, Autorità per le Garanzie nelle Comunicazioni, https://www.agcom.it/documents/10179/5491167/Allegato+22-4-2022/758b1aaa-de20-44b7-a0eb-92f67a4b1ee4?version=1.0, at 1.
115. *Ibid.*, at 2.
116. *Ibid.*, at 3.
117. *Ibid.*, at 7–8.

favours investments in very high-capacity networks and competition, aims to protect end-users, and clarifies the roles and tasks of MiSE, AGCOM, and the Italian National Cybersecurity Agency.

Said D.Lgs. 'establishes the specific rules on the protection consumers in the electronic communications sector as conditions accompanying general authorizations for the provision of electronic communications services'.[118] It also reaffirms the necessity for ISPs to obtain general authorization from MiSE,[119] referred to above.

§4. National Initiatives for Connectivity and Ultrabroadband

53. Multiple initiatives aimed at closing the digital divide and improving connectivity have been furthered in recent years. Among these are significant investments aimed at improving the economy and competitiveness, such as the Digital Agenda, the Digital Italy plan,[120] the 2021 'Recovery and Resilience Plan', and SNUBL, which already have and, in the future, will contribute to making progress in these areas.

The Italian Digital Agenda, situated under the 'Europe 2020' Strategy, established growth targets for Member States. In particular, the Digital Agenda aimed to 'leverage the potential of ICT technologies to foster innovation, progress and economic growth, having as its main objective the development of the Digital Single Market'.[121] Within this context, Italy developed the Italian Digital Agenda, its national approach to achieve the goals established in the European Agenda.[122] Developed together with the Conference of Regions and Autonomous Provinces, the Italian Digital Agenda, the Italian Strategy for Ultra-Broadband, and the Strategy for Digital Growth 2014–2020 'were prepared for the pursuit of the Digital Agenda goals'.[123]

The SNUBL Plan, implemented by MiSE, was approved on 3 March 2015; its aim is to reduce both the market and infrastructure gaps in the country by fostering 'more favourable conditions for the integrated development of fixed and mobile telecommunications infrastructures'.[124] To this end, the mission of Infratel Italia S.p.A., the 'in-house' company of MiSE, is that of 'tak[ing] care of the country's infrastructure programmes, in particular with reference to the development of the

118. *See* Art. 1, para. 3, of D.Lgs. 207/2021. Author's translation.
119. *See* Art. 11 of D.Lgs. 207/2021.
120. *See* Ministero per l'innovazione tecnologica e la transizione digitale, *Italia digitale 2026*, https://innovazione.gov.it/italia-digitale-2026/. *See also* Ministero dello Sviluppo Economico Dipartimento per le Comunicazioni (n.d.), *The 'Digital Italy' Plan,* https://www.mise.gov.it/images/stories/pdf_upload/DIGITAL-ITALY.pdf.
121. Ministero per la Pubblica Amministrazione, *Agenda digitale*, https://www.funzionepubblica.gov.it/digitalizzazione/agenda-digitale.
122. *Ibid.*
123. *Ibid.* Author's translation.
124. Ministero dello Sviluppo Economico, *Strategic Plan Banda Ultralarga: Introduction*, https://bandaultralarga.italia.it/en/introduction/.

ultra-broadband network and public Wi-Fi connection services within the framework of the Italian Ultra-Broadband Strategy'.[125] It is interesting to note that since the Ultra-Broadband plan has been active, as of August 2022, a total of 4,088 municipalities have entered into commercialization and 7,046 construction sites have been opened.[126]

In an effort to further promote the diffusion of broadband, with Legislative Decree 15 February 2016, no. 33, Italy effectively 'reduced the costs for laying cables and established the Networks Register for Infrastructure (SINFI), a dedicated instrument for implementing broadband strategy, managed by the Ministry of Economic Development'.[127]

In 2020, the Italian government announced the creation of AccessCo, formed through the merger of FiberCop (comprised of the telecommunications provider TIM's primary and secondary access network), Open Fiber (a company dedicated to fibre optics and owned by the *Cassa Depositi e Prestiti* – an investment firm under the control of the Ministry of Economy and Finance, and Enel, an Italian multinational manufacturer and distributor of electricity and gas).[128] Later the same year, the '*Autorità Garante della Concorrenza e del Mercato*' ('AgCM', i.e., the Italian Competition Authority) commenced an investigation into FiberCop.[129] The investigation was concluded in February 2022, with AgCM announcing that 'The commitments, positively assessed by the Authority, will make it possible to reduce the barriers to the acquisition of operators and to favour infrastructure.'[130]

The Italian Recovery and Resilience Plan includes 132 investments and 58 reforms supported by EUR 68.9 billion in grants and EUR 122.6 billion in loans with 25.1% of the plan being dedicated to the digital transition.[131] The Recovery and Resilience Plan promotes investments in several key areas, including:

(i) connectivity: promoting the deployment of high-capacity networks (fibre and 5G);
(ii) innovation of the production system and the digital transition: promoting investments in training activities, 4.0 technologies, and RDI;

125. *Ibid.*
126. Ministero dello Sviluppo Economico, *Piano Banda Ultralarga: i dati sullo stato di avanzamento al 31 agosto 2022*, 9.11.2022, https://bandaultralarga.italia.it/piano-banda-ultralarga-i-dati-sullo-stato-di-avanzamento-al-31-agosto-2022/.
127. Freedom House, *Freedom on the Net 2021: Italy*, 2021, https://freedomhouse.org/country/italy/freedom-net/2021.
128. *Ibid. See also* Italia Oggi, *Tlc, via libera di Cdp ad 'AccesCo', la società che gestirà la rete unica nazionale*, 31.8.2020, https://www.italiaoggi.it/news/tlc-via-libera-di-cdp-ad-accesco-la-societa-che-gestira-la-rete-unica-nazionale-202008311950195690.
129. AgCM, *I850 – ICA: investigation launched into contracts for the establishment of FiberCop*, 21.12.2020, https://en.agcm.it/en/media/press-releases/2020/12/I850.
130. AgCM, I850-I850B – Via libera a FiberCop. Accolti gli impegni di TIM, Fastweb, Tiscali e KKR presentati dopo l'avvio del procedimento, 24.2.2022, https://www.agcm.it/media/comunicati-stampa/2022/2/I850-I850B.
131. European Commission (n.d.), *Italy's recovery and resilience plan*, https://ec.europa.eu/info/business-economy-euro/recovery-coronavirus/recovery-and-resilience-facility/italys-recovery-and-resilience-plan_en.

(iii) digitalization of the Italian public administration, also by way of reforms which aim to:
   (a) ensure the timely and efficient procurement of ICT solutions;
   (b) remove obstacles to the adoption of cloud computing solutions by the public administration;
   (c) streamline bureaucracy which hinders the exchange of data between public administrations.

54. In the context of the National Recovery and Resilience Plan, pertaining to the Next Generation EU (NGEU) programme, lasting six years from 2021 through 2026, EUR 30.6 billion will be allocated through a complementary fund established by Decree-Law no. 59 of 6 May 2021.[132] The Plan specifically intends to contribute to reducing relevant gaps (including generational, gender-based, and territorial gaps).[133] Objectives of the Plan include (i) 'Digitisation, Innovation, Competitiveness, Culture'; (ii) 'Green Revolution and Ecological Transition'; (iii) 'Infrastructure for Sustainable Mobility; (iv) 'Education and Research'; (v) 'Inclusion and Cohesion'; and (vi) 'Health'.

Relevant recent initiatives which will also prove fundamental to digitalization in Italy include the:

(i) '*La Strategia Cloud Italia*' – the Italian Cloud Strategy – which, in collaboration with the '*Agenzia per la cybersicurezza nazionale*', the Italian National Cybersecurity Agency has worked to define a cloud strategy for the public administration;[134] and the
(ii) Strategic Program on Artificial Intelligence 2022–2024.[135]

55. In order to facilitate the installation of infrastructure and simplify related procedures, in 2021, the Italian legislator passed the '*Decreto Legge Semplificazioni-bis*' – Legislative Decree 31 May 2021, no. 77 – and Legislative Decree 8 November 2021, no. 207 (which transposes Directive (EU) 2018/1972). D.Lgs 77/2021 'further simplifies the authorisation procedure for the installation of electronic communications infrastructure and for digital infrastructure of buildings and real estate units'.[136] D.Lgs 207/2021 instead 'simplifies procedures for certain types of installations of electronic communications infrastructures'.[137]

Announced on 29 January 2022, the '*Fondo per la Repubblica Digitale*' ('Fund for a Digital Republic') provides EUR 350 million over a five-year period to fund

132. Ministero dell'Economia e delle Finanze, *The National Recovery and Resilience Plan (NRRP)*, 26.5.2021, https://www.mef.gov.it/en/focus/The-National-Recovery-and-Resilience-Plan-NRRP/.
133. *Ibid.*
134. More information on the Italian Cloud Strategy is available at the following link (in Italian): https://cloud.italia.it/strategia-cloud-pa/.
135. Italian Government, *Strategic Programme on Artificial Intelligence 2022–2024*, 24.11.2021, https://assets.innovazione.gov.it/1637777513-strategic-program-aiweb.pdf.
136. *See* European Commission, Digital Economy and Society Index (DESI) 2022: Italy, at 11.
137. *Ibid.*

projects that support digital transformation[138] and will surely also play a positive role in helping Italy to be on par with its Member State counterparts.

In terms of closing the digital skills gap, other initiatives include the *'Strategia Nazionale per le Competenze Digitali'*[139] ('National Strategy for Digital Skills') and its plan for operationalization,[140] which have been created in the context of the *'Repubblica Digitale'* ('Digital Republic') initiative 'chart a well-defined strategic path in digital skills policy, investing in more structural actions and ensuring relevance of ongoing initiatives'.[141]

Italy's efforts in terms of reforms and investment plans have thus far had a positive impact on connectivity within the country.[142] However, more progress will be necessary in terms of digitalization, digital skills, and connectivity to meet Europe's Digital Decade targets by 2030.

138. Ministero per l'innovazione tecnologica e la transizione digitale, *Nasce il Fondo per la Repubblica Digitale,* 29.1.2022, https://innovazione.gov.it/notizie/comunicati-stampa/nasce-il-fondo-per-la-repubblica-digitale/.

139. Ministero per l'innovazione tecnologica e la digitalizzazione, *Strategia Nazionale per le Competenze Digitali*, 16.7.2020, https://docs.italia.it/italia/mid/strategia-nazionale-competenze-digitali-docs/it/1.0/index.html.

140. Ministero per l'innovazione tecnologica e la transizione digitale, *Le azioni,* 16.7.2020, https://repubblicadigitale.innovazione.gov.it/it/le-azioni/#il-piano.

141. Giuseppe Iacono, *Italy marks sound progress in digital skills according to 2021 data by Eurostat*, 23.5.2022, .

142. *See* European Commission, *Digital Economy and Society Index (DESI) 2022: Italy*, https://digital-strategy.ec.europa.eu/en/policies/desi-italy, at 13.

Chapter 3. The Information and Communications Technology Market

§1. The Italian ICT Market in General

56. ISTAT, which stands for *'Istituto Nazionale di Statistica'* ('National Institute of Statistics'), is the Italian public research body that deals with general censuses of the population, services and industry, agriculture, sample surveys on households and general economic surveys at the national level. ISTAT issues an annual report concerning the use of ICTs by Italian companies.[143]

57. Moreover, Assintel (*'Associazione Nazionale Imprese ICT'*),[144] which is the national association for Italian ICT and Digital companies, issues a yearly report outlining the status and outlook of the ICT Business market in Italy. The latest report covers the year 2022.

In this Chapter, the latest ISTAT 2021 and 2022 reports, as well as the Assintel 2021–2023 report,[145] will be briefly summarized in order to provide a quick overview of the Italian ICT Market.

58. ICT spending of Italian companies is generally growing and will continue to grow, mostly thanks to the increased use of mobile devices and applications for collaboration which, together with the gradual migration of data from data centres to the cloud, are concrete steps in the evolution of corporate IT towards a more adaptive digital infrastructure ecosystem, capable of supporting continuous digital transformation.

In this context, additional drivers for innovation and ICT spending have been the COVID-19 pandemic, which has removed many of the barriers which prevented organizations from heavily investing in the ICT fields, and the related National Recovery and Resilience Plan,[146] which allocates a good deal of resources to digitalization and the digital transition. This has allowed the ICT sector to *see* an increase in investments even during the pandemic itself, in stark contrast with other sectors which saw (and are still seeing) a decrease in investments.

Particularly, the widespread adoption of remote work, which has risen in 2022 and now concerns seven out of ten Italian companies, and of cloud applications is pushing companies to adapt their investment strategies to cope with these changes, in particular by increasing the efforts to migrate old legacy platforms towards more agile and decentralized cloud solutions, with a view to also reduce costs and risks.

143. The ISTAT report for 2022 may be consulted at the following link: https://www.istat.it/it/files//2023/01/REPORTICTNELLEIMPRESE_2022.pdf, while the 2021 report in available at the following link: https://www.istat.it/it/files//2022/01/REPORT-ICT-NELLE-IMPRESE_2021.pdf.

144. Which can be translated as 'National Association of ICT Companies'. Assintel official website is available at the following link: https://www.assintel.it.

145. The Assintel report for 2021–2022 may be consulted at the following link: https://assintelreport.assintel.it/pages/home.

146. In Italy, the Plan is generally known as *'Piano Nazionale di Ripresa e Resilienza'* or 'PNRR'.

59. Another trend which is acquiring traction is cybersecurity, which companies are increasingly attentive to as a result of the increase in costly cyberattacks, particularly phishing and ransomware. In particular, cybersecurity is a growing concern, being perceived as a major threat by 45.1% of bigger companies, which have stipulated an insurance policy for cyberattacks, and by 14.4% of smaller ones.[147]

60. However, despite the general positive outlook of the ICT Business market in Italy, there are still relatively few companies that are willing to invest in the most innovative technologies, such as Artificial Intelligence, Robotics, and Augmented/Virtual Reality, while Internet of Things in gaining some traction mostly within the manufacturing industry.

61. Moreover, as will be seen in §3.I *infra*, there are still many differences in spending and investments among regions, with southern Italy generally lagging behind.

§2. The Level of Digitalization of Italian Enterprises

62. The overall level of digitalization of Italian enterprises may be summarized by taking into account some key indicators concerning small and medium-sized enterprises (SMEs), which by far constitute the majority of the Italian market.[148] These key indicators are summarized below, as reported within the ISTAT 2022 and 2021 reports.[149]

63. During 2022, 69.9% of Italian SMEs reached at least a basic level of 'digital intensity' (i.e., at least four of the twelve activities related to the adoption of ICTs,[150] while the EU 2030 target is 90%). This indicator places Italian companies in eight place in the European ranking, up from the tenth place which Italy held in 2021.

147. *See* the ISTAT report, *supra* n. 144.
148. *Ibid.*
149. ISTAT report, *supra* n. 144.
150. The 'Digital Intensity Index' or 'DII' is an index constructed at the level of microdata that measures the use by companies of twelve different digital technologies: (1) Percentage of connected employees > 50%; (2) presence of ICT specialists; (3) download speed > = 30 Mbit/s; (4) holding online meetings (e.g., via Skype, Zoom, MS Teams, WebEx, etc.); (5) informing employees on their cybersecurity obligations; (6) organizing trainings on ICT/IT matters for employees not specialized in ICT/IT fields; (7) implementing at least three ICT security measures; (8) documenting measures, practices or procedures on ICT security; (9) having employees with remote online access to e-mails, documents or online applications; (10) use of robots; (11) online sales value of at least 1% of total revenues (on total turnover); (12) having online sales greater than 1% of total revenues and whose value of web sales to private consumers (B2C) exceeds 10% of total online sales. The value for the index therefore varies from zero to twelve. The index identifies four digital intensities according to the number of activities carried out by companies: up to three activities (very low), from four to six (low), from seven to nine (high), from ten to twelve (very high).

During 2021, among companies with at least ten employees, 41.9% have purchased medium-high level cloud computing services and 51.9% at intermediate and sophisticated levels, while the EU average is 35% (the EU 2030 target is 75%).

The trend of the indicators of the digital transition estimated in 2021 shows, on the one hand, slow improvements – consistent with the EU average – in the area of electronic commerce of SMEs; on the other hand, important accelerations in the adoption of intermediate or sophisticated cloud services and in the use of at least two social media (27%; with an increase of ten percentage points from 2017 and of five percentage points from 2020).

64. The indicators of the Digital Economy Society Index for SMEs that sell online are improving very slowly. In 2020, the percentage of companies with at least ten employees who performed online sales continued to be low (18.4%), and although there was an increase of two percentage points compared to the previous year, it remains below the EU average (23%). A more consistent growth concerns companies with at least 250 employees who are also more active in the electronic sales market (44.5%, from 40.2% in 2019) compared to those with ten to forty-nine employees (17.2%, up from 15.2% in 2019). During 2022, the use of electronic commerce by SMEs has stagnated, with only 13% of SMEs having sold goods or services online for at least 1% of their revenue (only slightly up from 12.7% during 2021).

The propensity to sell online varies significantly between different economic sectors. The most active sectors in the e-commerce field include the hospitality sector (83.7%), publishing activities (73.1%), and travel agency services activities (47.8%). However, online sales are also widespread in telecommunications (30.1%), retail trade (31.0%) and wholesale (28.6%), food industries (28.5%), catering service activities (24.8%), and audio-visual activities (23.6%).

65. In the use of Internet of Things technologies, during 2021, Italian companies with at least ten employees are, overall, ranked eighth in Europe. In 2021, 32.3% of companies with at least ten employees used IoT devices (29% of the EU27 average).

Among the companies that have made use of the Internet of Things, the most frequent are those that use devices for the security of the company's premises, for example, intelligent or smart alarm systems (74.6%) and the maintenance of machines or vehicles through sensors monitored or controlled via the Internet (29.9%).

These instruments are mainly used in the energy sector (45.9%), real estate activities (42.5%), the manufacturing of coke and products deriving from oil refining (40.7%), the food industries (40.3%), telecommunications (39.8%), and electrical equipment manufacturing (39.6%).

The use of IoT devices varies considerably with respect to the size of the company, especially as companies with at least 250 employees, compared to those with less than 50 employees, leverage these intelligent technologies to improve production and management efficiency (respectively 59.0% and 30.5%).

§3. INVESTMENTS IN ICTS

66. The ICT market generated by Italian companies in 2021 has had a value of EUR 34.5 billion. In 2022, a growth of 5.4% is expected compared to 2021, which will lead the market to reach EUR 36.3 billion, to then exceed EUR 38 billion in 2023, thanks to a further growth of 4.9%.[151]

Figure 2 ICT Market Trend in Italy

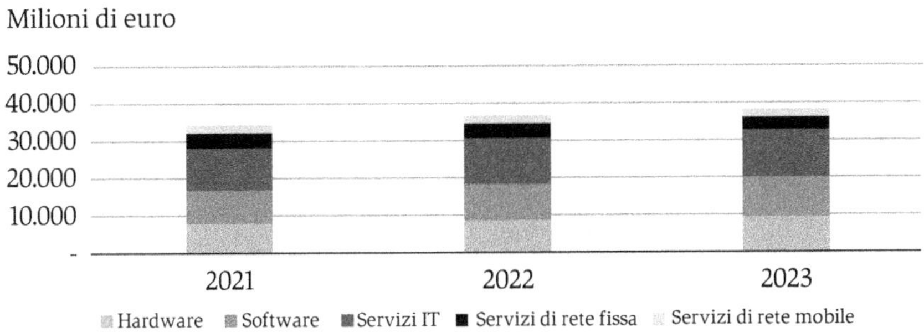

Source: IDC (Assintel Report, October 2022).

67. As shown in Figure 2, the ICT expenditure of Italian companies in 2022 stands at EUR 36.3 billion. IT Services, which include professional services dedicated to the development, integration and management of systems, solutions and applications, will generate a total expenditure of EUR 12.1 billion, which is equal to 33% of total ICT expenditure.

Over 51% of expenditure is instead absorbed by Hardware (EUR 9 billion) and Software (EUR 9.6 billion) which, compared to the previous year, have recorded very sustained growth, continuing to support the evolution of remote work, cloud migration of applications, and data centre transformation.

In percentage terms, spending on Telecommunications Services represents 15% of total investments by Italian companies for ICT, with a significant concentration in fixed network services (EUR 3.6 billion) compared to spending on mobile network services (EUR 2 billion), and a more moderate decrease compared to previous years.[152]

151. *See* the Assintel report, *supra* n. 146.
152. *Ibid.*

Figure 3 ICT Expenditure in Italy

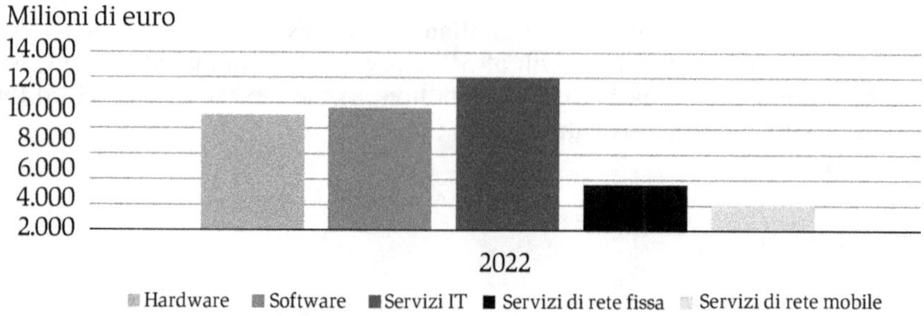

Source: IDC (Assintel Report, October 2022).

I. Regional Differences in Spending for ICTs

68. The ICT expenditure of companies by region – which is shown in Figure 3 – is influenced by the distribution of companies and institutions on the national territory. For this reason, over 45% of Italian ICT spending was concentrated in Lombardy and Lazio in 2022. The distribution of businesses by type and size also greatly influences expenditure in Emilia Romagna, Veneto and Piedmont, which overall account for 29% of ICT expenditure.

The remaining fifteen regions overall have a level of ICT investment which, albeit with different contributions, slightly exceeds 25% of total expenditure.[153]

153. *Ibid.*

Figure 4 The ICT Market per Region

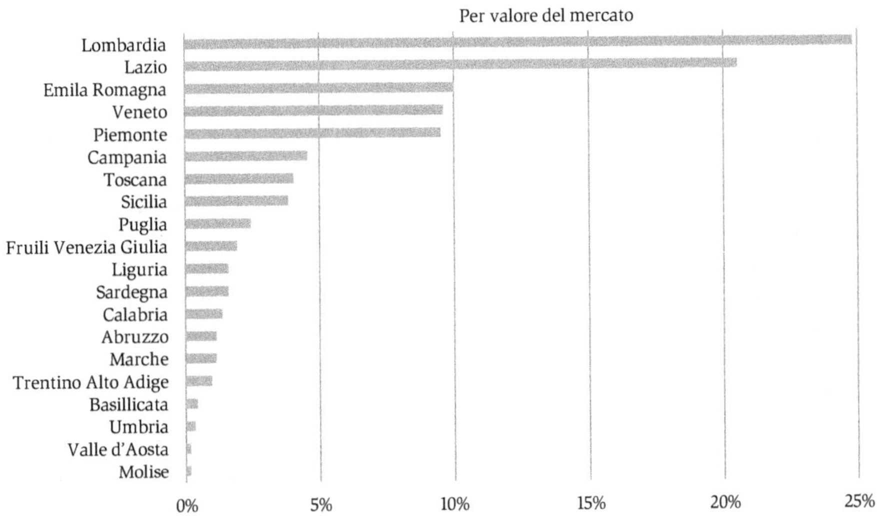

Source: IDC (Assintel Report, October 2022).

Chapter 4. E-Government

§1. The Digital Administration Code and Other Relevant Legislative Acts

69. The main legislative instrument on e-government within the Italian legal system is the Legislative Decree 7 March 2005, no. 82, titled *Codice dell'Amministrazione Digitale* ('Digital Administration Code' or 'CAD').

The CAD – which has been subject to numerous amendments over the years – regulates, in particular, digital citizenship and identity; relationships between public administrations; electronic and digital signatures; the requisites of validity, access retention and transmission of IT documents; the use and re-use of data by public administrations; online services rendered by the public administration; the development, acquisition and re-use of IT systems in public administrations; and the public connectivity system.

The CAD has both a vertical and a horizontal dimension, as it regulates not only the relationship between public bodies and between private parties and public bodies but also relationships between private parties with respect to rules concerning IT documents and electronic and digital signatures.

70. While the CAD has a general scope and endeavours to generally regulate the matter of digital administration, other more sectorial legislative acts exist, which complement the rules set forth by the CAD on specific points. This includes, for example, the Decree of the President of the Republic (D.P.R.) 11 February 2005, no. 68, on the use of Certified E-Mail, and Decree of the President of the Council of Ministers (D.P.C.M.) 25 March 2014, no. 85, which defines the characteristics of the digital identity and its use by public administrations.

71. Finally, sometimes, the rules set forth by the CAD have to be read in line with relevant EU legislation. This is true, notably, in the field of digital citizenship and identity, as well as in electronic and digital signatures, which are also covered by the eIDAS Regulation.[154]

I. Agency for Digital Italy ('AgID')

72. In 2012, the government issued Law Decree 9 February 2012, no. 5 (converted with amendments into Law 4 April 2012, no. 35) with the aim of introducing urgent measures on simplification and development, thereby including the enhancement of relations between the public administration and private parties through the development of innovative digital services. The Decree has laid the foundations for

154. Regulation (EU) no. 910/2014 of the European Parliament and of the Council of 23 Jul. 2014 on electronic identification and trust services for electronic transactions in the internal market and repealing Directive 1999/93/EC. OJ L 257, 28.8.2014.

the Italian Digital Agenda which, consistent with the European Digital Agenda, aims to modernize and enhance through the use of ICT technologies the Italian public administrations.

73. Subsequently, in order to ensure the fulfilment of the objectives of the Italian Digital Agenda, Law Decree 22 June 2012, no. 83 (converted with amendments by Law 7 August 2012, no. 134) has established *Agenzia per l'Italia Digitale* ('Agency for Digital Italy' or 'AgID'), which forms part of the Presidency of the Council of Ministers.

AgID is tasked with ensuring the digital coordination of the central, regional and local administration, in accordance with Article 117, paragraph 2, letter r) of the Constitution. Over the years, with various legislative acts, AgID has been assigned a number of specific tasks, among which, notably:[155]

(i) contributing to the diffusion of the use of information and communication technologies in order to foster innovation and economic growth;
(ii) elaborating instructions, technical rules and guidelines on the uniformity of languages, procedures, and standards for the full interoperability and consistency of the IT systems of the public administration;
(iii) monitoring the quality of services and the rationalization of IT spending by the public administration;
(iv) promoting and disseminating digital literacy initiatives.

§2. Digital Citizenship, Identity and Online Public Services

74. Digital citizenship and identity[156] are addressed by Articles 3 to 11 of the CAD, while the use of digital identity to enjoy online services is dealt with by Articles 63 to 66 of the CAD. In this respect, Article 3 sets forth a right for everyone to use the digital instruments regulated by the CAD vis-à-vis the public administration.

75. The most important instrument of digital identity is arguably the *Sistema Pubblico di Identità Digitale* ('Public System of Digital Identity' or 'SPID'), which was established by AgID to encourage the dissemination of online services and facilitate access to them by citizens and businesses (Article 64, paragraph 2-*bis*, of the CAD), and which consists of an open set of public and private entities which, subject to accreditation by AgID, according to the procedures defined with a D.P.C.M.,[157] identify users to allow them access to online services (Article 64, paragraph 2-*ter*, of the CAD).

---

155. Cf. AgID's official website: https://www.agid.gov.it/it/agenzia/strategia-quadro-normativo.
156. 'Digital identity' is defined by Art. 1, para. 1, letter u-*quater* of the CAD as 'the computerized representation of the correspondence between a user and their identifying attributes, verified through the datasets collected and recorded in digital form according to the procedures established by Art. 64 of the CAD'. Author's translation.
157. The relevant D.P.C.M. has been adopted in 2014, i.e., D.P.C.M. 85/2014, which defines the characteristics of the digital identity and its use by public administrations. Moreover, in line with Art.

In practical terms, the SPID is a login system that enables private parties (either natural or legal persons) to access most online public services with a single digital identity. The SPID is issued, at the request of the private party, by an accredited identity provider, i.e., a legal entity accredited by AgID,[158] based on procedures which aim to unequivocally identify the applicant.

The number of SPID users, although low in the years following its release in March 2016, has steadily increased overtime and received a considerable boost in the context of the COVID-19 pandemic, given the widespread digitalization which the pandemic has brought about: as of 11 January 2023, SPID digital identities in Italy exceeded 33.5 million.[159] SPID has been used to make more than a billion accesses to online public services in 2022, almost doubling the figure registered in 2022.[160]

76. Access to online public services can also take place, pursuant to Article 66 of the CAD, by using the *Carta d'Identità Elettronica* ('Electronic Identity Card' or 'CIE'), which is the identity document which incorporates elements for the physical identification of the holder, issued on IT support by the municipal administrations, with the main purpose of demonstrating the identity of its owner (Article 1, paragraph 1, letter c, of the CAD).

77. Article 64-*bis* of the CAD requires public bodies to make their services available by means of SPID, while both public bodies and accredited identity providers are required to project and develop services and interfaces which are interoperable.

SPID and CIE may be used, for example, to formally file a request for change of residence, request the issuing of an official certificate, book a medical appointment, send one's tax declaration, consult one's social security position, request access to bonuses, etc.[161]

4, para. 2, of said D.P.C.M., AgID has adopted a Regulation concerning the implementing modalities of SPID, which can be accessed here: https://www.agid.gov.it/sites/default/files/repository_files/regolamento_modalita_attuative_spid_2.0.pdf.

158. There are currently twelve accredited identity providers, as listed by AgID in its official website (https://registry.spid.gov.it/identity-providers): Aruba S.p.A., EtnaHitech S.C.p.A., InfoCamere S.C.p.A., InfoCert ID, Intesa ID, Lepida ID, Namirial ID, Poste ID, Sielte ID, SPIDItalia Register.it, TeamSystem ID, TIM ID.

159. This data is provided by the official website of AgID: https://www.agid.gov.it/it/agenzia/stampa-e-comunicazione/notizie/2023/01/11/piu-miliardo-accessi-tramite-spid-2022.

160. *Ibid.*

161. *Ibid.*

§3. Relationships Between Private Parties, and Between Private Parties and Public Administrations: The IT Document and Electronic Signatures, Certified E-Mail and the Digital Domicile

78. As anticipated, some of the legal institutions established and regulated by the CAD have relevance not only for the relationship between private parties and the public administrations but also between private parties themselves.

I. The IT Document and Electronic Signatures

79. In this respect, the IT document is defined by Article 1, paragraph 1, letter p, of the CAD as 'the electronic document that contains the computer representation of legal acts, facts or legally relevant data'.[162] The provision of a definition of an IT document serves the purpose of clarifying that the creation and use of IT documents are allowed and recognized and have legal effects within the Italian legal system.

80. However, in order for the IT document to be unequivocally attributed to a person and to have *tout court* legal value in some specific circumstances, it needs to be signed with an electronic signature. In this respect, the CAD foresees four different types of electronic signatures, each one of which has its own degree of legal value.

81. Three types of electronic signatures are the same as those which were envisaged by the eIDAS Regulation, i.e., the simple, advanced, and qualified electronic signatures.

Moreover, the CAD envisages a fourth and more robust type of electronic signature, i.e., the digital signature. This type of signature finds its definition within Article 1, paragraph 1, letter s, of the CAD, which defines the digital signature as:

> [A] particular type of qualified signature based on a cryptographic key system, a public and a private one, related to each other, which allows the owner of the electronic signature through the private key, and to a third party through the public key, respectively, to make manifest and to verify the origin and integrity of an IT document or a set of IT documents.[163]

82. As regards the simple electronic signature, Article 20, paragraph 1-*bis* of the CAD provides that its evidentiary value can be freely decided by the judge. As a result, there is no guarantee that an IT document signed with a simple electronic signature will have any evidentiary value in case of a dispute in court.

Concerning the advanced electronic signature, the qualified electronic signature and the digital signature, Article 20, paragraph 1-*bis* of the CAD provides that 'the

162. Author's translation.
163. *Ibid.*

IT document satisfies the requirement of written form, and has the legal value foreseen by Article 2702 of the Civil Code, when signed with digital signature, another type of qualified electronic signature or advanced signature … .'[164] In this case, the judge has, therefore, no possibility to assess the evidentiary value of the advanced electronic signature, qualified electronic signature and digital signature, given that this assessment has already been carried out by the legislator: as a result, the evidentiary value of these types of electronic signatures is always guaranteed by the legal system.

Some specific types of contracts,[165] when executed in the form of IT documents, are deemed legally valid only when signed with a digital signature, pursuant to Article 21, paragraph 2-bis, and Article 1350 of the Civil Code. The digital signature is, therefore, the strongest type of electronic signature to be present within the Italian legal system.

83. As will be seen in §4., *infra*, the use of electronic signatures is also highly relevant in the context of the Telematic Civil Process.

II. Certified E-Mail ('PEC') and the Digital Domicile

84. The '*Posta Elettronica Certificata*' ('Certified E-Mail' or 'PEC') is defined by Article 2, paragraph 1, letter v-*bis*, of the CAD, as 'a system of communication capable of certifying the sending and receipt of an electronic mail message, as well as to provide a receipt which are opposable to third parties'.[166]

85. Similarly, to the issuing of SPID credentials, PEC accounts may be supplied only by accredited private entities (the 'PEC Operator', defined in Article 2, paragraph 1, letter u-*bis*, of the CAD) which must fulfil specific technical and professional requirements and is subject to supervision and enforcement by AgID. This is due to the fact that the PEC has to guarantee certainty of sending and the guaranteed receipt of communications, as outlined by the definition above, which is achieved by means of technical measures.

86. The use of PEC is strictly related to the Digital Domicile, which is defined by Article 1, paragraph 1, letter n-*ter*, of the CAD as 'an electronic address elected at a certified e-mail service or certified electronic delivery certificate service, as defined by the … eIDAS Regulation, [is] valid for the purposes of electronic communications having legal value'.

The indication of a Digital Domicile is generally not compulsory but rather voluntary (Article 6-*quater* of the CAD), except for public bodies, professionals and companies, which are required to indicate a Digital Domicile to be registered within the publicly accessible National Index of PEC Addresses ('*Indice Nazionale degli*

164. *Ibid.*
165. Such as contracts concerning the rental or purchase of real estate, contracts concerning the establishment of corporations, etc.
166. Author's translation.

Indirizzi PEC' or 'INI-PEC')[167] and, for public bodies, the Index of Public Administrations ('*Indice delle Pubbliche Amministrazioni*' or 'IPA').[168]

87. Article 6, paragraph 1 of the CAD provides that when the PEC is sent to a Digital Domicile, the legal value of a PEC is equivalent to the use of registered postal mail with acknowledgement of receipt, except when otherwise provided by the law, in particular, the date and time of transmission and receipt of the IT document sent via PEC are opposable to third parties if the technical requirements for the valid issuing of the PEC are fulfilled.

As shall be seen in the following paragraph, the use of the PEC is also highly relevant in the context of the Telematic Civil Process.

88. According to AgID, which updates this information every two months, as of June 2022, there are more than 14 million PEC addresses, and during the months of May and June 2022, almost 500 million PEC messages have been exchanged.[169]

§4. The Telematic Civil Process ('PCT')

89. The Telematic Civil Process ('*Processo Civile Telematico*' or 'PCT') consists of a set of rules aimed at regulating the digitalization of the performance of activities and the writing of deeds in the context of civil procedure.

90. The origins of the PCT can be traced back to the early two-thousands, with Decree of the President of the Republic (DPR) 13 February 2001, no. 123, whose aim is to regulate the use of ICT tools in the context of civil and administrative procedures. For several years after the adoption of DPR 123/2001, the PCT saw a slow implementation phase, initially limited to experimentations in some Italian civil courts, with mixed results.[170]

Finally, Law Decree 24 June 2014, no. 90, rendered the use of PCT compulsory for some types of civil proceedings, starting from 30 June 2014. During the following years, the Italian legislator has progressively widened the scope of the mandatory use of the PCT which now includes, *inter alia*, the filing of appeals by injunctions, the deposit of endo-processual acts both for ordinary Tribunals and Court of Appeals, real estate litigation.

91. Operationally, the PCT is usually understood as including:[171]

167. The INI-PEC is publicly accessible at the following link: https://www.inipec.gov.it.
168. The IPA is publicly accessible at the following link: https://indicepa.gov.it/ipa-portale/consultazione/domicilio-digitale/ricerca-pec.
169. This data is provided by the official website of AgID: https://www.agid.gov.it/it/piattaforme/posta-elettronica-certificata/statistiche-utilizzo-pec.
170. Maribel Maini, *La sperimentazione del processo civile telematico*, 1–2 Informatica e diritto 399, 400 (2007).
171. *See* the official website of the Italian Bar Association: https://www.consiglionazionaleforense.it/pct/-/asset_publisher/2wDhXcMQ34b0/content/processo-civile-telematico-cos-e.

(i) the online consultation of the procedural file, which is possible for lawyers, expert witnesses, as well as for the private parties of a proceeding;[172]
(ii) the telematic filing and transmission of documents between the lawyer and the judicial authority;
(iii) the electronic payment of the unified contribution.

92. The preparation of judicial documents takes place by using a specific software, named 'File Editor of the Telematic Civil Process' ('*Redattore atti del Processo Civile Telematico*') which is foreseen by Ministerial Decree 21 February 2011, no. 44, and whose technical specifications are regulated by the Provision of the Ministry of Justice of 16 April 2014.[173] Article 12 of the Provision expressly states that the documents may be signed both by using a qualified electronic signature or by digital signature (for which *see* §3.I, *supra*).

Finally, the filing and transmission of the documents take place by means of the PEC (for which *see* §3.II, *supra*), as every lawyer is under an obligation to have a PEC address.

172. In this case, the citizen who is party in a civil litigation may access the judicial documents using their SPID credentials (for which *see supra* §2).
173. The text of the provision may be found here: https://pst.giustizia.it/PST/resources/cms/documents/Estratto_Gazzetta_Ufficiale_99_2014.pdf. This provision is arguably the most important source which regulates the PCT.

Part I. Privacy Protection in Italy

Chapter 1. Privacy Protection in the Constitution

§1. The Italian Constitution: A Brief Overview

93. The Italian constitution[174] entered into force on 1 January 1948, after long and complex discussions which took place within the Constitutional Assembly ('*Assemblea Costituente*').[175] The Assembly was elected on 2 June 1946, in the first free generalized elections after the fall of fascism and the end of World War II. The final text of the Constitution was approved by more than 90% of the Assembly components, despite the latter being composed of many political forces with stiff differences among them.[176]

94. This circumstance led to a number of characteristics which are inherent to the Italian Constitution. In particular, it is a 'long' Constitution, given that such wide *consensus* could only be reached by adding the different instances, values and interests of each political force. It is also an 'open' Constitution because a number of its provisions leave their implementation to ordinary legislation. Moreover, many articles provide strong protections to political minorities, either directly or indirectly.

Lastly, and more relevant for the purposes of this volume, the Constitution does not provide for a 'closed list' of fundamental rights and freedoms which are granted constitutional protection. Rather, while indeed some specific fundamental rights are expressly recognized by Articles 1 to 54, the Constitution adopts an open-ended model where new fundamental rights are derived by the jurisprudence of the Constitutional Court on the basis of Article 2,[177] which states that (free translation), 'The

174. The official English language translation of the Constitution of the Italian Republic is available on the Italian Senate's website at: https://www.senato.it/documenti/repository/istituzione/costituzione_inglese.pdf. All direct quotations from the Constitution within this volume are taken from the official translation.

175. The minutes of the discussion (in Italian) are available online at the following URL http://leg16.camera.it/516?conoscerelacamera=118.

176. Roberto Bin & Giovanni Pitruzzella, *Diritto Costituzionale* 138–139 (Giappichelli Editore 20th ed. 2019).

177. Paolo Grossi, *L'invenzione del diritto* (2017); Augusto Barbera, *Commentario della Costituzione* (Giuseppe Branca ed., 1950), 80 et seq. Another mechanism which permits the Constitution to stay up to date with the emergence of new fundamental rights is Art. 117, which allows human rights treaties and conventions that have been executed and ratified by the Italian Republic (such as, most

Republic recognizes and guarantees the inviolable rights of man, both as an individual and in the social formations where his personality develops, and requires the fulfilment of the mandatory duties of political, economic and social solidarity'. This 'open clause' mechanism has allowed the Italian Constitution to stay up-to-date overtime and introduce new generations of fundamental rights within the Italian constitution, which were not yet recognized when the Constitution was adopted in 1948.

95. Concerning constitutional justice, Articles 134–137 provide for the institution of a Constitutional Court ('*Corte Costituzionale*'), which has the power to invalidate or amend the provisions of ordinary laws which are deemed to be contrary to the Constitution. Alleged unconstitutional law provisions may be referred to the Court by any ordinary or administrative judge, as well as by the State against regional laws and by the Regions against state laws or other regions laws. The Court is composed of fifteen judges, which remain in their position for nine years and cannot be re-appointed. One-third of the judges are nominated by the Parliament, a third by the President of the Republic and a third by the supreme ordinary and administrative judiciary.[178]

§2. The Right to Privacy and Personal Data Protection Within the Italian Constitution

96. The right to privacy is not expressly recognized by the Italian Constitution, given that, as indicated above, the latter does not expressly list all fundamental rights and freedoms which are recognized and protected at a constitutional level. However, some of the fundamental rights which are expressly recognized by the Constitution provide some indirect protection to the right to privacy. In particular, such indirect protection may be found in the protection of personal freedom (Article 13), the right to personal domicile (Article 14), the right to liberty and secrecy of correspondence (Article 15), as well as the freedom of thought (Article 21) intended in its negative dimension, i.e., the right to maintain one's thoughts and ideas confidential.[179]

I. Early Judgments: The Emergence of the Right to Confidentiality

97. Against this background, the Italian Constitutional Court has recognized the existence of a right to privacy – labelled as the right to confidentiality ('*diritto alla riservatezza*') – in the context of various decisions concerning the freedom of the

---

notably, the European Convention on Human Rights and Fundamental Freedoms) to be granted quasi-constitutional force: *see*, for a general overview, Part I, Ch. 2, *infra*.

178. Article 135, para. 1, of the Constitution.

179. *See*, e.g., Licia Califano, Trasparenza e privacy nell'evoluzione dell'ordinamento costituzionale, 31 Giornale di Storia Costituzionale 77 (2016), passim.

press, starting from the 1970s.[180] In particular, with judgment 122/1970, and later with judgment 38/1973, the Court has held that the right to confidentiality has constitutional protection and that it may be carved out from Article 2 of the Constitution, read in conjunction with Articles 3[181] and 13.

98. These judgments, however, did not define the right, nor did they outline its scope of application. It was only in 1975 that the Supreme Court of Cassation, with its judgment of 27 May 1975, no. 2129 provided a definition of the right to confidentiality, which it defined as (free translation): 'The protection of those situations and circumstances which are strictly personal and familiar which, even if they have taken place outside of the home, do not have for the others a socially significant interest … '. As can be appreciated from this notion, such a right covers the static and negative aspects of the right to privacy, similar to the 'right to be let alone' carved out by Warren and Brandeis in their 1890 article for the Harvard Law Review,[182] albeit, as can be seen from the above definition, the right to confidentiality recognized by the Supreme Court of Cassation is wider in scope, given that it also covers facts and circumstances which takes place outside of the personal domicile. Even in the light of this judgment, no right to personal data protection existed in the Italian constitutional order at that time.

II. The Emergence of the Right to Personal Data Protection Within the Italian Legal System

99. During the 1980s, however, things slowly started to change. In 1981, Italy signed the Council of Europe's ('CoE') Convention for the Protection of Individuals with regard to Automatic Processing of Personal Data ('Convention 108'),[183] i.e., the first binding international legal instrument which recognized the right to personal data protection, thereby starting a process which would later lead to the right of personal data protection being recognized as having a constitutional status. However, despite having signed the Convention, Italy did not ratify it at the time and failed to adopt a general legislation aimed at regulating the automated processing of personal data, which was expressly required by the Convention itself.

100. Despite this setback, during the 1990s, the Constitutional Court refined, expanded and evolved the right to privacy first envisaged by the Supreme Court of

180. Nadia Zorzi Galgano et al., *Persona e Mercato dei Dati. Riflessioni sul GDPR* 5–6 (1st ed. 2019).
181. Article 3 sets forth the right to formal equality before the law (para. 1), as well as the right to 'substantive equality' (para. 2). *See,* e.g., Bin & Pitruzzella, *supra* n. 177, 515–521.
182. Samuel D. Warren & Louis D. Brandeis, *The Right to Privacy,* 4 Harvard Law Review 193, (1890).
183. Council of Europe, *Convention for the Protection of Individuals with Regard to Automatic Processing of Personal Data,* Council of Europe Treaty Series 108 (1981). Convention 108 requires parties to it 'to take the necessary steps in their domestic legislation to apply the principles it lays down in order to ensure respect in their territory for the fundamental human rights of all individuals with regard to processing of personal data'. Also note that Italy has been party to Convention 108 since 1 Jul. 1997. For more information, *see* Convention 108 and Protocols, Council of Europe, https://www.coe.int/en/web/data-protection/convention108-and-protocol.

Cassation in 1975, encompassing under this concept not only the safeguard of confidentiality but also the protection of personal data.[184] In particular, with its judgment 139/1990, the Constitutional Court recognized that (free translation): 'The principles which safeguard individual privacy … are present, in almost identical form, in the legal orders of all the civil nations.' This judgment allowed the Court to implicitly recognize the protection of personal data as being encompassed within the right to confidentiality and therefore protected under the Constitution,[185] as the facts of the case concerned a legislative provision, Legislative Decree 6 September 1989, no. 322, which prohibited the national statistical office from communicating or disseminating the data related to Italian residents to the public, except in aggregated and anonymous form.[186]

101. In light of this recognition, the Court has proceeded, in the following years, in upholding the right to confidentiality in the context of the interception of telephone calls (judgments 366/1991 and 81/1993), as well as of the protection of the private domicile against video surveillance (judgment 135/2002).[187] Meanwhile, the Italian legislator adopted the first encompassing legal instrument for the protection of personal data, i.e., Law 31 December 1996, no. 675,[188] in the context of the transposition of Directive/95/46/EC.[189] After the enactment of Directive 2002/58/EC[190] (so-called ePrivacy Directive and hereinafter referred to as such within this volume), L. 675/1996 would later be reorganized within Legislative Decree 30 June 2003, no. 196, titled 'Personal Data Protection Code' (and hereinafter referred to as such within this volume), which has undergone numerous amendments through the years and is still in force today.[191]

---

184. *See*, e.g., Califano, *supra* n. 180, at 84; Zorzi Galgano et al., *supra* n. 181.
185. Paola Patatini & Fulvio Troncone, *L'oscuramento dei dati personali nei provvedimenti della Corte costituzionale*, Servizio Studi Corte Costituzionale (dicembre 2020), https://www.cortecostituzionale.it/documenti/convegni_seminari/STU%20316_Oscuramento_dati_personali.pdf, 19–21.
186. The Court upheld the validity of this provision.
187. Califano, *supra* n. 180, at 85. More generally on case law concerning video surveillance in Italy, *see* Paolo Balboni, *Video Surveillance and Related Privacy and Data Protection Issues: The Italian Experience* (Sjaak Nouwt, Berend R. de Vries, & Corien Prins (eds.), Reasonable Expectation of Privacy? Eleven Country Reports on Camera Surveillance and Workplace Privacy, T.M.C. Asser Press, The Hague), 293 – 322.
188. Before the enactment of this law, some legal provisions aimed at protecting privacy and personal data could be found (and can still be found) in the L. 300/1970 (so-called *Statuto dei Lavoratori*, i.e., 'Workers Statute'), in particular within its Art. 4, which prohibits the employer from monitoring the activities of its employees, and Art. 8, which prohibits the employer from carrying out investigations concerning the employee's religious beliefs, trade union membership and, in general, in facts not relevant to the evaluation of the employee's performance.
189. Directive 95/46/EC of the European Parliament and of the Council of 24 Oct. 1995 on the protection of individuals with regard to the processing of personal data and on the free movement of such data, OJ L 281, 23.11.1995.
190. Directive 2002/58/EC of the European Parliament and of the Council of 12 Jul. 2002 concerning the processing of personal data and the protection of privacy in the electronic communications sector (Directive on privacy and electronic communications), OJ L 201, 31.7.2002.
191. The Personal Data Protection Code had been thoroughly overhauled in 2018, with D.Lgs. 101/2018, in order to bring it in line with the GDPR. *See* Part II, Ch. 1, §1.

102. Despite being adopted in order to transpose the above-mentioned two European Directives, the adoption of L. 675/1996 and D.Lgs. 196/2003 has arguably accelerated the elaboration and emergence of personal data protection as a fundamental right. In particular, with its judgment 5658/1998, the Supreme Court of Cassation listed L. 675/1996 among the legislative instruments which reflect the willingness of the legislator to provide active protection to the right to confidentiality, including the protection of personal data, while at the same time recalling its previous jurisprudence in order to confirm that such a right is also directly protected by the Constitution, especially in the light of its Article 2.

103. Article 1 of the original text of the Personal Data Protection Code[192] expressly recognized the protection of personal data as a fundamental right of the individual, thereby using the exact same wording which may be found in Article 8 of the Charter of Fundamental Rights of the European Union.[193] Article 2 provided that the processing of personal data shall take place in accordance with the fundamental rights and freedoms of data subjects, especially with regard to confidentiality, personal identity and the right to personal data protection. Given the same wording used, as well as the fact that the Personal Data Protection Code was aimed at transposing EU Law on personal data protection (at that time, the two Directives mentioned above), it can be argued that the right set forth within Article 1 of the original text of the Personal Data Protection Code is the same as the one recognized by European Union primary law, i.e., by Article 8 of the Charter and Article 16 TFEU. As a result, the right to personal data protection in force within the Italian constitutional order can be similarly conceptualized as the right to assert one's control over one's personal data, thereby going beyond the right to privacy intended as the mere and static 'right to be let alone'.

104. Finally, with its judgment 271/2005, the Constitutional Court finally recognized the constitutional standing of the provisions of the Personal Data Protection Code – thereby including Article 1 – and, as a result, of the right to personal data protection within the Italian constitutional order.[194]

III. The Limits of the Right to Confidentiality and to Data Protection

105. In its subsequent judgments, the Constitutional Court has confirmed the existence of the right to confidentiality and data protection within the Italian constitutional order.[195] Moreover, the Court has clarified the limits of the two rights, with particular regard to their balancing vis-à-vis transparency in the public sector.

192. Before being repelled by the 2018 reform: *see* Part II, Ch. 1, §1.
193. Charter of Fundamental Rights of the European Union, OJ C 326, 26.10.2012.
194. Califano, *supra* n. 180, at 85.
195. Patatini & Troncone, *supra* n. 186, at 21.

106. With judgment 165/2008, the Court stated that the right to confidentiality is not absolute and may be subject to derogations and limitations in order to be balanced with other rights and values protected by the Constitution, such as the principles of publicity and transparency of the public administrative activity, which are a corollary of the democratic principle[196] and of the principle of the good functioning of the public administration.[197]

According to the Court, the publication – and therefore the processing – of personal data in order to achieve the above-mentioned aims amounts to a legitimate purpose of processing. In this respect, the Court clarified that the relevant processing of personal data is legitimate insofar as it is limited to what is strictly necessary to fulfil such purposes, with a view to provide minimal interference to the right of confidentiality and data protection. In any case, it is necessary that the interference with such rights is provided for by law and amounts to 'a measure which, in a democratic society, is necessary for national security, public security, the economic well-being of the country, the protection of public order and the prevention of criminal offenses, as well as the protection of the rights and freedoms of others'.[198]

107. In 2019, the Court notably applied these principles with its judgment 20/2019, again in a case concerning transparency in the context of public administration. In particular, Legislative Decree 25 May 2016, no. 97, was subject to scrutiny from the Court; this decree mandated that all the income earned and estate properties owned by publicly elected officials, public directors and close family members[199] had to be published online. The purpose of this publication was to allow Italian citizens to verify whether those persons benefited from increases in income and assets, including through the spouse or other close relatives, and whether such increases were consistent with the remuneration received through public funds for the position held.[200]

In this context, from a theoretical perspective, the Court asserted that – in light of technological developments – today, the right to confidentiality encompasses the right to control the flow of one's personal information,[201] thereby recognizing the right to personal data protection as being a subset of the constitutionally-protected right to confidentiality. Subsequently, the Court reiterated that the pursuit of objectives of transparency in the exercise of public functions and offices for the public benefit is a legitimate aim which – in principle – may be balanced (and therefore may legitimize interferences with) the right to confidentiality and data protection. However, the pursuit of these purposes must take place through the disclosure of personal information which are reasonably and effectively connected to the exercise

196. Such principle is recognized under Art. 1 of the Constitution.

197. Which is indirectly protected by Art. 97 of the Constitution.

198. Author's translation. Constitutional Court judgment 165/2008, para. 5.1.

199. Albeit, for the latter category, the publication was subject to the family member's consent; however, the possible denial of consent has still to be published.

200. Nicolò Zanon, Privacy e trasparenza in conflitto: il caso della pubblicazione on line dei dati reddituali e patrimoniali dei dirigenti della pubblica amministrazione, (12.10.2019) https://www.cortecostituzionale.it/documenti/relazioni_internazionali/RelazioneZANON_Lisbona10-12ottobre2019.pdf, 9.

201. Constitutional Court judgment 20/2019, para. 2.2.

of control from the general public, both on the correct pursuit of institutional functions and on the correct use of public resources, with the ultimate aim of combating public perception of corruption.

In this respect, the Court held that the publication of amounts related to the performance of public office, as well as that of service trips and missions paid with public funds, amounted to a measure genuinely necessary to pursue such legitimate aim, given that it enables the possibility of widespread control by those same recipients of the services provided by the public administration, concerning the way in which public resources are spent and the results achieved by the administration. However, the same could not be held concerning the publication of income and real estate data (both of the public directors and of their closest relatives), in addition to the information relating to salaries and other sums received by public directors for their office.

Chapter 2. National Application of European and International Conventions (Incl. National Jurisprudence Regarding ECHR Article 8)

§1. INTRODUCTION

108. International conventions to which the Italian Republic is a signatory, European Union regulations, and national law are sources of private international law in Italy.[202] Multiple international multilateral and European conventions are in force in the country,[203] e.g., the 1951 Refugee Convention and its 1967 Protocol, the Convention on the Law Applicable to Contractual Obligations 1980, also known as the 'Rome Convention', the Vienna Convention on the International Sale of Goods of 1980, the Hague Divorce Convention of 1970, etc.[204]

109. Italy is a founding member of the CoE,[205] having joined on 5 May 1949,[206] and the Italian Republic is furthermore a signatory to the European Convention on Human Rights ('ECHR'),[207] the CoE's fist 'convention and the cornerstone of all its activities'.[208] In addition to the ECHR, over two hundred international treaties have been agreed upon in the context of the CoE.[209] Along these lines, Italy is party to numerous conventions, including the Budapest Convention,[210] 'Convention 108'[211] and more recently, its modernized version, Convention 108+.

202. *Which country's law applies?* European Judicial Network (in civil and commercial matters) (22 Dec. 2021), https://e-justice.europa.eu/340/EN/which_country_s_law_applies?ITALY&member=1.
203. *Ibid.*
204. *Ibid.*
205. Note that 'The Council of Europe (CoE) is an Intergovernmental Organisation based in the Palace of Europe in Strasbourg (France). It was established by the Treaty of London of 5 May 1949 by ten founding States (Belgium, France, Luxembourg, Netherlands, United Kingdom, Denmark, Norway, Ireland, Italy and Sweden) with the aim of creating a common democratic and legal space in Europe, guaranteeing respect for human rights, democracy and the rule of law.' For more information, *see Council of Europe,* Ministero degli Affari Esteri e della Cooperazione Internazionale https://www.esteri.it/en/politica-estera-e-cooperazione-allo-sviluppo/organizzazioni_internazionali/council-of-europe/.
206. *Italy,* Council of Europe, https://www.coe.int/en/web/portal/italy.
207. Italy signed the European Convention on Human Rights on 4 Nov. 1950 and it was ratified on 16 Oct. 1955. https://www.echr.coe.int/Documents/Facts_Figures_Italy_ENG.pdf.
208. *See A Convention to protect your rights and liberties*, Council of Europe, https://www.coe.int/en/web/human-rights-convention#:~:text=A%20Convention%20to%20protect%20your,prerequisite%20for%20joining%20the%20Organisation. Also *see The ECHR and Italy: Facts and Figures*, Council of Europe (February 2022), https://www.echr.coe.int/Documents/Facts_Figures_Italy_ENG.pdf.
209. *Impact of the European Convention on Human Rights,* Council of Europe, https://www.coe.int/en/web/impact-convention-human-rights#/.
210. Council of Europe, *Convention on Cybercrime*, Council of Europe Treaty Series 185 (2001).
211. *See supra* n. 184.

Italian Ambassador Michele Giacomelli, the Permanent Representative of Italy to the Council of Europe, deposited the ratification document of the Amending Protocol to the Convention for the Protection of Individuals with regard to the Processing of Personal Data (CETS 223) on 8 July 2021.[212]

Moreover, Italy, like all EU Member States, is required to observe the principles and respect the rights included in the Charter of Fundamental Rights of the European Union[213] (hereinafter the 'Charter') which can be thought of as the 'EU's bill of human rights', in cases where 'they are acting within the scope of binding EU law'.[214] Sometimes, the provisions of the Charter 'are sufficiently precise and unconditional, they can have a direct effect at the national level – for instance in national courtrooms. Charter provisions that are 'principles' can only be invoked before a court if implemented by legislative or executive acts'.[215]

For the purpose of clarity, it is necessary to briefly explain the relationship between the ECHR and the Charter.[216] Article 52(3) ('Scope and Interpretation') states that:

> In so far as this Charter contains rights which correspond to rights guaranteed by the Convention for the Protection of Human Rights and Fundamental Freedoms, the meaning and scope of those rights shall be the same as those laid down by the said Convention. This provision shall not prevent Union law providing more extensive protection.[217]

212. *Italy, a 12th ratification for Convention 108+*, Council of Europe (8 Jul. 2021), https://www.coe.int/en/web/data-protection/-/italy-a-12th-ratification-for-convention-10-1.
213. Of particular relevance with respect to the topic at hand are Arts 7 and 8 of the Charter which concern the 'Respect for private and family life' and the 'Protection of personal data', respectively. Note that the European Parliament, Commission and the Council of the EU proclaimed the Charter in December 2000 and that it became legally binding on 1 Dec. 2009. *See* p. 6, *The EU Charter of Fundamental Rights in Italy,* European Union Agency for Fundamental Rights (2019), https://fra.europa.eu/sites/default/files/fra_uploads/fra-2019-eu-charter-in-italy_en.pdf.
214. The Charter of Fundamental rights includes fifty articles that concerns substantive rights and principles, and general provisions in fourth articles. For more information *see ibid.*, at 2.
215. *Ibid.* Also note that 'national courts do sometimes use the Charter to interpret or further develop national law, even outside the scope of EU law' and that 'in Italy, some Charter rights appear not to be fully mirrored in national constitutional law – for instance, the right of access to placement services (Art. 29), protection in the event of unjustified dismissal (Art. 30), consumer protection (Art. 38), right of access to documents (Art. 42) and the right not to be tried or punished twice for the same criminal offence (Art. 50). The absence of certain rights from a constitutional text by no means implies that they are not protected by the legal order. However, explicit guarantees in a constitutional text make these rights more visible and so also more accessible. In this sense, the Charter can strengthen less well-known rights.' Also *see ibid.* (https://fra.europa.eu/sites/default/files/fra_uploads/fra-2019-eu-charter-in-italy_en.pdf), at 5.
216. The European Charter became legally binding in European Union Member States upon the entrance in to force of the Lisbon Treaty. *EU Charter of Fundamental Rights,* European Union Agency for Fundamental Rights, https://fra.europa.eu/en/eu-charter#:~:text=The%20Charter%20of%20Fundamental%20Rights,Lisbon%20on%201%20December%202009.
217. European Union, Charter of Fundamental Rights of the European Union, 26 Oct. 2012, 2012/C 326/02.

110. It is also relevant to recall that when it comes to the issue of data protection, for example, the Charter provides more extensive protections to the right than the Convention does.[218]

§2. The Italian Constitution and the European Convention on Human Rights

111. In terms of national law, the Italian legal system and, more specifically, the Italian Constitution provides for 'the protection of all rights and fundamental freedoms included in relevant international standards, such as the European Convention on Human Rights and Fundamental Freedoms, the Human Rights Universal Declaration or the International Covenant on Civil and Political Rights'[219] of which the ECHR is of particular relevance, also having a so-called super-legislative rank.[220] The Italian Constitution, which contains 139 articles and 18 'Transitional and final Provisions', came into effect in 1948.[221] Two parts of the Italian Constitution deal with fundamental rights: Articles 1–12 ('Fundamental Principles') and Articles 13–54 (Part I, 'Rights and Duties of the Citizens').[222] However, other fundamental rights can be found in various other articles of the Constitution. To this end, *see* in this volume Part I, Chapter 1, *supra*.

In Italy and with respect to the protection of human rights in the national legal system, it is the Italian Constitutional Court that handles infringements at the constitutional level,[223] and the same Court has the exclusive competence to carry out 'the judicial review of legislation on the ground on conventionality'.[224]

---

218. Note that 'in many contexts it may not be possible to directly invoke the Charter – for instance, because the respective Charter provision is a principle and not a right and was not implemented by a legislative or executive act; or is otherwise not directly applicable; or does not apply at all because the case at hand falls outside the scope of EU law. In any case, the Charter increases the visibility of rights. It explicitly spells out rights and principles that are often not expressly laid out in other international human rights documents, such as the ECHR … ' *See supra* n. 214 (https://fra.europa.eu/sites/default/files/fra_uploads/fra-2019-eu-charter-in-italy_en.pdf), at 4.
219. Ministry of Foreign Affairs and International Cooperation, Inter-ministerial Committee for Human Rights, *Italy's Contribution on 'Cultural Rights and Public Spaces'* (June 2019), https://www.ohchr.org/sites/default/files/Documents/Issues/CulturalRights/Call/7_ITALY.docx.
220. *See* Alessia Cozzi et al., *Comparative study on the implementation of the ECHR at the national level*, Council of Europe (2016), https://rm.coe.int/16806fbc14, at 44.
221. Mario Einaudi, *The Constitution of the Italian Republic*, 42 American Political Science Review no. 4 (1948): 661–76.
222. *See supra* n. 214 (https://fra.europa.eu/sites/default/files/fra_uploads/fra-2019-eu-charter-in-italy_en.pdf), at 3.
223. *See supra* n. 220 (Ministry of Foreign Affairs and International Cooperation, Inter-ministerial Committee for Human Rights, *Italy's Contribution on 'Cultural Rights and* Public (June 2019), https://www.ohchr.org/sites/default/files/Documents/Issues/CulturalRights/Call/7_ITALY.docx), at 2.
224. Cozzi et al., *supra* n. 221, at 44. Also note that, 'When the interpretation in conformity with the Convention is not possible, ordinary courts must make a referral to the Constitutional Court, in order to evaluate the consistency of the internal norm with the ECHR' and that 'the Italian Constitutional Court recognises a prominent role to the ECtHR interpretation, but eventually it is for the Constitutional Court to strike the fair balance between all the rights and the general interests at stake.'

Neither the Charter nor the ECHR are directly referred to in the Italian Constitution. They are, nonetheless, binding for Italy pursuant to Articles 10,[225] 11[226] and 117[227] of the Italian Constitution.[228] The reform of the Italian constitution in 2001,[229] in fact, vests legislative powers 'in the State and the Regions in compliance with the Constitution and with the constraints deriving from EU legislation and international obligations' under the amended Article 117, paragraph 1, of the Constitution. As scholars have pointed out, the addition of this Article guarantees compliance with the obligations of the ECHR at the constitutional level in Italy and 'as a consequence, that a conflict between a rule of domestic law and a rule of international treaty law, in particular of the ECHR, amounts to a violation of Article 117(1)'.[230]

Along these lines, the Italian Constitutional Court in its Decision no. 311 of 2009, in stating that 'the domestic judge, as the common judge of the Convention, has the duty to apply the relevant rules, as interpreted by the Strasburg Court', confirmed that:

> *112.* [T]he competence of the ordinary courts to apply the ECHR is limited only by the existence of a conflict with a domestic law provision and by the impossibility of solving this conflict by way of interpretation. Accordingly, the domestic judge should be seen as fully competent to apply the ECHR in all cases when he is not bound to raise the plea of unconstitutionality before the Corte Costituzionale.[231]

225. Article 10 of the Italian Constitution reads: 'The Italian legal system conforms to the generally recognised principles of international law. The legal status of foreigners is regulated by law in conformity with international provisions and treaties. A foreigner who, in his home country, is denied the actual exercise of the democratic freedoms guaranteed by the Italian constitution shall be entitled to the right of asylum under the conditions established by law. A foreigner may not be extradited for a political offence.'
226. Article 11 of the Italian Constitution reads, 'Italy rejects war as an instrument of aggression against the freedom of other peoples and as a means for the settlement of international disputes. Italy agrees, on conditions of equality with other States, to the limitations of sovereignty that may be necessary to a world order ensuring peace and justice among the Nations. Italy promotes and encourages international organisations furthering such ends.'
227. 'Legislative powers shall be vested in the State and the Regions in compliance with the Constitution and with the constraints deriving from EU legislation and international obligations.'
228. *See supra* n. 214 (https://fra.europa.eu/sites/default/files/fra_uploads/fra-2019-eu-charter-in-italy_en.pdf), at 3. It should also be noted that the Charter 'benefits from the strength of EU law, which often has direct effect and, in principle and unlike international law, must be granted supremacy over national law. However, in many contexts it may not be possible to directly invoke the Charter – for instance, because the respective Charter provision is a principle and not a right and was not implemented by a legislative or executive act; or is otherwise not directly applicable; or does not apply at all because the case at hand falls outside the scope of EU law.' Also *see ibid.*, at 4.
229. *See* Andrea Caligiuri & Nicola Napoletano, *The Application of the ECHR in the Domestic Systems*, 20 The Italian Yearbook of International Law Online 125, 135 (2010).
230. *Ibid.*
231. *Ibid.*, at 141.

§3. Italy and the European Convention on Human Rights

113. The ECHR, the official name of which is 'The Convention for the Protection of Human Rights and Fundamental Freedoms', opened for signature on 4 November 1950 in Rome, Italy.[232] It came into force on 3 September 1953[233] and has been amended several times.[234] Italy implemented the ECHR within the national legal system through Law 4 August 1955, no. 848, making it part of ordinary Italian law.[235] To this end, it is cited in multiple cases of the Italian Courts, some of which will be dealt with below.

Article 8 of the Convention concerns the 'Right to respect for private and family life'[236] and is of particular relevance to the area of privacy, as affirmed by case law of the European Court of Human Rights ('ECtHR'), also known as the 'Strasbourg Court'.[237] The purpose of Article 8 ECHR 'is to protect against arbitrary interferences with private and family life, home, and correspondence by a public authority'.[238] In terms of national application, it is also relevant to note that '[w]hile the

232. Convention for the Protection of Human Rights and Fundamental Freedoms (European Convention on Human Rights, as amended) (ECHR), available at: https://www.echr.coe.int/pages/home.aspx?p=basictexts.

233. *Ibid.*

234. As the official document of the Convention notes at 3, 'The text of the Convention is presented as amended by the provisions of Protocol no. 15 (CETS no. 213) as from its entry into force on 1 August 2021 and of Protocol no. 14 (CETS no. 194) as from its entry into force on 1 June 2010. The text of the Convention had previously been amended according to the provisions of Protocol No. 3 (ETS no. 45), which entered into force on 21 September 1970, of Protocol No. 5 (ETS no. 55), which entered into force on 20 December 1971, and of Protocol No. 8 (ETS no. 118), which entered into force on 1 January 1990, and comprised also the text of Protocol No. 2 (ETS no. 44) which, in accordance with Article 5 paragraph 3 thereof, had been an integral part of the Convention since its entry into force on 21 September 1970. All provisions which had been amended or added by these Protocols were replaced by Protocol No. 11 (ETS no. 155), as from the date of its entry into force on 1 November 1998. As from that date, Protocol No. 9 (ETS no. 140), which entered into force on 1 October 1994, was repealed and Protocol No. 10 (ETS no. 146) lost its purpose.'

235. *See* Caligiuri & Napoletano, *supra* n. 230, at 135.

236. The full text of Art. 8 reads as follows, '1. Everyone has the right to respect for his private and family life, his home and his correspondence. 2. There shall be no interference by a public authority with the exercise of this right except such as is in accordance with the law and is necessary in a democratic society in the interests of national security, public safety or the economic well-being of the country, for the prevention of disorder or crime, for the protection of health or morals, or for the protection of the rights and freedoms of others.'

237. *See* Privacy and data protection: Explanatory Memorandum, Council of Europe, https://www.coe.int/en/web/freedom-expression/privacy-and-data-protection-explanatory-memo. Also note, as explained in the memorandum, 'Private life is a notion not susceptible to exhaustive definition' and 'Many activities of users will involve some form of automatic processing of personal data; examples include the use of browsers, e-mail, instant messages, voice-over Internet protocols, social networks and search engines as well as cloud data storage services. Convention 108 covers all operations carried out in the Internet, such as collection, storage, alteration, erasure and retrieval or dissemination or personal data.' It should be noted that these two rights, the rights to privacy and to data protection, are two distinct rights established in the EU Charter of Fundamental Rights, but the Convention does not specifically include a right to data protection as covered in Convention 108. Despite this, scholars have pointed out that in, e.g., *Amann v. Switzerland*, no. 27798/95, §65, Eur. Ct. H.R. 2000-II; *Rotaru v. Romania* [GC], no. 28341/95, §43, Eur. Ct. H.R.2000-V, the Court has 'applied Article 8 of the European Convention on Human Rights (covering the right to

choice of the means to secure compliance with Article 8 in the sphere of protection against acts of individuals is, in principle, within the State's margin of appreciation, effective deterrence against grave acts, where fundamental values and essential aspects of private life are at stake, requires efficient criminal law provisions'.[239]

In the country, as mentioned above, the Italian Constitutional Court has established that Article 117, paragraph 1, of the Italian Constitution, ensures compliance with the ECHR obligations at the constitutional level.[240]

114. According to the Public Relations Unit of the CoE's executive body, the Committee of Ministers, decisions of the ECtHR have 'led to various reforms and improvements in Italy', an example of which is the 2013 decision of the Constitutional Court which decided that an individual who had been abandoned at birth could be provided with access to information about their birth mother; the Italian legislator then established this right in law in 2015.[241]

115. Other case law of relevance to this volume can be found in the Supreme Court of Cassation Section I Judgment no. 19761 of 9 August 2017, in which the theme of data protection under Article 8 ECHR was examined. In this specific case, the Italian Court determined that an individual (the sole director and liquidator of a bankrupt company) did not have the right for their data contained in a public register maintained by the Chamber of Commerce of Lecce to be erased, insofar as it was considered that such publication in the Registry of Businesses corresponded to a legal obligation which is also in the interest of society at large. In its decision, the Court noted the relevance of affirming the legal principle that:

---

privacy) to give rise to a right of data protection as well.' *See* Juliane Kokott & Christoph Sobotta, *The Distinction Between Privacy and Data Protection in the Jurisprudence of the CJEU and the Ecthr*, 3 International Data Privacy Law 222, 223 (2013).

238. *See* at 8, *Guide on Article 8 of the European Convention on Human Rights*, European Court of Human Rights (31 Aug. 2021), https://www.echr.coe.int/documents/guide_art_8_eng.pdf.

239. *Ibid.*

240. *See* Caligiuri & Napoletano, *supra* n. 230. Also note, as pointed out by the authors, 'Before the constitutional reform of 2001, the Corte di Cassazione, in its Decision of 10 July 1993 no. 2194, issued in the Medrano case, recognized to the ECHR rules "a particular force of resistance in respect to ordinary subsequent laws". Moreover, the *Corte Costituzionale* (19 Jan. 1993, no. 10) stated that the rules of international treaty law introduced in the domestic legal system 'derive from an atypical competence of the State, as such insusceptible of being abrogated or modified by means of ordinary law'.

241. *See supra* n. 209, at 5 (*The ECHR and Italy: Facts and Figures*, Council of Europe (February 2022), https://www.echr.coe.int/Documents/Facts_Figures_Italy_ENG.pdf). Note that this case, *Godelli v. Italy*, the ECtHR unanimously held that there had been a violation of Art. 8 ECHR, considering that 'a fair balance had not been struck between the interests at stake since the legislation, in cases where the mother had opted not to disclose her identity, did not allow a child who had not been formally recognised at birth and was subsequently adopted to request either non-identifying information about his or her origins or the disclosure of the birth mother's identity with the latter's consent'. For more information on the case, *see Confidentiality of information concerning a child's origins: the Italian system does not take account of the child's interests,* Registrar of the European Court of Human Rights, ECHR 347 (2012), https://hudoc.echr.coe.int/eng#{%22itemid%22:[%22003-4089584-4796295%22]}.

In the light of the regulatory framework and the tasks institutionally pursued by the Chambers of Commerce in keeping the Registry of Businesses, responding to a legal obligation, the registration and preservation in the Registry itself of information relating to the office of director and liquidator, held by a person in a company, even if it was later first declared bankrupt and then deleted from the Registry of Businesses, as the requirements of commercial publicity prevail over the interest of the private individual to prevent it, is legitimate, functional to the reasons of certainty in commercial relations that the establishment of the Registry of Businesses satisfies.[242]

116. The Court, therefore, determined that the above is in line with Article 8, paragraph 2, ECHR,[243] and the case law of the ECtHR because Italian law (*see* Articles 2383, 2475 and 2487-*bis* of the Civil Code) requires its publication also because such publication is necessary and proportionate to protect collective interests in a democratic society.

117. In Judgment no. 17383 of 20 August 2020 of the Italian Supreme Court of Cassation, Civil Section VI,[244] the Court determined that non-material compensable damages provided under the since repealed Article 15 of the Personal Data Protection Code,[245] while consisting of harms to the fundamental rights of individuals as established under Article 8 ECHR and Articles 2 and 21 of the Italian Constitution, still requires the severity and seriousness of the harm or damage to be verified – i.e., 'a loss of a personal nature actually suffered by the person concerned'. Indeed, the Court determined the necessity to balance the right with the principle of solidarity established under Article 2 of the Italian Constitution, stating that 'the principle of tolerance of minimum damage is an intrinsic precipitate, which determines unjustifiable damage of the right and not the mere violation of the requirements established by Article 11 of the Personal Data Protection Code,[246] but only that which significantly affects its effective scope determines an unjustifiable damage to the

242. Author's translation.

243. Article 8, para. 2, reads: 'There shall be no interference by a public authority with the exercise of this right except such as is in accordance with the law and is necessary in a democratic society in the interests of national security, public safety or the economic well-being of the country, for the prevention of disorder or crime, for the protection of health or morals, or for the protection of the rights and freedoms of others.'

244. Cassazione civile sez. VI, 20.8.2020, (ud. 14/01/2020, dep. 20/08/2020), no. 17383. *See* Rassegna mensile della giurisprudenza civile della Corte Suprema di Cassazione: Provvedimenti pubblicati luglio – agosto 2020, Ufficio del Massimario e Ruolo, https://www.cortedicassazione.it/cassazione-resources/resources/cms/documents/RASSEGNA_MENSILE_LUGLIO-AGOSTO_2020.pdf. Note that in this case, the Court of Rome had 'rejected the claim brought by Associazione Professionale Studio tecnico di Progettazione G.L. and F.G. and A.L. against B.N. L. s.p.a. concerning the violation of the duty of secrecy of banking information in relation to a registered letter sent at the associated firm, without an envelope and folded back on itself containing the revocation of the credit lines granted within the five-day period.'

245. Despite the fact that Art. 15 of the Italian Personal Data Protection Code has been repealed, it is reasonable to maintain that the logic of the Court can apply to the provisions of Art. 82 GDPR concerning the 'Right to compensation and liability'. *See*, in this volume, Part VIII, Ch. 5, §2.

246. This Article has been repealed by D.Lgs. 101/2018.

right'.[247] In short, the Supreme Court of Cassation in Judgment no. 17383 confirms that the required factual analysis remains anchored in the concrete material event 'brought to judicial cognition and its having matured in a given temporal and social context' to determine whether or not the minimum tolerable threshold is met. In this case, the Court dismissed the appeal and ordered the appellant to pay the costs of the proceedings.

118. Similarly, in its Judgment no. 16402 of 10 June 2021,[248] the Supreme Court of Cassation decided in a case that dealt with non-pecuniary damages compensable under the since repealed Article 15 of the Personal Data Protection Code in cases where a fundamental right protected by Articles 2 and 21 of the Italian Constitution and Article 8 of the ECHR have been violated. Again, the Court decided that the offence must have a concrete impact on the right at hand and that 'privacy damage, like any non-pecuniary damage, does not exist in "*re ipsa*", as the indemnifiable damage is not identified with the mere injury of the interest protected by the law, but with the consequences of such injury, although it can also be proven through presumptions'.

Therefore, the Court once again confirmed its precedent and reiterated the requirement to have proof of concrete damages suffered as opposed to a mere violation of law in order for compensation to be awarded in case of damages suffered following violations of data protection rights, such as those enshrined under Article 8 ECHR. The Court furthermore stated that a mere allegation of damages causing distress 'constitutes a generic and apodictic assertion unsuitable even for an understanding of the reasons for such distress' and logically that the negative consequences suffered as a result of unlawful processing must be specified and proven, also though a presumption.

119. The Constitutional Court in its Judgment no. 20 of 21 February 2019 – already analysed within §2.II of the previous Chapter – deals with transparency in the exercise of public functions. More specifically, in this decision, the Court demonstrated its desire to protect fundamental rights to the maximum extent possible also with respect to cooperation between courts and tribunals as established by recent case law.[249] In doing so, it held that the public administration was no longer under the 'obligation to publish, on the Internet, personal data on the income and assets of public-sector managers, except for those in top-ranking positions'.[250]

---

247. Author's translation.
248. Supreme Court of Cassation, no. 16402/2021, sect. civ.
249. Gian Luigi Gatta, *The Report on the Activities of the Italian Constitutional Court in 2019*, Criminal Justice Network (1 May 2020), https://www.criminaljusticenetwork.eu/en/post/the-report-on-the-activities-of-the-italian-constitutional-court-in-2019.
250. Ufficio Stampa della Corte Costituzionale, Public-Sector Managers – Unconstitutionality of the General Obligation to Publish Data on Income and Assets on the Internet: The Obligation Applies only to Top-Ranking Positions (21 Feb. 2019) https://www.cortecostituzionale.it/documenti/download/pdf/Dirigenza_pubblica_sent_20_del_2019_Zanon.pdf.

In this case, as already seen, the Court dealt with the constitutional legitimacy of Article 14, paragraph 1-*bis*, of D.Lgs. 33/2013,[251] which calls for compensation of any nature connected to the office and the costs of service trips and missions paid with public funds to be published. Notably, in determining that the balance between the right to confidentiality of personal data and the right of citizens to freely access data and information relating to the public administration to be 'unreasonable', the Court also made specific reference to Article 8 ECHR by means of Article 117, paragraph 1, of the Italian Constitution.

120. Finally, it is also interesting to note that the GPDP in its 'Guidelines Applying to the Use of E-Mails and the Internet in the Employment Context' of 1 March 2007, refer to the case law of the ECtHR in its analysis of the processing of employee data, noting that 'The personal data at issue may concern, in addition to work-related information, the private life and/or personal sphere of both employees and third parties' and that 'the line between these two areas is at times difficult to draw.'[252]

§4. VIOLATIONS OF ARTICLE 8 ECHR BY THE ITALIAN REPUBLIC

121. The Convention is interpreted by the Strasbourg Court. As of February 2022, in over 70% of the decisions of the ECtHR concerning Italy, at least one violation of the ECHR has been found by the Court; 7.49% of cases have found a violation concerning Article 8.[253] The vast application of Article 8 – which the Court of Strasbourg has interpreted broadly over the years, encompassing obligations towards States which are well beyond the right to privacy and data protection[254] – should be considered in this analysis, however, leading to the majority of cases to be of limited relevance for the purposes of this volume.

122. One case of interest where Italy was found to have violated Article 8 ECHR is found in the *Enea v. Italy*[255] case which concerned the interception of mail

251. Article 14, para. 1-*bis*, reads as follows, 'Public administrations shall publish the data referred to in paragraph 1 for holders of administrative, managerial or management or government offices however denominated, unless they are awarded free of charge, and for holders of offices managerial positions, in any capacity conferred, including those conferred discretionally by the political steering body without public selection procedures.'

252. GPDP, *Guidelines Applying to the Use of E-Mails and the Internet in the Employment Context*, 1.3.2007, https://www.garanteprivacy.it/home/docweb/-/docweb-display/docweb/1408680#nota2.

253. *See supra* n. 209, at 5 (*The ECHR and Italy: Facts and Figures*, Council of Europe (February 2022), https://www.echr.coe.int/Documents/Facts_Figures_Italy_ENG.pdf).

254. *See*, for a quick review, Bart Van Der Sloot, *Editorial*, 8 European Data Protection Law Review 167, (2022).

255. *Enea v. Italy* [GC], no. 74912/01, Eur. Ct. H.R.

directed towards prisoners.[256] More specifically, in this case, the ECtHR determined that the Italian Prison Administration Act,[257] which, according to the Italian Authorities, justified the monitoring of correspondence, violated Article 8 ECHR because said Act 'did not regulate either the duration of the measure or the reasons capable of justifying it, and did not indicate with sufficient clarity the scope and manner of exercise of the discretion by the competent authorities, thus not offering the minimum degree of protection against arbitrariness required by the rule of law'.[258]

As also mentioned in the preceding Section of the Chapter, the *Godelli v. Italy* case of 2013 is of interest and led to legislative changes in the Republic.[259] Mrs Godelli, abandoned by her mother and at age 10, discovered that she had been adopted, but her adoptive parents refused to provide her with any information about her origins.[260] After their death, Mrs Godelli attempted to find out more about her origins but was unable to as her biological mother had decided to keep her identity secret, in line with Article 28, paragraph 7, of Law 26 May 1984, no. 183 (Law on the right of the minor to know their origins). The Court found that the Italian law had failed to balance Mrs Godelli's right to access and her biological mother's right to remain anonymous; voting six to one, the Strasbourg judges found that Article 8 of the Convention had been violated. Following the decision, with Judgment no. 278/2013, the Italian Constitutional Court declared the part of the law to be unconstitutional, specifically with reference to the part which does not foresee that the judge may consult the mother when the child seeks information on their origin.[261]

---

256. *See*, Ivana Roagna, *Protecting the Right to Respect for Private and Family Life under the European Convention on Human Rights*, Council of European Human Rights Handbooks, Council of Europe: Strasbourg (2012), https://www.echr.coe.int/LibraryDocs/Roagna2012_EN.pdf, at 38.
257. L. 354/1975.
258. *See Enea v. Italy* (*supra* n. 256), §39.
259. *Godelli v. Italy*, no. 33783/09, Eur. Ct. H.R.
260. *Woman's legal fight to find out about her origins,* Council of Europe, https://www.coe.int/en/web/impact-convention-human-rights/-/woman-s-legal-fight-to-find-out-about-her-origins.
261. *Ibid.*

Chapter 3. Privacy in Electronic Communications (National Transposition of the ePrivacy Directive)

§1. INCLUSION WITHIN THE PERSONAL DATA PROTECTION CODE

123. The Italian law provisions concerning privacy in electronic communications and which transpose the ePrivacy Directive are included within the Personal Data Protection Code. In particular, they are found within Title X on 'Electronic communications' and Chapter I on 'Electronic Communications Services', encompassing Articles 121 to 132-*ter*.[262] An important revision of this Title was made in 2012, with Legislative Decree 28 May 2012, no. 69, where the provisions of Title X were amended in order to reflect the modifications to the ePrivacy Directive made by Directive 2009/136/EC.[263]

Title X was further amended in the context of the 2018 reform with Legislative Decree 10 August 2018, no. 101, with a view of bringing the Title – along with the rest of the Personal Data Protection Code – in line with the GDPR. However, given that the Title is expressly aimed at transposing the ePrivacy Directive within the Italian legal order, this has led some authors to question the legitimacy of the amendments provided to this Chapter by the reform. This is because, in some cases, the alterations have gone beyond the mere replacement of legal cross-references which were strictly necessary to reflect the direct applicability of the GDPR.[264]

Other minor amendments have been made over time in relation to specific articles. The latter revision has taken place in 2021, with Law Decree 30 September 2021, no. 132, as enacted and amended by Law 23 November 2021, no. 178, which has modified the rules governing judicial requests to access traffic data.[265]

---

262. Before the 2018 reform, the Chapter was divided into three Chapters, i.e., the aforementioned Ch. I, titled 'Electronic Communications Services', a Ch. II, titled 'Internet and Electronic Networks' and a Ch. III, titled 'Video-Surveillance'. The last two Chapters have been repealed by D.Lgs. 51/2018 and, as a result, Title X is now composed only of Ch. I.

263. Directive 2009/136/EC of the European Parliament and of the Council of 25 Nov. 2009 amending Directive 2002/22/EC on universal service and users' rights relating to electronic communications networks and services, Directive 2002/58/EC concerning the processing of personal data and the protection of privacy in the electronic communications sector and Regulation (EC) no. 2006/2004 on cooperation between national authorities responsible for the enforcement of consumer protection laws, OJ L 337, 18.12.2009.

264. *See*, for example, Luca Bolognini & Enrico Pelino, *Codice Privacy: tutte le novità del D.lgs. 101/ 2018* (Giuffré Francis Lefebvre, 2019), at 58–61. The authors highlight, in particular, the fact that the law with which the Parliament had delegated the Government to amend the Data Protection Code did not envisage the possibility of materially amending the provisions which transposed the ePrivacy Directive.

265. *See infra* in this Ch. 3, §4.IV.

§2. Scope of Application and Relevant Definitions

124. According to Article 121, paragraph 1, of the Personal Data Protection Code, Title X applies to: 'the processing of personal data in connection with the provision of publicly accessible electronic communications services on public communications networks, including public communications networks supporting data collection and identification devices'.

The scope of application thereby closely reflects the one set forth in Article 3, paragraph 1, of the ePrivacy Directive.

Concerning the legal definitions, Article 1, paragraph 1-*bis*, provides a list of definitions used within Title X, which are substantially the same as those provided at the European level in Article 2 of the ePrivacy Directive and in Article 2 of Directive 2002/21/EC;[266] the only possible exception is the notion of 'contracting party', defined as: 'any natural or legal person, body or association who or which is party to a contract with the provider of publicly available electronic communications services for the supply of such services, or is anyhow the recipient of such services by means of pre-paid cards', which slightly differs from the notion of 'subscriber' set out in Article 2, letter (k) of Directive 2002/21/EC.[267]

§3. Cookie Law

I. Relevant Legislation and Guidance

125. Article 122, paragraph 1, of the Personal Data Protection Code, transposes Article 5, paragraph 3, of the ePrivacy Directive quite literally.[268] Instead, paragraph 2 adds that: 'With a view to giving the consent referred to in paragraph 1 above, specific configurations of software or devices may be used that should be user-friendly as well as unambiguous vis-à-vis the contracting party or user.' In 2021, the GPDP updated its guidance on Article 122 of the Personal Data Protection Code[269] with a view to clarifying its relationship with the relevant GDPR provisions – with specific regard to those on consent and transparency – with its 10 June 2021 Guidelines on the use of cookies and other tracking tools (hereinafter, the 'Cookie Guidelines').[270]

266. Directive 2002/21/EC of the European Parliament and of the Council of 7 Mar. 2002 on a common regulatory framework for electronic communications networks and services (Framework Directive), OJ L 108, 24.4.2002.

267. 'Any natural person or legal entity who or which is party to a contract with the provider of publicly available electronic communications services for the supply of such services'.

268. Article 122, para. 1, provides that: 'Storing information, or accessing information that is already stored, in the terminal equipment of a contracting party or user shall only be permitted on condition that the contracting party or user has given his consent after being informed in accordance with simplified arrangements. This shall be without prejudice to technical storage or access to stored information where they are aimed exclusively at carrying out the transmission of a communication on an electronic communications network, or insofar as this is strictly necessary to the provider of an information society service that has been explicitly requested by the contracting party or user to provide the said service. In order to determine the simplified arrangements referred to herein, the Garante shall also take account of the proposals put forward by the nationally most representative

The Cookie Guidelines are meant to provide an overview of the law applicable to cookies and other tracking tools and to outline the appropriate arrangements applicable to the provision of information to users and for obtaining the consent of data subjects, where necessary. In particular, while recognizing that Article 95 GDPR prescribes that the GDPR 'shall not impose additional obligations on natural or legal persons in relation to … matters for which they are subject to specific obligations with the same objective laid down in Directive 2002/58/EC', the GPDP recalls that the GDPR is:

> [I]ntended to expand and enhance the power of the individual to organise and control the processing of his or her personal information, in particular by supplementing the definition of consent contained in Directive 95/46/EC; by clarifying that the data subject's indication of consent to the processing of his or her personal data must be not only free, specific and informed, as was already the case with the Directive, but also 'unambiguous'; and by requiring that the concrete, effective implementation of data protection principles is achieved by design and by default.[271]

126. Moreover, the GPDP recognizes that not only cookies[272] but also other tracking technologies fall under the scope of Article 122 of the Personal Data Protection Code. Such tracking technologies can be broadly categorized as either being 'active identifiers' – thereby including cookies – or 'passive identifiers', which encompass the use of fingerprinting techniques.[273] Publishers are, therefore, required to implement both active and passive identifiers in accordance with Article 122, as interpreted by the Cookie Guidelines.

---

consumer and industry associations involved in order to also ensure that the mechanisms implemented make the contracting party or user actually aware.'

269. The GPDP had already adopted Decision no. 229 of 8 May 2014 aimed at identifying simplified arrangements for providing online information to users on the cookies stored on their terminals by visited websites as well as providing appropriate guidance on how to obtain the users' consent, where required by the law. Being adopted in 2014, the Decision failed to take into account the reinforced transparency and consent requirements provided by the GDPR. This situation became especially relevant in the light of the 2019 CJEU 'Planet49' judgment, which clarified that GDPR consent requirements also apply in the context of the use of cookies and other tracking technologies, despite their use being regulated under the ePrivacy Directive. *See* Case C-673/17, *Bundesverband der Verbraucherzentralen und Verbraucherverbände –Verbraucherzentrale Bundesverband eV v. Planet49 GmbH*, 01.1.2019, ECLI:EU:C:2019:801.

270. The Cookie Guidelines are available at following URL: https://www.garanteprivacy.it/home/docweb/-/docweb-display/docweb/9677876#english.

271. *Ibid.*, para. 1.

272. 'Cookies' are defined in para. 1 of the Cookie Guidelines as: '[T]ext strings that the websites visited by the user (so-called "publisher" or "first party" websites) or else different websites or web servers (so-called "third parties") place and store within a terminal device in the user's possession – whether directly as is the case with publisher websites, or indirectly as is the case with "third parties", i.e. through the intermediation of the publisher websites.'

273. 'Fingerprinting Techniques' are defined by the Cookie Guidelines as 'a technology to identify the user's device by collecting all or part of the information on the specific user-selected configuration of that device'; *see ibid.*, para. 1.

127. For the sake of simplicity, within this Chapter, we shall refer to both active and passive identifiers as 'cookies'.

II. Cookies Exempted from Consent: Technical and Analytical Cookies

128. According to the Cookie Guidelines, in line with Article 122 of the Personal Data Protection Code, cookies that are used to carry out the transmission of a communication over an electronic communications network or which are strictly necessary for the provider of an information society service explicitly requested by the contracting party or user do not require the latter's prior consent.[274] As a result, those cookies can be lawfully served as soon as the user or contracting party lands on the website, even without further actions being carried out by the user.

While technical cookies do not require users' prior consent, they still need to be listed in the general information notice or on the homepage of the website.[275] However, websites that only serve technical cookies are not obliged to also implement a cookie banner.[276]

129. In framing the technical cookie category, however, the GPDP goes further than the letter of Article 122, thereby stating that cookies and other tracking technologies which are used solely 'to assess the effectiveness of an information society service provided by a publisher, to design a website or to help measure its "traffic" – i.e., the number of visitors, possibly broken down by geographical area, time slot or other characteristics' – may be equated to technical cookies and, therefore, implemented without user's prior consent.

This is, however, only possible where specific measures are taken by the publisher in order to comply with the data protection by design and by default principle (Article 25 GDPR), as well as the data minimization principle (Article 6, paragraph 1, letter c, GDPR).[277] Such measures are aimed to significantly reduce the identification potential of analytics cookies and prevent the data subject from being singled out, and they include the following:

(i) masking out appropriate portions of the IP address in the cookie;[278]

274. *See ibid.*, para. 4.
275. *See, ibid.*, paras 5 and 7.1. This approach seems to be in line with the 'Planet49' CJEU judgment (*supra* n. 270), which specifically requires publishers to include 'the duration of the operation of cookies and whether or not third parties may have access to those cookies' (para. 81).
276. *Ibid.*, para. 7.1: 'Where only technical cookies or similar tools are implemented, their presence may be referred to on the home page or else in the general information notice without the need to display ad-hoc banners that users will then have to remove/deactivate'.
277. *Ibid.*, para. 7.2.
278. In particular, according to the GPDP (*ibid.*, para. 7.2): 'Taking into account the 32-bit IPv4 representation of IP addresses, which are usually represented and used as a sequence of four dot-separated decimal numbers between 0 and 255, one of the measures that can be implemented in order to benefit from the said exemption is the masking out of at least the fourth component of the address, which creates a 1/256 (approximately 0.4%) uncertainty in attributing the cookie to a specific data subject.

(ii) in case of third-party cookies, such third parties which provide web measurement services to the publishers shall not match the data, even if minimized according to point (i) above, nor shall they disseminate such data to other third parties.[279]

130. Being equated by the GPDP to the 'technical cookie' category, analytics cookies which fulfil the conditions set out above still need to be mapped in the website's information notice or homepage while not necessarily requiring prior consent in order to be used. Again, if a website only serves this type of cookie, it does not need to implement a cookie banner.

131. Perhaps surprisingly, despite having crafted the analytical cookies classification, the GPDP specifies that the 'technical cookies' category should be construed narrowly,[280] since the law is 'framed unquestionably in such a way as to generally ban any processing of data subjects' information – except for certain situations that are set out in a stringent, highly specific manner and do not lend themselves to a looser interpretation based on analogy'. It follows that all cookies which do not fall within the technical and analytical category outlined above should be considered to be subject to consent, as specified in the following paragraph.

III. Cookies Subject to Consent: Profiling Cookies

132. According to the GPDP, so-called profiling cookies are:

> [U]sed to trace specific actions or recurring behavioural patterns in the use of the offered functionalities back to specific, identified or identifiable individuals for the purpose of grouping the different profiles within homogeneous, multi-sized clusters; this is aimed in turn to enable the controller to, *inter alia*, provide increasingly customized services beyond what is strictly necessary for the delivery of the given service and also send targeted advertising messages, i.e., messages that are in line with the preferences expressed by the user in the context of their web-browsing activities.[281]

Similar procedures should be adopted with regard to IPv6 addresses, which have a very different structure and a significantly larger addressing space since they consist of 128-bit binary numbers.'

279. According to the GPDP, however (*ibid.*, para. 7.2): 'This is without prejudice to the production of statistics based on minimized data across several domains, websites or apps that can be traced back to the same publisher or publishing group. However, statistical analyses concerning several domains, websites or apps that can be traced back to one single controller can be considered lawful even in the absence of the aforementioned minimization measures – on condition [sic] such analyses are performed by way of the controller's own resources and do not turn into activities that go beyond statistical counting and take on ultimately the features of processing operations aimed to enable business-related decision-making.'

280. *See, a contrario, ibid.*, para. 4.

281. *Ibid.*, para. 4.

133. This type of cookie may only be used by the publisher with prior user or contracting party's consent. As a result, such cookies may not be served as soon as the user lands on the website but only after they have provided valid consent in light of the GDPR requirements, as will be seen in the following section.

IV. Consent Validity Requirement

134. The GPDP recognizes that the 'consent' referred to by Article 122 of the Personal Data Protection Code has the same validity requirements as those set out under the GDPR.[282] The GPDP has thus proceeded to lay down the interpretation of such requirements in the context of the use of profiling cookies.

In this respect, the GPDP leverages Article 25 GDPR, in particular the 'data protection by default' principle, in order to stress the importance that 'by default, no cookies or tools other than technical ones are placed on the user's device when that user first accesses a website, and that no other active or passive tracking technique is used at that time'.[283]

A. Cookie Banner Requirements

135. While conceding that the freedom to conduct a business and the accountability principle mean, as a rule, that a controller is able to implement the arrangements that it considers most suited to achieve compliance with data protection legislation, the GPDP recommends all website operators to – upon the user's landing in the website – immediately show a banner which size shall be sufficient to interrupt user's experience, while avoiding the risk to inadvertently activate the banner's commands, in order to allow the user to freely decide whether to express consent to the installation of profiling cookies.[284]

136. The Cookie Guidelines further detail the requirements of such banner, aimed at allowing the user to express an affirmative and informed action in case they want profiling cookies to be used. Such requirements include:[285]

(i) a warning that if the banner is closed by clicking on the 'X' at its top right corner,[286] the default settings are left unchanged and, therefore, browsing can continue without cookies or other tracking tools other than technical ones;

282. *Ibid.*, para. 5.
283. *Ibid.*, para. 7.1.
284. *Ibid.*
285. *Ibid.*
286. According to the GPDP, (*ibid.*, para. 7.1): 'The command in question will have to be as visible as any other commands or buttons that may be used to flag other choices available to the users, which will be detailed below. In other words, the mechanism to enable continued browsing without giving any consent will have to be as user-friendly and accessible as the one in place for giving one's consent.'

(ii) a minimal information notice to the effect that the website uses, if any, technical cookies or other technical tools and may, only after obtaining the user's consent, also use profiling cookies or other tracking tools in order to send advertisements and/or customize its services;

(iii) a link to the privacy policy or to a second-layer extended information notice – which should be one-click away through a link to be placed in the footer of any page of the domain accessed by the user – where at least all the information referred to in Articles 12 and 13 of the Regulation is provided clearly and thoroughly, including with regards to technical cookies or tools;

(iv) a command button through which consent can be given by accepting the installation of all cookies or the use of other tracking tools;

(v) a link to an additional dedicated area of the website where the user can individually select the list of third parties and the cookies – possibly grouped into homogeneous categories – to which the user chooses to consent.

137. In case the user decides to provide their consent to the use of profiling cookies, the affirmative action with which the user has expressed such consent shall be appropriately documented and recorded by the data controller.[287]

138. Alternatively, if the user opts to close the banner by clicking on the 'X' at its top-right corner, according to the GPDP, this shall be interpreted as a wish from the user to keep the default settings of the banner, i.e., to refuse to provide their consent.[288] As a result, in this case no profiling cookies can be installed on the user's device. The refusal shall then be recorded and documented by the data controller as well, with a view to avoiding excessive reiteration of consent requests, as seen in more detail §3.IV.D, below. In any case, the user shall be free to change their previous choice, e.g., by providing their consent at a later stage or withdrawing the consent already provided: this should be achieved by means of a clearly visible link or button to be added in the footer of the website, which gives access to an ad-hoc area where the user may revisit their choices at any time.[289]

B. Scrolling as a Means of Valid Consent

139. According to the Cookie Guidelines, and in line with EDPB guidance on consent,[290] scrolling may not per se amount to a valid consent, as it fails to meet the standards of validity set forth by the GDPR.[291] However, the GPDP takes the view that scrolling may be implemented as part of a broader mechanism aimed at signifying the user's consent to the use of profiling cookies, while the publisher remains

287. *Ibid.*, para. 7.1.
288. *Ibid.*
289. *Ibid.* The GPDP suggests that such link or button is named as 'Change your mind on cookies' or similar wording.
290. European Data Protection Board, *Guidelines 05/2020 on consent under Regulation 2016/679*, para. 86, available at https://edpb.europa.eu/sites/default/files/files/file1/edpb_guidelines_202005_consent_en.pdf.
291. *Ibid.*, para. 6.1.

responsible for demonstrating that such a process complies with the stringent requirements for consent validity set forth by the GDPR, under the principle of accountability.[292]

Unfortunately, no further examples of any such mechanism are given by the GPDP within the Cookie Guidelines, nor in any other provision.

C. Cookie Walls

140. The GPDP defines 'Cookie Walls' as 'a "take it or leave it" mechanism in which the user is obliged to give his or her consent to the reception of cookies or other tracking tools – since failing to do so will prevent him or her from accessing the site'.[293] Again, in line with EDPB guidance on consent,[294] according to the GPDP, this practice is – as a rule – not in line with applicable legislation as it is contrary to the requisite of 'free' consent outlined under Article 4, no. 11, GDPR.

An exception to this rule is where the publisher provides the option of accessing 'equivalent content' to the data subject which refuses the installation of profiling cookies; whether the exception may apply is to be verified on a case-by-case basis and in the light of data protection principles, with particular regard to lawfulness, fairness and transparency.[295] It is, therefore, advisable that publishers who wish to leverage such exceptions proceed to document their decision in the context of a data protection impact assessment.

D. Reiteration of Consent Requests

141. As indicated above, publishers are required to document and record not only the user's consent but also the negative choice made by the user, both for accountability purposes and in order to avoid the excessive reiteration of consent requests in case the user returns to the website multiple times.[296] In this respect, according to the GPDP, the cookie banner should not be presented again to the user who has refused provision of consent for a minimum of six months after such refusal has taken place, except where one of the following events takes place:[297]

(i) one or more of the circumstances of the processing changes significantly, so that the banner also serves the specific as well as necessary purpose of informing exactly about the changes in question, e.g., regarding any of the 'third parties';

292. *Ibid.*
293. *Ibid.*
294. *See supra* n. 291, paras 39–41.
295. *Ibid.*, para. 6.1.
296. *Ibid.*, para 7.1. In particular, the GPDP suggests that the choice be recorded via a first-party technical cookie, even though the publisher is free to choose other means to achieve this result, in light of the principle of accountability.
297. *Ibid.*, para. 6.2.

(ii) it is impossible for the website operator to be aware that a cookie has already been stored on the device in order to be re-transmitted to the site that generated it on the occasion of a subsequent visit by that user. This is the case, for instance, where the user chooses to delete the cookies lawfully stored in his/her device, and the controller is unable to keep track of the user's intention to stick to the default settings and accordingly to continue browsing without being tracked.

§4. Processing of Traffic Data

I. Relevant Legislation

142. The Italian legislation concerning the processing of traffic data can be found in various sources.

Within the Personal Data Protection Code, those sources are found in Articles 123 and 132, titled respectively 'Traffic Data' and 'Traffic Data Retention for Other Purposes'. The former lays down general rules concerning the ordinary processing and retention of traffic data, while the latter establishes the processing and retention of traffic data for purposes of prevention and prosecution of crimes.

Aside from the Personal Data Protection Code, the processing of traffic data is addressed by three other important sources:

(i) Legislative Decree 30 May 2008, no. 109, which specifies the categories of traffic data which are subject to the rules set forth by Articles 123 and 132 of the Personal Data Protection Code and provides further specifications concerning the processing of traffic data.
(ii) The GPDP provision named 'Secure Retention of Telephone and Internet Traffic Data – 24 July 2008',[298] which lays down the security measures that data controllers who process traffic data must introduce and maintain.
(iii) Article 24 of the Law 20 November 2017, no. 167, which determines the period of time for which traffic data must be retained by the provider for purposes of prevention and prosecution of crimes.

II. Definition of 'Traffic Data' and Scope of Application

143. As anticipated above, the definition of traffic data is set forth within Article 121, letter h) of the Personal Data Protection Code and closely reflects the definition provided by the ePrivacy Directive, i.e., 'any data processed for the purpose of the conveyance of a communication on an electronic communications network or for the billing thereof'.

Such definition being quite broad and generic, the Italian legislator has provided for another, more specific, definition in Article 1 of the D.Lgs. 109/2008, which

298. Available online at https://www.garanteprivacy.it/home/docweb/-/docweb-display/docweb/1542849.

delimits 'traffic data' as (author's translation) 'any data undergoing processing for the purpose of transmitting a communication on an electronic communications network or related invoicing, thereby including the data necessary to identify the subscriber or user'. For further clarity and specification, a detailed categorization of which data items amount to 'traffic data' is found within Article 3 of the D.Lgs. 109/2008. This Article classifies traffic data within the following categories (author's translation):

(i) Data which are necessary to identify the source of a communication.
(ii) Data which are necessary to identify the recipient of a communication.
(iii) Data which are necessary to determine the date, time, and duration of a communication.
(iv) Data which are necessary to determine the type of communication.
(v) Data which are necessary to determine the communication equipment of the users, actual or presumed.
(vi) Data which are necessary to determine the location of the user equipment used for mobile communication.

144. Article 3 further provides an analytical list of detailed data items which are included in each category.

145. In light of the applicable provisions set out above, the scope of application of the rules on the processing of traffic data is limited to providers of a public communications network or publicly available electronic communications services when they provide either e-mail, Internet connectivity, telephone (mobile or landline), SMS, MMS or fax transmission services.

It follows that the rules on the processing of traffic data do not apply in instances where the electronic communication service is provided by a data controller who does not fall into the above-mentioned categories and as part of a merely ancillary service, such as a restaurant or hotel which provides complimentary wi-fi to its customers.

III. Processing of Traffic Data for 'Ordinary Purposes'

146. Article 123, paragraphs 1 and 2, of the Personal Data Protection Code, provide that, as a general rule, traffic data may only be processed and retained for billing purposes, in particular, to provide evidence in case an invoice is challenged by the contracting party or in order for the service provider to pursue payment. Traffic data processed for this purpose may be retained for up to six months after the data has been generated, without prejudice to further retention as may be necessary on a case-by-case basis for pursuing or defending against specific claims.

147. According to paragraph 3, traffic data may also be processed for marketing purposes and in order to provide value-added services,[299] but only when the contracting party has provided their consent. In this case, the data may be retained for the amount of time necessary to pursue the stated purpose for which consent has been obtained.

148. Concerning transparency obligations, paragraph 4 of Article 123 provides that, in addition to the information set forth in Articles 13 and 14 GDPR, the data controller must also inform the contracting party or user of the nature of the traffic data processed as well as on the duration of the processing for the purposes referred to above.

IV. Processing of Traffic Data for Purposes of Prevention and Prosecution of Crimes

149. Article 132, paragraph 1, of the Personal Data Protection Code, read together with Article 24 of L. 167/2017, mandates that traffic data, as well as data related to unsuccessful calls, must be retained by the relevant service provider for seventy-two months (i.e., six years) for purposes of prevention and prosecution of crimes. During this period of time, the service provider must make the traffic data available to Italian judicial authorities upon lawful request from the latter. In particular, according to paragraph 3 of Article 132, such requests:

(i) may only concern criminal offences that are punished by imprisonment for a maximum term of not less than three years[300] (including life imprisonment), or else offences consisting in serious threats or harassment or causing serious private nuisance by means of the telephone;
(ii) may only concern criminal offences for which there is sufficient circumstantial evidence;
(iii) shall be authorized by a reasoned order of the competent judge,[301] except in cases where there is an urgent need to act and there are reasons to believe that

299. Article 121, para. 1-*bis*, lett. l), of the Personal Data Protection Code, in line with Art. 2, lett. (g), of the ePrivacy Directive, defines value added services as 'any service which requires the processing of traffic data or location data other than traffic data beyond what is necessary for the transmission of a communication or the billing thereof'. Recital 18 of the ePrivacy Directive clarifies that 'Value added services may, for example, consist of advice on least expensive tariff packages, route guidance, traffic information, weather forecasts and tourist information'.

300. Such period is to be determined in accordance with s. 4 of the Criminal Procedure Code.

301. Prior to the amendments to Art. 132 of the Personal Data Protection Code carried out with D.L. 132/2021, the request could be authorized by reasoned decree of the public prosecutor, and in some cases also by the defence counsel. The prior provision was arguably in breach of EU data protection law, in particular in light of the CJEU's judgment in Case C-746/18, *H. K. v. Prokuratuur*, 2.3.2021, ECLI:EU:C:2021:152, where the Court held that access to traffic data shall be subject to authorization by an independent third party, such as the judge, while the public prosecutor – being party to the proceeding – has no sufficient independency. Accordingly, D.L. 132/2021 referred to the above-mentioned CJEU judgment in its preamble, thereby expressly aiming to bring Art. 132 of the Personal Data Protection Code in line with EU Law.

any delay may seriously undermine the investigations, in which case the public prosecutor may acquire the data directly, pursuant to a reasoned order.[302]

150. Moreover, pursuant to paragraph 4-*ter* and 4-*quater* of Article 132, Italian law enforcement authorities[303] may, in order to carry out pre-trial investigations, order the relevant provider to retain and protect telematic traffic data for no longer than ninety days, which may be extended up to six months on specific grounds to be justified. The relevant provider shall then comply without delay and forthwith give assurances to the requesting authority as to their compliance while also keeping the order at issue and any related activity confidential. Finally, according to paragraph 4-*quinquies*, the relevant law enforcement authority shall notify the order in writing without delay, and in any case, within forty-eight hours, to the competent public prosecutor, who shall endorse the order if it deems that the relevant preconditions are fulfilled. The measures shall cease to be enforceable if they are not endorsed.

151. Finally, in accordance with Article 4 of D.Lgs. 109/2008, on the 30th of June of each year, the service provider which is subject to traffic data retention obligations shall send to the Ministry of Justice for the subsequent forwarding to the European Commission, the following information:

(i) the total number of cases in which the provider has granted access to traffic data relating to the competent authorities;
(ii) the period of time between the date of storage of traffic data and that of the request by the competent authorities;
(iii) cases in which it was not possible to satisfy the requests for access to the traffic data.

152. In addition to this annual reporting obligation, pursuant to Article 132-*bis*, paragraph 2, of the Personal Data Protection Code, the GPDP may also request the relevant service provider to disclose information on the number of requests received, the legal justification invoked, and the relevant response.

V. Security Measures Applicable to the Processing of Traffic Data

153. Article 132-*bis*, paragraph 1, of the Personal Data Protection Code sets out the obligation for providers which are subject to data retention and access rules to

302. The public prosecutor's reasoned order shall then be communicated immediately, and at all events by no later than forty-eight hours, to the judge that is competent for granting the relevant authorization. The judge shall decide in the subsequent forty-eight hours whether to validate the said request with a reasoned order. If the public prosecutor's order is not upheld by the judge, the data thus acquired may not be used (Art. 132, para. 3-*bis* of the Personal Data Protection Code).

303. In particular, the Minister for Home Affairs or the heads of the central offices specializing in computer and/or IT matters from the State Police, the Carabinieri, and the Financial Police as well as the other entities mentioned in para. 1 of s. 226 of the implementing, consolidating, and transitional provisions related to the Criminal Procedure Code as per D.Lgs. no. 271/1989.

adopt internal procedures to meet the requests made in compliance with the provisions that envisage access to traffic data. Moreover, Article 132, paragraph 5, of the Personal Data Protection Code, mandates the GPDP to adopt a decision of a general nature, laying down the security measures to safeguard data subjects whose traffic data are processed for purposes of prevention and prosecution of crimes. Such measures are currently listed in detail within the above-mentioned GPDP provision named 'Secure Retention of Telephone and Internet Traffic Data – 24 July 2008.'[304]

Among the security measures listed in the 2008 GPDP decision, the most important ones applicable to the processing of traffic data for 'ordinary purposes'[305] are arguably:

(i) access to traffic data by the service provider's authorized persons may take place only with strong authentication systems in place;
(ii) keeping a register of technical accesses for extraordinary reasons, in case of absence of access by means of strong authentication;
(iii) separation of the technical functions of assigning authentication credentials and identification of authorization profiles from those of technical management of systems and databases;
(iv) rendering the traffic data immediately unavailable for processing upon expiry of the established terms;
(v) logging of the activities carried out by the service providers' authorized persons on the traffic data: recording, in a specific audit log, of the operations carried out on the traffic data and on the other personal data connected to them;
(vi) adequately documenting the information systems used for the processing of traffic data according to the principles of software engineering.

154. The security measures applicable to the processing of traffic data for purposes of prevention and prosecution of crimes[306] are the same as those applicable to the processing for 'ordinary purposes' but, in addition, include the following:

(i) one of the strong authentication techniques shall be based on the elaboration of biometric characteristics of the person in charge;
(ii) adoption, for data retention, of IT systems which are physically distinct from those used to process traffic data for 'ordinary purposes';[307]

---

304. *See supra* n. 299.
305. *See* Part I, Ch. 3, §4.III, *supra.*
306. *See* Part I, Ch. 3, §4.IV, *supra.*
307. More precisely, the traffic data stored for a period not exceeding six months from their generation can be processed for purposes of prevention and prosecution of crimes both by providing for their processing with the same storage systems used for 'ordinary purposes', and by providing for their duplication, with separate storage from traffic data processed for 'ordinary purposes'. The computer equipment used for the processing of traffic data exclusively for purposes of prevention and prosecution of crimes shall be located within areas with selected access and equipped with electronic control devices or surveillance procedures that involve the registration of the identification data of the persons having access to the data, with indication of the relevant time references. In the

(iii) specifically designate the authorized persons who can access the traffic data stored for purposes of prevention and the prosecution of crimes;[308]
(iv) provide the authorized persons with periodic trainings;
(v) carry out, at least annually, an internal control activity to check compliance with organizational, technical and security measures regarding the processing of traffic data; the controls shall also include *a posteriori* controls, on a sample basis or on any alarm deriving from alerting and anomaly detection systems, on the legitimacy and lawfulness of access to traffic data carried out by the persons in charge, on the integrity of the data and the IT procedures used for their processing. Periodic checks shall also be carried out on the effective deletion of data after the retention periods have elapsed. The control activity shall be adequately documented;
(vi) protect traffic data processed for exclusive purposes of justice with cryptographic techniques.

155. Finally, Article 132-*ter* of the Personal Data Protection Code – introduced in the context of the 2018 reform – has clarified that the processing of traffic data and, more generally, the processing carried out by providers of publicly available electronic communications services is in any case subject to the risk-based approach to security measures set forth by Article 32 GDPR. In other words, Article 132-*ter* refers to the rules on security measures in the context of the ePrivacy Directive transposition to those set forth by the GDPR.[309] As a result, the provider is not only required to adopt the security measures set forth by the 2008 GPDP provision but also to assess (and document) whether those measures are adequate to the effective risk, to be assessed in light of the relevant elements indicated in Article 32 GDPR. The service provider shall then adopt further security measures if deemed necessary.

VI. Data Breach Reporting Rules for Providers of Publicly Available Electronic Communication Services and Other Transparency Obligations

156. Prior to the 2018 reform, Article 32-*bis* of the Personal Data Protection Code – now repealed by D.Lgs. 101/2018 – specifically regulated data breach documentation and reporting obligations for providers of publicly available electronic communication services, with a view to transposing Article 4, paragraph 3, of the

case of the processing of telephone traffic data exclusively for purposes of prevention and prosecution of crimes, the access control must include a biometric recognition procedure. Finally, the provider shall adopt suitable measures to guarantee the restoration of access to traffic data in the event of damage to the data or to the electronic tools in a period of time compatible with the rights of the data subjects and, in any case, not exceeding seven days.

308. This obligation is set forth by both Art. 123, para. 5, and Art. 132-*ter*, para. 3, of the Personal Data Protection Code.

309. Bolognini & Pelino, *Codice Privacy: tutte le novità del D.lgs. 101/2018* 58–61 (Giuffré Francis Lefebvre, 2019), at 58.

ePrivacy Directive, as amended by Directive 2009/139/CE.[310] The repealing of Article 32-*bis* in the context of the 2018 reform implies that data breaches suffered by providers of publicly available electronic communication services – even those concerning traffic data – are now subject to the general obligations set forth under Articles 33–34 GDPR.[311]

157. Another important transparency obligation, however, 'survived' the 2018 reform: according to the current text of Article 132-*quater* of the Personal Data Protection Code – which aims to transpose Article 4, paragraph 2, of the ePrivacy Directive – the provider of a publicly available electronic communications service is required to 'inform subscribers and, where possible, users, using clear language that is appropriate and suitable by having regard to the age and the category of the data subject receiving such information and taking special care in case children are involved, whether there is a particular risk of network security breach'. Moreover, in case the aforementioned risk falls outside the scope of application of the measures that the provider is required to take pursuant to Article 132-*ter*, paragraphs 2, 3 and 5, then 'the provider shall specify all the possible remedies and the expected costs. Similar information shall be provided to the Garante and the Authority for Communications Safeguards'.

§5. Unsolicited Communications and Processing of Personal Data Within Public Directories (Referral)

158. The Italian legislator has transposed Articles 12 and 13 of the ePrivacy Directive within Articles 129 and 130 of the Personal Data Protection Code. These provisions will be examined within Part III, Chapter 2, §2, as they concern the legal bases applicable to the processing of personal data.

§6. Itemised Billing

159. The Italian legislator has transposed Article 7 of the ePrivacy Directive within Article 124 of the Personal Data Protection Code. This Article enables the contracting party to 'receive, upon request and free of charge, detailed proof of the

310. In line with para. 4 of such Article, the GPDP had adopted in 2013 the general provision named 'Implementing Measures with Regard to the Notification of Personal Data Breaches – 4 April 2013 [2414592]' (available at https://www.garanteprivacy.it/web/guest/home/docweb/-/docweb-display/docweb/2414592), with a view to further clarify the breach documentation and reporting obligations. In line with the repealing of Art. 32-*bis* by the legislator, the GPDP has repealed the aforementioned general provision, with its decision of 30 Jul. 2019 (doc. web 9126951, available at https://www.garanteprivacy.it/home/docweb/-/docweb-display/docweb/9126951).

311. According to Bolognini & Pelino, *Codice Privacy: tutte le novità del D.lgs. 101/2018* 58–61 (Giuffré Francis Lefebvre, 2019), at 59–60, the repealing of Art. 32-*bis* and the fact that data breaches suffered by providers of publicly available electronic communication services are now subject to general GDPR rules amount to a violation of European Union Law, as Italy has failed to transpose the specific data breach reporting obligations set forth by the ePrivacy Directive, which – as *lex specialis* – should prevail over the GDPR.

items making up the bill, in particular concerning date and starting time of a conversation, selected numbers, type of numbering, place, duration and units charged for each conversation'.

At the same time, Article 124 aims to safeguard the right to privacy of users and contracting parties by providing that, on the one hand, such services and communications, as well as the communications required to implement alternative payment methods, shall not be displayed in the documents sent to contracting parties concerning the communications performed. On the other hand, the final three digits of the called numbers shall not be displayed in contracting parties' bills; a contracting party may request communication of the full numbers relating to the communications at stake for the sole purpose of specifically challenging either the accuracy of certain charges or charges relating to limited periods.

Pursuant to paragraph 5 of Article 124, the GPDP may, however, authorize the service provider to report the full numbers in the bills.

160. Concerning service provision and payment, the provider of publicly available electronic communications service is required 'to enable users to perform communications and request services from any terminal equipment – free of charge and using simple means – by availing themselves of alternative payment methods, including anonymous methods, such as credit cards, debit cards or pre-paid cards'.

§7. Calling Line Identification Requirements and Exceptions for Nuisance and Emergency Calls

161. Article 125 of the Personal Data Protection Code transposes Article 8 of the ePrivacy Directive quite literally, without any particular deviation from the latter's text, thereby granting to users and contracting parties the possibility to eliminate the presentation of calling line identification, free of charge and by using simple means.

The only noteworthy difference is the specific exemption set forth in paragraph 1 of Article 126, pursuant to which the possibility to eliminate the presentation of calling line identification on a per-call or per-line basis does not apply to providers of telemarketing activities, as the latter are subject to the specific requirements set out in Article 2 of Law 11 January 2018, no. 5, which requires them to adopt specific telephone numbers when calling users for telemarketing purposes.[312] The aim of this latter norm is to allow users to quickly identify incoming calls which are of a commercial nature, without having to answer the call.

162. The exceptions to the possibility of eliminating the presentation of calling line identification set out in Article 10 of the ePrivacy Directive have been transposed within Article 127 of the Personal Data Protection Code, which contains both the exception for nuisance calls and the one for emergency calls. As regards the former, paragraphs 1 and 2 provide that the recipient of nuisance calls may request the provider to override, on a temporary basis, the elimination of the presentation of calling line identification and store the data concerning the origin of the incoming

312. *See also* Part III, Ch. 2, §2.

call; to this end, the provider shall make available transparent procedures to contracting parties and may charge amounts not exceeding the costs actually incurred.

Such exception may only concern the time ranges during which the nuisance calls take place and for no longer than fifteen days. The request has to be made in writing and shall specify the manner in which the nuisance calls are received, and if the request is made by phone, it shall be followed up in written form to the service provider within the following forty-eight hours. The data stored pursuant to the request may then be communicated to the contracting party, where the latter declares that they will only use them to protect themselves against nuisance calls.

163. Concerning the exception for emergency calls, paragraph 4 of Article 127 mandates the provider to 'set out transparent procedures in order to ensure that the services authorized to deal with emergency calls may override, on a per-line basis, the elimination of the presentation of calling line identification and, if necessary, process location data notwithstanding the temporary denial or absence of consent of the contracting party or user'.

§8. Location Data Other than Traffic Data

164. Processing of location data – other than traffic data – relating to users or contracting parties of public communications networks or publicly available electronic communications services is regulated by Article 126 of the Personal Data Protection Code, which transposes Article 9 of the ePrivacy Directive without particular deviations from the latter's text, thereby establishing that such data 'may only be processed when they are made anonymous, or with the prior consent of the users or contracting parties, which may be withdrawn at any time, to the extent and for the duration necessary for the provision of a value-added service'.

The only relevant difference concerns the security measures, which may be found in paragraph 4 of Article 126, where the Italian legislator has mandated the service provider to 'ensure identification of the authorised persons accessing the data also by means of automated search operations'. This specific security measure is without prejudice to the obligation of the relevant provider to fulfil the requirements set forth by Article 32 GDPR.

§9. Automatic Call Forwarding

165. Article 128 of the Personal Data Protection Code has transposed Article 11 of the ePrivacy Directive quite literally, thereby providing that: 'the provider of a publicly available electronic communications service shall take the measures required to allow each contracting party, free of charge and using simple means, to stop automatic call forwarding by third parties to his/her own terminal'.

Chapter 4. Other Relevant National Legal Provisions Regarding the Protection of Privacy

§1. Obligations of Professional Secrecy (Including Equivalent Obligations of Secrecy)

166. As will be seen in greater detail in Part X, Chapter 1, §1, of this volume, there are various provisions concerning professional secrecy in the Italian legislative framework. Such provisions are found in the Personal Data Protection Code (Article 138), the Criminal Code (Article 622), and the Criminal Procedure Code (Article 200). The latter two provisions, in particular, provide the cases in which witnesses in a criminal proceeding may refuse to answer questions due to their relationship with the suspect or profession.

Generally speaking, the unjustified violation of professional secrecy (i.e., violation of professional secrecy outside of the specific cases set forth by the law) is considered a crime pursuant to Italian criminal law.

167. The provisions of the Personal Data Protection Code on professional secrecy, instead, limit protection of professional secrecy only to the journalistic activity and, in particular, to the source of information, which the journalist is not bound to disclose even in the case of a request of access from the data subject pursuant to Article 15 GDPR.

§2. Churches and Religious Associations

168. As will be seen more specifically in Part X, Chapter 2, §2, of this volume, in Italy, according to the General Authorization of the GPDP no. 3, the members of religious associations may process special categories of personal data of their members according to the rules and provisions of the Authorization, which also constitutes the legal basis for such processing activities.

169. In addition, as shall be seen in §3 of the Chapter, the Catholic Church – as a sovereign legal entity – has approved a complete body of internal data protection rules by means of the General Decree no. 389/2018 of the Italian Conference of Bishops ('*Conferenza Episcopale Italiana*', abbreviated as 'CEI'), which replaced the previous General Decree no. 1285 of 20 October 1999 and which aims to apply Article 91 GDPR. The Decree is a complete discipline governing ecclesiastic data processing activities that reflects most of the provisions of the GDPR. The power to enforce this discipline is, however, conferred to the GPDP.

170. Finally, the GPDP has adopted over the years some noteworthy decisions concerning, *inter alia*, requests for deleting one's personal data from the Church's baptismal records, examined in §4 of Chapter 1.

§3. Law Enforcement Agencies

171. Part X, Chapter 3 of this contribution deals with Legislative Decree 18 May 2018, no. 51, in which the Italian legislator has provided a complete framework to regulate the data protection rules to be followed during criminal investigations, thereby transposing Directive (EU) 2016/680. D.Lgs. 51/2018 applies to the fully or partially automated processing of personal data of natural persons and the non-automated processing of personal data of natural persons contained in or intended for a filing system carried out by the competent authorities for the purpose of the prevention, investigation, detection, and prosecution of crimes, or the execution of criminal sanctions, including the safeguarding against and preventing threats to public safety.

172. This Decree reflects the obligations to be followed in the processing activities mentioned above to guarantee and safeguard the rights of data subjects, in particular, their right to personal data protection. The GPDP is the competent authority for ensuring the respect of those provisions.

§4. National Security Services

173. As will be seen in greater detail in Part X, Chapter 4 of this contribution, even if the GDPR does not apply to activities concerning national security (since such activities fall outside European Union Law), Article 58 of the Personal Data Protection Code includes some specific provisions pertaining to the processing of personal data for purposes of national security and defence (in continuity with the provisions which were already set out in the Personal Data Protection Code, before the direct applicability of the GDPR).

174. In addition to the provision mentioned above, the legislator also provided a specific discipline to address the activities processed by some of the bodies responsible for National Security. In particular, these are Article 26 of Law 3 August 2007, no. 124, Article 160, paragraph 4, of the Personal Data Protection Code, and the provisions of D.Lgs. 51/2018 (where compatible).[313] It is also provided that detailed rules for implementing these provisions will be contained in a regulation adopted by a D.P.R. upon a proposal submitted by the Minister of Defence.

§5. Other Specific Regimes

175. Dealt with in Part X, Chapter 5, §1, of this volume, the protection of the individual's rights, as well as, more generally, their privacy, is recognized by some criminal provisions. In particular, some of them are found in the Criminal Code; others are provided by the Personal Data Protection Code. In addition, some of these

313. *See* §3 of this Ch. 4 and *infra* Part X, Ch. 3, of this volume.

provisions, according to Legislative Decree 8 June 2001, no. 231, also punish the legal entity that commits those crimes in the interest or to the advantage of the entity itself.

In the same D.Lgs. 231/2001, regulations on the whistleblowing system for private legal entities are found, as shall be seen in §2. The Italian legislator has transposed Directive (EU) 2019/1937[314] concerning whistleblowing in 2023, in particular with D.Lgs. n. 24/2023.

176. Another point of attention concerns more specifically the Italian regulation of wiretapping, which shall be examined in §3 of Chapter 5. The full discipline of these means of evidence-seeking is contained in the Code of Criminal Procedure which has recently been modified to give greater guarantees to persons who may be wiretapped even if they are not involved in the investigation. The entire procedure is, therefore, now provided for in a specific preliminary phase, during which irrelevant conversations are eliminated before they can be made public.

177. Finally, §4 of Chapter 5 deals with the recent introduction of a discipline against cyberbullying provided by Law 29 May 2017, no. 71, also deserves attention due to its impact on privacy regulation under Italian law. The 2017 law has, in particular, provided some guarantees and safeguards for victims of certain acts of cyberbullying.

314. Directive (EU) 2019/1937 of the European Parliament and of the Council of 23 Oct. 2019 on the protection of persons who report breaches of Union law, PE/78/2019/REV/1, OJ L 305, 26.11.2019.

Part II. National Data Protection Law

Chapter 1. Background: General Description of the National Data Protection Law (+ Short Presentation of Other Relevant National Legislation)

178. The first comprehensive legislation on the processing of personal data in Italy was Law 31 December 1996, no. 675, concerning the protection of individuals and other subjects regarding the processing of personal data. The L. 675/1996 was issued to implement Directive 95/46/EC of the European Parliament and of the Council (on the protection of individuals with regard to the processing of personal data and on the free movement of such data).[315] Then, after just over five years (considering that L. 675/1996 came into force in 1997), the Italian legislator carried out a comprehensive reform of the matter which resulted in Legislative Decree no. 196 of 30 June 2003: indeed, named the 'Personal Data Protection Code' ('*Codice* in materia *di protezione dei dati personali*', in Italian) and usually referred to as the 'Privacy Code' ('*Codice Privacy*', in Italian).

The Personal Data Protection Code is organized in three parts:

(i) the first part, containing general provisions, is divided into seven titles;
(ii) the second part contains specific provisions necessary to comply with a legal obligation or for performance of a task carried out in the public interest or related to the exercise of official authority, as well as provisions for processing referred to in Chapter IX of the GDPR;
(iii) the third part contains provisions about remedies and sanctions.

179. The Personal Data Protection Code has been amended several times, most recently in 2021.[316] After the reform enacted by means of Legislative Decree 18 May 2018, no. 51 and of Legislative Decree 10 August 2018, no. 101, the Personal Data Protection Code now contains provisions to adapt the national legislation to the GDPR and to derogate the latter where this is allowed. Other strategic matters concerning personal data protection are also included or referred to in the Personal Data Protection Code, as illustrated in Article 154, related to the tasks of the GPDP.

315. Directive 95/46/EC of the European Parliament and of the Council of 25 Oct. 1995, OJ L 281, 23.11.1995.
316. The Personal Data Protection Code has been amended by way of D.L. 139/2021, as subsequently enacted via L. 205/2021, and the amendments made by way of D.L. 132/2021, as subsequently enacted via L. 178/2021.

Indeed, the GPDP shall also perform supervisory or assistance tasks concerning personal data processing as provided for by laws ratifying international agreements and conventions or otherwise by European Union regulations, for example, with regard to:

(i) Regulation no. 1987/2006 on the establishment, operation and use of the second-generation Schengen Information System (SIS II) and Council Decision 2007/533/JHA on the establishment, operation and use of the second-generation Schengen Information System (SIS II).
(ii) Regulation 2016/794 on the European Union Agency for Law Enforcement Cooperation (Europol).
(iii) Provisions of Chapter IV of Convention no. 108 on the protection of individuals with regard to the automated processing of personal data, as adopted in Strasbourg on 28 January 1981 and implemented by Law 21 February 1989, no. 98, being the authority designated for the purpose of inter-state cooperation pursuant to Article 13 of said Convention.
(iv) Regulation 767/2008 of the European Parliament and of the Council concerning the Visa Information System (VIS) and the exchange of data between Member States on short-stay visas (VIS Regulation) and Council Decision 2008/633/JHA concerning access for consultation of the Visa Information System (VIS) by designated authorities of Member States and by Europol for the purposes of the prevention, detection, and investigation of terrorist offences and of other serious criminal offences.

180. The Personal Data Protection Code – and specifically its Title X named 'Electronic communications' of its second part – also implements Directive 2002/58/EC on the processing of personal data and the protection of private life in the electronic communications sector.[317]

181. Before the 2018 reform arising from the GDPR, the Personal Data Protection Code was complemented by:

(i) Annex B related to minimum security measures.
(ii) Annex C related to non-occasional processing for judicial sector or police purposes.[318]

182. Today, the Personal Data Protection Code is only complemented by Annex A,[319] which contains:

317. Directive 2002/58/EC of the European Parliament and of the Council of 12 Jul. 2002 concerning the processing of personal data and the protection of privacy in the electronic communications sector (Directive on privacy and electronic communications), OJ L 201, 31.07.2002. As outlined *supra*, Part I, Ch. 3.
318. Annexes B and C were repealed by Art. 27 of D. Lgs. 101/2018.
319. The Rules of Conduct replaced the Annex A1, A2, A3, A4 and A6 of the Personal Data Protection Code as set for by the Art. 20, para. 4, of D.Lgs. 101/2018. As announced by the GPDP in its newsletter no. 454 of 21 Jun. 2019, Annex A7, which contained the Rules of Conduct for the Processing of Personal Data to the Purpose of Commercial Information, has been replaced by the Codes of

(i) the Rules of Conduct for the Processing of Personal Data in the Exercise of the Journalistic Activity;
(ii) the Rules of Conduct for the Processing for Archiving Purposes for the Public Interest or for Historical Research Purposes;
(iii) the Rules of Conduct for Processing for Statistics and Scientific Research Purposes within the National Statistical System;
(iv) the Rules of Conduct concerning Processing for Statistics and Scientific Research Purposes;
(v) the Rules of Conduct concerning the Processing of Personal Data carried out to Conduct Defensive Investigations or to Exercise or Defend a Right in a Judicial Context.[320]

183. In addition to the Personal Data Protection Code and its Annex A, Italian data protection law includes other provisions concerning personal data processing, which are issued or approved by the GPDP. In particular, it is relevant to consider:

(i) General decisions and orders issued by the GPDP.[321]
(ii) General authorizations.
(iii) Guidelines.[322]
(iv) Injunctions and orders (against specific organizations).[323]

Conduct prepared by the National Association between Commercial Information and Credit Management, https://www.garanteprivacy.it/web/guest/home/docweb/-/docweb-display/docweb/9586215.

320. The Rules of Conduct – Annex A of the Personal Data Protection Code are available at: https://www.garanteprivacy.it/codice.

321. Some important general decisions include: GPDP, *Measures and arrangements applying to the controllers of processing operations performed with the help of electronic tools in view of committing the task of system administrator*, 27.11.2008, doc. web no. 1628774, https://www.garanteprivacy.it/web/guest/home/docweb/-/docweb-display/docweb/1628774; GPDP, *Provvedimento del Garante sulla notifica delle violazioni dei dati personali (data breach) – 30 luglio 2019*, 30.7.2019, doc. web no. 9126951, https://www.garanteprivacy.it/home/docweb/-/docweb-display/docweb/9126951; GPDP, *Prescrizioni in materia di circolazione delle informazioni in ambito bancario e di tracciamento delle operazioni bancarie – 12 maggio 2011*, 12.5.2011, doc. web. no. 1813953, https://www.garanteprivacy.it/home/docweb/-/docweb-display/docweb/1813953; GPDP, *General Application Order Concerning Biometrics*, 12.11.2014, doc. web 3590114, https://www.gpdp.it/web/guest/home/docweb/-/docweb-display/docweb/3590114; GPDP, *Documento di indirizzo su designazione, posizione e compiti del Responsabile della protezione dei dati (RPD) in ambito pubblico*, 29.04.2021, doc. web 9589104, https://www.garanteprivacy.it/web/guest/home/docweb/-/docweb-display/docweb/9589104.

322. Some important GPDP's guidelines are: GPDP, *Guidelines on the use of cookies and other tracking tools – 10 June 2021*, 10.06.2021, doc. web no. 9677876, https://www.garanteprivacy.it/web/guest/home/docweb/-/docweb-display/docweb/9677876 (for which *see supra* Part I, Ch. 3, §3); GPDP, *Guidelines on the Electronic Health Record and the Health File – 16 july 2009*, 16.7.2019, doc. web no. 1672821, https://www.garanteprivacy.it/web/guest/home/docweb/-/docweb-display/docweb/1672821; GPDP, *Guidelines on Marketing and against Spam – 4 July 2013*, 4.7.2013, doc. web no. 4304228, https://www.garanteprivacy.it/web/guest/home/docweb/-/docweb-display/docweb/4304228 (for which *see infra* Part III, Ch. 2, §2).

323. Please note that while such provisions do not have general applicability, they need to be taken into account as they contain prescriptions for processing that other organizations may do in the same or similar manner.

(v) Rules of Conduct, which apply to specific sectors.[324]
(vi) Codes of Conduct, in case the data controller or processor has decided to adhere.[325]

184. The Personal Data Protection Code is destined to receive new updates, even if only to adapt it to new standards and provisions that will be introduced by the forthcoming ePrivacy Regulation.

324. Cf. Part VI, §1 *infra.*
325. The updated list of Italian Codes of Conduct is available at the following link https://www.gpdp.it/codici-di-condotta. On 9 Mar. 2023, the GPDP approved the Code of Conduct for Telemarketing and teleselling activities; however, its effectiveness is subject to the conclusion of the accreditation process of the monitoring body https://www.garanteprivacy.it/web/guest/home/docweb/-/docweb-display/docweb/9868813 *See also infra*, part VI).

Chapter 2. Scope of the National Law (Material, Personal, Territorial)

§1. Introduction

185. Regarding the material, personal, and territorial application of the Personal Data Protection Code, a preliminary remark must be made: Article 5 of the Personal Data Protection Code, which regulated the subject matter and scope of application of the Code, was repealed by the Legislative Decree 10 August 2018, no. 101, in the context of the 2018 Data Protection Reform.

In this respect, it should also be kept in mind that the Personal Data Protection Code is intended to both complement the GDPR and transpose the ePrivacy Directive,[326] whose scope of application substantially equates to that of the GDPR in light of its Article 1, paragraph 2, which states that 'The provisions of this Directive particularise and complement [the GDPR].'[327]

As a consequence, it should be considered that when the GDPR and the ePrivacy Directive apply in accordance with the criteria defined within the GDPR itself,[328] in light of its internal references to the complementary legislation of Member States, the Personal Data Protection Code will also apply in these areas. However, it remains to be seen in which specific cases the Personal Data Protection Code applies, as opposed to other Member States' data protection legislation which also complements the GDPR or transposes the ePrivacy Directive.

186. Considering this premise, in order to identify the criteria for the material, personal, and territorial application of the Personal Data Protection Code, it is arguably necessary to refer to the criteria defined by the GDPR. This is further confirmed by the fact that, with respect to its scope of application, Article 1 of the Personal Data Protection Code (titled 'Scope') refers to the GDPR by establishing that 'Personal data shall be processed in accordance with the provisions of Regulation (EU) 2016/679 of the European Parliament and of the Council, of 27 April 2016, hereinafter the "Regulation", and with this Code, by respecting human dignity and the rights and fundamental freedoms of the individual.'

§2. Personal and Material Scope of Application

187. Concerning the personal and material scope of application, the Personal Data Protection Code does not deviate from the GDPR nor from the ePrivacy Directive's scope of application; therefore, it applies in the same cases provided therein.

326. In this respect, *see* in this volume: Part I, Ch. 3, *supra*.
327. It should be noted that, while the text of the Article expressly references 'Directive 95/46/EC', after the direct applicability of the GDPR this must be read in light of the latter's Art. 94, para. 1: '*References to the repealed Directive shall be construed as references to this Regulation*'.
328. For the GDPR: Art. 2, as regards the material scope of application, and Art. 3, as regards the territorial scope of application; for the ePrivacy Directive: Art. 1, establishing both its relevant scope and aim.

188. An exception to the above notably takes place in the context of the processing of personal data of deceased persons, which the GDPR expressly excludes from its scope of application. According to Recital 27 of the GDPR, 'This Regulation does not apply to the personal data of deceased persons'; however, 'Member States may provide for rules regarding the processing of personal data of deceased persons.'

The Italian legislator has, in fact, decided to provide for specific rules concerning personal data related to deceased persons within Article 2-*terdecies* (titled 'Rights concerning deceased persons'). However, rather than extending all EU and Italian data protection provisions to personal data of deceased persons, this Article only regulates the rights provided under Articles 15–22 GDPR, which exercise is granted to 'any entity having a vested interest or acting to protect the data subject as the latter's agent, or else on household-related grounds deserving protection'.

§3. Territorial Scope of Application

189. As indicated above, the 2018 reform has repealed Article 5 of the Personal Data Protection Code, which was used to set forth its scope of application. Concerning specifically the *territorial* scope of application, paragraph 1 of said Article stated that 'This code regulates the processing of personal data carried out by anyone established in the State or in a place of the State however subject to sovereignty, including where the processing takes place abroad.'

Considering the fact that the legislator has not replaced the repealed Article 5 with other provisions, in order to determine the scope of application of the Personal Data Protection Code, it is arguably necessary to refer to the general principles of Public International Law, as well as to Article 3 of the GDPR, interpreting it with a view to determining the territorial scope of application of the Personal Data Protection Code (as opposed to the GDPR itself), vis-à-vis other Member States' national data protection law.

190. Concerning the relevant principles of Public International Law, an important role is played by the *principle of territoriality*, according to which no law enacted by a state may generally produce effects outside the territory of that State, and that in any case of extra-territorial effect, there needs to be a link (which can be either subjective, e.g., the nationality of the person involved, or objective, e.g., the place of performance of a service or the place where a damage occurs) to allow the application of a given law to a given circumstance.[329]

As regards Article 3 of the GDPR, it lays down the following criteria which trigger the GDPR (and, as seen above, the ePrivacy Directive) territorial scope of application, including the processing of personal data which:

329. It should be noted that general principles of Public International Law currently in force are automatically recognized and given constitutional status within the Italian legal system, pursuant to Art. 10, para. 1, of the Italian Constitution. *See* Bin & Pitruzzella, *supra* n. 177, at 336.

(i) Takes place in the context of the activities of an establishment of a controller or a processor in the Union, regardless of whether the processing takes place in the Union or not.
(ii) Concerns data of data subjects who are in the Union and is performed by a controller or processor not established in the Union, where the processing activities are related to:
   (a) the offering of goods or services, irrespective of whether a payment of the data subject is required, to such data subjects in the Union; or
   (b) the monitoring of their behaviour as far as their behaviour takes place within the Union.
(iii) Is carried out by a controller not established in the Union but in a place where Member State law applies by virtue of public international law.

191. By applying the principle of territoriality, read together with Article 3 GDPR, it may be argued that the criteria which trigger the territorial scope of application of the Personal Data Protection Code may be carved out to include the processing of personal data which:

(i) Takes place in the context of the activities of an establishment of a controller or a processor in Italy, regardless of whether the processing takes place in Italy or not.
(ii) Concerns data of data subjects who are in Italy and is performed by a controller or processor not established in Italy, where the processing activities are related to:
   (a) the offering of goods or services, irrespective of whether a payment of the data subject is required, to such data subjects in Italy; or
   (b) the monitoring of their behaviour as far as their behaviour takes place within Italy.
(iii) Is carried out by a controller not established in Italy, but in a place where Italian law applies by virtue of public international law.

192. In other words, the territorial scope of application of the Personal Data Protection Code mirrors the criteria set forth in Article 3 GDPR. This conclusion is in line with the aim of the Personal Data Protection Code, which is to complement the GDPR and to transpose the ePrivacy Directive.

193. The conclusion is that the Personal Data Protection Code also applies extraterritorially in the cases referred to under point (ii), letters a. and b. above – thereby including where the data controller is established in another Member State – is also arguably in line with the Court of Justice of the European Union's (CJEU's) Weltimmo judgment.[330] In this judgment, the Court held that a Member State supervisory authority is entitled to pursue enforcement actions and to apply its relevant national data protection law, where the data controller processes personal data in the context of the provision of services within a Member State. Although this judgment

330. Case C-230/14, *Weltimmo s.r.o. v. Nemzeti Adatvédelmi és Információszabadság Hatóság*, 1.10.2015, ECLI:EU:C:2015:639.

took place in the context of the now-repealed Directive 95/46/EC, it may be argued that its principles remain sound even after the direct applicability of the GDPR.

I. Relevant GPDP's Decisions

194. In 2016, in a decision against Facebook Italy S.r.l., the GPDP[331] has notably applied the CJEU's Weltimmo judgment. Although the decision refers to the Personal Data Protection Code in the version prior to the 2018 reform, it is interesting to note that the GPDP has also applied extra-territorially to Italian data protection law.

In particular, the GPDP ruled that Facebook Italy S.r.l., which carried out marketing activities on behalf of Facebook Ireland Ltd., although not carrying out any data processing activities on Italian territory (as such data were processed in the context of the activities of the Irish establishments of Facebook Ireland Ltd.), nevertheless carries out activities which are economically connected to Facebook Ireland Ltd. and therefore, the jurisdiction is rooted in the territory of the Italian State.[332] As a consequence, the Personal Data Protection Code was applied to the case at hand.

331. GPDP, *Provvedimento dell'11 febbraio 2016*, 11.2.2016, doc. web no. 4833448, https://www.gpdp.it/web/guest/home/docweb/-/docweb-display/docweb/4833448.

332. *Ibid.*, paras 18–19: '(18) Whereas, in order to ensure that individuals are not deprived of the protection to which they are entitled under this Directive, any processing of personal data in the Community must be carried out in accordance with the law of one of the Member States; whereas, in this connection, processing carried out under the responsibility of a controller who is established in a Member State should be governed by the law of that State; (19) Whereas establishment on the territory of a Member State implies the effective and real exercise of activity through stable arrangements; whereas the legal form of such an establishment, whether simply branch or a subsidiary with a legal personality, is not the determining factor in this respect; whereas, when a single controller is established on the territory of several Member States, particularly by means of subsidiaries, he must ensure, in order to avoid any circumvention of national rules, that each of the establishments fulfils the obligations imposed by the national law applicable to its activities.'

Chapter 3. Concepts (National Jurisprudence: Also Previous to the GDPR -, DPA Opinions + Divergent and Additional Definitions)

§1. The Concepts of 'Communication' and 'Dissemination' of Personal Data

195. In particular, Article 2-*ter* of the Personal Data Protection Code gives particular and detailed relevance to the concepts of communication and dissemination of personal data.[333] Article 2-*ter*, letter 4) of the Personal Data Protection Code states:

(a) 'Communication' shall mean disclosing personal data in whatever manner, including by making available, interrogating or creating links to such data, to one or more identified entities other than the data subject, the controller's representative in the EU, the processor or the latter's representative in the EU, and the persons authorised to process personal data under the controller's or processor's authority in pursuance of Article 2-quaterdecies.
(b) 'Dissemination' shall mean disclosing personal data in whatever manner, including by making available or interrogating such data, to unidentified entities.

196. This distinction is applied in other articles of the Personal Data Protection Code, but it should not be applied technically to the GDPR: in fact, the GDPR does not give a specific definition of communication and dissemination, but rather it considers both to be processing operation under its Article 4, no. 1. In other words, the Italian legislator has isolated the 'communication' and 'dissemination' of personal data as two specific processing operations, subjecting them to specific provisions in instances regulated throughout the Personal Data Protection Code.

197. In this respect, it is noteworthy to examine Article 96 of the Personal Data Protection Code, which regulates the processing of personal data relating to students. Except for personal data referred to in Articles 9 and 10 of the GDPR, the institutions of the Italian national education system and training centres – both public and private – may communicate or disseminate, also to private entities and by electronic means, on the data subjects' request, data on the evaluation and marks obtained by students, in order to facilitate training and professional integration, also abroad. The purpose of Article 96 must be referred to in the information provided to data subjects pursuant to Article 13 GDPR. The Italian legislator also specifies that students' personal data may subsequently be processed only for the same purposes indicated in Article 96.

333. It should be noted that the definitions of 'communication' and 'dissemination' of personal data were present in the former Art. 4 ('Definitions') of the Personal Data Protection Code, with the same wording, also before the 2018 reform.

198. Another important instance where the concepts of 'communication' and 'dissemination' are used by the Italian Legislator can be found in the very same Article which lays down the two definitions, i.e., Article 2-*ter* (titled 'Legal basis to process personal data for the performance of a task carried out in the public interest or in the exercise of official authority'), which shall be examined in Part III, Chapter 2, V, *infra*.

199. The two concepts are also leveraged in a few more instances, particularly in Article 137 concerning journalism, freedom of expression and information,[334] in Article 61, which regulates the use of public information and rules of conduct, as well as in Articles 100, 102 and 106 concerning processing for archiving purposes in the public interest, scientific or historical research purposes or statistical purposes,[335] while the concept of 'communication' is used in Article 127 which concerns nuisance and emergency calls.[336]

200. The concept of 'dissemination' is leveraged in Article 2-*septies* concerning the processing of genetic data, biometric data, and data relating to health in order to generally ban the dissemination of such data, as well as in the context of Article 144-*bis* against so-called revenge porn. Finally, the same concept forms part of a provision which lays down a criminal offence, i.e., Article 167-*bis*, named 'Unlawful communication and dissemination of personal data that are processed on a large scale.'[337]

201. The Italian legislator has also laid down other concepts within the Personal Data Protection Code in the context of the transposition of the ePrivacy Directive, contained in its Title X, named 'Electronic communications', Chapter I, named 'Electronic Communications Services', as seen in Part I, Chapter 3, *supra*, such concepts do not deviate from the definitions provided by the ePrivacy Directive and are therefore not specific to Italian legislation.

The only exception to this is arguably the distinction between 'telephone' and 'internet' traffic data, which derives from Directive 2006/24/EC and which is still set forth within Article 1 of Legislative Decree 10 August 2018, no. 101, and within the GPDP decision titled 'Secure Retention of Telephone and Internet Traffic Data – 24 July 2008.' Although the Directive has been invalidated by the judgment of the CJEU in 2014,[338] the relevant definitions set forth by Italian law are still valid and applicable in Italy. Until 2017, Article 132 of the Personal Data Protection Code concerning traffic data retention obligations for purposes of combating crime, provided for two retention periods for telephone and internet traffic data; however, the

334. Which shall be examined *infra* in Part IX, Ch. 1, II.
335. Which shall be examined *infra* in Part IX, Ch. 5.
336. Which has been examined *supra* in Part I, Ch. 3, VII.
337. Which shall be examined *infra* in Part VIII, Ch. 6.
338. Joined Cases C-293/12 and C-594/12, *'Digital Rights Ireland Ltd v. Minister for Communications, Marine and Natural Resources and Others and Kärntner Landesregierung and Others'*, 8.4.2014, ECLI:EU:C:2014:238.

distinction between the two concepts has lost much of its relevance after the Legislator has enacted the Law 20 November 2017, no. 167, which established the retention period for all types of traffic data in seventy-two months.

§2. The Person Authorized to Process Personal Data

202. Article 2-*quaterdecies* of the Personal Data Protection Code[339] provides that tasks and functions related to the processing of personal data may be assigned by the data controller or processor to individuals who are expressly designated and who act under the authority of the data controller and data processor, similar to the provision of Article 29 GDPR.

These persons – usually labelled 'persons authorized to process personal data' ('*persone autorizzate al trattamento*') or 'persons in charge of the processing' ('*incaricati al trattamento*')[340] – are therefore tasked, within the scope of their internally assigned duties and delegated powers, to implement the data controller or processor instructions, privacy policies and procedures, thereby ensuring internal compliance with privacy rules. The designation and instruction of such individuals represent the adoption of additional organizational measures, which are relevant in terms of accountability and data security.

The specific tasks and functions – and the related level of internal responsibility – allocated by the data controller or processor to these individuals may vary in accordance with the role they play within the relevant organization.

§3. The 'Internal Data Processor'

203. Prior to the 2018 reform, in particular, the adoption of D.Lgs. 101/2018, which amended the Personal Data Protection Code, Article 4, paragraph 1, letter g), of the Personal Data Protection Code laid down the notion of 'data processor', defined as 'the natural person, legal person, public administration and any other body, association or body appointed by the owner to process personal data'.[341]

204. Aside from the possibility of the data processor being an entity different from the data controller, the definition left open the possibility of the data processor being a natural person acting under the authority of the data controller (e.g., an employee).

339. This provision reads as follows: '1. The controller or processor may provide under their own responsibility and within the framework of the respective organisation that specific tasks and functions relating to the processing of personal data be allocated to expressly designated natural persons acting under the controller's or processor's authority. 2. The controller or processor shall set out the most appropriate arrangements to authorise the persons acting under their authority to process personal data.'

340. This last expression draws from Italian legal tradition, where Art. 4, para. 1, lett. h), of the Personal Data Protection Code, now repealed, laid down that definition.

341. Author's translation.

As a result, in the Italian data protection theory[342] and practice, the internal data processor was identified as the person within the structure of the data controller who was in charge of and/or carried out specific data protection activities on behalf of the controller, but in a higher-level position and with more responsibility than the person in charge of the processing.[343]

In practice, the internal data processor had a certain discretion in determining the means and, to a small extent, the purposes of the processing according to the instructions defined by the data controller. In fact, this role had to be compatible with the previous European Union legislation on data processors, i.e., Directive 95/46/EC, which the Personal Data Protection Code aimed to transpose.

205. However, after the direct applicability of the GDPR and the 2018 reform, Article 4 of the Personal Data Protection Code has been repealed. Moreover, the GDPR now provides some obligations that are directly applicable to the data processor provided precisely for an external data processor and not for an internal data processor: some of these obligations are, for example, the register of processing operations (Article 30, paragraph 2, GDPR), the appointment of a DPO (Article 37 GDPR) or of the EU representative (Article 27 GDPR). As observed by some authors,[344] these obligations are clearly incompatible with the possibility of the data processor being internal to the data controller's organization.

As a result, the concept of internal data processor is generally considered to be incompatible with the new rules introduced by the GDPR and by the revised Personal Data Protection Code and has, therefore, been abandoned in practice.

342. Laura Greco, Il nuovo Rregolamento Europeo sulla privacy e sulla protezione dei dati personali 267 (Giusella Finocchiaro ed., Zanichelli editore 2017).

343. Giovanni M. Riccio, *La nuova disciplina europea della privacy* 46 (Salvatore Sica, Virgilio D'Antonio & Giovanni M. Riccio eds, CEDAM 2016).

344. Enrico Pelino, *Il Regolamento Privacy Europeo* 148 (Luca Bolognini, Enrico Pelino & Camilla Bistrolfi eds, Giuffrè Francis Lefebvre, 2016).

Chapter 4. Minors

§1. Provisions of the Italian Data Protection Code Relating to Minors

206. The Italian Personal Data Protection Code regulates the personal data of minors within Part I, Title I, with Article 2-*quinquies*, titled 'Child's Consent in Relation to Information Society Service' and within Part II, Title I, with Article 50, titled 'Reports or Images Concerning Underage Persons.'

§2. Child's Consent in Relation to Information Society Service

207. Article 2-*quinquies*, paragraph 1, of the Personal Data Protection Code, specifies Article 8 GDPR[345] by establishing that:

> Pursuant to Article 8(1) of the Regulation, a child aged above 14 years may give his or her consent to the processing of his or her personal data in relation to the offer of information society services directly to him or her. Regarding such services, the personal data of a child aged below 14 years may be processed lawfully in accordance with Article 6(1), letter a) of the Regulation if the consent is given by the holder of parental responsibility over the child.

208. The Italian legislator has therefore decided, in the context of the 2018 reform, to bring to *14 years* the minimum age, where children may be able to express a valid consent in relation to the offer of information society services.

209. Complementing the above provision, paragraph 2 of Article 2-*quinquies* provides that:

> [I]n relation to the offer of the services referred to in paragraph 1 directly to a child, the controller shall provide any information and communication relating to the processing activities concerning that child by using clear and plain language, in an especially concise, exhaustive, easily accessible and intelligible form, so as to make the child's consent meaningful.

210. Therefore, in order to be able to express valid consent, the minor must be adequately informed about the processing of their personal data, which is usually achieved by means of a privacy policy conceived to be specifically directed at children in a way that allows them to easily understand its content.[346]

---

345. In line with the possibility for Member States to provide a different age for valid child's consent in this area, pursuant to Art. 8, para. 1 GDPR.

346. It has been observed that this provision does not add nor specify anything in respect to the rules and principles concerning the requirements of enhanced transparency towards children already set forth by the GDPR; rather, the provision only repeats existing GDPR provisions: Bolognini & Pelino, *Codice Privacy: tutte le novità del D.lgs. 101/2018* 58–61 (Giuffré Francis Lefebvre, 2019), at 46.

211. It should be noted that the above framework seems consistent with the indications provided by Recital 58 GDPR.

I. Other Italian Law Provisions Concerning Publication or Dissemination of Images of Children

212. Article 50 of the Italian Personal data protection Code provides that it is forbidden to:

> [P]ublish and disseminate, by any means whatsoever, reports or images allowing an underage person to be identified, which is referred to in Section 13 of Presidential Decree No 448 of 22 September 1988, shall also apply if an underage person is involved for whatever reason in judicial proceedings concerning non-criminal matters. Violation of the prohibition referred to herein shall be punished in pursuance of Section 684 of the Criminal Code.

213. Italian law lays down further provisions aimed at protecting the right to privacy of individuals, which may have an impact on the publication or dissemination of reports or images allowing an underage person to be identified. Such provisions shall be examined *infra* in Part IX, Chapter 1, of this volume, as they arguably aim to balance freedom of expression vis-à-vis the protection of children's privacy.

§3. GPDP Decisions on Children's Consent in Relation to Information Society Services: The Case of TikTok

214. The provisions referred to above have been clarified and applied by the GPDP in several decisions.

Following reports sent to the GPDP by some consumer protection associations relating to possible privacy risks posed in relation to the TikTok social media platform, the GPDP, in January 2020, sent a letter to the EDPB, communicating the need for coordinated action between the European authorities.[347] Following this request, a specific taskforce was set up in order to coordinate the activities of the European authorities with respect to the company, whose headquarters were established in the USA at the time. After August 2020, the Company, in a press release,[348] announced the decision to establish a new Data Centre in Ireland to be used for the service provided to all users in the EEA and Switzerland in order to mitigate the risks in terms of transfers of personal data to the USA, following the CJEU 'Schrems II' judgment of 17 July 2020.[349]

---

347. GPDP, *TikTok: the Italian DPA calls for an EU taskforce*, 24.1.2020, doc. web no. 9249681, https://www.garanteprivacy.it/web/guest/home/docweb/-/docweb-display/docweb/9249681.

348. Tik Tok, https://newsroom.tiktok.com/it-it/al-via-il-nuovo-data-center-europeo-in-irlanda (in Italian).

349. Case C-311/18, *Data Protection Commissioner v. Facebook Ireland Ltd., Maximilian Schrems*, 17.7.2020, ECLI:EU:C:2020:559.

215. At the national level, the GPDP, after launching an investigation in March 2020 aimed at highlighting a series of processing activities deemed to not be in compliance with the legislation on the protection of personal data, on 22 December 2020 issued a formal complaint against TikTok Technology Ltd. (established in Ireland), accusing the latter of the violation of some provisions of the GDPR. Strong criticalities were found as regards the methods of registration to the social network, which did not ensure adequate forms of protection for minors. The ban on enrolment under the age of 13, established by the social network, is, in fact, easily circumvented once a false date of birth is entered.[350]

According to the GPDP, TikTok failed to prevent underage children from registering on the social network, nor did it verify that the national provisions were respected, which provide for the consent of parents or those with parental responsibility for the minor who is under 14 years of age to register on social networks. In addition, the GPDP contested the ways in which the privacy policy was provided, the transfer of data to third countries, the retention period, and compliance with the principles of data protection by design and by default.

216. Moreover, after a tragic event that involved a 10-year-old girl from Palermo, who allegedly lost her life by participating in a challenge on the social network, the GPDP adopted an emergency measure pursuant to Article 66 of the GDPR to limit the processing of data by TikTok for users whose age cannot be ascertained.[351] TikTok Ireland, following the measure, collaborated with the GPDP and declared its willingness to comply with the order received through a media awareness campaign.

In particular, the company decided to send an 'in app' message to all Italian users, asking them to indicate their date of birth again before continuing to use the service. Additionally, as stated by TikTok, once a user under the age of 13 is identified, the company has undertaken to remove the account without allowing new attempts at registering to be made.

TikTok also improved the reporting function that allows users to indicate the presence on the platform of users under 13 years of age and has undertaken to consider, in perspective, the possibility of using artificial intelligence as an additional tool to support user age verification.

217. This urgent measure was followed by another urgent measure motivated by the critical issues identified with regard to the adequacy of the mechanisms envisaged for age verification, also, in this case, providing the company with a deadline, 22 April 2021, to comply with the indications provided by the GPDP.[352] Following

350. GPDP, *Tik Tok Endangers Children's Privacy: Italian Dpa Initiates Proceedings Against the Social Network*, 22.12.2020, doc. web no. 9508923, https://www.garanteprivacy.it/web/guest/home/docweb/-/docweb-display/docweb/9508923#en.

351. GPDP, *Provvedimento del 22 gennaio 2021*, 22.1.2021, doc. web no. 9524194, https://www.garanteprivacy.it/home/docweb/-/docweb-display/docweb/9524194.

352. GPDP, *Provvedimento del 25 marzo 2021*, 25.3.2021, doc. web no. 9574709, https://www.garanteprivacy.it/home/docweb/-/docweb-display/docweb/9574709.

this provision, the GPDP requested information on how to register and verify the age of users also with respect to other platforms.[353]

218. The problem of lack of proper age verification mechanisms was recalled in another urgent measure issued against TikTok, whereby the GPDP stated that using personal data stored in users' devices to profile them and send them personalized advertising without users' explicit consent is unlawful.[354]

In that decision, the GPDP pointed out, *inter alia*, that the absence of certain elements for the identification of persons over the age of majority would risk involving in the profiling activity not only persons under the age of 18 but also those under the age of 14, for whom consent of the exercisers of parental responsibility would be required, and, hypothetically, also minors under the age of 13, for whom access to the platform would be prohibited entirely.

As a result of the GPDP's decision, TikTok decided to suspend the shift to legitimate interest as the legal basis for sending personalized advertising to people over the age of 18.[355]

§4. GPDP Decisions on the Dissemination of Children's Personal Data on Social Networks

219. The GPDP has adopted several decisions in the context of the dissemination of personal data belonging to children on social networks generated from complaints concerning the publication of personal data (e.g., comments, photographs) on social networks, in particular, Facebook, Instagram, and YouTube.

220. In this respect, the GPDP has clarified that the provisions that apply to the publication of personal data on social networks are those set out under Articles 136 and following the Personal Data Protection Code, since the broad wording of those provisions permits the extension of the guarantees and derogations established therein regarding the protection of personal data to data published on social networks.[356]

For the personal information published through social media, similarly to what happens in the case of the dissemination for journalistic purposes, it is therefore not necessary to collect the consent of the person concerned, provided that the publication of such information is supported by adequate purposes of public interest.[357]

---

353. GPDP, *Relazione annuale 2020*, 2.7.2021, doc. web no. 9676435, https://www.garanteprivacy.it/web/guest/home/docweb/-/docweb-display/docweb/9676435 at 134 and 135.
354. GDPD, *Provvedimento del 7 luglio 2022*, 7.7.2022, doc. web no. 9788429, https://www.garanteprivacy.it/web/guest/home/docweb/-/docweb-display/docweb/9788429.
355. GPDP, *Comunicato stampa, Tik Tok rinvia la pubblicità basata sul legittimo interesse. Per il Garante privacy 'una decisione responsabile'*, 12 luglio 2022, doc. web no. 9789143, https://www.garanteprivacy.it/web/guest/home/docweb/-/docweb-display/docweb/9789143.
356. In this respect, *see also infra* Part IX, Ch. 1, §6.
357. GPDP, *Annual Report for 2020*, 2.7.2021, doc. web no. 9676435, https://www.garanteprivacy.it/web/guest/home/docweb/-/docweb-display/docweb/9676435, at 133.

221. In applying the principle of the essentiality of information in the context of social media, the GPDP has, for example, imposed a fine of EUR 50,000 on the Mayor of Messina for having published videos and images of minors and other individuals with social and economic difficulties on his public Facebook page, portraying those individuals as alleged perpetrators of crimes, thereby exposing them to the harmful comments of other social network users. In the case in question, the GPDP concluded that such publication was not justified by reasons of public and social interest (and thereby violated the principles of lawfulness and accuracy), went beyond the limitations set out under Article 137, paragraph 3, of the Personal Data Protection Code, and represented a violation of the principles set out under Articles 7, 8, 9, and 10 of the Deontological Rules.[358]

358. GPDP, *Ordinanza ingiunzione – 13 maggio 2021*, 13.5.2021, doc. web no. 9670001, https://www.garanteprivacy.it/web/guest/home/docweb/-/docweb-display/docweb/9670001.

Part III. General Principles

Chapter 1. Data Quality Principles

222. Regarding the principles of lawfulness, fairness and transparency, it is worth pointing out that some Italian authors considered these three fundamental aspects of the processing in a single 'teleological' perspective, and this is the reason they are all grouped in a single provision (Article 5(a) GDPR). In this sense, lawfulness can be considered a relative concept, as it requires, at the same time, to assess the effectiveness of transparency and fairness in relation to a processing activity which involves a data subject.[359]

However, by analysing the differences between lawfulness and fairness, it can be maintained that lawfulness is limited to the respect of the applicable law provisions by the data controller in the context of the processing activities carried out by the latter. Furthermore, the fines issued by the GPDP with regard to the lawfulness of data processing demonstrate that the violation of this principle is linked to a case-by-case analysis, and it needs to be considered together with other equal-ranking principles, as shall be seen below.

Concerning a digital imprinting system, the GPDP stated that the lawfulness of the system is also to be assessed by having regard to other features related to compliance with the data minimization, proportionality, purpose specification, and fairness principles, as well as with data quality requirements.[360]

223. Further considerations regarding the principles of lawfulness, fairness, and transparency can be found in other relevant fines issued by the GPDP. One of them relates to the collection of personal data from third parties for telemarketing purposes. The GPDP states that the principles of lawfulness, fairness, and transparency are not respected when a data controller acquires personal data from third-parties for its autonomous marketing purpose without a specific data subject's consent

359. Luca Bolognini & Enrico Pelino, *Codice della disciplina privacy* (Giuffrè Francis Lefebvre, 2019), at 86.

360. GPDP, *Use of Fingerprints for Assiduity Control at the Workplace*, 21.7.2005, doc. web no. 1166892, https://www.garanteprivacy.it/web/guest/home/docweb/-/docweb-display/docweb/1166892, para. 4.

which clearly indicates the recipient(s) of such data. In particular, the GPDP clarified that the collection of consent by a mere indication of indefinite categories of recipients cannot be considered in line with the principles of lawfulness, fairness and transparency.[361]

224. In another relevant sanction, the GPDP considered that the principles of fairness and purpose limitation were violated in the case of a data controller which carried out a processing activity by formally qualifying the communication as a 'service communication', even if the latter included promotional offers for the data subjects despite their refusal to receive promotional communications.[362]

225. Regarding respect to the principle of purpose limitation, in another fine issued in recent years, the GPDP noted that the statement of the purposes of the processing carried out by the data controller did not appear to be supported by the stringent requirements of specificity. Even more so, considering that 'sensitive' data might be involved, the purposes of the relevant processing should have been described with the necessary precision: on the one hand, to allow data subjects to express their consent in a free and informed manner and, on the other hand, to allow the competent authorities to verify compliance with the above-mentioned requirements and with the additional provisions on the matter, with particular regard, for example, to the principle of data minimization.[363]

226. From another perspective, the GPDP recently investigated the collection of personal data via web scraping in a recent sanction issued against Clearview AI.[364] The findings showed that the company infringed several fundamental data protection principles, including the principles of transparency, purpose limitation, and storage limitation. The GPDP concluded that a violation of the principle of transparency had taken place by considering that, on the one hand, the company failed to adequately inform users, who had no contact with the company and were neither directly informed of its processing activities nor were they able to receive any information by consulting the company's website. On the other hand, a violation of the principle of purpose limitation was integrated as the company processed users' data for a purpose other than those which they had made available online. In this case, the GPDP clarified that the public nature of the personal data (which were images

361. GPDP, *Ordinanza di ingiunzione nei confronti di Iren Mercato S.p.A. – 13 maggio 2021*, 13.5.2021, doc. web no. 9670025, https://www.garanteprivacy.it/web/guest/home/docweb/-/docweb-display/docweb/9670025, para. 2.2.1.

362. GPDP, *Provvedimento correttivo e sanzionatorio nei confronti di TIM S.p.A.*, 15.1.2020, doc. web no. 9256486, https://www.garanteprivacy.it/web/guest/home/docweb/-/docweb-display/docweb/9256486, para. 3.2.

363. GPDP, *Provvedimento del 10 gennaio 2019*, doc. web no. 9080914, para. 5, https://www.garanteprivacy.it/web/guest/home/docweb/-/docweb-display/docweb/9080914. *See also* GPDP, *Ordinanza ingiunzione nei confronti di Facebook Ireland Ltd e Facebook Italy s.r.l. – 14 giugno 2019*, doc. web no. 9121486, https://www.garanteprivacy.it/web/guest/home/docweb/-/docweb-display/docweb/9121486.

364. GPDP, *Ordinanza ingiunzione nei confronti di Clearview AI – 10 febbraio 2022*, doc. web no. 9751362, para 3.6.1, https://www.garanteprivacy.it/home/docweb/-/docweb-display/docweb/9751362.

of the data subjects) is not sufficient to assume that data subjects could reasonably expect that their personal data may be used for other purposes (in the case at stake, facial recognition purposes). Moreover, the public nature of the personal data does not automatically entitle the data controller to lawfully and freely re-use this data. Lastly, as the GPDP ascertained that the company had not established any data storage period, a violation of the storage limitation principle has been deemed to have occurred as well.

227. Interesting insights regarding the interpretation of the data protection principles, thereby including their balancing vis-à-vis other laws, can also be shown by taking into account the relevant case law of the Supreme Court of Cassation. In one of its judgments, the Court examined the relationship between the national civil procedural rules and the general data protection rules by assessing the necessity to use personal data which had been unlawfully collected or processed as evidence in legal proceedings. The Court concluded by confirming this possibility, taking into account that the right to the protection of personal data is not an absolute right, and it must be balanced against other fundamental rights in accordance with the principle of proportionality.[365] This approach is also confirmed by Article 2-*decies* of the Italian Personal Data Protection Code currently in force, which states that any personal data that is processed in breach of the relevant provisions on the protection of personal data may not be used, except as provided for in Article 160-*bis* of the Italian Data Protection Code (which states that the validity, enforceability and admissibility in judicial proceedings of records, documents and measures based on the processing of personal data that is not compliant with the law shall continue to be regulated by the relevant procedural law provisions).[366]

228. On the balancing criterion and the principle of minimization as a limit to the processing of personal data, even if carried out for relevant reason of public interest, another decision of the Supreme Court of Cassation is relevant. In particular, it was clarified that it cannot be held that a bank has breached applicable data protection law merely because it provided the persons acquiring credit with information concerning the debtor and which are instrumental in the assignment of the credit, such as the debtor's debt situation, the location of the property used to secure the credit, etc., where no proof is provided that the communication to third parties took place in breach of the principle of minimizing the use of personal data.[367]

From the public interest perspective, it is interesting to note a judgment in which the Court confirmed that the presence of the 'public interest' may justify an important exception to the principle of storage limitation. The Court based its reasoning on Article 99 of the Italian Data Protection Code, which states that:

(i) processing of personal data for archiving purposes in the public interest, scientific or historical research purposes or statistical purposes

365. Supreme Court of Cassation, no. 8459/2020, civ. sect.

366. *See* Bolognini & Pelino, *Codice Privacy: tutte le novità del D.lgs. 101/2018* 58–61 (Giuffré Francis Lefebvre, 2019), at 89.

367. Supreme Court of Cassation, no. 34113/2019, civ. sect.

may be carried out also for longer than is necessary for achieving the individual purposes for which the data had been previously collected or processed.

(ii) Where the processing of personal data is terminated, for whatever reason, such data may be kept or transferred to another data controller for archiving purposes in the public interest, scientific or historical research purposes or statistical purposes.

229. Therefore, the Court concluded that personal data processed for the purposes of carrying out a public selection process can be retained for a further period following the conclusion of the public competition, even if the processing for this purpose has ceased. Indeed, the notion of 'public interest' implies that a lawful reason for further retaining and processing personal data may be the necessity of subsequent and further evaluations of the regularity of the selection process.[368]

368. Supreme Court of Cassation, no. 35095/2019, crim. sect.

Chapter 2. Legal Grounds

§1. Introduction

230. Before the direct applicability of the GDPR and the subsequent 2018 data protection reform, Italian data protection law adopted a clear 'consent-centric' approach in the context of legal grounds for processing personal data,[369] in particular, Article 24 of the Personal Data Protection Code, now repealed, provided that the processing of personal data by private and public entities alike was allowed only where the data subject had expressly consented to it, while Article 25 – titled 'Cases where the processing can be performed without consent'[370] – provided for specific exceptions to the general rule. As a result, consent was considered the principal legal basis, while the scope of application of other grounds for processing personal data was to be interpreted restrictively, as they were considered exceptions to a general rule.

231. After the direct applicability of the GDPR, legal grounds for processing personal data under the Italian data protection law are now those set forth by Article 6, paragraph 1, GDPR; this has also been recognized by the 2018 reform, which has repealed both Articles 24 and 25 of the Personal Data Protection Code. However, Italian data protection law has retained some specificities concerning, in particular, processing on the basis of consent,[371] which still partially reflects the pre-GDPR 'consent-centric' approach. Other specific provisions have been introduced by the 2018 reform as regards processing, which is necessary to comply with a legal obligation to which the controller is subject[372] and the processing for performance of a task carried out in the public interest or in the exercise of official authority vested in the controller.[373]

The specificities provided by Italian law relate, in particular, to the material scope of application of the legal bases indicated above.

§2. Consent for Marketing Activities

232. Concerning consent, most specificities revolve around the material scope of application of this legal basis in the context of direct marketing and marketing-related profiling. In particular, the GPDP has provided specific rules for data subject's consent in the context of direct marketing activities within the well-known 'Guidelines on Marketing and against Spam.'[374]

369. Bolognini & Pelino, *Codice Privacy: tutte le novità del D.lgs. 101/2018* 58–61 (Giuffré Francis Lefebvre, 2019), at 11–12.
370. Author's translation. In Italian, the Article was titled: 'Casi nei quali può essere effettuato il trattamento senza consenso'.
371. Article 6, para. 1, lett. a), GDPR.
372. Article 6, para. 1, lett. c), GDPR.
373. Article 6, para. 1, lett. e), GDPR.
374. GPDP, *Guidelines on Marketing and against Spam*, 4.7.2013, doc. web no. 4304228. Despite being adopted in 2013, i.e., before the direct applicability or even the entry into force of the GDPR, the

233. The Guidelines recognize that processing for direct marketing purposes carried out by means of automated tools[375] may only be performed with the contracting party's or user's prior consent,[376] given that such processing activity falls within the scope of Article 130, paragraphs 1 and 2, of the Personal Data Protection Code, which transposes Article 13 of the e-Privacy Directive. As a result, despite the possibility of performing direct marketing activities on the basis of the data controller's legitimate interest, recognized by Recital 47 GDPR,[377] data processing for direct marketing activities carried out by Italian-based data controllers may only be grounded on consent, aside from the specific exceptions provided for by national law, such as the so-called soft-opt in exception and the telephone operator exception (*see infra*).

Furthermore, it should be noted that the above rule to ground direct marketing processing activities on consent applies not only where the recipient of the marketing activities is a natural person but also where it is a legal person,[378] even though the latter category benefits from a limited pool of remedies, as legal persons may not exercise the rights provided by Articles 15–22 GDPR, nor can they lodge claims or complaints with the GPDP.[379]

I. Informed Consent in the Context of Marketing

234. Another specification provided by the 2013 Guidelines concerns transparency requirements, in order to ensure that consent is 'informed'. In particular, aside from the information set forth in Articles 13 and 14 of the GDPR,[380] data controllers should inform data subjects about the means which will be used to carry out marketing activities, in particular, whether the processing will be carried out through 'automated phone calls and similar arrangements such as faxes, emails,

Guidelines are still applicable and concretely applied by the GPDP in the context of its decisions, as they are deemed to be in line with the GDPR. *See*, for example: GPDP, *Decision 22 July 2021*, 4.7.2021, doc. web no. 9696708, https://www.garanteprivacy.it/web/guest/home/docweb/-/docweb-display/docweb/9696708.

375. That is, automated-calling systems, e-mails, SMS, MMS, telefax and similar systems (*see* Art. 130, paras 1 and 2, Data Protection Code).

376. *See* para. 2.5 of the 2013 Guidelines. The GPDP specifies that the requirement of consent applies also to data which are publicly available.

377. 'The processing of personal data for direct marketing purposes may be regarded as carried out for a legitimate interest'.

378. This outcome is a result of the fact that Art. 130 of the Data Protection Code refers not only to the 'user', but also to the 'contracting party'.

379. Such limitations as regards applicable remedies for legal persons have been also recognized by the 2013 Guidelines, *see* para. 2.1. According to the Guidelines, however, legal persons still have a few remedies at their disposal: 'Still, legal persons and similar entities may rely on the standard remedies made available by our legal system insofar as they are "contracting parties" – that is, they may seize judicial authorities under civil law to e.g. apply for injunctive orders or claim damages; if the preconditions set forth in Section 167 of Italy's Criminal Code are fulfilled, they may also lodge a criminal report and initiate criminal proceedings to obtain imposition of the applicable penalties. Moreover, they may benefit from the remedies this DPA is empowered to afford of its own motion – via prohibitory or injunctive orders and/or via the imposition of sanctions – if there is reason to believe that a given data processing operation is in breach of the law.'

380. Formerly, Art. 13 of the Personal Data Protection Code, repealed by D.Lgs. 101/2018.

SMS-messaging and MMS-messaging, as well as to conventional mechanisms such as paper mailing and operator-assisted calls'.

In addition, where the data controller wishes to leverage both conventional and automated means to carry out marketing activities, the information notice to be recalled within the marketing consent statement must specify that the right to object to marketing carried out through automated means also applies to conventional marketing and that the data subject may in any case exercise that right also partly, 'e.g., by objecting only to marketing communications via automated means'.[381]

II. Informed Consent in the Context of Marketing

235. Concerning the requirement that consent must be 'specific', the 2013 Guidelines clarify that – although connected to a broad common aim – direct marketing, profiling connected to marketing, and the disclosure of data to third parties for their own marketing purposes, each amount to a different processing purpose; as a result, each of these activities must be carried out on the basis of a separate consent from the contracting party or user.[382]

However, the Guidelines also recognize that 'marketing-related purposes are manifold as they include the delivery of advertising materials, direct selling, performance of market surveys, and commercial communications'. As a result, these specific purposes may be considered forming part of a broader 'marketing purpose' and may, therefore, be grounded on a single consent.[383] The same goes for direct marketing carried out on the basis of conventional (i.e., phone call operators and paper mail) and automated means (i.e., automated-calling systems, e-mails, SMS, MMS, telefax and similar systems), which can be based on the same consent for the general marketing purpose.[384]

In any case, as indicated above in Chapter 2, §2.02.A,[385] in order for consent to be 'informed' (and, therefore, valid), the consent statement must specify which means of the processing are going to be leveraged by the data controller, as well as the fact that the contracting party or user has the right to object to the processing in its entirety, or only as regards one or more of the means leveraged by the data controller.[386]

III. Consent to the Disclosure of Data to Third Parties for their Own Marketing Activities

236. As indicated in Chpater 2, §2.02.B,[387] disclosure of data to third parties for their own marketing purposes amounts to a different processing activity than direct

381. *See* para. 2.6.2 of the 2013 Guidelines.
382. *See* para. 2.6.1 of the 2013 Guidelines.
383. *Ibid.*
384. *See* para. 2.6.2 of the 2013 Guidelines.
385. *See supra* §2.02.A within this Ch. 2.
386. That is, conventional or automated means. *See Ibid.*
387. *See supra* §2.02.B within this Ch. 2.

marketing or profiling. As a result, this distinct activity must be grounded on a specific consent. In addition, in order for such consent to be 'informed' and therefore valid, the information notice must also 'specify the individual third parties or else the respective (business or commodity) categories – e.g., "financing", "publishing", "clothing"'.[388]

237. If the above conditions are fulfilled and the third parties are named individually, the latter – as autonomous data controllers – may process the data for their marketing purposes, mentioned by the first data controller which disclosed the data in the first place and do not need to provide an additional information notice to the data subjects.[389] Otherwise, the third parties may carry out their own marketing activities, but only after having provided the data subjects with their own information notices. In both cases, however, the third-party recipients must provide their contact details in order for data subjects to be able to exercise their data protection rights.

IV. Consent for Profiling Activities Related to Marketing

238. As already seen above, in the 2013 Guidelines, the GPDP clarified that profiling activities,[390] even where related to marketing purposes (usually, with the aim of serving personalized advertising to the user), amount to a different processing activity than direct marketing itself. As a result, profiling needs to be grounded on another legal basis, different from the one leveraged by the data controller to perform direct marketing activities. In this respect, given the inherent intrusiveness of profiling, as well as the risk that such activity may pose for the rights and freedoms of data subjects, the GPDP has consistently held that profiling should be based on the data subject's consent. This approach has been reiterated by the GPDP multiple times, not only within the already mentioned 2013 Guidelines but also in the

388. *See* para. 2.6.3 of the 2013 Guidelines. It should be noted that the requirement to disclose the individual name of the recipients or the business or commodity categories seems to be in line with the more recent Arts 13(1)(e) and 14(1)(e) GDPR, as interpreted by the A29WP Guidelines on Transparency, although such guidelines arguably raise the transparency bar to an extent, as the data controller is required to disclose 'the type of recipient (i.e., by reference to the activities it carries out), the industry, sector and sub-sector and the location of the recipients' (*see* the Annex to the Guidelines on Transparency).

389. *Ibid.* Again, this provision seems to be in line with the more recent Art. 14, para. 5, lett. (a), GDPR, which does not require the further provision of information on the processing, insofar as 'the data subject already has the information'.

390. While, before the direct applicability of the GDPR, Italian legislation adopted a specific definition of 'profiling', both within Art. 71, para. 1, lett. d), of the Personal Data Protection Code and within the 'Linee guida in materia di trattamento di dati personali per profilazione on line', 19 Mar. 2015, doc. web 3881513, as of today the applicable definition of 'profiling' within Italian data protection law is arguably the one adopted under Art. 4, para. 4, GDPR.

'Guidelines on processing of personal data for online profiling'[391] and in the previous 'Loyalty cards and safeguards for consumers: guidelines applying to loyalty programmes.'[392]

Based on the aforementioned orientation, it may be held that under Italian data protection law, the performance of profiling activities aimed at carrying out personalized direct marketing activities requires the data controller to acquire two different consents from the same data subjects:

(i) A consent to the performance of direct marketing activities.
(ii) A consent to (marketing-related) profiling.

V. Exceptions to Consent for Marketing Activities: The 'Soft Opt-In' Exception

239. The Italian legislator has transposed the so-called soft opt-in exception to consent, provided by Article 13, paragraph 2, of the e-Privacy Directive, within Article 130, paragraph 4,[393] of the Personal Data Protection Code.

The provision has been transposed without particular specifications. As indicated by the 2013 Guidelines, which provide the GPDP's interpretation of the soft opt-in exception:

> If the data controller uses, to directly sell own services or products, the e-mail contact information that was made available by the data subject within the framework of the sale of a product or service, that controller may do without the data subject's consent – providing the product or service in question is similar to the one previously sold and the data subject does not object to the use of his/her data after being informed appropriately.[394]

VI. Consent in the Context of Marketing Activities Carried Out by Means of Telephone Operators and Postal Mail

240. While it may be held that Italian data protection law adopts a 'consent-centric' approach in the context of direct marketing activities by requiring, as a rule,

391. Author's translation.
392. GPDP, *Loyalty cards and safeguards for consumers: guidelines applying to loyalty programmes*, 24.02.2005, doc. web no. 1109624.
393. 'Subject to paragraph 1, where a data controller uses, for direct marketing of his/her own products or services, electronic contact details for electronic mail supplied by a data subject in the context of the sale of a product or service, said data controller may fail to request the data subject's consent, on condition that the services are similar to those that have been the subject of the sale and the data subject, after being adequately informed, does not object to said use either initially or in connection with subsequent communications. The data subject shall be informed of the possibility to object to the processing at any time, using simple means and free of charge, both at the time of collecting the data and when sending any communications for the purposes referred to in this paragraph.'
394. Paragraph 2.7 of the 2013 Guidelines.

an opt-in in order to ground the legitimacy of direct marketing activities which involve the processing of personal data, the opposite is true when such activities are carried out by means of telephone operators and postal mail, as long as the data used for marketing are included within paper or electronic directories available to the public. In this respect, the Italian legislator has leveraged the possibility provided within Article 13, paragraph 3, of the e-Privacy Directive,[395] which leaves each Member State the choice of whether to subject those marketing activities to an 'opt-in' or 'opt-out' model, thereby choosing the latter.

In particular, Article 130, paragraph 3-*bis*, of the Personal Data Protection Code provides that the use of telephone and postal mail for the purpose of sending advertising or direct sales material or to carry out market research or commercial communication towards contracting parties[396] whose data are included within paper or electronic directories available to the public is permitted where the contracting party has not objected to such processing. The right to object, or 'opt-out', may be exercised by the contracting party by registering in a public opposition registry (*'Registro delle Opposizioni'*), as shall be seen in the next section.

VII. The Opposition Registry

241. The opposition registry was adopted, initially, with D.P.R. 7 September 2010, no. 178, with a view to putting into effect the above-mentioned opt-out right in favour of contracting parties whose telephone and mail[397] data is present within paper or electronic public directories. The contracting parties who wish to opt-out from marketing activities carried out through telephone operators and postal mail may, therefore, subscribe to the registry; otherwise, if their data are present within paper or electronic public directories, they may be subject to marketing by means of phone calls and paper mail.

In order to leverage the possibility of reaching out to those contracting parties, the operator must register itself within the opposition registry, subject to a fee,[398] to be able to consult the registry and, therefore, check the numbers and/or postal addresses that the operator itself holds against the registry. The consultation of the registry by an operator is effective for fifteen days for telephone calls and thirty days in the case of postal marketing.

395. 'Member States shall take appropriate measures to ensure that, free of charge, unsolicited communications for purposes of direct marketing, in cases other than those referred to in paragraphs 1 and 2, are not allowed either without the consent of the subscribers concerned or in respect of subscribers who do not wish to receive these communications, the choice between these options to be determined by national legislation'.

396. This definition encompasses both natural and legal persons and is therefore broader than the notion of 'data subject' adopted by Art. 4, para. 1, GDPR.

397. Although, concerning mail data, the possibility for the contracting party to subscribe to the opposition registry has been enacted much later, with D.P.R. 8 Nov. 2018, no. 149, which amended the 2010 D.P.R.

398. The relevant fees can be consulted here: https://www.registrodelleopposizioni.it/it/operatori/home-operatori.

From the above arrangements, it follows that the operator may leverage two different legal bases in order to perform phone calls with operators and postal mail activities, depending on the source of the data used to carry out such activities:[399]

(i) if the data have been gathered from a public directory, the operator can perform marketing activities, provided that it has checked the opposition registry within a timely manner and the user has not opted-out from the activity;
(ii) if the data have not been gathered from a public directory, the operator must have acquired a GDPR-valid consent before the processing takes place.

242. Overtime, however, and especially from 2016 onwards, the aim of the registry has expanded.

In this respect, with Law 11 January 2018, no. 5, and D.P.R. 27 January 2022, no. 26, the Italian legislator has extended the possibility to subscribe to the registry – starting from July 2022 – also to contracting parties whose telephone number (both landline and mobile) are not present within public directories. In this case, however, the effect of the subscription to the opposition registry is not to opt-out from receiving marketing communications; rather, by subscribing to the registry, the contracting party signifies the withdrawal of all the consents previously expressed, with any form or means and by any operator, in relation to the processing of the contracting party's landline or mobile telephone number for marketing purposes (thereby including disclosure of the number to third parties for their own marketing purposes).[400]

§3. Consent for the Use of Cookies and Other Tracking Technologies

243. Article 122 of the Personal Data Protection Code, which transposes Article, paragraph 3, of the e-Privacy Directive, mandates that the storage of information in the terminal equipment of a contracting party or a user or access to information already stored is only permitted on condition that the contracting party or user has given their consent, after being informed in a simplified manner. The aforementioned rule does not apply in cases where the storage or access to information already stored within the terminal equipment is aimed solely at carrying out the transmission of a communication over an electronic communications network or to the extent strictly necessary for the provision of an information society service explicitly requested by the contracting party or by the user.

While the Italian transposition of Article 5, paragraph 3, of the e-Privacy Directive, does not differ significantly from the text of the Directive, the GPDP has adopted a peculiar interpretation of Article 122, already addressed in Part I, Chapter 3, §3, *supra*.

---

399. Luana Patti, Privacy e Libero Mercato Digitale: Convergenza tra Regolazioni e Tutele Individuali nell'Economia Data-Driven 114 (Luca Bolognini ed., 2021).

400. *See* Art. 1, para. 5, of L. 5/2018. The same provision lays down an exception to this general right of withdrawal, which shall not apply to any consents given in the context of specific contractual relationships in place, or ceased by no longer thirty days, concerning the supply of goods or services, for which the right to withdraw consent is in any case assured by simplified means.

§4. Validity of Consent in Relation to the Offer of Information Society Services Directly to a Child

244. The Italian legislator has leveraged the opportunity set forth by Article 8 GDPR, which leaves to Member States the possibility to provide by law an age lower than 16 years for consent provided by a child for the processing of their personal data in relation to the offer of information society services[401] directly[402] to a child, provided that such lower age is not below thirteen years.[403]

In this respect, Article 2-*quinquies*, paragraph one, of the Personal Data Protection Code – introduced by the 2018 reform – has lowered the age to 14 years for children's consent provided in relation to an information society service to be valid. Furthermore, Article 2-*quinquies*, paragraph 1, clarifies that when the child is less than 14 years of age, the processing of personal data referred to above is lawful only when consent is provided by the parent or guardian.

Finally, the second paragraph of Article 2-*quinquies* provides that the data controller which seeks the child's consent, referred to in paragraph 1, must use particularly clear and simple language which should be concise and exhaustive, easily accessible, and understandable by the child, in order for consent to be meaningful.[404]

§5. Processing for Compliance with a Legal Obligation or for the Performance of a Task Carried Out in the Public Interest or in the Exercise of Official Authority

245. In accordance with Article 6, paragraphs 2[405] and 3[406] GDPR, the Italian legislator has introduced more specific provisions to adapt the application of the

---

401. The notion of 'information society service' is set forth by Directive 98/35/CE, as amended by Directive 98/48/CE: 'any service normally provided for remuneration, at a distance, by electronic means and at the individual request of a recipient of services.'
402. The use of the word 'directly' is generally interpreted as meaning that the child should be the one directly requesting, and using, the service, as a user or contracting party. *See* Bolognini & Pelino, *Codice Privacy: tutte le novità del D.lgs. 101/2018* 58–61 (Giuffré Francis Lefebvre, 2019), at 45.
403. The protection of minors under Italian data protection law is more generally addressed *supra* in Part II, Ch. 4, §1.
404. It has been observed that this provision does not add nor specify anything in respect to the rules and principles concerning the requirements of enhanced transparency towards children already set forth by the GDPR; rather, the provision only repeats Arts 12–14 and Recital 84 GDPR: Bolognini & Pelino, *Codice Privacy: tutte le novità del D.lgs. 101/2018* 58–61 (Giuffré Francis Lefebvre, 2019), at 46.
405. 'Member States may maintain or introduce more specific provisions to adapt the application of the rules of this Regulation with regard to processing for compliance with points (c) and (e) of paragraph 1 by determining more precisely specific requirements for the processing and other measures to ensure lawful and fair processing including for other specific processing situations as provided for in Chapter IX.'
406. 'The basis for the processing referred to in point (c) and (e) of paragraph 1 shall be laid down by: (a) Union law; or (b) Member State law to which the controller is subject. The purpose of the processing shall be determined in that legal basis or, as regards the processing referred to in point (e) of paragraph 1, shall be necessary for the performance of a task carried out in the public interest

legal bases set forth by Article 6, paragraph 1, letter c) and letter e), GDPR, i.e., respectively, where the processing is necessary for compliance with a legal obligation to which the controller is subject and where the processing is necessary for the performance of a task carried out in the public interest or in the exercise of official authority vested in the controller.

246. Concerning both legal bases referred to above, the Italian legislator has included the new Article 2-*ter* within the Personal Data Protection Code, which aims to specify – and therefore restrict – its scope of application. The Article titled 'Legal basis to process personal data for the performance of a task carried out in the public interest or in the exercise of official authority' has been introduced in the context of the 2018 reform and has been amended, lastly, with Law Decree 8 October 2021, no. 139, converted into law with amendments by Law 3 December 2021, no. 205.

The first paragraph of Article 2-*ter* provides that only national law,[407] regulations,[408] and administrative instruments of a general nature[409] may provide the basis for the processing referred to in Article 6, paragraphs 2 and 3, GDPR. While Article 2-*ter* restricts the applicability of the two legal bases in question only to the aforementioned legal acts, it should be noted, however, that the provision does not require that the data controller wishing to leverage the legal bases in question be a public authority.

As a result, under Italian data protection law, such legal bases may be leveraged by public and private entities alike, as long as the processing is grounded within national formal law, regulations or administrative instruments of a general nature.

247. In addition to the above, paragraph 1-*bis* of Article 2-*ter* – introduced in 2021 with the aforementioned Law Decree[410] with a view to broaden the possibility for public authorities to leverage the two GDPR legal bases in question – provides

---

or in the exercise of official authority vested in the controller. That legal basis may contain specific provisions to adapt the application of rules of this Regulation, *inter alia*: the general conditions governing the lawfulness of processing by the controller; the types of data which are subject to the processing; the data subjects concerned; the entities to, and the purposes for which, the personal data may be disclosed; the purpose limitation; storage periods; and processing operations and processing procedures, including measures to ensure lawful and fair processing such as those for other specific processing situations as provided for in Chapter IX. The Union or the Member State law shall meet an objective of public interest and be proportionate to the legitimate aim pursued.'

407. In the context of Italian constitutional law, the concept of law ('*legge*') is usually understood as encompassing: (i) ordinary legislation ('*legge in senso formale*') adopted by the Italian Parliament; (ii) legislative decrees enacted by government on the basis of a general law ('*legge quadro*') adopted by the Parliament, under Art. 76 of the Constitution; (iii) law decrees ('*decreti legge*') enacted by government in cases of urgency, under Art. 77 of the Constitution. Bin & Pitruzzella, *supra* n. 177, at 367–368 and 384–401.

408. Regulations ('*regolamenti*') are secondary sources of law, which validity depends on them being in line with the law. *Ibid.*, at 411–421.

409. Administrative instruments of a general nature ('*atti amministrativi generali*') are usually defined as acts adopted by the public administration, which are intended to apply to the general public. *Ibid.*, at 421–422.

410. D.L. 139/2021, converted into law with amendments by L. 205/2021.

that when the processing of personal data is carried out by a public authority,[411] the processing is also legitimate where it is necessary to perform a task carried out in the public interest or in the exercise of official authority conferred to the public authority. However, paragraph 1-*bis* further specifies that it shall be applied in compliance with Article 6 GDPR in order to ensure that their application will not be detrimental to the protection of the rights and freedoms of data subjects.[412]

Finally, the 2021 reform has also provided specific rules concerning the lawfulness of the communication and dissemination[413] of personal data taking place in the context of the performance of a task carried out in the public interest or in the exercise of official authority – by private or public entities alike. In particular, paragraph 2 of Article 2-*ter* provides that the communication of personal data, other than special categories of personal data referred to in Article 9 GDPR and criminal convictions and offences referred to in Article 10 GDPR, may take place if the communication occurs in accordance with paragraph 1 or 1-*bis* of Article 2-*ter*.

According to paragraph 3 of Article 2-*ter*, personal data may be disseminated or communicated to entities that intend to process such data for purposes other than the performance of a task carried out in the public interest or in the exercise of official authority, only if the communication takes place in accordance with paragraph 1 or 1-*bis* of Article 2-*ter*. In this case, moreover, the GPDP shall be notified at least ten days prior to commencement of the communication or dissemination.

411. More specifically, a public administration referred to in s. 1(2) of D.Lgs. 165/2001 – including the independent administrative authorities and the administrative bodies listed in s. 1(3) of L. 196/2009, – as well as by a State-owned company or a company managing public services owned by a local authority as referred to in D. Lgs. 175/2016, whereby processing related to activities performed on unregulated markets shall be excluded as for publicly owned companies.

412. This last part has been amended by L. 205/2021, while the original provision enacted with D.L. 205/2021, allowed the public authority to determine itself the purpose of the processing, consistently with the public task or power exercised.

413. For the notion of 'communication' and 'dissemination' of personal data within Italian data protection law, please *see infra* Part II, Ch. 3.

Chapter 3. Special Categories of Data

§1. The Notion and Protection of 'Data Relating to Health' under the Jurisprudence of the Supreme Court of Cassation

248. Several judgments of the Supreme Court of Cassation have strengthened the protection of health data and extended the relevant notion, as can be observed in the following cases:

249. With judgment no. 30981/2017, the Court established that personal data capable of revealing health status may be processed only by using technical means, such as encryption techniques, that do not allow for the identification of data subjects .

Moreover, the Court has interpreted extensively the notion of 'data relating to health' provided by Article 4, no. 15, GDPR: in particular, the Court stated that even the mere indication to the law that recognizes the health allowance in favour of the beneficiary is capable of revealing the health status of the beneficiary of the allowance.

As a result, such indication amounts to 'data relating to health', thereby triggering the application of Article 9 GDPR.

250. With judgment no. 9382, dated 4 April 2019, the Supreme Court of Cassation stated that, in principle, the privacy of health data prevails over administrative transparency.

The Court, therefore, considered the sanction against a public administration that divulged information about the health status of one of its employees to be legitimate. In this respect, the Court also stated, regarding data related to health, that: 'the protection of sensitive data prevails over a generic need for administrative transparency, both in terms of the constitutional profile of the assessment of the interests at stake and in terms of the substantive circumvention of the applicable law on the protection of personal data, in particular in the case of sensitive data, where a generic need for administrative transparency should not prevail'.[414]

251. In its judgment no. 16816, dated 26 June 2018, concerning the disclosure of a child's disability condition by means of posting such information on the school bulletin board for the purpose of the ranking of admission to a school privilege, the Supreme Court of Cassation further clarified the scope of application of the notion of 'data relating to health'. In particular, the Court stated that information concerning the health of a child amounts to personal and sensitive data and, as such, asserted its protection under the Italian Personal Data Protection Code.

More interestingly, the Court noted that this protection extends not only to the child but also to individuals who have family or domestic relationships with the child. This is because a family member's disability implicitly exposes a condition of weakness or social hardship of the other persons who are part of the family.

414. Author's translation.

As a consequence, a family member's disability is potentially capable of exposing the other family members to disadvantages or discrimination. Applying this principle, the Court ruled that the family could pursue damages following the unlawful disclosure of the child's disability.

§2. Processing of Special Categories of Personal Data for Objectives of Relevant Public Interest

252. Article 2-*sexies*, paragraph 1, of the Personal Data Protection Code implements and specifies Article 9, paragraph 2, letter g), GDPR, i.e., the legal basis concerning the processing of special categories of personal data for objectives of relevant public interest. Article 2-*sexies* lists the specific cases in which there is a relevant public interest and in which public and private entities may process such data.

This norm restricts the scope of the above-mentioned GDPR provision, as on the one hand, it specifies that, aside from EU law, the reasons for public interests shall be found only in a law, a regulation, or an administrative instrument of a general nature; on the other hand, the provision specifies that, in order to integrate the relevant GDPR legal basis, such normative sources shall also specify 'what types of data may be processed, what processing activities may be performed and what substantial public interest reasons justify the processing along with the suitable, specific measures to safeguard the data subject's fundamental rights and interests'.

253. Paragraph 2 of Article 2-*sexies* further provides some examples where substantial public interest shall be considered to exist; however, as this list is without prejudice to paragraph 1, it is not comprehensive, but it only servers as a reference for future interventions of the Legislator, as also indicated in the GPDP's Official Opinion on the Personal Data Protection Code reform.[415]

254. Finally, it is interesting to note that paragraph 1-*bis* of Article 2-*sexies*, which has been added by Law Decree 8 October 2021, no. 139, converted into law with amendments by Law 3 December 2021, no. 205, directly provides for an instance where processing of special category data (in particular, data relating to health) is lawful for objectives of relevant public interest. In particular, the paragraph provides that:

> [D]ata relating to health shall be processed, after removing directly identifying information, by the Ministry of Health, the Istituto Superiore di Sanità [Higher Institute for Health], the National Agency for regional healthcare services, the Italian Medicine Agency, the National Institute for the promotion of health in migrant populations and for the fight against poverty-related diseases, and by Regions, with regard to the individuals using the respective services, also by

415. GPDP, *Parere sullo schema di decreto legislativo recante disposizioni per l'adeguamento della normativa nazionale alle disposizioni del Regolamento (UE) 2016/679*, 22.5.2018, doc. web no. 9163359 https://www.garanteprivacy.it/home/docweb/-/docweb-display/docweb/9163359.

way of the interlinking at national level of the individual information systems of the National Health Service including Electronic Health Records (FSE), which shall serve purposes compatible with those underpinning the processing at issue, in accordance with the purposes officially pursued by each of the aforementioned entities as well as with the arrangements and for the purposes set out in a decree by the Minister of Health, under the terms of paragraph 1 hereof, subject to an opinion given by the Garante, pursuant to the provisions made in the Regulation, this Code, the Digital Administration Code referred to in legislative decree no. 82 of 7 March 2005, and the interoperability guidelines issued by the Agency for Digital Italy.

§3. Further Conditions, Including Limitations, with Regard to the Processing of Genetic Data, Biometric Data or Data Concerning Health

255. According to Article 9, paragraph 4, GDPR, Member States may maintain or introduce further conditions, including limitations, with regard to the processing of genetic data, biometric data, and data concerning health or sexual orientation. Such data are also known, in the Italian privacy discourse, as so-called super-sensitive data, a subset of the special categories of personal data (formerly named, in the context of Directive 95/46/EC and the pre-2018 reform Personal Data Protection Code, 'sensitive data').[416] The Italian Legislator has put in place specific provisions which give effect to Article 9, paragraph 4, GDPR, also by referring to general decisions adopted by the GPDP.

Regarding genetic data, biometric data and data concerning health, Article 2-*septies* of the Personal Data Protection Code provides that such data may be lawfully processed according to:

(a) one of the conditions set out in paragraph 2 of Article 9 GDPR;
(b) the safeguards provided through a general decision issued every two years by GPDP.

256. According to paragraph 3 of Article 2-*septies*, before being adopted, the draft general decision shall undergo public consultation, lasting for a period of at least sixty days. Moreover, according to paragraph 2, the GPDP general provision shall take into account:

(a) the guidelines, recommendations and best practices published by the European data protection board and the best practices concerning the processing of personal data;
(b) the scientific and technological developments in the sector addressed by the safeguards;
(c) the interest in the free movement of personal data in the EU.

---

416. Bolognini & Pelino, *Codice Privacy: tutte le novità del D.lgs. 101/2018* 58–61 (Giuffré Francis Lefebvre, 2019), at 28–29.

257. Moreover, pursuant to paragraph 5, the safeguards included in the general decision shall be adopted in respect of each category of personal data by having regard to the specific purposes of the processing and may provide for additional conditions to be fulfilled in order for the processing to be lawful, with particular regard to security measures, enabling selective access to data, and safeguarding data subject rights.

258. As regards the 'safeguards concerning genetic data and the processing of data relating to health for prevention, diagnosis and treatment purposes as well as the safeguards referred to in paragraph 4, letters b) ad c) above', paragraph 6 requires that the safeguards 'shall be adopted after hearing the Ministry of Health, which shall obtain, for that purpose, an opinion from the *Consiglio Superiore di Sanità* ("Higher Council for Healthcare")'.

Concerning genetic data, 'the safeguards may provide for relying on the data subject's consent as an additional measure to protect the data subject's rights in case a particular high risk exists'.

In relation to biometric data, paragraph 7 of Article 2-*septies* includes an exception to the general GDPR prohibition of processing such data. The exception applies where the processing of biometric data takes place in the context of procedures enabling physical or logical access to data by authorized personnel, in the case where biometric access is deemed necessary by the data controller or data processor as part of the security measures pursuant to Article 32 of the GDPR. This provision is, therefore, aimed at allowing data controllers and processors to leverage the use of biometric access controls, where this is appropriate as part of the security measures adopted to protect personal data.

259. Finally, the Italian legislator has strengthened the protection for genetic data, biometric data, and data concerning health by including an express ban on the dissemination of such data within paragraph 8 of Article 2-*septies*. Exceptions to this ban are arguably Article 9, paragraph 2, letter a), (data subject's consent) and e), GDPR (data made manifestly public by the data subjects).

§4. General GPDP Authorizations Concerning the Processing of Special Categories of Personal Data

260. Over the years, the GPDP has issued general authorizations with respect to the processing of special categories of personal data in certain areas, thereby establishing further specific rules for processing special categories of personal data for those areas.[417]

In the context of the 2018 reform, Article 21, paragraph 1, of Legislative Decree 10 August 2018, no. 101, mandated the GPDP to adopt a general decision in order to identify which obligations, among those set forth in the general authorizations

417. The general authorizations currently in force may be found at the following URL within the GPDP official website: https://www.garanteprivacy.it/home/provvedimenti-normativa/provvedimenti/autorizzazioni.

already adopted by the GPDP, were to be deemed compatible with the GDPR and, therefore, still in force within the Italian legal system.

261. A number of already existing authorizations were eventually confirmed – and, in some cases, amended or supplemented – by the GPDP with its Decision no. 146 of 5 June 2019.[418] The most relevant elements contained in the authorizations adopted by the GPDP are indicated below.[419]

262. It is relevant that in relation to the processing of health-related data in the healthcare sector, the GPDP has provided public clarifications regarding the application of the existing regulatory framework in this area.[420] In this respect, it is important to note that the GPDP specifies that processing for 'purposes of care', on the basis of Article 9(2)(h) and (3) of the GDPR, are properly those carried out by (or under the responsibility of) healthcare professionals, bound to professional confidentiality, or by other individuals also bound to confidentiality obligations.

Unlike the previous legal framework, healthcare professionals no longer have to acquire the patient's consent for processing necessary to provide healthcare services requested by patients, regardless of whether healthcare professionals operate as freelance professionals (in a medical practice) or within a public or private health care facility.[421]

263. The GPDP also specifies, with reference to the healthcare sector, that processing related to the use of medical apps for promotional or commercial purposes to legal entities or for commercial or electoral purposes by healthcare professionals and those carried out through the Electronic Health Record always requires the explicit consent of the data subject.

I. General Authorization No. 3/2016 on the Processing of Sensitive Data by Associations and Foundations

264. The GPDP has expanded the scope of General Authorization no. 3/2016 regarding the processing of special categories of personal data by associations,

418. GPDP, *Provvedimento recante le prescrizioni relative al trattamento di categorie particolari di dati, ai sensi dell'art. 21, comma 1 del d.lgs. 10 agosto 2018*, n. 101, 5.6.2019, doc. web no. 9124510, https://www.garanteprivacy.it/home/docweb/-/docweb-display/docweb/9124510.

419. Authorization no. 1/2016 on the processing of sensitive personal data in the context of the employment relationship and Authorization no. 1/2016 on the processing of personal data in the context of scientific research shall be examined, respectively, *infra* in Part IX, Ch. 4 and 5.

420. GPDP, *Chiarimenti sull'applicazione della disciplina per il trattamento dei dati relativi alla salute in ambito sanitario, 7 marzo 2019*, doc. web no. 9091942, https://www.garanteprivacy.it/home/docweb/-/docweb-display/docweb/9091942.

421. Author's translation.

foundations, churches and religious associations or communities, extending it to all third-sector operators in Italy.[422]

265. According to the provisions of the aforementioned Authorization, special categories of personal data may be processed specifically for cultural, religious, political, trade union, sporting or competitive purposes, as well as for purposes of education, scientific research, advocacy, environmental protection, etc. These purposes need, however, to be identified by provision of law, the internal memorandum of association, the articles of association or the national collective agreement, as applicable.

The same processing activities may also be carried out to exercise the right of access to data and administrative documents within the limits established by the relevant laws.[423]

266. Of relevance is also Article 2, paragraph 4, which states that personal data referring to associates or members may be communicated to other associates, even in the absence of the consent of the persons concerned, provided that said communication is provided for by the internal memorandum of association or by provision of law and that the modalities of use of the data are made known to the data subjects when issuing the information notice pursuant to Article 13 of GDPR.

II. General Authorization No. 6/2016 on the Processing of Sensitive Data by Private Investigators

267. General Authorization no. 6/2016 applies to entities that exercise private investigation activities by having obtained the necessary prefecture license pursuant to Article 134 del Royal Decree (R.D.) 18 June 1931, no. 773, as subsequently amended.[424]

268. Concerning the purposes of the processing, special categories of personal data can be processed by private investigators, alternatively:

(i) in order to allow the entity who confer the task to the investigator to have their right ascertained, exercised or defended in the context of judicial proceedings which, in case of processing of genetic data relating to the health,

422. GPDP, *Allegato 1, 2. Prescrizioni relative al trattamento di categorie particolari di dati da parte degli organismi di tipo associativo, delle fondazioni, delle chiese e associazioni o comunità religiose (aut. gen. n. 3/2016), in Provvedimento recante le prescrizioni relative al trattamento di categorie particolari di dati, ai sensi dell'art. 21, comma 1 del d.lgs. 10 agosto 2018*, n. 101, 5.6.2019, doc. web no. 9124510, *https://www.garanteprivacy.it/home/docweb/-/docweb-display/docweb/9124510. See also infra* Part X, Ch. 1.

423. *See infra* Part IX, Ch. 2.

424. GPDP, *Allegato 1, 3. Prescrizioni relative al trattamento di categorie particolari di dati da parte degli investigatori privati (aut. gen. n. 6/2016), in Provvedimento recante le prescrizioni relative al trattamento di categorie particolari di dati, ai sensi dell'art. 21, comma 1 del d.lgs. 10 agosto 2018*, n. 101, 5.6.2019, doc. web no. 9124510, https://www.garanteprivacy.it/home/docweb/-/docweb-display/docweb/9124510.

sexual life or sexual orientation, must be of equal rank to that of the subject to whom the data refer, or consist of a right of the personality or another fundamental right or freedom;

(ii) on behalf of a lawyer in the context of a criminal proceeding, to search and identify elements in favour of their client, to be used solely for the purpose of exercising their rights in court.

269. The following are the specific obligations addressed to private investigators, found in Article 3, paragraph 3, of the Authorization:

(a) private investigators cannot undertake investigations, searches or other forms of data collection on their own initiative but only on the basis of a specific assignment given in writing, including by a defending lawyer;
(b) the private investigator must personally carry out the assignment received and may not make use of other investigators not named in the assignment;
(c) the assignment shall specifically mention the right to be exercised in court or the criminal proceedings to which the investigation is connected, as well as the main elements of fact that justify the investigation and the reasonable term within which the assignment shall be concluded;
(d) once the specific investigative activity has been concluded, the processing must end in any form whatsoever, except for the prompt communication to the defending lawyer or to the entity who conferred the assignment, who may allow, also during the assignment, the temporary storage of strictly personal material of the persons who carried out the activity, for the sole purpose of demonstrating the lawfulness and correctness of their work;
(e) genetic, biometric and health data can be communicated to the competent authorities only for purposes of prevention, investigation or repression of crimes.

III. General Authorization No. 8/2016, on the Processing of Genetic Data

270. Authorization no. 8/2016 aims to implement Article 9, paragraph 4, GDPR, by establishing specific obligations for the processing of genetic data.[425]

Concerning its scope of application, it should be noted that the GPDP considers the authorization to be applicable also to biological samples, genetic tests, and pharmacogenetic and pharmacogenomic tests.

271. The most relevant provisions concerning the custody and security of genetic data and biological samples, found in Article 4, paragraph 2, of the General Authorization, are the following:

425. GPDP, *Allegato 1, Prescrizioni relative al trattamento dei dati genetici (aut. gen. no. 8/2016), in Provvedimento recante le prescrizioni relative al trattamento di categorie particolari di dati, ai sensi dell'art. 21, comma 1 del d.lgs. 10 agosto 2018*, n. 101, 5.6.2019, doc. web no. 9124510, https://www.garanteprivacy.it/home/docweb/-/docweb-display/docweb/9124510.

(a) access to the premises shall be controlled, *inter alia,* by electronic means with specific identification procedures, including biometric devices. Persons admitted, in whatever capacity, after closing time, are to be identified and their personally identifiable information registered;
(b) the storage, use and transport of biological samples shall be carried out in a way that guarantees their quality, integrity, availability and traceability;
(c) the transfer of genetic data by means of electronic messaging systems, including e-mail, shall be carried out with the following precautions: transmission of the data shall take place in the form of an attachment and not as text included in the body of the message; the data shall be encrypted, taking care to make the cryptographic key known to the recipient by means of communication channels other than the one used for data transmission; use of protected communication channels; protection of the attachment by means of suitable methods for preventing the unlawful or accidental acquisition of the transmitted data, such as a password for opening the file made known to the recipient by means of communication channels other than those used for data transmission. The use of web application-type communication channels is also permitted, where they provide for the use of protected transmission channels, taking into account the state of the art of technology, and where they guarantee, after verification, the digital identity of the server providing the service and of the client station from which the data is accessed, using digital certificates issued in accordance with applicable law, by a certification authority;
(d) genetic data and biological samples contained in lists, registers or databases are processed using encryption or pseudonymisation techniques in order to render them temporarily unintelligible even to those authorized to access them and to make it possible to identify the persons concerned only where necessary.

272. Of relevance is also paragraph 5 of Article 4, which mandates the acquisition of data subject's in the following circumstances:

(a) where the purpose of the processing is the protection of the health of a third party, which shall moreover be of the same genetic lineage as the data subject whose consent is sought;[426]
(b) the performance of genetic tests as part of defensive investigations or for the exercise, establishment or defence of a right in the context of judicial proceedings, unless otherwise provided by law;
(c) to perform genetic tests for purposes of family reunification. In this case, the data subjects are required to declare whether or not they want to know the results of test, including any unexpected news concerning them, if such news amounts to a concrete and direct benefit for the data subject in terms of therapy, prevention, or awareness of reproductive choices;
(d) scientific and statistical research purposes not provided for by law.

426. *See* Art. 4, para. 7, discussed *infra*.

273. Article 4, paragraph 5.1, specifically regulates the case in which the opinions of the child whose genetic data are processed may be taken into account. In particular, it is provided that the child's opinion, to the extent that their age and degree of maturity so permit, is, where possible, taken into account, the best interests of the child being paramount in all cases. In other cases of legal incapacity, processing is allowed if the purposes pursued are of direct benefit to the data subject and his or her opinion is, where possible, taken into account, provided that the interest of the legally incompetent person prevails in all cases.

The same provision states that concerning genetic data relating to an unborn child, consent may be validly provided by the mother. In the event that the processing carried out through prenatal tests may also reveal genetic data relating to the future onset of pathology of the father, prior consent of the latter is also necessary.

274. Of relevance is also the regulation on the processing of genetic data of a third party. According to Article 4, paragraph 7, of the General Authorization, the processing of genetic data for the purpose of protecting the health of a third party may be carried out if the third party belongs to the same genetic lineage as the data subject and with the data subject's consent. If the data subject's consent is not provided or cannot be provided, the processing may be carried out only with regard to available genetic data if it is indispensable to enable the third party to make an informed reproductive choice or is justified by the need for preventive or therapeutic measures for the third party.

275. Without prejudice to Article 4, paragraph 5, discussed *supra,* the Authorization provides for specific provisions on consent within Article 4, paragraph 11.2. In particular, genetic data and biological samples of persons who are unable to give their consent due to legal incompetence may be processed for purposes of scientific research that do not directly benefit the persons concerned, only if the following conditions are cumulatively met:

(a) the research is aimed at improving the health of another person belonging to the same age group, suffering from the same pathology, or in the same condition as the data subject, and the research programme is subject to a reasoned, positive opinion of the competent ethics committee;
(b) research with the same purpose may not be carried out by processing data relating to persons who can give their consent;
(c) consent to the processing is obtained from the person legally exercising parental authority, or from a close relative, a family member, a cohabiting partner or, in their absence, from the person responsible for the facility where the data subject is staying;
(d) the research does not entail significant risks to the dignity, rights and fundamental freedoms of the data subject.

276. The foregoing is without prejudice to the need to take into account, where possible, the opinion of the minor or the legally incompetent person.

Chapter 4. Personal Data Relating to Criminal Convictions and Offences

277. This section examines the instances where Italian data protection law allows for the processing of personal data related to criminal convictions and offences pursuant to Article 10 GDPR.

The Italian legal landscape, and specifically Italian data protection law, strictly limits the possibilities of processing data related to criminal convictions and offences.

§1. Processing of Data Related to Criminal Convictions and Offences in the Work Context

278. Before the direct applicability of the GDPR, employers in Italy could request certificates of criminal records (*certificato del casellario giudiziale*[427]) and certificates of pending charges (*certificato dei carichi pendenti*[428]) from applicants or employees according to General Authorization no. 7/2016[429] of the GPDP. In particular, in light of this authorization, employers could request the data subject provide their certificate of pending charges and criminal records before commencing their work for the purposes of running background checks on them.

279. After the direct applicability of the GDPR, and in light of the stricter regime outlined within Article 10, the GPDP issued a decision[430] pursuant to Article 21(1) of the Personal Data Protection Code, outlining which General Authorizations published before the GDPR are still to be considered valid. One of the authorizations that were declared to no longer be in force is Authorization no. 7/2016

427. The certificate of criminal records contains indications on provisions related to criminal, civil, and administrative decisions concerning the person and can be obtained by the data subject by submitting a request to the Public Prosecutor's Office (*Procura della Repubblica Presso il Tribunale*) of the Court that has jurisdiction over the place of residence of the data subject. More information is available at the following link (in Italian): https://www.giustizia.it/giustizia/page/it/certificato_casellario_giudiziale.

428. The certificate outlines any pending criminal proceedings against a person, and can be obtained by the data subject by submitting a request to the Public Prosecutor's Office (*Procura della Repubblica Presso il Tribunale*) of the Court that has jurisdiction over the place of residence of the data subject. The certificate reports the proceedings pending at that office as well as those in progress at the anti-mafia district prosecutors' offices (DDA). More information is available at the following link (in Italian): https://www.giustizia.it/giustizia/it/mg_3_3_3.wp.

429. *See* the GPDP's Authorization o. 7 of 2016 – GPDP, *Autorizzazione al trattamento dei dati giudiziari da parte di privati, di enti pubblici economici e di soggetti pubblici*, 15.12.2016, doc. web. no. 5803630, https://www.garanteprivacy.it/web/guest/home/docweb/-/docweb-display/docweb/5803630.

430. *See* GPDP, *Provvedimento recante le prescrizioni relative al trattamento di categorie particolari di dati, ai sensi dell'art. 21, comma 1 del d.lgs. 10 agosto 2018, n. 101*, 05.12.2016, doc. web. no. 9124510, https://www.garanteprivacy.it/web/guest/home/docweb/-/docweb-display/docweb/9124510.

mentioned above, given that Article 10 of the GDPR allows the processing of data related to criminal convictions and offences only where this is allowed by a specific national law authorizing it.

In line with Article 10 GDPR, Article 2-*g* of the Personal Data Protection Code holds that the processing of data related to criminal convictions and offences that 'is not carried out under the control of official authority shall be allowed solely if it is authorized by a law or, where so provided for by law, by a regulation providing for appropriate safeguards for the rights and freedoms of data subjects, in accordance with Article 10'.[431] In sum, in order for the processing of data related to criminal convictions and offences to be considered lawful under Italian data protection law, it is necessary that either a primary or a secondary source of Italian law permits such processing.[432]

280. In Italy, at present, the processing of data related to criminal convictions and offences in the private employment context is allowed only pursuant to Article 25-a of Presidential Decree no. 313 of 14 November 2002, which allows for the processing of such data for running background checks on employees whose professions entail contact with minors (e.g., school teachers), but only to verify that the data subject has not been convicted for crimes related to minors (e.g., crimes related to child pornography, the sexual abuse of children, etc.).

In the specific area of recruitment, the above-mentioned provision is also taken into account in the recently approved Code of Conduct for Employment Agencies[433] drafted pursuant to Article 40 of the GDPR, which prohibits the collection of an employment candidate's personal data related to criminal convictions and offences, except when the candidate is applying for a job position that involves contact with minors.

281. In addition, for public employees, according to Legislative Decree no. 165 of 30 March 2001, which provides for 'General provisions concerning employment at public entities', integrity checks by means of the provision of the certificate of pending charges and criminal records are allowed.

282. According to Article 2-g(2) of the Personal Data Protection Code, in the absence of a law or regulation, it is up to the Minister of Justice to regulate instances where the processing of data related to criminal convictions and offences is allowed in the private sphere, pursuant to Article 10 GDPR.

---

431. *See* Art. 2-g of the Italian Personal Data Protection Code.
432. *See supra* n. 408 above.
433. *See* GPDP, *Provvedimento dell'11 gennaio 2024 – Codice di condotta per il settore delle APL*, 11.01.2024, doc. web. no. 9983415, https://www.garanteprivacy.it/documents/10160/0/Assolavoro+-+Codice+di+condotta+per+il+settore+delle+APL.pdf/7e5a388b-b21f-261a-2e77-47aaf4182b45?version=1.0.

The Ministry prepared a draft Decree, of which the GPDP issued a favourable opinion,[434] pointing out the necessary amendments and additions. To date, the aforementioned D.M. has not been concretely implemented, as it has not yet been enacted.

283. In light of this regulatory deficiency, pursuant to Article 22, paragraph 12, of D.Lgs. 101/2018:[435]

> Until the date of entry into force of the decree of the Minister of Justice referred to in Article 2-g(2)(6), of the Code on the Protection of Personal Data, referred to in Legislative Decree no. 196 of 2003, to be adopted within eighteen months from the date of entry into force of this decree, the processing of data referred to Article 10 of Regulation (EU) 2016/679 is allowed when it is carried out in implementation of protocols of understanding for the prevention and combating of organized crime, entered into with the Ministry of the Interior or Prefectures – UTG, subject to the opinion of the Data Protection Authority, which specifies the type of data processed and the operations that can be performed.

284. The GPDP's opinion on the 'Processing of judicial data carried out by private parties in the implementation of protocols entered into for the prevention and combating of organized crime phenomena'[436] established that, until the Government enacts the aforementioned Decree, the protocols are in the meantime to be considered compatible with the provisions of Article 10 of the GDPR, insofar as they comply with the principles of the GDPR. In particular, in cases where certificate of pending charges and criminal records must be requested pursuant to the so-called Anti-Mafia Code (Legislative Decree no. 218 of 15 November 2012), such protocols must provide for compliance with the principle of minimization, the prohibition of dissemination of such information, the requirement to inform the data subjects of the processing activities performed according to Articles 13 and 14 of the GDPR, the requirement to publish such protocols, to keep the information collected only for the time strictly necessary for the execution of the requirements of the Anti-Mafia Code, and compliance with the principle of segregation of access.

---

434. *See* GPDP, *Parere su uno schema di regolamento recante l'individuazione dei trattamenti di dati personali relativi a condanne penali e reati e delle relative garanzie appropriate ai sensi dell'articolo 2-octies, comma 2, del Codice – 24 giugno 2021*, 24.06.2021, doc. web. no. 9682603, https://www.garanteprivacy.it/home/docweb/-/docweb-display/docweb/9682603.

435. Author's translation.

436. *Ibid. See* GPDP, *Parere relativo al trattamento di dati giudiziari effettuato da privati in attuazione dei protocolli d'intesa stipulati per la prevenzione e il contrasto dei fenomeni di criminalità organizzata*, 22.07.2021, doc. web. no. 9693175, https://www.garanteprivacy.it/home/docweb/-/docweb-display/docweb/9693175.

§2. Processing of Data Related to Criminal Convictions and Offences in the Context of Public Tenders

285. Another case in which the certificate of pending charges and criminal records may be required concerns public tenders, as provided for in Articles 94 et seq. of Legislative Decree no. 36 of 31 March 2023. According to these provisions, in order for a company to participate in a tender, it must prove that it meets certain requirements and, in particular, that it does not meet the exclusion criteria which, in most cases, are related to convictions in relation to the criminal felonies outlined in such provisions.

§3. Processing of Data Related to Criminal Convictions and Offences in the Context of Anti-money Laundering Provisions

286. Another instance in which the processing of criminal data is allowed is under Legislative Decree no. 231 of 21 November 2007, which establishes anti-money laundering provisions (*see also* Article 2-g(m) of the Personal Data Protection Code). Specifically, for companies that operate in the financial sector, banks, accountants and, in specific cases, lawyers may process criminal information if the latter is publicly available. Otherwise, access to business information, according to the Code of Conduct on business information,[437] does not include the processing of criminal records.

§4. Processing of Data Related to Criminal Convictions and Offences by Lawyers

287. Before the GDPR became directly applicable, the now invalidated Authorization no. 7/2016 was also valid for criminal data processing activities performed by lawyers. Now that the Authorization is no longer in force, lawyers can process personal data under a specific law that authorizes them to do so.

288. In particular, Article 2-g(e) of the Personal Data Protection Code provides that the processing of criminal records is possible in the case of 'Establishing, exercising or defending a legal claim.'

Based on that provision, where the client asks for the assistance of a lawyer – which in a criminal proceeding is mandatory, since self-representation is not possible – the legal basis authorizing the criminal data processing activity may be found in Article 10 of the GDPR, read together with Article 2-g(e) of the Personal Data Protection Code, as well as Articles 96 and 97 of the Italian Criminal Procedure Code.

437. *See* GPDP, *Deliberazione del 12 giugno 2019 – Codice di condotta per il trattamento dei dati personali in materia di informazioni commerciali*, 12.06.2019, doc. web no. 9119868, https://www.garanteprivacy.it/home/docweb/-/docweb-display/docweb/9119868.

§5. PROCESSING OF DATA RELATED TO CRIMINAL CONVICTIONS AND OFFENCES BY INVESTIGATIONS AGENCIES

289. With regard to investigation agencies, the GPDP has published the 'Rules of ethics regarding the processing of personal data carried out to perform defensive investigations or to assert or defend a right in court.'[438]

The data processing activities related to criminal convictions and offences are admitted by Article 2-g(g) of the Personal Data Protection Code, which provides that such processing is lawful when 'carrying out investigations or searches or collecting information on behalf of third parties under the terms of Section 134 of the consolidated statute on public security'.[439]

---

438. Author's translation. *See* GPDP, *Regole deontologiche relative ai trattamenti di dati personali effettuati per svolgere investigazioni difensive o per fare valere o difendere un diritto in sede giudiziaria pubblicate ai sensi dell'art. 20, comma 4, del d.lgs. 10 agosto 2018, n. 101 – 19 dicembre 2018*, 19.12.2018, doc. web no. 9069653, https://www.garanteprivacy.it/home/docweb/-/docweb-display/docweb/9069653.

439. Author's translation.

Part IV. Data Subject Rights

Chapter 1. Right to Be Informed

290. With regard to the exercise of privacy rights, there are no significant discrepancies between the Italian data protection framework and the GDPR. However, thanks to the legislative intervention of the Italian legislator and the GPDP, it is possible to rely on some useful operational clarifications that could facilitate the practical application of the provisions established by the European Union Legislator.

291. This is the case of the right to be informed, in respect of which the Personal Data Protection Code provides for the following exceptions related to special processing situations:

(i) Articles 77 to 80 and 82 of the Personal Data Protection Code, related to specific arrangements to inform the data subject and process personal data concerning the healthcare sector.
(ii) Article 110-*bis* of the Personal Data Protection, regarding further processing of personal data by third parties for scientific research or statistical purposes.
(iii) Article 111-*bis* of the Personal Data Protection Code, on information regarding received *curriculum vitae*.

§1. Right to Be Informed in the Healthcare Sector

292. Articles 77 to 82 of the Personal Data Protection Code provide for specific arrangements in order to inform data subjects pursuant to Articles 13 and 14 GDPR and to process personal data for the following categories:

(i) healthcare professionals, such as general practitioners and paediatricians;
(ii) public and private organizations providing healthcare and welfare services;
(iii) competent services or departments of public bodies that deal with healthcare or social protection and welfare;
(iv) cases of emergency situations and protection of health and bodily integrity.

293. With regard to general practitioners and paediatricians, Article 78 of the Personal Data Protection Code provides that:

> The information may be provided as regards the overall personal data processing operations that are required for diagnosis, assistance and treatment activities … to safeguard the data subject's health or bodily integrity, such activities being performed at the data subject's request or else being known to the data subject in that they are carried out in his/her interest.

294. Moreover, information shall be given with regard to data collected from third parties and, preferably, in writing. The information shall also analytically highlight the data processing operations that may entail specific risks for the data subject's rights and fundamental freedoms and dignity (e.g., for scientific research purposes including clinical drug testing, within the framework of tele-aid or telemedicine services, to supply other goods or services to the data subject via electronic communication networks).

295. Article 79 of the Personal Data Protection Code provides that public and private organizations providing healthcare and welfare services may adopt the same specific arrangements provided by Article 78 of the Personal Data Protection Code with regard to different services also provided by different divisions and units within the organizations or in specified hospitals or local branches of such organizations. In the health sector, it may be considered that the status of data controller should not automatically follow the legal subjectivity of the entity but rather the individual structures managed by the same company.[440]

296. Pursuant to Article 82 of the Personal Data Protection Code, in cases of medical emergency and/or related to public hygiene, the information may be given after the relevant service has been provided, without delay, whenever the competent authority has issued a contingent emergency order.

The same modalities may be used in case the data subject is physically impaired, legally incapable or unable to distinguish right and wrong (and the information cannot be provided, where so required, to a designated person) and when a serious, impending and irreparable risk to the data subject's health or bodily integrity exists. This provision is particularly relevant as Law Decree 9 March 2020, no. 14, on 'Urgent provisions for the strengthening of the National Health Service in relation to the COVID-19 emergency'[441] and its amendments allowed for simplified rules for the protection of personal data which processing is based on Article 9, paragraph 2, letter I, GDPR.

These rules, however, were temporary and have been applied for the duration of the state of emergency in Italy (until 31 March 2022). Moreover, Article 14 provides that, pursuant to Article 23, paragraph 1, letter e, GDPR, and without prejudice to the provisions of Article 82 Personal Data Protection Code, the entities referred to in paragraph 1 of said Article 14 may omit the information referred to in

---

440. Bolognini & Pelino, *Codice Privacy: tutte le novità del D.lgs. 101/2018* 58–61 (Giuffré Francis Lefebvre, 2019). The analysis of privacy roles, in fact, should be performed on a factual, rather than a formal analysis of the actual influence on the purposes and means of processing.
441. Author's translation.

Article 13 GDPR or provide simplified information, subject to oral communication to the data subjects of the relevant limitation.

297. In this regard, the GPDP published a dedicated decision titled 'Clarifications on the application of the provisions for the health data processing in the health sector'[442] dated 7 March 2019. The GPDP clarified that the data subject should receive the information pursuant to Articles 13 and 14 GDPR in a concise, transparent, intelligible and easily accessible form, using clear and plain language as well as in a sequential manner, as in the healthcare services sector a plurality of data controllers carry out many complex data processing operations.

298. This means that a public or private healthcare facility could provide (e.g., at the time of admission) only information relating to processing activities that fall within the ordinary activity of providing healthcare services and information relating to particular treatments and related activities (e.g., the provision of medical devices, online delivery of medical reports, scientific research purposes, electronic health records, the use of medical applications for purposes other than telemedicine, etc.) at a later stage on the basis of specific supplementary information and only to patients actually interested in such services and in receiving further treatments. This allows data subjects to pay more attention to the most significant information concerning the processing of their data, thus raising their awareness.[443]

§2. Right to Be Informed in the Context of Further Processing for Scientific Research or Statistical Purposes

299. Article 110-*bis* sets out restrictions on the GDPR provisions in case of further processing of personal data for scientific research purposes by third parties (so-called secondary use). Pursuant to Article 110-*bis*, the GPDP may authorize further processing of personal data processed by third parties for scientific research purposes or statistical purposes. The third parties that mainly carry out the scientific/statistical research activities (data controllers different from the one that collected the data on the basis of the first processing)[444] should be able to process such personal data without the obligation to provide a specific privacy notice in case providing the notice would prove impossible, or would involve a disproportionate effort, or would make it impossible, or seriously jeopardize the attainment of the research objectives. The above is without prejudice to the adoption of appropriate measures to protect the rights, freedoms and legitimate interests of the data subject, including preventive forms of data minimization and anonymization. In order to perform such processing, the third party may also request a specific authorization

442. Author's translation, as no official translation of the GPDP decision is available.
443. GPDP, *Chiarimenti sull'applicazione della disciplina per il trattamento dei dati relativi alla salute in ambito sanitario*. 7.3.2019, doc. web no. 9091942, https://www.garanteprivacy.it/web/guest/home/docweb/-/docweb-display/docweb/9091942.
444. Bolognini & Pelino, *Codice della disciplina privacy* (Giuffrè Francis Lefebvre, 2019), at 157.

from the GPDP, whose deadline for replying is set at forty-five days according to the so-called silence-rejection mechanism.[445]

§3. Right to Be Informed: Information Regarding Received CVs

300. Article 111 of the Personal Data Protection Code provides that if a candidate sends an unsolicited CV for the purpose of possible recruitment, the information shall be provided by the data controller at the moment of the first contact with the candidate. The same provision is confirmed in the GPDP's 'Decision on the requirements for the processing of special categories of data, pursuant to Article 21(1) of Legislative Decree no. 101 of 10 August 2018.'[446]

---

445. In other words, the authorization is assumed to be rejected if the relevant timeline elapses without any response from the GPDP.

446. GPDP, *Provvedimento recante le prescrizioni relative al trattamento di categorie particolari di dati, ai sensi dell'art. 21, comma 1 del d.lgs. 10 agosto 2018*, n. 101, 5.6.2019, doc. web no. 9124510, https://www.garanteprivacy.it/web/guest/home/docweb/-/docweb-display/docweb/9124510.

Chapter 2. Right of Access

§1. Educational Material from the GPDP on the Right of Access

301. While the right of access to personal data within the Italian legal framework is generally regulated by Article 15 GDPR, the GPDP dedicated a webpage[447] on its official website to informational material that explains the right of access in the Italian context. The GPDP, by means of various information sheets, aims at explaining in simple language the topic of the right of access, from a more general perspective (sheet on the right of access) to more detailed specific cases, such as the right of access to administrative documents, simple or general civic access, and the right of access concerning deceased persons.[448]

302. With its information sheet on the right of 5access,[449] the GPDP aims to provide data subjects with a brief and clear guide that describes the key points of the right of access as regulated by the GDPR, also enriching the EU legal framework with some additional provisions set out in Italian law. In particular, the GPDP highlights the following aspects of interest:

(i) the right of access may be exercised not only by the data subject but also by their representative. Under Italian law, a representative is generally considered to be a natural or legal person to whom power of attorney is conferred by the right holder or by the law.[450] Without dwelling on the regulation of the power of attorney within Italian law, it should be noted that this power does not have any effect unless it is conferred in the form required by law for the legal act to be performed;[451]

(ii) the request for access may be addressed to the data controller (i.e., a company, the Public Administration, a freelance professional, etc.), also by addressing the request directly to the data protection officer, where appointed;

(iii) the data subject's request does not necessarily require a motivation;

(iv) the data subject generally does not have to cover the costs of making a request for access. However, if the data subject's requests are manifestly unfounded, excessive or repetitive, the data controller may charge a reasonable fee, taking into account the costs incurred in providing the information; and

(v) the right of access may be subject to certain exceptions as well as specific limitations where its exercise may affect the rights and freedoms of other persons. In addition to the provisions of the GDPR, some limitations to the right of access are provided for in Articles 2-*undecies* and 2-*duodecies* of the Personal Data Protection Code.[452] The right of access may be restricted, for

447. https://www.garanteprivacy.it/home/i-miei-diritti/diritti/diritto-di-accesso.
448. *See infra*, §2 in this Ch. 2, on the right of access concerning deceased persons.
449. https://www.garanteprivacy.it/garante/document?ID=9506347.
450. *See* Arts 1387 et seq. of the Italian Civil Code.
451. As required, in particular, by Art. 1392 of the Italian Civil Code.
452. *See*, concerning the restrictions to data subjects' rights, *infra*, Part IV, Ch. 8.

instance, where it could cause actual and concrete prejudice to the conduct of defensive investigations or the protection of a right in a court proceeding.

In addition to this, the GPDP recently published a set of frequently asked questions on schools and privacy titled *'Scuola e privacy: Domande più frequenti'*, of which some questions pertain to the right of access.[453] The GPDP, in this information, specifies that:

(i) the right of access to the personal data of students can be exercised by directly contacting school that acts as the data controller;
(ii) it is possible to access administrative documents held by the school, but this should be done pursuant to Law 27 August 1990, no. 241 (Articles 22 and following), and not pursuant to Article 15 GDPR.

§2. Access to Data Concerning Deceased Persons

303. Special regulation of the right of access is foreseen in Article 2-*quaterdecies* of the Personal Data Protection Code[454] in the event that the requested data concerns deceased persons.[455] Even though this provision applies to all data subject rights provided by Articles 15–22 GDPR, the right of access is arguably the most important instance where Article 2-*quaterdecies* may find application.

304. The GPDP, through an information sheet published on its website,[456] summarizes the special rules governing the right of access to information of deceased persons in simple language, highlighting the following:

453. GPDP, *Scuola e privacy. Domande più frequenti*, https://www.garanteprivacy.it/home/faq/scuola-e-privacy.
454. Article 2-*quaterdecies* of the Personal Data Protection Code states: '1. The rights referred to in Articles 15 to 22 of the Regulation concerning the personal data of deceased persons may be exercised by any entity having a vested interest or acting to protect the data subject as the latter's agent, or else on household-related grounds deserving protection. 2. Exercise of the rights referred to in paragraph 1 shall not be allowed where so provided for in a law or if the data subject has banned such exercise expressly by means of a written statement submitted or communicated to the controller with regard to the direct offer of information society services. 3. The data subject's intention to ban exercise of the rights referred to in paragraph 1 must be unambiguous, specific, free and informed. The ban may apply to the exercise of some of the rights referred to in the said paragraph. 4. The data subject has the right to at any time revoke or amend the ban referred to in paragraphs 2 and 3. 5. The ban shall in no case result into detrimental effects to the exercise by third parties of property rights arising from the data subject's decease or of the right to defend a legal claim'.
455. In this respect, it should be noted that the GDPR does not apply to data relating to deceased persons, as recognized by Recital 27. However, Member States remain free to enact national rules concerning the processing of data concerning deceased persons.
456. https://www.garanteprivacy.it/garante/document?ID=9530351.

(i) the right of access concerning the personal data of deceased persons may be exercised by any entity having a vested interest or acting to protect the data subject as the latter's agent, or else on household-related grounds deserving protection; and
(ii) the exercise of the right of access may not be allowed where so provided for in law or if the data subject has banned such exercise expressly by means of a written statement submitted or communicated to the controller, where the processing concerns the direct offer of information society services. Nevertheless, it is specifically stated that the ban shall in no case result in detrimental effects to the exercise by third parties of property rights arising from the data subject's death or of the right to defend a legal claim.

305. For all matters not expressly provided for in Article 2-*quaterdecies* of the Personal Data Protection Code, the general rules provided by the GDPR apply with reference to, for example, the information that can be requested, to whom the request should be made, the timeframe within which the controller must acknowledge the Trequest and the possibility of lodging a complaint in the event of failure to acknowledge the request.

§3. Access to Banking Data

306. It is interesting to highlight the differences under the Italian legal framework between the right of access under Article 15 of the GDPR and the right of access to banking documents, which is governed by a special regulation contained in Article 119 of Legislative Decree no. 385/1993, as subsequently amended, i.e., the text of the Consolidated Banking Law ('*Testo Unico Bancario*' hereinafter 'TUB'). Since the scope of the aforementioned provision partially overlaps with the right of access to personal data under the GDPR, this paragraph aims to outline the characteristics of the two rights and how they should be coordinated in case of exercise of data subjects' rights towards data controllers in the banking sector.

307. Article 119 of the TUB, titled 'Periodic Communications to Customers', in its paragraphs 1, 2 and 3, requires banks to provide detailed information concerning the conduct of the banking relationship.

Paragraph 4, in turn, states that the client, or the person who succeeds the client in any capacity, and the person who takes over the administration of the client's property, has the right to obtain, at their own expense, within a reasonable period of time and in any case not later than ninety days, copies of the documentation pertaining to individual transactions carried out in the last ten years. The provision further goes on to specify that the client may be charged only for the cost of producing such documentation.

308. Given the above, it is clear that the two rights have different scopes and requirements. Nevertheless, coordination between the right to access bank documents and the right to access personal data has been undertaken by the GPDP itself, which has published relevant FAQs on its website[457] for this purpose, containing clarifications on the following aspects:

(i) the right of access to banking documents entails the right to know all the personal data contained in the documents in the possession of the bank where the person holds a bank account, securities deposit, etc;
(ii) the account holder cannot request account statements from the bank by relying on the right of access to personal data provided by Article 15 of the GDPR. In this case, however, the application must be submitted pursuant to Article 119 of the TUB, which has different scope and requirements;
(iii) the account holder may also obtain a full copy of the documentation in the bank's possession, but again, the request must be submitted on the basis of Article 119 of the TUB, since it cannot be based, due to its different scope, on the right of access provided for by the GDPR;
(iv) in the event of a request for access to personal data on the basis of the GDPR, the bank is instead only obliged to provide a copy of the personal data being processed;
(v) the account holder, as a data subject, may request any personal data concerning them from the bank, such as, for example, information relating to transactions carried out (such as call recordings of trading orders) or personal data that the bank may have collected in order to perform the client's investment orders;
(vi) as to the procedure to follow in submitting a request to the bank for access to personal data, the FAQs recall that it is necessary to forward such a request by expressly specifying that it is formulated pursuant to Article 15 of the GDPR;
(vii) the information may be obtained free of charge. However, in the event of a request for additional copies, the data controller may charge a reasonable fee;
(viii) in the event that the bank refuses to provide the data or does not allow the request for reasons of difficulty in extracting the information, the data subject may lodge a complaint with the GPDP to obtain an injunction ordering the bank to provide the requested data;
(ix) moreover, the bank is obliged to disclose the requested information in a comprehensible manner and is obliged to provide, if necessary, the criteria and parameters for understanding the meaning of any codes associated with the information. Again, if the bank fails to do so, the data subject may insist on requesting further clarification or lodge a complaint with the GPDP.

457. https://www.garanteprivacy.it/faq/accesso-ai-dati-bancari.

§4. Access to Personal Data and Access to Administrative Documents (Referral)

309. The relevant topic of access to personal data and access to administrative documents expressly addresses *infra* in this Volume, within Part IX, Chapter 2.

§5. Relevant Decisions of the GPDP on the Right of Access

310. For the sake of thoroughness, it is worth going through some interesting decisions of the GPDP on the right of access to understand its position and approach in applying the Regulation provided for by Article 15 of the GDPR and the relevant provision set out in Italian law.

311. In a recent decision, the GPDP fined an important telecommunications service provider, TIM S.p.A., for failing to release information that the data subject requested to defend himself in a criminal lawsuit.[458] Going into more detail, the data subject, as a holder of two telephone lines, needed to collect information to be produced in a criminal trial in support of his defence to prove that he had nothing to do with the facts he was being charged with. Having received no response from the company to his repeated requests, he approached the GPDP, requesting that it order TIM to hand over the requested telephone records in time for the criminal trial hearing.

The company defended itself by justifying the failure to ensure the timely exercise of right of access due, first, to formal irregularities in the data subject's request, claiming that the attached ID card was not legible, and second, due to technical and organizational issues within the company.

The GPDP's reply to the company's defence has more points of interest: first, the GPDP stated that the technical problems mentioned by the company in the management of the data subject's requests could not in any case have a negative impact on the right of access and on the effective control and availability of his data, especially if this is necessary to defend the accused in a criminal trial; and second, that the attempts to contact the data subject to supplement his request, moreover almost twenty days after it was sent, cannot be considered an adequate effort to 'facilitate the exercise of data subject's right', as stated by Article 12, paragraph 2, letter f), GDPR.

Considering the above, the GPDP fined the company for infringing the fundamental right of access set out in Article 15 of the GDPR.

312. In another decision dated 13 March 2022,[459] the GPDP condemned the conduct of a data controller that had indeed provided information to the data subject

458. GPDP, *Ordinanza ingiunzione nei confronti di Tim S.p.A. – 11 novembre 2021*, 11.11.2021, doc. web no. 9722894, https://www.garanteprivacy.it/web/guest/home/docweb/-/docweb-display/docweb/9722894.

459. GPDP, *Ordinanza ingiunzione nei confronti di Medicina & Lavoro s.r.l. – 13 gennaio 2022*, 13.1.2022, doc. web no. 9744655, https://www.garanteprivacy.it/web/guest/home/docweb/-/docweb-display/docweb/9744655.

but in a way that did not comply with Article 15. In this case, the data subject submitted the request asking for a copy of their medical records retained by the data controller, but the response was not adequate, since it provided only general indications on how to obtain such data upon payment of the production costs.

A second request sent by the data subject one day later remained unanswered.

The GPDP, therefore, fined the controller as a consequence of its inadequate reply, basing the decision on two main arguments. First, the right of access under Article 15 of the GDPR includes the right for data subjects to have access to the information in their medical records, as also recognized by Recital 63 of the GDPR. Second, the GPDP recalled that the data controller may 'charge a reasonable fee taking into account the administrative costs of providing the information' but only 'where requests from a data subject are manifestly unfounded or excessive' (*see* Article 12, paragraph 3, letter a), GDPR). Now, since this was not an unfounded or excessive request, nor was there any reason to refuse access due to the administrative fees to be covered, the GPDP declared the processing to be unlawful.

313. Finally, in another decision dated 27 January 2022,[460] the GPDP fined the data controller for taking incomplete action on the request of the data subject.

On this occasion, although the data subject requested both access to his personal data and their deletion, the data controller only took action with regard to the second request. This incomplete response given by the data controller, which erased the information but failed to provide access to it under Article 15 GDPR, was declared unlawful by the GDPD, since it made it impossible for the data subject to exercise that right and deprived him of control over his personal data.

314. In June 2022, the GPDP imposed a sanction of EUR 70,000 on Unicredit S.p.A. for failing to provide a complete, intelligible, and easily accessible response to a request submitted by one of its employees for access to data processed as part of the employment relationship.[461]

More specifically, the employee at stake had made a very generic request to access all his personal data pursuant to Article 15 GDPR. The employer replied, confirming that the request was being worked on, and asked the data subject to complete a module that specified the data requested in more detail. However, the employee failed to complete the form. According to the employer, the request made by the data subject was to be considered unfounded, given the generic nature of the request, together with the failure to complete the requested module. The GPDP, however, stated that the completion of modules to specify data subjects' requests can be considered an adequate organizational measure but that the data controller should not condition the management of the data subject's request on the prior submission of a specific form, and that requests submitted in free form shall always be satisfied.

460. GPDP, *Ordinanza ingiunzione nei confronti di T.S.M. s.r.l. – 27 gennaio 2022*, 27.1.2022, doc. web no. 9746068, https://www.garanteprivacy.it/web/guest/home/docweb/-/docweb-display/docweb/9746068.

461. GPDP, *Ordinanza ingiunzione nei confronti di Unicredit S.p.A. – 16 giugno 2022*, 13.5.2023, doc. web no. 9795350, https://www.garanteprivacy.it/web/guest/home/docweb/-/docweb-display/docweb/9795350.

In addition to this, after the proposal of the complaint by the data subject, the employer replied to the data subject request, sending a very large number of documents and generically referring to the information notice provided to the data subjects. This way of replying was deemed inadequate by the GPDP because:

(i) the considerable number of documents shared with the complainant had not been provided in a manner that facilitated access and understanding by the data subject;
(ii) the response did not contain the information on data processing requested by the employee under Article 15 of the GDPR, given that the mere reference to the information notice does not satisfy this requirement, as also confirmed by the EDPB in its Guidelines on data subject rights.[462]

315. In another decision dated 15 September 2022, the GPDP imposed a fine of EUR 40,000 on FCA Italy S.p.A. because an employee had requested access to personal data processed in the context of his employment relationship, and the controller had failed to comply with this request in a timely manner, contrary to the requirements of Articles 12 and 15 GDPR.[463] More specifically, it was only after a complaint had been filed with the GPDP and the related administrative proceedings had been initiated that the employer provided effective feedback to the data subject by sending documentation containing the requested personal data, declaring that it did not process any more data than what it transmitted.

Furthermore, concerning the means to provide the employee with the response to his request, the GPDP considered the reply that the employer claimed to have provided by means of periodical meetings that the employee had with the HR department was inadequate, also considering that such meetings were cancelled due to the COVID emergency. Since the data subject had expressly requested a reply via certified electronic mail, the GPDP clarified that a written reply should have been provided within the deadline set forth in Article 12 GDPR.

In specifying the criteria applied to define the amount of the sanction, the decision clarifies that the GPDP took into consideration:

(i) the fact that FCA had already received another sanction for failure to adequately reply to a data access request;[464] and
(ii) the size of the company, the number of employees and customers employed, and, therefore, the relevance of the processing carried out within the scope of

462. EDPB, *Guidelines 01/2022 on data subject rights – Right of access*, 28.3.2023, https://edpb.europa.eu/our-work-tools/our-documents/guidelines/guidelines-012022-data-subject-rights-right-access_en.

463. GPDP, *Ordinanza ingiunzione nei confronti di FCA Italy S.p.A. – 15 settembre 2022*, 15.1.2022, doc. web no. 9827119, https://www.garanteprivacy.it/web/guest/home/docweb/-/docweb-display/docweb/9827119.

464. GPDP, *Ordinanza ingiunzione nei confronti di FCA Italy s.p.a. – 16 dicembre 2021*, 16.12.2021, doc. web no. 9742908, https://www.garanteprivacy.it/web/guest/home/docweb/-/docweb-display/docweb/9742908.

its business, in consideration of which FCA Italy S.p.A. should have put in place appropriate measures to adequately respond to requests for the exercise of rights.

316. Finally, in another decision dated 1 December 2022, the GPDP fined Amazon Italia Logistica S.r.l. EUR 20,000.[465] A former employee had requested documents from the controller. Specifically, various professional certificates obtained during the employment relationship were requested but were not supplied in due time. During its investigation, the GPDP found that the controller had not sufficiently fulfilled its obligation to comply with the data subject's request for access. More specifically:

(i) the employer gave access to only one of the certificates, claiming that the others were not at its disposal; the GPDP observed that Article 12(4) GDPR had not been respected, given that the provision of the documents occurred only after the data subject had made the complaint, without replying to the request in a timely manner;

(ii) the employer objected that when the employee requested the documents, no reference had been made to any exercise of the data subject's right and that the request had not been sent to the specific address dedicated to data subjects' requests. Instead, it had merely been addressed to the HR department. The GPDP observed that the objections made by the employer were irrelevant and that a violation of Article 15 GDPR had occurred given that, as also specified in the EDPB's Guidelines 01/2022, 'data subjects are not required to specify the legal basis in their request' and 'if the controller has doubts as to which right the data subject wishes to exercise, it is recommended to ask the data subject making the request to explain the subject matter of the request'. In addition to this, concerning the recipient of the request, the GPDP deemed the fact that the request had not been sent to the dedicated address, given that the GDPR does not provide for specific modalities that the data subjects must observe when exercising their rights and the information notice provided for to employees suggested to send data subject requests to the dedicated address or to the HR department.

465. GPDP, *Ordinanza ingiunzione nei confronti di Amazon Italia Logistica s.r.l. – 1 dicembre 2022*, 13.05.2023, doc web. no. 9843805, https://www.gpdp.it/web/guest/home/docweb/-/docweb-display/docweb/9843805.

Chapter 3. Rights of Rectification

317. There are no significant differences or novelties in the Italian data protection legal framework with respect to the regulatory framework introduced at the European level with the GDPR. However, the GPDP has provided useful operational clarifications for the practical application of such provisions, thanks to its relevant decisions concerning the exercise of this right.

§1. The Limits of the Right of Rectification: Objectively Ascertainable Elements

318. With respect to the right of rectification under Article 16 GDPR, in a Decision dated 27 January 2022, the GPDP investigated the balance between the right at stake vis-à-vis freedom of expression. In this specific case, GPDP received a complaint,[466] pursuant to Article 77 GDPR, in which a data subject requested the publisher of a newspaper, among others, to rectify the description of the judicial case in which he had been involved years before, as reported in an article. In this regard, the GPDP clarified that Article 16 GDPR only applies in order to rectify objective elements and not subjective or evaluative ones. In fact, with regard to the request for rectification that the data subject filed to the GPDP (i.e., aimed at obtaining the correction of information deemed to be untrue), the Italian DPA determined that, since it cannot be ascertained objectively, such request should be filed with the publisher on the basis of the provisions of Law 8 February 1947, no. 48 (the so-called Press Law).[467]

§2. Right of Rectification in the Field of Medical, Biomedical and Epidemiological Studies and Research

319. The Personal Data Protection Code also enforces the data subject's right of rectification in two very specific circumstances:

(i) the field of study and research pursuant to Article 100 of the Personal Data Protection Code;
(ii) the field of medical, biomedical and epidemiological research pursuant to Article 110 of the Personal Data Protection Code.

320. Article 100 on 'Data Concerning Studies and Researches' states that data subjects may exercise their data protection rights – except for the rights of access

466. GPDP, *Provvedimento del 27 gennaio 2022*, 27.1.2022, doc. web no. 9747871.
467. *See* Art. 8 of L. 47/1948, which states that the editor shall be obliged to have included in the newspaper or periodical or news agency, free of charge, the declarations or corrections of persons whose images have been published or to whom acts or thoughts or statements have been attributed that they consider to be damaging to their dignity or contrary to the truth, provided that the declarations or corrections do not contain any content liable to criminal prosecution.

and portability – in relation to the communication or disclosure of their personal data processed for studies and research purposes. These rights must be exercised in the manner set out in Article 100, paragraph 4-bis, of the Personal Data Protection Code, i.e., in accordance with the arrangements set out in the relative applicable codes of conduct. However, at the time of writing, no codes of conduct have been adopted in this area.[468]

321. Article 110, paragraph 2, of the Personal Data Protection Code, in line with the provisions of Article 89, paragraph 2, GDPR, provides for certain exceptions to the right of rectification in the case of processing operations in the field of medical, biomedical and epidemiological research.[469]

In fact, where a data subject exercises his/her right to rectification pursuant to Article 16 GDPR regarding processing operations in the context of medical, biomedical and epidemiological research, any rectification or completion of such data shall be recorded without modifying the data, but only insofar the rectified or completed data do not produce significant effects on the outcome of the research.

468. Roberto D'Orazio et al., *Codice della privacy e data protection* (Giuffrè ed. 2021), at 1313–1316.
469. *Ibid.*, at 1369–1376.

Chapter 4. Right to Erasure

§1. The Right to Erasure in the Italian Legal System

322. The right to erasure has not received a specific regulation under Italian data protection law, as this right is already comprehensively provided and regulated under Article 17 GDPR. However, the GPDP has issued its 'Guide to the application of the European Regulation on the protection of personal data',[470] which is intended to provide an overview of the main issues that businesses and public bodies must bear in mind when complying with the GDPR.

323. Moreover, the GPDP has developed a substantial and interesting jurisprudence concerning this right, especially in the context of its balancing vis-à-vis other fundamental rights and freedoms. The debate on the right to erasure in Italy has found fertile ground in the journalistic sector, which is part of the broader right to freedom of expression. In particular, focus shall be steered towards the balance between the right to erasure under Article 17 GDPR and another constitutionally recognized right, i.e., the right to freedom of the press, as protected under Article 21 Italian Constitution.[471]

§2. The Right to Erasure vis-à-vis the Freedom of the Press

324. In its milestone judgment no. 19681 of 22 July 2019, the Supreme Court of Cassation, after a brief *excursus* on the most relevant sources of law and case law in Italy on the freedom of the press,[472] illustrates how the scope of the freedom of the press – though recognized at the constitutional level pursuant to Article 21 Italian Constitution – is not without limits. In fact, three conditions must be met in order for the freedom of the press to be lawfully exercised:

(i) social utility of the information;
(ii) objective description of the facts;
(iii) the form through which the information is delivered, which must always respect the dignity of the person.[473]

470. Author's translation. The Guide, with specific regards to some data subjects rights, may be find at the following URL (Italian only): https://www.garanteprivacy.it/home/i-miei-diritti/diritti/.
471. *See also*, for a general overview of processing rules for journalistic purposes, *infra*, Part IX, Ch. 1.
472. As for legal provisions, *see* Arts 2, 3 and 21 of the Italian Constitution; the so-called Press Law – L. 47/1948; Code of conduct concerning the processing of personal data in the exercise of journalistic activity. As for case law references, *see inter alia* Supreme Court of Cassation, no. 5658/1998, civ. sect.; Supreme Court of Cassation, no. 10690/2008, civ. sect.; Supreme Court of Cassation, no. 5525/2012, civ. sect.; Supreme Court of Cassation, no. 16111/2013, civ. sect.; Supreme Court of Cassation, no. 12834/2014, civ. sect.
473. *See* Supreme Court of Cassation, no. 19681/2019, un. civ. sect.

325. The scope of the right to erasure is therefore connected, in a dialectic manner, to the scope of the freedom of the press. In particular, the former is to be considered prominent when there is no longer any appreciable social utility in informing the public, where the news is to be considered outdated or no longer reflecting the current situation because it has not been updated, or where the exposition of the facts is not commensurate with the need for information and has caused damage to the dignity of the persons concerned.[474] In such a case, the right to erasure shall not apply, in the light of the relevant exemption provided by Article 17, paragraph 3, letter a, GDPR, which states that the right shall not apply when the processing is necessary 'for exercising the right of freedom of expression and information'.

These are the boundaries within which the Court has acknowledged the application of the right to erasure, clarifying that time changes the relationship between the opposing rights, generally tilting the balance in favour of the right to erasure. Therefore, with the exception of the case of a person who plays a particular public role or when news maintains a public interest over time, the publication of information concerning a specific person, over a long period of time, of facts and events that concern them, violates the right to be forgotten.[475]

I. The Different Facets of the Right to Be Forgotten

326. In the same judgment, the Court has also specified that the right to be forgotten refers to at least three different subjective situations, which are recognized by the Italian legal system:[476]

(i) the right to be forgotten of those who wish not to ***see*** news relating to events legitimately published (i.e., 'disseminated', according to Italian privacy discourse)[477] in the past, published again, after a certain amount of time has elapsed between the first and second publication;
(ii) the right to be forgotten connected to the use of the Internet and the availability of news on the web, consisting in the contextualization of the publication, which legitimately took place many years earlier in a different context; and
(iii) the right to be forgotten dealt with in the 'Google Spain' judgment of the CJEU, in which the data subject claims the right to de-list news relating to him or her from search engines.

327. Judgment no. 19681 of 22 July 2019 concerns the first of the three situations listed above, i.e., the scenario in which the legitimacy of the subsequent publication of what has already been disclosed is at issue. In this judgment, the Court

474. *Ibid.*
475. *Ibid.*
476. *Ibid.*
477. *See also*, for a general overview of legal concepts and definition relevant to Italian data protection law, *infra* Part II, Ch. 3.

also states that, in relation to a past event, new elements may intervene, rendering the news relevant at a later date. In this sense, its publication after a long period of time still amounts to exercising the right of freedom of the press.

According to the Court, since the right to publish again a certain piece of information already published in the past is unquestioned, such a right is not absolute, and the judge is called upon to assess the concrete and current public interest when mentioning the identifying elements of the persons to whom those facts and events refer to. Moreover, further publication may be deemed lawful only if it refers to persons who are currently of interest to the public, whether for reasons of fame or because of the public role they play. Where this is not the case, the right to confidentiality of the data subject prevails with respect to past events that may harm their dignity and of which collective memory has been extinguished.

Chapter 5. Right to Restriction

328. The right to restriction is part of the new generation of data subject rights and has a precautionary connotation, with its main function being to provide the data subject with a tool to exercise effective control over their data. The right to restriction subjects the data to a constraint of unusability and inaccessibility, which is necessarily temporary and instrumental with respect to the possible subsequent rectification or erasure. It also entails obligations and responsibilities for the owner, including custody. The right provided by Article 18 GDPR reproposes, under a different name, the essential features of what was previously referred to within Directive 95/46 as the 'blocking of personal data', translated in Italian – starting from the Italian version of Directive 95/46 – with the term '*congelamento*' (i.e., 'freezing').[478]

The repealed Article 4(1)(o) of the former Personal Data Protection Code defined 'blocking' as the conservation of personal data with temporary suspension of any other processing, a definition which remains relevant and adapted to today's content. With regard to the right to restriction, there are no specific legal provisions under national Italian law. However, there is relevant case law provided by the GPDP. The GPDP has, in fact, expressed a constant jurisprudential orientation, stating that the right to restriction may represent a measure against the further diffusion of data or images in the context of a proceeding.[479]

478. Article 12, lett. b), Directive 95/46/EC. However, under the Directive the right to restriction was not expressly labelled as such; it is instead possible to find the origin of the right to restriction in Art. 15 of Regulation (EC) no. 45/2001 on the processing of personal data carried out by the EU institutions, denominated as 'blocking'.

479. Among many decisions, *see* GPDP, *Provvedimento del 25 marzo 2019*, 25.3.2019, doc. web no. 9114178.

Chapter 6. Profiling

§1. Introduction

329. The Italian legal framework does not contain any specific dispositions dedicated to profiling and automated decision-making.

In particular, Italy has not enacted any legal provision capable of amounting to a relevant exception to the prohibition of automated decision-making established under Article 22, paragraph 2, letter b), GDPR.[480] Therefore, Italian-based data controllers may take automated decisions pursuant to Article 22 GDPR only where necessary for entering into, or performance of, a contract between the data subject and a data controller (Article 22, paragraph 2, letter a), GDPR), or on the basis of data subject's express consent (Article 22, paragraph 2, letter c), GDPR).[481]

330. Nevertheless, there are a number of recent decisions of the GPDP concerning profiling and automated decision-making activities carried out on personal data that are worth analysing.

§2. Relevant Decisions from the GPDP on Profiling

331. The first two cases which are analysed below regard two major food delivery companies that were fined by the GPDP for profiling riders' data in violation of the GDPR and infringing their rights as data subjects.

The third case concerns an Italian University which was fined for using behavioural and facial recognition software aimed at verifying the correctness of students' conduct during examinations performed remotely due to the lockdown caused by the COVID-19 emergency.

Lastly, a GPDP ruling containing points of interest for the purposes of this chapter concerning the social network TikTok, which was fined for unlawfully profiling users in order to send them personalized advertising content, is dealt with.

I. Decision Against Foodinho

332. The decision against Foodinho S.r.l. (a company belonging to the Glovo group of undertakings),[482] albeit being later annulled by the Milan Court on grounds

480. Pursuant to which the automated decision is lawful where 'is authorised by Union or Member State law to which the controller is subject and which also lays down suitable measures to safeguard the data subject's rights and freedoms and legitimate interests'.

481. For a general overview of national Member States' laws that have implemented the GDPR in the field of automated decision-making, *see* Gianclaudio Malgieri, *Automated decision-making in the EU Member States: The right to explanation and other 'suitable safeguards' in the national legislations*, 35 Computer Law & Security Review 1 (2019).

482. *See* GPDP, *Ordinanza ingiunzione nei confronti di Foodinho s.r.l. – 10 giugno 2021*, 10.6.2021, doc. web no. 9675440, https://www.garanteprivacy.it/home/docweb/-/docweb-display/docweb/9675440.

of the excessiveness of penalties imposed by the GPDP,[483] is of significant relevance since, for the first time, the GPDP thoroughly investigated the processing of riders' data carried out by 'instant' delivery providers. As other 'instant' delivery providers, Foodinho delivers, by way of a digital platform, food or other goods supplied by retailers following orders placed by customers and, to that end, the company relies on natural persons (so-called riders) who deliver the goods to final customers.

333. The inspection carried out by the GPDP against the company in question established several infringements of GDPR provisions, also with regard to profiling and automated decision-making which the company employed to manage its relationship with riders, especially as regards the allocation of deliveries.

In investigating the processing activities carried out by Foodinho, the GPDP focused its attention on the meticulous collection and automated processing of riders' data – without human intervention – in order to assign them a rating, with a view to automatically determine how orders were allocated to riders and the hierarchy in the booking of their shifts, thereby triggering the application of Article 22 GDPR, as the activity arguably had a significant effect on the riders, similar to a legal decision.

334. First, it was found that the GDPR provisions, which require data subjects to be properly informed about the processing activities carried out on their data, were violated, namely:

(i) Article 5, paragraph 1, letter a) GDPR was infringed in respect of the transparency principle on account of the failure to specify the actual arrangements for processing location data, the categories of data collected with particular regard to the data on the conversations via chats, e-mails and/or phone calls with the call centre, and the evaluation of riders by retailers and customers.

(ii) Article 13, paragraph 2, letter f) GDPR was infringed since the information notice provided did not refer to any automated processing activities, including profiling and 'no meaningful information was provided regarding the logic of the processing and the importance and consequences of such processing for data subjects' (author's translation). Indeed, such activities were carried out and were intended to score riders and rank them in terms of priority in booking the time slots as determined by the company for sending delivery orders, thus violating the above-mentioned provision.

335. Second, the company, through the meticulous collection and processing of riders' data, carried out automated processing activities, including profiling, both within the framework of the so-called excellence system and as part of the order allocation system.

483. *See* https://legalcommunity.it/hogan-lovells-con-foodinho-glovo-per-lannullamento-di-sanzione-privacy-da-26-milioni/.

336. Using the 'excellence system', riders were assigned scores based on the application of an algorithm that penalized riders who did not accept orders in time or refused them and favoured those who accepted on time or delivered the most orders. The score took into account orders actually delivered, check-in within the booked slot a few minutes after the start of the time slot, and acceptance within thirty seconds of the order being placed. However, the functioning of the order allocation system depended on an algorithm that took into account several pieces of information, such as the rider's geographic location taken from the GPS of the device, details on the handling of the order in progress and those already placed, feedback from customers and partners, remaining battery level of the device, etc.

According to the GPDP, by doing so, the company carried out discriminatory profiling activities that significantly affected the lives of the data subject, by granting or denying the very possibility of receiving orders and, therefore, of obtaining employment.

Considering the above, the GPDP noted that while one of the exemptions provided for by Article 22 GDPR applied to the specific processing, which was necessary for the performance of a contract between the parties (Article 22, paragraph 2, letter a), GDPR), it did not appear that the company implemented suitable measures 'to safeguard the data subject's rights and freedoms and legitimate interests, at least the right to obtain human intervention … to express his or her point of view and to contest the decision' and, as a result, Foodinho had breached Article 22 GDPR.

337. Lastly, the GPDP pointed out that the technology used, such as the mobile app to be installed on riders' smartphones, the geolocation system, and the operation of the platform itself, required the execution of a data protection impact assessment pursuant to Article 35 of GDPR. Such an assessment was also necessary due to the performance of automated processing, including profiling activities, which might raise risks to riders' rights, as it concerns the 'assessment of personal aspects, in particular by analysing or predicting aspects concerning professional performance, … reliability or behavior, location or movements, in order to create or use personal profiles'.

338. For the sake of completeness, it should also be noted that the GPDP, in view of the established equivalence of riders to employees under the law, found a breach of the applicable employment laws regulating remote surveillance of employees[484] as well as of the provisions protecting labour on digital platforms.[485] In conclusion, for the violations described above, the GPDP imposed an administrative fine in addition to several corrective measures, amounting to EUR 2.6 million.

484. In particular, L. 300/1970 (so-called *Statuto dei Lavoratori*, i.e., 'Workers Statute').
485. *See* D.Lgs. 81/2015.

II. Decision Against Deliveroo

339. Most of the reasonings expressed by the GPDP against Foodinho are also contained in its decision against Deliveroo, a company also active in the field of 'instant' delivery.[486] Also, in this case, the investigations carried out by the GPDP concerning the processing of riders' data revealed numerous and serious violations of EU and national data protection laws, applicable employment laws,[487] and provisions protecting labour on digital platforms.[488]

340. More specifically, the infringements attributed to Deliveroo were concerned, among others, with the lack of transparency of the algorithms used to manage riders, both for the allocation of orders and the booking of shifts. As a consequence, the GPDP fined Deliveroo EUR 2.5 million and imposed several corrective measures on Deliveroo to be implemented to comply with GDPR provisions.

More specifically, with reference to profiling activities, the company was ordered to put in place appropriate measures:

(i) to protect the rights, freedoms and legitimate interests of the data subject, and at least the right to obtain human intervention on the part of the data controller, to express their opinion and to object to the decision, in relation to automated processing, including profiling;[489]
(ii) to periodically verify the correctness and accuracy of the results of the algorithmic systems also to ensure that the risk of errors is minimized;
(iii) aimed at introducing tools to avoid improper and discriminatory uses of feedback-based reputational mechanisms. Such a check has to be repeated each time the algorithm is modified with regard to the use of feedback for the calculation of the score.

III. Decision Against Bocconi University

341. Another interesting decision of the GPDP concerns the use of a behavioural and facial recognition software implemented by the Bocconi University of Milan.[490]

342. During the GPDP's investigation, it emerged that the University used a remote supervision system for written examinations called 'Respondus'. The use of

486. *See* GPDP, *Ordinanza ingiunzione nei confronti di Deliveroo Italy s.r.l. – 22 luglio 2021*, 22.7.2021, doc. web no. 9685994, https://www.garanteprivacy.it/home/docweb/-/docweb-display/docweb/9685994.
487. In particular, the Workers Statute (L. 300/1970).
488. *See* D.Lgs. 81/2015.
489. *See* Art. 22, para. 3, GDPR.
490. *See* GPDP, *Ordinanza ingiunzione nei confronti di Università Commerciale 'Luigi Bocconi' di Milano – 16 settembre 2021*, 16.9.2021, doc. web no. 9703988, https://www.garanteprivacy.it/home/docweb/-/docweb-display/docweb/9703988.

the Respondus software was aimed at verifying the correctness of students' behaviour during examinations conducted remotely due to the lockdown caused by the COVID-19 emergency. The software captured video images and images of the student's screen by identifying and flagging the moments when unusual and/or suspicious behaviour was detected by video recording, and snapshots were taken at random intervals to keep track of abnormal behaviour such as eyes not looking at the monitor, face partially absent from the picture, face missing, etc. At the end of the examination, the system processed the video, inserting warning signals in correspondence to possible improper behaviour and assigning, among other things, a so-called Review Priority, so that the professor, or the individual acting on their behalf, could then assess whether an impermissible action had been committed during the test.

343. In relation to such a data processing activity, the GPDP found several infringements of data protection laws.

344. The conduct of the University was first of all criticized for not having provided the students, as data subjects, with adequate information on the functioning of the Respondus software, as well as with information on the processing activities carried out through it, such as the tracking of the student's behaviour during the test (i.e., facial position, disconnections from the Internet network, attempts to use the mouse or trackpad to switch from one application to another or to exit the system, and applications in use on the device) subsequent profiling activities, and audio-video recording of the examination. Nor was there any mention in the privacy notice of the photograph taken by the system at the beginning of the test of the student, who was asked to produce an identity document and take a panoramic shot of their surroundings.

In light of the foregoing, the GPDP stated that, although the processing in question did not result in a fully automated decision-making process under Article 22 GDPR, since the software did not automatically impart punishments or take any other decisions autonomously, the data subjects had not received the necessary information that made the logic on which the operation of the supervisory system was based explicitly known.

Thus, the GPDP determined that the processing carried out by the University did not comply with the principles of lawfulness, transparency and fairness laid down in GDPR.[491]

345. Second, with specific reference to the analysis of students' behaviour during the examination, the GPDP, after having carefully examined the functioning of the Respondus software, considered that this resulted in a partially automated processing operation for the analysis of the behaviour of the data subjects which involved the profiling of students, i.e., the automated processing of personal data for

491. Article 5, para. 1, lett. a), and Art. 13 GDPR.

the purpose of evaluating personal aspects relating to a natural person and, in particular, as in the case at stake, for analysing aspects concerning that natural person's behaviour or reliability, thereby amounting to a profiling activity under the GDPR.[492]

The GPDP pointed out that such processing could lead to detrimental consequences for the data subject, such as the invalidation of an examination, which is in violation of the principle of non-discrimination. Therefore, such data processing, in order to be lawful, should have been necessary for the performance of a task carried out in the public interest and should therefore be provided for by a rule of law or regulation[493] which, however, was absent in the case at stake.

346. Considering all the above reasons, Bocconi University was imposed an administrative fine of EUR 200,000 for having processed students' data in breach of Articles 5, paragraph 1, letter a), and 6 GDPR. The University was furthermore ordered to cease the processing activities and to communicate the corrective measures implemented in the following month to the GPDP.

IV. Decision Against TikTok

347. With the order issued towards TikTok,[494] a popular social media platform, the GPDP once again warned data controllers against profiling users in order to send 'personalized' advertising based on legitimate interest.

348. More precisely, in June 2022, the social network announced a change to its privacy policy by communicating its intention to start providing personalized advertising to users aged over 18 years old, consisting of showing them personalized advertising content according to the activity of the users on the TikTok app, grounding such data processing on its legitimate commercial interest under Article 6, paragraph 1, letter f), GDPR.

In response to this proposed change, the GPDP initiated an investigation which revealed that:

(i) With a high degree of probability, activities were carried out for the purpose of 'personalizing' advertising, which is likely to involve the use of cookies or other tracking techniques (including those of third parties).
(ii) With a high degree of probability, profiling operations that also involved automated decision-making processes pursuant to Article 22 of GDPR were carried out in the absence of measures required to protect data subjects' rights and freedom.

---

492. Article 4, para. 4), GDPR.
493. Article 6, para. 1, lett. e), and para. 3, Recital 72 GDPR, as well as Art. 2-*quater* of the Personal Data Protection Code.
494. GPDP, *Provvedimento del 7 luglio 2022*, 7.7.2022, doc. web no. 9788429, https://www.garanteprivacy.it/home/docweb/-/docweb-display/docweb/9788429.

(iii) In the information notice, the right to object to such a processing activity was not adequately highlighted, as it is merely mentioned the specific processing in a generic way at the end of the text, without any direct link with the activity of personalized advertising.

349. With specific regard to the legal basis of the legitimate interest, the GPDP referred to the previous opinion of the WP29 on the concept of legitimate interest[495] which, although based on Article 7 of the repealed Directive 95/46/EC, the GPDP still considered sound.

Taking into account the aforementioned guidance, the GPDP found it difficult for the data controller to justify the use of legitimate interest as a legal basis for intrusive profiling and tracking practices for marketing or advertising purposes. The GPDP stressed that the legitimate interest of the data controller cannot make profiling lawful if the processing falls within the scope of Article 22, paragraph 1, GDPR.

350. Finally, in its warning addressed to the social network, the GPDP also drew attention to the absence of certain elements for the identification of the age of the user. This could also involve persons under the age of 18, for whom parental consent should have been required, and, in the case of minors under the age of 13, for whom access to the platform should have been completely prohibited.[496]

In light of the foregoing, the GPDP issued a formal warning to TikTok, pointing out that the provision of 'personalized' commercial advertising to users over the age of 18, through profiling of their behaviour within the social network, at least to the extent to which it is based on so-called automatically collected information and stored on the users' device, could not be based on legitimate interest, as this activity was in breach of Article 6 GDPR, Article 5, paragraph 3 of the e-Privacy Directive and Article 122 of the Personal Data Protection Code.

The company later overturned its decision, thereby continuing to serve personalized advertising on the basis of consent.

§3. Period of Storage of Data for Profiling Purposes: Useful Decisions from the GPDP

351. In addition to the decisions described above, there are some further GPDP decisions pertaining specifically to the retention period of personal data processed for profiling purposes that the GPDP has issued before the entry into force of the GDPR that can still be useful to data controllers that wish to motivate, for accountability purposes, their decisions pertaining data storage.

495. Article 29 Working Party, *Opinion 06/2014 on the notion of legitimate interests of the data controller under Article 7 of Directive 95/46/EC* (844/14/EN WP 217), https://ec.europa.eu/newsroom/article29/items/611236/en.

496. On this point, *see infra* in this Part IV, Ch. 4, § 3.

352. More specifically, the pre-2018 reform Personal Data Protection Code established, under Article 17, the 'preliminary verification' mechanism, pursuant to which certain data processing activities could be performed only after authorization from the GPDP. In particular, this was required in case where the data controller intended to put in place several types of data processing that could potentially trigger risks to the rights and freedom of the data subjects, including the processing of personal data by automated means for profiling purposes.

353. For this reason, the GPDP has issued several decisions in response to requests by data controllers for the extension of data storage periods for profiling purposes. In order to better understand such decisions and why they can still be useful after the entry into force of the GDPR, the guidelines issued in 2005 by the GPDP on fidelity programmes are worth mentioning,[497] since such guidelines contain relevant dispositions on data retention periods for marketing and profiling purposes.

354. First, it should be noted that the guidelines applied to processing operations are carried out in connection with the issuance of loyalty cards. With reference to data retention periods, the guidelines provided that:

> the detailed data on the items purchased by identifiable customers may be retained for profiling or marketing purposes for no longer than twelve or twenty-four months, respectively, as of their storage, subject to their being actually anonymized in such a way as to prevent data subjects from being identified also indirectly and/or via interconnections with other databases [sic].[498]

355. Even if the guidelines at stake specifically referred to data processing operations carried out in the context of fidelity programmes, such retention periods were (and still are) considered a 'best practice' among data controllers; as a consequence, data controllers who wished to retain personal data for longer periods than those provided by the guidelines, had to request an extension of such period, sending a 'preliminary notification' to the GPDP under Article 17 of the Personal Data Protection Code and motivating why they needed longer retention periods in order to fulfil the purposes for which the personal data were originally collected. Hence, the GPDP issued several decisions in which it accepted or rejected such requests for the extension of retention periods.

356. After the entry into force of the GDPR, Article 17 of the Personal Data Protection Code, along with the 'preliminary notification' mechanism, was repealed, and the evaluations that were requested from the GPDP by means of the 'preliminary notification' shall now be performed by data controllers themselves, pursuant

497. GPDP, *Loyalty cards and safeguards for consumers: guidelines applying to loyalty programmes – 24 Feb. 2005*, 24.2.2005, doc. web no. 1109624, https://www.garanteprivacy.it/web/guest/home/docweb/-/docweb-display/docweb/1109624.

498. *See Ibid.*, para. 9.

to the principle of accountability provided for by Article 24 GDPR, or in the context of a Data Protection Impact Assessment under Article 35 GDPR. This means that data controllers shall define and apply data retention periods and be able to demonstrate that such periods are in compliance with the principle of storage limitation under Article 5, paragraph 1, letter e) of the GDPR. As a consequence, the arguments in favour of the extension of retention periods contained in the GPDP's decisions issued before 2018 can still be very useful to data controllers in motivating their established data retention periods.

For this reason, it is interesting to provide an overview of such decisions, taking into consideration the different data retention periods admitted by the GPDP for profiling activities in different industry sectors.

357. In the fashion sector, for instance, different data controllers selling medium to high-range products, such as Salvatore Ferragamo,[499] Diesel,[500] Marni,[501] Pianoforte,[502] PC S.r.l.,[503] Staff,[504] etc., obtained an extension of the data retention period of up to seven years for the purchase data of customers, processed for profiling purposes connected to personalized marketing.

The reason for granting the extension was that having taken into consideration the average period of repurchase of the products at stake, typically one purchase per season, a one-year profiling exercise would not be enough to fulfil the purpose. In this respect, it is worth mentioning that the GPDP rejected the request for an extension to seven years made by a data controller in the make-up sector.[505]

---

499. GPDP, *Trattamento dei dati personali della clientela per finalità di profilazione e marketing. Verifica preliminare presentata da Salvatore Ferragamo S.p.A. – 30 maggio 2013*, 30.5.2013, doc. web no. 2547834, https://www.garanteprivacy.it/web/guest/home/docweb/-/docweb-display/docweb/2547834.

500. GPDP, *Verifica preliminare. Estensione dei tempi di conservazione di dati personali riguardanti la clientela per attività di profilazione e di marketing – 22 maggio 2018*, 22.5.2018, doc. web no. 9019902, https://www.garanteprivacy.it/web/guest/home/docweb/-/docweb-display/docweb/9019902.

501. GPDP, *Verifica preliminare. Estensione dei tempi di conservazione dei dati personali riguardanti la clientela per attività di profilazione e di marketing – 22 maggio 2018*, 22.5.2018, doc. web no. 9019882, https://www.garanteprivacy.it/web/guest/home/docweb/-/docweb-display/docweb/9019882.

502. GPDP, *Verifica preliminare. Estensione dei tempi di conservazione di dati personali riguardanti la clientela per attività di profilazione e di marketing – 22 maggio 2018*, 22.5.2018, doc. web no. 9020270: https://www.garanteprivacy.it/web/guest/home/docweb/-/docweb-display/docweb/9020270.

503. GPDP, *Verifica preliminare. Estensione dei tempi di conservazione di dati personali riguardanti la clientela per attività di profilazione e di marketing – 22 maggio 2018*, 22.5.2018, doc. web no. 9020250: https://www.garanteprivacy.it/web/guest/home/docweb/-/docweb-display/docweb/9020250.

504. GPDP, *Verifica preliminare. Estensione dei tempi di conservazione di dati personali riguardanti la clientela per attività di profilazione e di marketing – 22 maggio 2018*, 22.5.2018, doc. web no. 9020242, https://www.garanteprivacy.it/web/guest/home/docweb/-/docweb-display/docweb/9020242.

505. GPDP, *Verifica preliminare. Estensione dei tempi di conservazione di dati personali riguardanti la clientela per attività di profilazione e di marketing – 22 maggio 2018*, 22.5.2018, doc. web no. 9022048, https://www.garanteprivacy.it/web/guest/home/docweb/-/docweb-display/docweb/9022048.

358. In the automotive sector, different data controllers obtained an extension of the data retention period of up to ten years for profiling purposes.[506] Once again, the extension was motivated by the average time of repurchase of cars by clients, that would have rendered the profiling activities based on personal data less than ten years old useless.

Similar motivations were used in the decisions in favour of some jewellery brands, where the same period of retention of ten years was granted by the GPDP.[507]

359. Finally, the longest data retention period was admitted by the GPDP in the real estate sector, where the GPDP accepted the request for extension of data retention period for profiling purposes up to twenty years.[508] In this decision as well, the extension of up to twenty years was justified by the fact that typically, clients turn to real estate agencies once or twice every ten years per property purchase; this means that a period of storage of personal data for profiling purposes shorter than twenty years would impact the usefulness of the profiling activities.

360. In conclusion, even if the decisions at stake were issued by the GPDP before the entry into force of the GDPR, the motivations contained therein can still be very useful today to data controllers that wish to motivate their decisions on data retention periods with respect to compliance with the storage limitation principle in internal documents, policies and procedures, for accountability reasons.

§4. Classification under the Code of Conduct for Telemarketing and Teleselling

361. This section contains a description of a data processing activity called 'classification' which may not be considered profiling according to the dispositions of the Code of Conduct for telemarketing and teleselling activities approved by the GPDP.

In March 2023, the GPDP approved the Code of Conduct for telemarketing and teleselling activities, that will enter into force after a monitoring body pursuant to

---

506. *See*, for example: GPDP, *Verifica preliminare. Prolungamento dei tempi di conservazione dei dati personali riferiti alla clientela per il loro utilizzo a fini di profilazione e di promozione commerciale profilata – 18 aprile 2018*, 18.4.2018, doc. web no. 8997404, https://www.garanteprivacy.it/web/guest/home/docweb/-/docweb-display/docweb/8997404; GPDP, *Verifica preliminare. Prolungamento dei tempi di conservazione dei dati personali riferiti alla clientela per il loro utilizzo a fini di profilazione e di promozione commerciale profilata – 9 maggio 2018*, 9.5.2018, doc. web no. 8998319, https://www.garanteprivacy.it/home/docweb/-/docweb-display/docweb/8998319.

507. GPDP, *Trattamento e conservazione di dati personali della clientela per finalità di profilazione. Verifica preliminare richiesta da Bulgari S.p.A. – 24 aprile 2013*, 24.4.2013, doc. web no. 2499354, https://www.garanteprivacy.it/web/guest/home/docweb/-/docweb-display/docweb/2499354.

508. GPDP, *Conservazione dei dati personali riguardanti la clientela per attività di profilazione e di marketing – 30 giugno 2016*, 30.6.2016, doc. web no. 5411203, https://www.garanteprivacy.it/web/guest/home/docweb/-/docweb-display/docweb/5411203.

Article 41 of the GDPR has checked the compliance of the Code of Conduct and after its publication in the Official Journal.[509]

The Code of Conduct confirms the definition of profiling contained in Article 4 GDPR[510] but also contains some additional specifications which, according to the authors, are worth mentioning in this Chapter.

362. First, the Code of Conduct clarifies under Article 12, paragraph 4, that profiling activities for marketing purposes requires a specific and distinct consent, separate from the consent for the performance of promotional activities. However, the same Article specifies that the activity of 'classifying' data subjects does not require specific and separate consent, provided that such activity does not involve profiling in any way.

More specifically, according to Article 2, paragraph 2, letter l) of the Code of Conduct, 'classification' refers to the operation of merely extracting macro-categories of data subjects from databases through queries to partition the data in the database (e.g., age group, gender, area of residence, nationality), without performing additional processing operations consisting of profiling activities such as developing conclusions regarding personal aspects relating to a data subject, such as purchasing preferences, interests, tastes and habits, online behaviour, location or movements.

363. This specification is arguably quite relevant for data controllers who use simple personal information about the data subjects (e.g., area of residence, nationality) to extract clusters of recipients of marketing communications. Given the approval from the GPDP of the Code of Conduct, it is reasonable to maintain that such activity does not require specific consent and is not to be classified in itself as 'profiling' under the meaning of Article 4(4) GDPR, unless the controller performs additional processing activities that entail profiling, such as predicting the data subjects' interests.

Similar to what happens with the information about the purchased good or service under Article 130, paragraph 4 of the Italian Personal Data Protection Code, the classification activity at stake could be based on legitimate interest, and the data controller should perform a legitimate interest assessment, in which the organization clarifies exactly what personal data are used for the classification and motivates why the activity does not entail profiling. It remains intended that the controller should apply adequate organizational measures to allow data subjects to opt out of such processing.

---

509. GPDP, *Provvedimento di approvazione del codice di condotta per le attività di telemarketing e teleselling presentato dalle associazioni promotrici – 9 marzo 2023,* 9.3.2023, doc web no. 9868813, https://www.garanteprivacy.it/web/guest/home/docweb/-/docweb-display/docweb/9868813.

510. *See* Art. 2, para. 2, letter m), of the Code of Conduct for telemarketing and teleselling activities.

Chapter 7. Right to Object

364. As regards the right to object, there are no specific legal provisions or relevant case law in Italy. However, the GPDP has issued its 'Guide to the application of the European Regulation on the protection of personal data',[511] which is intended to provide an overview of the main issues that companies and public bodies must bear in mind when complying with the GDPR, and which also cover an explanation of the right to object.

511. Author's translation. The Guide, with specific regards to some data subjects rights, may be find at the following link and is in Italian only: https://www.garanteprivacy.it/home/i-miei-diritti/diritti/.

Chapter 8. Restrictions (National Implementation of Article 23 of the GDPR)

§1. Provisions of the Personal Data Protection Code Relating to Restrictions on the Rights of Data Subjects

365. The Personal Data Protection Code provides restrictions to the exercise of data subjects' rights within Part I, Title I, Chapter III, with Article 2-*undecies* titled 'Restriction to the rights of data subjects' and Article 2-*duodecies* titled 'Restrictions based on judicial grounds'. Both provisions were adopted in the context of Article 23 GDPR, which allows Member States to – *inter alia* – restrict 'by way of a legislative measure the scope of the obligations and rights provided for in Articles 12 to 22'.

I. Ordinary Restrictions to Data Subjects' Rights

366. Article 2-*undecies* provides that the rights referred to in Articles 15 to 22 of the GDPR may not be exercised by making a request to the controller or lodging a complaint with a supervisory authority[512] if the exercise of those rights may prove factually, effectively detrimental to a number of values protected by law.

A. *Anti-money Laundering Provisions*

367. Articles 15 to 22 GDPR may not be exercised if they may prove detrimental to the interests safeguarded by anti-money laundering provisions.[513]

368. In Italian law, money laundering is a crime provided for in Article 648-*bis* of the Criminal Code, which punishes both 'whoever substitutes or transfers money, goods or other benefits deriving from a non-culpable crime' and 'those who hinder the identification of the criminal origin of the money'.[514] Anti-money laundering legislation is mainly based on D.Lgs. 231/2007, which in turn transposes European Directive 2005/60/EC.[515] The Decree introduced a series of provisions into national law in order to protect the stability and integrity of the economic and financial system. That piece of legislation was most recently amended by Legislative Decree 4 October 2019, no. 125, and the related implementation provisions issued by the

512. *See*, Art. 77 GDPR.
513. Article 2-*undecies*, para. 1, lett. a), of the Personal Data Protection Code.
514. *See* Art. 648-*bis* of the Criminal Code. Author's translation.
515. Directive 2005/60/EC of the European Parliament and of the Council of 26 Oct. 2005 on the prevention of the use of the financial system for the purpose of money laundering and terrorist financing, OJ L 309, 25.11.2005.

Ministry of Economy and Finance, by the Financial Information Unit (FIU) for Italy and by the supervisory authorities of the sector.[516]

369. Anti-money laundering involves a series of activities that must be carried out by professionals (notaries, lawyers, accountants, financial intermediaries, etc.) and credit institutions, such as banks and Italian post offices.

The main obligations established by the law include:

(i) Passive collaboration aimed at guaranteeing in-depth knowledge of customers through their identification and retention obligations of documents relating to the transactions carried out.

(ii) Active collaboration aimed at identifying and reporting suspicious money laundering operations.

(iii) A third fundamental requirement concerns the reporting to the *Unità di Informazione Finanziaria per l'Italia* (Financial Information Unify for Italy, 'UIF') of suspicious money laundering operations. A suspicious transaction is an operation that, due to its characteristics, size, nature or any other circumstance, induces the operator in the bank to know, suspect or have reasonable grounds to suspect that money laundering is taking place, that it has been carried out, or that attempted money laundering, or terrorist financing operations have been ascertained. In this case, a report must be sent to the FIU without delay.

B. *The Interests Safeguarded by the Provisions Aimed to Support Victims of Extortion*

370. Articles 15 to 22 GDPR may not be exercised if they may prove detrimental to the interests safeguarded by the provisions aimed at supporting victims of extortion.[517]

371. In Italian law, extortion is a crime provided for in Article 629 of the Criminal Code, which punishes anyone who, by means of violence or threat, forces someone to do or omit something or procures for themselves or others an unjust profit that causes damage to others.

Law 23 February 1999, no. 44, containing 'Provisions concerning the Solidarity Fund for the victims of extortion and usury requests', introduced various provisions to benefit those damaged by usurious or extortionate activities. In fact, the aforementioned law expanded the subjective and objective scope of usability of the donation of a sum of money to contribute to the compensation for the pecuniary damage suffered by also setting precise limits and conditions. In addition to the temporal and territorial limitation provided for in Article 2 of L. 44/1999, for which donations are

516. *UIF: Unità di Informazione Finanziaria per l'Italia, Normativa Nazionale*, https://uif.bancaditalia.it/normativa/norm-antiricic/index.html?com.dotmarketing.htmlpage.language=102&dotcache=refresh#NormNaz.

517. Article 2-*undecies*, para. 1, lett. b) of the Personal Data Protection Code.

granted in relation to harmful events occurring in the territory of the State after 1 January 1990, the same Law establishes the subjective requirements and conditions for obtaining the donation.[518]

C. The Activities of Parliamentary Inquiry Committees as Set up Pursuant to Article 82 of the Constitution

372. Articles 15 to 22 GDPR may not be exercised if they may prove detrimental to the activities of parliamentary inquiry committees as set up pursuant to Article 82 of the Constitution.[519]

373. The activities of parliamentary inquiry committees are set up pursuant to Article 82 of the Italian Constitution, dealing with issues of public interest. The Constitution, to this end, allows the Italian Parliament to create specific inquiry committees (*Commissioni d'Inchiesta*) that pursue the aim of investigating aspects of general interest so as to report them to Parliament. In order to proceed with the inquiries, each Chamber, by majority, must appoint a commission formed with proportional criteria, that is, criteria which reflects the composition of the political forces present in it. Once its work is finished, the Commission presents a report to the Plenary Assembly of the Parliament, which is then discussed and voted on.[520]

D. The Activities Carried Out by a Public Body for Some Specific Financial Purposes

374. Articles 15 to 22 GDPR may not be exercised if they may prove detrimental to the activities carried out by a public body other than profit-seeking public bodies, where those activities are expressly provided for by a law for purposes relating exclusively to monetary policies, the system of payments, the oversight over credit and financial brokers and markets, and the protection of market stability.[521]

This provision is aimed at balancing the data protection rights of the individual and the public needs dictated by specific legislative provisions.

375. An example of this is found in credit legislation, where the GPDP has approved the 'Code of conduct for information systems managed by private entities in terms of consumer credit, reliability and punctuality in payments',[522] aimed at

518. Maurizio Villani, *Fondo di solidarietà per le vittime di richieste estorsive ed usura*, 11.6.2018, https://www.diritto.it/fondo-solidarieta-le-vittime-richieste-estorsive-ed-usura/.
519. Article 2-*undecies*, para. 1, lett. c) of the Personal Data Protection Code. Article 82 of the Italian Constitution reads: 'each Chamber can arrange inquiries on matters of public interest. To this end, it appoints a Commission from among its members formed to reflect the proportion of the various groups. The Commission of Inquiry carries out investigations and examinations with the same powers and the same limitations as the judicial authority'. Authors' translation.
520. Federico Del Giudice, *Compendio di diritto Costituzionale* 15 (Giuridiche Simone, 2020).
521. Article 2-*undecies*, para. 1, lett. d) of the Personal Data Protection Code.
522. *See infra* Part VI, §5.

strengthening both the protection of consumers registered in credit databases as well as in terms of transparency of the functioning of the algorithms that analyse the 'financing' risk, which usually takes place in the context of Credit Information Systems (*Sistemi di Informazione Creditizia*, 'SIC'). SICs are databases that contain information relating to requests for loans, in particular those on payments, delays or non-fulfilment of instalments. These databases are managed by subjects who make this information available to other subjects, such as credit institutions, financial institutions, sellers who sell goods in instalments, etc., who are then able to evaluate the circumstances of a loan based on the information present in the SIC.

E. *The Performance of Investigations by Defence Counsel or the Exercise of a Legal Claim*

376. Articles 15 to 22 GDPR may not be exercised if they may prove detrimental to the performance of investigations by defence counsel or the exercise of a legal claim.[523]

The foundation of the criminal defence investigation is identified in the right of defence, recognized by the Italian Constitution as inviolable in every state and degree of the criminal procedure, pursuant to Article 24, paragraph 2, of the Italian Constitution. The purposes of defensive investigations are described in Article 327-*bis* of the Code of Criminal Procedure, where it is stated that the defendant has the right to carry out investigations to search and identify evidence in favour of their client.[524]

377. The interviewing of possible witnesses and related suspects is arguably the most important of the investigative acts. Article 391-*bis* of the Italian Code of Criminal Procedure regulates three methods of acquisition and provides for a core of provisions common to all cases. The modalities consist of carrying out an interview, taking information to be recorded, and issuing written documentation.

F. *Confidentiality Regarding the Identity of Whistle-Blowers*

378. Articles 15 to 22 GDPR may not be exercised if they may prove detrimental to the confidentiality regarding the identity of whistle-blowers[525] pursuant to Legislative Decree no. 24 of 10 March 2023, which transposes Directive (EU) 2019/1937.[526]

523. Article 2-*undecies*, para. 1, lett. e) of the Personal Data Protection Code.
524. Paolo Tonini, *Manuale Breve di diritto processuale penale* 498 (Giuffrè Francis Lefebvre, 2022).
525. For an analysis of the Italian Regulation on Whistleblowing, *see supra* Part X, Ch. 5, § 2.
526. Directive (EU) 2019/1937 of the European Parliament and of the Council of 23 Oct. 2019 on the protection of persons who report breaches of Union law, OJ 305/17, 26.11.2019.

379. Legislative Decree 24/2023 protects those who report violations they have come to be aware of, also in the context of a private employment relationship (so-called whistleblowing). The current legislation, consequently, imposes on public and private entities the obligation to create specific procedures and dedicated channels that allow those who intend to do so to report unlawful conduct, guaranteeing the confidentiality of the identity of the reporting subject. Furthermore, in order to avoid retaliation by the employer against the whistle-blower who makes a report, the legislation provides for certain measures, such as reinstatement in the post of work and compensation for damages, as well as a series of penalties applicable in the event that the whistle-blower suffers discriminatory acts or retaliatory actions.

(i) the scope of the Legislative Decree 24/2023 is broader than the previous legislation;[527] as it:
  - (i) refers not only to violations of European Union law but also to violations of national law already specified for the public sector, by Law 190/2012 and for the private sector, by Law 179/2017;
  - (ii) expands the definition of whistleblowing to categories that had hitherto remained excluded by national law, such as former employees and job applicants, self-employed, freelancers, consultants, volunteers, trainees, shareholders and stakeholders;
  - (iii) extends the protection of whistle-blowers in the private sector to all companies that employed an average of fifty or more employees in the past year;
  - (iv) applies to both personnel of the Public Administration and personnel of Companies subject to public control, as well as personnel of companies that provide goods and services or perform works for the Public Administration;
  - (v) prohibits revealing the reporter's identity even in criminal and accounting proceedings and in disciplinary proceedings.

380. In this regard, the exceptions to the exercise of data subjects' rights in this instance are, therefore, aimed at safeguarding the confidentiality of the whistle-blower, so that the facts they have reported may not be disclosed to those to whom the reporting refers (which may, for example, happen if the latter exercise the right of access under Article 15 GDPR).[528]

527. Law 30 Nov. 2017, no. 179.
528. Subparagraph f) of Art. 2– undecies has been amended following the approval of the Legislative Decree 24/2023 in order to reflect the substantial changes introduced with the transposition of the European directive.

G. Protected Interests Regarding Taxation and the Performance of Activities Aimed at Preventing and Countering Tax Evasion

381. Articles 15 to 22 GDPR may not be exercised if they may prove detrimental to the protected interests regarding taxation and the performance of activities aimed at preventing and countering tax evasion.[529]

382. The aim of this provision, which was added in 2019 by Article 1, paragraph 681, of Law 27 December 2019, no. 160, is safeguarding the confidentiality of the enforcement activities carried out by the Tax Revenue Agency (*Agenzia delle Entrate*), which may be endangered by the exercise of data subjects' rights.[530]

H. Procedural Provisions

383. Article 2-*undecies*, paragraph 3, provides that in the cases listed, with the exception of the activity of parliamentary inquiry commissions, rights are exercised in accordance with the provisions of the law or regulations governing the sector, which must at least include measures aimed at regulating the areas referred to in Article 23, paragraph 2.[531]

In those instances, exercise of the data subject rights can, in any case, be delayed, limited or excluded with motivated communication and delivered without delay to the interested party, unless the communication could compromise the purpose of the limitation for the time and to the extent that this constitutes a necessary and proportionate measure, taking into account the fundamental rights and legitimate interests of the data subject, in order to safeguard the interests at issue in the context of the relevant exceptions indicated in paragraph 1 of Article 23.

In such cases, the rights of the data subject can also be exercised through the GPDP with the modalities referred to in Article 160 of the Personal Data Protection Code. In this case, the GPDP shall inform the data subject of having carried out all the necessary checks or having carried out a review of the decision of not allowing the data subject to exercise their rights, as well as the fact that the data subject has the right to judicial redress.

529. Article 2-*undecies*, para. 1, lett. f-*bis* of the Personal Data Protection Code.

530. GPDP, *Relazione annuale 2021*, 7.7.2022, doc. web n. 9787195, https://www.garanteprivacy.it/web/guest/home/docweb/-/docweb-display/docweb/9787195, at p. 39.

531. 'In particular, any legislative measure referred to in paragraph 1 shall contain specific provisions at least, where relevant, as to: (a) the purposes of the processing or categories of processing; (b) the categories of personal data; (c) the scope of the restrictions introduced; (d) the safeguards to prevent abuse or unlawful access or transfer; (e) the specification of the controller or categories of controllers; (f) the storage periods and the applicable safeguards taking into account the nature, scope and purposes of the processing or categories of processing; (g) the risks to the rights and freedoms of data subjects; and (h) the right of data subjects to be informed about the restriction, unless that may be prejudicial to the purpose of the restriction.'

II. Restrictions to Data Subjects' Rights Based on Judicial Grounds

384. Pursuant to Article 23, paragraph 1, letter f), GDPR, Article 2-*duodecies* of the Personal Data Protection Code introduces limitations to the exercise of data subjects' rights in the context of proceedings before the ordinary judicial authority, the Higher Council of the Judiciary or other self-governing bodies, as well as the Ministry of Justice.

The scope, expressly set out in the last paragraph of Article 2-*duodecies* is as follows:

> [P]rocessing activities on judicial grounds shall mean any processing of personal data that is related to the handling of cases and disputes at judicial level, the processing activities carried out with regard to the legal status and payment conditions applicable to the judiciary, and the processing activities that are carried out in connection with inspections concerning judicial offices. Judicial grounds do not include the standard management and administrative activities concerning staff, equipment or facilities providing this is not prejudicial to the confidentiality of instruments that are related directly to the handling of proceedings at judicial level.

Procedurally, the data subjects whose rights are not fulfilled may leverage Article 160 of the Personal Data Protection Code, as seen in the previous paragraph.

385. The aim of the restrictions to the exercise of data subjects' rights is to guarantee the independence of the judiciary and judicial proceedings from possible interference as a consequence of the exercise of the rights of data subjects. This balancing of conflicting interests is very delicate, and even within applicable general lines, it should take into account the specificities of the individual case in the assessment of the effective prejudice to the independence of the judiciary, without prejudice to the essential content of the right to the protection of personal data.[532]

§2. GPDP Decisions on Processing Operations Carried Out in the Context of Restrictions to the Rights of Data Subjects

386. The rules summarized above have been clarified and applied by the GPDP in several decisions.

For instance, in the insurance sector, numerous complaints were received by data subjects whose request to exercise the right of access under Article 15 GDPR to documents containing medical evaluations was rejected by the data controller.[533] In particular, many access requests related to litigation or pre-litigation situations between the insurance company (as data controller) and the data subject, so that the

532. Bolognini & Pelino, *Codice Privacy: tutte le novità del D.lgs. 101/2018* 58–61 (Giuffré Francis Lefebvre, 2019), at 69.

533. GPDP, *Annual Report for 2020,* 2.7.2021, doc. web no. 9676435, https://www.garanteprivacy.it/web/guest/home/docweb/-/docweb-display/docweb/9676435, 179–180.

exercise of the right of access. Therefore, the GPDP held that such requests were liable for falling within the restriction set forth in letter e) of Article 2-*undecies*, that is, the exercise of the right of access may prove detrimental to the performance of investigations by defence counsel or the exercise of a legal claim.

Part V. Duties of Controllers and Processors

Chapter 1. National Rules Regarding Duties of Controllers

§1. INTRODUCTION

387. Preliminarily, it should be noted that the Italian data protection framework does not envisage specific provisions concerning additional duties for data controllers, in addition to those provided by the GDPR and the other relevant EU data protection law provisions. However, as a matter of fact, further obligations which controllers are required to fulfil may be found in some of the GPDP's provisions, outlining further requirements to be met by data controllers while carrying out certain processing activities, especially in the context of direct marketing activities.

388. One of the most controversial issues for data controllers is the prior and indiscriminate sharing of personal data between market players while carrying out marketing activities. Hence, the following paragraphs briefly outline the main requirements to adhere to, on the one hand, to share personal data with third parties so that the latter can process them for their autonomous promotional purposes and, on the other hand – from the opposite perspective of the recipient of such data – to be able to correctly carry out direct marketing initiatives, once the personal data has been so acquired (so-called lead acquisition).[534]

389. The main requirements relating to the activity of transferring personal data to third parties and lead acquisition can already be found in the Guidelines on Marketing and Against Spam (hereinafter, only 'Guidelines').[535] Since the Guidelines at stake are from 2013, they are to be interpreted in the light of the current legal framework as well as of the most recent decisions issued by the GPDP, which have clarified their scope of application after the entry into force of the GDPR.[536]

534. ICTLC Italy, *The legality of disclosure by transmission of personal data for direct marketing purposes under Italian data protection law*, ICTLC (26 Feb. 2022), https://www.ictlc.com/the-legality-of-disclosure-by-transmission-of-personal-data-for-direct-marketing-purposes-under-italian-data-protection-law/?lang=en.

535. *See* in this regard Art. 22, para. 4, of D.Lgs. 101/2018, whereby as from 25 May 2018, the measures of the GPDP continue to apply, insofar as they are compatible with the Regulation and with the provisions of [the same D.Lgs. 101/2018].

536. GPDP, *Ordinanza ingiunzione nei confronti di Sky Italia S.r.l.*, 16.9.2021, doc. web no. 9706389, https://www.garanteprivacy.it/home/docweb/-/docweb-display/docweb/9706389; GPDP, *Ordinanza di ingiunzione nei confronti di Iren Mercato S.p.A. – 13 maggio 2021*, 13.5.2021, doc. web

§2. Transfer of Personal Data to Third Parties for Their Autonomous Direct Marketing Purposes

390. The GPDP establishes that – in order to carry out processing operations whose purpose is the transfer of data to third parties for their autonomous direct marketing purposes – the transferor must:

(i) adequately describe such purpose in its privacy policy pursuant to Article 13 GDPR;
(ii) indicate within the privacy policy each of the third-party data transferees or, alternatively, the economic or product categories to which they belong (e.g., 'finance', 'publishing', 'clothing', etc.);
(iii) acquire specific consent for the communication[537] (and/or transfer) of personal data to third parties for promotional purposes, which is to be separate from the consent leveraged by the data controller to carry out its promotional activities;[538]
(iv) be able to provide evidence of the consent(s) collected for the communication of the data.[539] Pursuant to point ii. above, it shall be noted that the wording 'third party' is to be understood in a broad sense and also with reference to cases where the third-party transferee belongs to the same business group to which the transferor belongs.[540] In general, the subjects belonging to the

no. 9670025, https://www.garanteprivacy.it/web/guest/home/docweb/-/docweb-display/docweb/9670025; GPDP, *Ordinanza ingiunzione nei confronti di Enel Energia S.p.a. – 16 dicembre 2021*, 16.12.2021, doc. web no. 9735672, https://www.garanteprivacy.it/web/guest/home/docweb/-/docweb-display/docweb/9735672.

537. For the notion of 'communication' pursuant to Italian Data Protection Law, *see supra* Part II, Ch. 3., § 1.

538. *See also*, on this point, *supra* Part III, Ch. 2.

539. In the *Ordinanza ingiunzione nei confronti di Enel Energia* (*supra* n. 537) the GPDP stated that the principle of accountability – outlined both in a legal perspective (Art. 5, para. 2, and Art. 24 GDPR) and in a more modern technological dimension (Art. 25) – implies the overcoming of an exclusively formalistic logic of adaptation to the laws, imposing on the data controller to prepare systematic mechanisms of assessment, also beforehand and afterwards, of the respect of the regulations in matters of personal data protection by all the subjects involved in the chain of the processing that concern him, which can be attributed to him or which can bring advantages, also of an economic nature. It should also be noted that in *Ordinanza ingiunzione nei confronti di Sky Italia* (*supra* n. 537), the GPDP states that the entire structure of the GDPR is based on the accountability of the data controller. The latter, in view of the circumstance that the personal data of the persons contacted who have subscribed to the promotional offers are destined to be included in corporate databases, should adopt measures of particular guarantee in order to prove that the contracts and activations recorded in its systems originate from contacts made in full compliance with the provisions on the protection of personal data, in particular those of Arts 5, 6 and 7 GDPR relating to consent.

540. In this sense *see*, by way of example: GPDP, *Guiding Principles Applying to the Processing of Employees' Personal Data for the Purpose of Managing Employment Relations in the Private Sector*, 23.11.2006, doc. web no. 1427027, https://www.garanteprivacy.it/web/guest/home/docweb/-/docweb-display/docweb/1427027; GPDP, *Prescrizioni in materia di circolazione delle informazioni in ambito bancario e di tracciamento delle operazioni bancarie – 12 maggio 2011*, 12.5.2011, doc. web no. 1813953, https://www.garanteprivacy.it/home/docweb/-/docweb-display/docweb/1813953; GPDP, *Titolarità del trattamento di dati personali in capo ai soggetti che si avvalgono di agenti*

same group of undertakings must be considered – as a rule – as autonomous and distinct data controllers when they process personal data for their own marketing purposes.[541]

391. Under point iii. above, it is worth outlining that the consent initially given by a data subject to an entity also for third parties' promotional activities cannot extend its effectiveness to subsequent communications to further data controllers, either by the transferor or by the third-party transferee, since such communication would not be based on the necessary, specific, and informed consent of the data subject.[542]

§3. Lead Acquisition

392. As far as lead acquisition activities are concerned, it must be borne in mind that the point of view is complementary with §2 *supra*, since the focus is now on the obligations that the entity receiving the personal data is bound to respect.

393. In order to carry out a lawful lead acquisition activity, on the one hand, the data subjects must be previously informed by the transferor – pursuant to Article 13 GDPR – about the purpose of communicating the personal data to third parties for their autonomous marketing purposes (as seen above), but, on the other hand, they must also be informed by the transferee about the subsequent processing operations that will be carried out on such data.

As a matter of fact, third parties are allowed to send promotional communications to the data subjects only against the issuance of the third party's own privacy notice pursuant to Article 14 GDPR.[543]

394. As far as the legal basis of the subsequent processing carried out by the transferee is concerned, the GPDP has clarified the limits of the simplification provided for by the Guidelines issued in 2013, i.e., the possibility for the transferee to not require, in turn, a further consent for the performance of direct marketing activities. The transferees may refrain from requesting a new consent only to the extent

---

per attività promozionali – 15 giugno 2011, 15.6.2011, doc. web no. 1821257, https://www.garanteprivacy.it/home/docweb/-/docweb-display/docweb/1821257.

541. *See* para. 2.6.3 of the Guidelines for more details. In this sense, it would not be sufficient to indicate in the privacy notice that the companies to which the personal data are transferred also include companies belonging to the same group of undertakings as the transferor company, being instead necessary that the company name or, alternatively, the economic or product categories to which they belong, are indicated also for such entities. In *Ordinanza ingiunzione nei confronti di Enel Energia* (*supra* n. 537), the GPDP specified that a single consent to the disclosure of data for promotional purposes also by group companies, parent companies, subsidiaries and affiliates and commercial partners, cannot be considered either specific or free and does not constitute an appropriate legal basis for the above-mentioned processing, pursuant to Art. 6 GDPR. Furthermore, in the absence of a clear identification of the recipients, a consent linked to processing operations that can be referred to an indeterminate number of subjects cannot be considered informed.

542. *See*, ex multis, Ordinanza di ingiunzione nei confronti di Iren Mercato S.p.A. (*supra* n. 537).

543. *See* Ordinanza ingiunzione nei confronti di Sky Italia (*supra* n. 537).

that, while carrying out direct marketing campaigns, they intend to make use of automated tools (such as, for example, e-mail, SMS, and MMS). Thus, the transferee must obtain a new consent to proceed with the sending of promotional communications in all cases where the transferee intends to use non-automated contact tools (e.g., telephone with operator or paper mail).[544]

395. As a corollary of the accountability principle, to prevent an endless 'chain' of liabilities in the context of the data processing,[545] the GPDP has emphasized that it is necessary for a data controller to provide evidence of the overall assessments carried out on the characteristics of the processing activities, on the related risks, and on the effectiveness and adequacy of the measures adopted on a case-by-case basis – effectiveness and adequacy that cannot be tested and demonstrated without structured and systematic assessment mechanisms. The transferee is, therefore, required to adopt safeguards to prove that personal data and related consents have been collected in full compliance with data protection provisions by the transferor, including safeguards that can ensure (and monitor over time) the proper handling of consents.[546]

As a consequence, it is advisable for the transferee to request the sharing of the consents collected by the transferor in order to be able to demonstrate the lawfulness of marketing data processing on the basis of the data (and related consents) so obtained.

544. *See Ibid.*

545. *See Ordinanza ingiunzione nei confronti di Enel* (*supra* n. 537).

546. *See* GPDP, *Ordinanza ingiunzione nei confronti di Wind Tre S.p.A. – 9 luglio 2020*, 9.7.2020, doc. web no. 9435753, https://www.garanteprivacy.it/home/docweb/-/docweb-display/docweb/9435753. Specifically, the transferee must check that the data subjects have correctly had access the privacy notice, in accordance with the procedures described above, given consent to receive promotional communications from third parties, and that they are not registered in the '*Registro Pubblico delle Opposizioni*' (*see*, on this point, *supra*, Part III, Ch. 2, §2.VII) or have objected to the processing in question; these checks must be carried out by means of special procedures for filtering contact lists.

Chapter 2. National Rules Regarding Joint Controllers

396. Italian data protection law does not provide for specific rules concerning joint controllership, while GPDP's decisions regarding joint controllership are not numerous and are merely incidental. Accordingly, the GPDP's guidance on the duties and obligations of such actors is scarce. However, the GPDP's decisions of 11 November 2021, no. 9736936[547] and 18 April 2019, no. 9105201[548] are worth mentioning.

397. According to the former, the Italian DPA stated that, with specific reference to a joint controllership agreement pursuant to Article 26 GDPR, for the sake of greater transparency, it is important that the joint controllers specify in detail their respective roles and relationships as to the purposes and means of the processing activity. In particular, the parties should clearly describe the underlying data flows and the powers granted to each party (in particular, as to the appointment of any data processors).[549]

In this context, it is also deemed necessary that the privacy notices – especially in cases where they are issued pursuant to Article 14 GDPR – provide a clear indication of the ways in which the data subjects may exercise, towards the joint controllers, the rights set out in Articles 15 to 22 GDPR.[550]

398. The second decision concerns electoral propaganda and political communication activities. The GPDP pointed out that such activities often involve several actors, especially for the acquisition of personal data from third parties who make available information relating to data subjects (e.g., mobile telephone numbers, e-mail or postal addresses, etc.) and that it is also possible that such third parties might directly send political communications to data subjects.[551] Hence, when the services at stake are provided by third parties, the latter may, in specific cases, be appointed as joint controllers of the processing or as mere processors, depending on their actual degree of discretion and the processing activities carried out. In particular, they might be appointed as joint controllers when, in addition to directly providing for the sending of communications, they use databases in their possession and/or in any case when they have, jointly with the data controller, decision-making power over the purposes and means of the relevant processing.[552]

However, in such a case, although the activities relating to database management, collection of consent and sending of communications are the responsibility of the third party, political parties, political movements, committees of promoters and

547. GPDP, *Provvedimento dell'11 novembre 2021*, 11.11.2021, doc. web no. 9736936, https://www.garanteprivacy.it/web/guest/home/docweb/-/docweb-display/docweb/9736936.

548. GPDP, *Provvedimento in materia di propaganda elettorale e comunicazione politica*, 18.4.2019, doc. web no. 9105201, https://www.garanteprivacy.it/web/guest/home/docweb/-/docweb-display/docweb/9105201.

549. GPDP, *Provvedimento dell'11 novembre 2021*, *supra* n. 548, para. 3.3.

550. *Ibid.*, para. 3.3.

551. GPDP, *Provvedimento in materia di propaganda elettorale*, *supra* n. 549, para. 4.

552. *Ibid.*, para. 4.

supporters, and individual candidates are responsible for verifying the actual fulfilment of the third parties obligations under the legislation.[553]

The verification, depending on the case, should concern, in the case of small databases (in the amount of a few hundred or a thousand personal data records), all the data subjects involved or, in the case of larger databases, at least an objectively relevant sample with respect to the quantity of data, and should also concern the quality, with reference to the accuracy, correctness and updating of the processed data.[554]

In particular, the assignee must verify that:[555]

(i) the assignor has provided the data subject with the information pursuant to Article 13 GDPR, also with regard to the purpose of communicating his data to third parties in the political and/or propaganda sector;
(ii) the same party has acquired from the data subject a specific consent for the communication to third parties for the purposes of electoral propaganda and related political communication.

399. However, it is not necessary to acquire specific consent to leverage one or more channels (e-mail, SMS, telephone calls with operator, fax, paper mail) used to pursue such purposes. In any case, consent must be given clearly and freely and, to this end, formulated in differentiated terms with respect to the various other purposes that may be pursued (e.g., that of sending advertising, direct sales, or market research material; that of profiling; that of communication to third parties for their promotional or profiling purposes).[556]

553. *Ibid.*
554. *Ibid.*
555. *Ibid.*
556. *Ibid.*, para. 2. In this respect, for an overview on Italian data protection rules regarding consent for marketing and promotional activities *see supra* Part III, Ch. 2, II.

Chapter 3. National Rules with Regard to Processors

§1. The Data Processor in General

400. This section identifies some topics of interest concerning the figure of the data processor (identified under Articles 4(7) and 28 of the GDPR), without going over the specific applicable legal provisions. As identified in several Opinion of GPDP, such as the 'Opinion on the subjective qualification for privacy purposes of the Supervisory Bodies (ODV) provided for in Article 6, Legislative Decree no. 231 of 8 June 2001,'[557] a data processor is an entity called upon to carry out processing on behalf of the controller. The data processor may be considered legally distinct from the controller but acts on behalf of the latter in accordance with the instructions given by the data controller (Article 28 GDPR).

The appointment of the data processor must take the form of a contract (or other legal act in accordance with national law) and must exhaustively cover at least the matters referred to in Article 28, paragraph 3, GDPR in order to demonstrate that the controller provides 'sufficient guarantees' such as, in particular, the nature, duration and purpose of the processing operation or operations assigned, the categories of data to be processed, the appropriate technical and organizational measures to allow compliance with the instructions given by the controller and, in general, with the provisions contained in the GDPR (*see* the Guide to the application of the European Data Protection Regulation[558] issued by the GPDP).

401. Consequently, companies that perform services in outsourcing for other entities must be appointed as data processors as stated, among many decisions, in the Injunction order against Region Lazio – 14 January 2021 no. 9.[559] In this injunction, the GPDP took the opportunity to clarify that even in cases where the supplier

557. Author's translation. GPDP, *Parere sulla qualificazione soggettiva ai fini privacy degli Organismi di Vigilanza previsti dall'art. 6, d.lgs. 8 giugno 2001*, n. 231, doc. web no. 9347842, https://www.garanteprivacy.it/home/docweb/-/docweb-display/docweb/9347842. *See also* § 2. Some Specific Qualifications Decided by the GPDP: Labour Consultants and Members of Companies' Supervisory Bodies.

558. GPDP, *supra* n. 512.

559. *See*, for example, GPDP, *Ordinanza ingiunzione nei confronti di Regione Lazio – 14 gennaio 2021*, 14.1.2021, doc. web no. 9542113, https://www.gpdp.it/web/guest/home/docweb/-/docweb-display/docweb/4833448: this case showed that the Lazio Region had failed to appoint the call centre as data processor. *See also, inter alia*: GPDP, *Titolarità del trattamento di dati personali in capo ai soggetti che si avvalgono di agenti per attività promozionali – 15 giugno 2011*, 15.6.2011, doc. web no. 1821257, https://www.garanteprivacy.it/web/guest/home/docweb/-/docweb-display/docweb/1821257; GPDP, *Unsolicited Telephone Services: Enhancing the Safeguards for Citizens – 16 February 2006*, 16.2.2006, doc. web no. 1242592, https://www.garanteprivacy.it/web/guest/home/docweb/-/docweb-display/docweb/1290823; GPDP, *Servizi postali: Poste Italiane resta titolare del trattamento anche in caso di appalto – 29 aprile 2009*, 19.4.2009, doc. web no. 1617709, https://www.garanteprivacy.it/web/guest/home/docweb/-/docweb-display/docweb/1617709; GPDP, *Prescrizioni in materia di circolazione delle informazioni in ambito bancario e di tracciamento delle operazioni bancarie – 12 maggio 2011*, 12.5.2021, doc. web no. 1813953, https://www.garantepr

(a call centre) is located outside the European Union, if it carries out processing on behalf of the data controller, it must be appointed as a data processor.[560]

The data controller is responsible for the actions of the data processor. In fact, the aforementioned injunction clarifies that the data controller is the subject with whom the decisions on the purposes and means of the processing of personal data of the data subjects rest, in addition to a 'general responsibility' for the processing carried out (*see* Article 5, paragraph 2, GDPR, on accountability and Article 24 GDPR), also when these are carried out by other subjects on its behalf (*see* Recital 81, Article 4, paragraph 8, and Article 28 GDPR).[561] The appointment of the data processor also ensures the legitimacy of the disclosure of personal data between the data controller and the data processor.

402. With regard to the clauses that should be contained in the (contractual) act appointing the data processor, it is important to point out that there is a Commission Implementing Decision (EU) 2021/915 of 4 June 2021 on standard contractual clauses between data controllers and data processors pursuant to Article 28 paragraph 7, GPDP and Article 29 paragraph 7 of Regulation (EU) 2018/1725 of the European Parliament and of the Council. This provides precise guidance on the content of the clauses.[562]

403. It is important to bear in mind that the definition of the role of data processor is substantive and not formal. Therefore, the parties could also formalize a contractual relationship where they self-identify as acting both as autonomous data controllers, but if, in substance, one party acts as a data processor, substance prevails over form. For example, if a data processor decides the purposes of the processing, it acts as a data controller, as stated in Article 28, paragraph 10, GDPR. The privacy roles defined by the parties in written agreements are, therefore, only of presumptive value, as the GPDP is able to re-assert their privacy roles on the basis of a factual evaluation. Recently, the Italian Court of Cassation has stated that:

> The person who acts for his own purposes, which exceed those included in the appointment agreements, automatically becomes a 'controller', de facto, since he is autonomously and arbitrarily defining the means and purposes of the personal data processing operations, disregarding the provisions of the controller, with all the responsibilities that such conduct entails (*see* Italian Court of Cassation 23.7.2021, no. 21234).

ivacy.it/web/guest/home/docweb/-/docweb-display/docweb/1813953. *See also*, with specific reference to the Single Reservation Centres: GPDP, *Relazione annuale 2016*, 6.6.2017, doc. web n. 6458231, https://www.garanteprivacy.it/web/guest/home/docweb/-/docweb-display/docweb/6458231, at 61–62.

560. *See*, for example, GPDP Provision of 10 Oct. 2013, doc. web no. 2724806.

561. *See*, for example, GPDP Provision of 17 Sep. 2020, doc. web no. 9461168., https://www.garanteprivacy.it/web/guest/home/docweb/-/docweb-display/docweb/9461168.

562. *See* the full text here: https://eur-lex.europa.eu/legal-content/IT/TXT/PDF/?uri=CELEX:32021D0915&from=IT.

404. In particular, the decision clarifies that it is necessary that the actual data processing by the person in charge be carried out in compliance with the instructions given by the controller, with the consequence that, where there is no such compliance, the person in charge may be recognized as the actual controller, concretely responsible for the processing, by reason of the decision-making and managerial autonomy manifested in having disregarded the instructions given by the controller.[563]

§2. Some Specific Qualifications Decided by the GPDP: Labour Consultants and Members of Companies' Supervisory Bodies

405. In some cases, it is not easy to identify whether an entity is acting as a data processor or as a data controller because it seems that the data processor defines – at least to some extent – the purposes of the processing.[564] There are specific decisions of the GPDP on this point, with reference to certain professional activities, as will be seen below.

406. Regarding labour consultants,[565] the GPDP clarifies that a distinction must be made between the activity in which the employment consultant processes the data of its employees or clients (where those are natural persons) in its capacity as a professional – as this is an activity that is regulated for tax purposes – and the different activity for which the consultant processes the data of the client's employees. In the first case, the labour consultant acts in full autonomy and independence, precisely determining the purposes and means of processing the client's data for the management and fulfilment of her activity. For this part of her activity, therefore, the labour consultant acts as a data controller, since she performs a merely executive activity of processing on behalf of her client, but at the same time, she exercises a completely autonomous decision-making power on the purposes and means of the processing.

563. Author's translation.

564. With reference to the role of the lawyer, *see* GPDP, *Albi e ordini professionali – Chiarimenti sui principali adempimenti in materia di protezione di dati personali nello svolgimento dell'attività forense*, 3.6.2004, doc. web no. 1007280, https://www.garanteprivacy.it/web/guest/home/docweb/-/docweb-display/docweb/1007280, where the GPDP states that: 'Bars and professional associations – Clarifications on the main requirements for the protection of personal data in the performance of legal activities' (author's translation) which defines the lawyer as autonomous data controller since they carry out activities independently, deciding autonomously on the means and purposes of processing and having the contract of mandate as the legal basis. However, the activity of consultancy outside the contract of mandate is different, and according to most authors would fall within the activity of the data processor, such as in case of consultancy activities that law firms carry out on behalf of the data controller; *see also*, *inter alia*, Bolognini & Pelino, Codice della disciplina Privacy (Giuffré Francis Lefebvre, 2019). The National Bar Association ('Consiglio Nazionale Forense'), has also addressed this topic in a document available at the following link in Italian only: https://www.consiglionazionaleforense.it/documents/20182/445621/IL+GDPR+E+L%27AVVOCATO/ef231b75-2066-43df-8d88-570bf0ea98b3.

565. GPDP, *Risposta a un quesito relativo al ruolo del consulente del lavoro dopo la piena applicazione del Regolamento (UE) 679/2016*, 22.1.2019, doc. web no. 9080970, https://www.garanteprivacy.it/home/docweb/-/docweb-display/docweb/9080970.

Conversely, in the second case (i.e., processing the personal data of the client's employees), the correct qualification is that of a data processor, as the activity is characterized by the performance of activities delegated by the data controller. The data controller, because of its own organizational choices, may identify a subject who is particularly qualified to perform these activities (in terms of specialist knowledge, reliability, and structure made available, *see* Recital 81 GDPR), delimiting the scope of the respective powers and providing specific instructions on the processing to be performed. Therefore, the client is the subject who, in the light of the concrete context in which the processing takes place, takes the basic decisions relating to the purposes and means of processing lawfully carried out, grounded on one of the legal bases identified by the law (Articles 6 and 9 GDPR).[566] Labour consultants, as certified professionals, apply their specific sectoral rules in order to correctly fulfil their obligations, but it is still the employer who entrusts the consultant with the relevant task and, therefore, determines the purposes of the processing. For these reasons, the consultant acts as a data processor in the case set out above.

In this same decision, the GPDP, under the rules applicable prior to the 2018 reform, and after assessing the concrete elements of the activity carried out, has referred to several decisions where the GPDP has determined that the following entities normally play the role of the data processor: the parent company delegated by its subsidiaries and affiliated companies to carry out labour law's obligations, social security and social assistance activities for employees,[567] the entity which provides geographic location services,[568] electronic mail services,[569] and security services.[570]

407. A much-discussed case in Italian legal doctrine is the data protection role of the supervisory body ('*Organismi di Vigilanza*' or 'ODV'), established under D.Lgs. 231/2001 and which has the task of supervising the functioning and observance of the company internal compliance framework aimed at preventing the commission of crimes.[571]

Regarding this matter, the debate concerned whether the members of supervisory bodies could be identified as autonomous data controllers because of the power of

---

566. *Ibid.*

567. GPDP, *Linee-guida per il trattamento di dati dei dipendenti privati,* 23.11.2006, doc. web no. 1364099, https://www.garanteprivacy.it/web/guest/home/docweb/-/docweb-display/docweb/1364099, para. 3.2.

568. *See* GPDP, *Vehicle Geo-Location and Employer-Employee Relations – 4 October 2011*, 04.10.2011, doc. web no. 2444921, https://www.garanteprivacy.it/web/guest/home/docweb/-/docweb-display/docweb/2444921, para. 5.2.; GPDP, *Localizzazione di veicoli aziendali – 28 giugno 2018*, 28.06.2018, doc. web no. 9023246, https://www.garanteprivacy.it/web/guest/home/docweb/-/docweb-display/docweb/9023246; GPDP, *Provvedimento del 19 luglio 2018*, 19.7.2018, doc. web no. 9039945, https://www.garanteprivacy.it/web/guest/home/docweb/-/docweb-display/docweb/9039945.

569. GPDP, *Accesso alla posta elettronica dei dipendenti – 22 dicembre 2016*, 22.12.2016, doc. web no. 5958296, https://www.garanteprivacy.it/web/guest/home/docweb/-/docweb-display/docweb/5958296, para. 3.4.

570. GPDP, *Impianto di videosorveglianza installato presso una farmacia – 20 novembre 2014*, 20.11.2014, doc. web no 3671057, https://www.garanteprivacy.it/web/guest/home/docweb/-/docweb-display/docweb/3671057.

571. GPDP, *supra* n. 558.

initiative and control entrusted to them or as data processors, given that it is the company that decides which personal data the ODV processes, based on the risk areas identified. This debated has become outdated after the entry into force of the GDPR, since the GDPR appears to have superseded the figure of the internal data processor,[572] qualifying the data processor as an entity which can only be external to the data controller's structure.[573] Some have argued that such members are neither controllers nor processors because the ODV would be an integral part of the company and would identify with it, so it would not need to be appointed.[574] In light of the internal nature of the ODV members vis-à-vis the company, some influential authors have also identified the members of the ODV as persons authorized to process personal data, pursuant to Article 29 GDPR and Article 2-*quaterdecies*, paragraph 2, of the Personal Data Protection Code.[575]

Within the aforementioned Decision, the GPDP has adhered to this latter view.[576] As a consequence, members of the ODV shall not be qualified as external data processors, nor as autonomous or joint controllers with the company, but rather as persons authorized to process personal data.

§3. The Duty of Supervision of the Data Controller Towards the Data Processors: *Culpa in Eligendo* and *Culpa in Vigilando*

408. Another fundamental element to be taken into consideration concerns the supervision that the data controller should exercise over the activity of the data processor. Potentially, the controller can be held liable for *culpa in eligendo* if it chooses, for example, a data processor that does not offer sufficient guarantees pursuant to Articles 28, paragraph 1, and 32 GDPR, but also for *culpa in vigilando*, if the data controller does not supervise the activity carried out by the processor after the latter has been assigned with the task.

409. Regarding *culpa in eligendo*, the reference is Recital 81 of the GDPR and Article 28, paragraph 1, GDPR, which states that 'the controller shall use only processors providing sufficient guarantees to implement appropriate technical and organizational measures in such a manner that processing will meet the requirements of this Regulation and ensure the protection of the rights of the data subject'. For instance, the existence of ISO certifications (e.g., ISO/IEC 27001 or UNI EN ISO 9001, but also the Technical Guidelines for the implementation of minimum security measures for Digital Service Providers drafted by ENISA or D.P.C.M. 81/2021 setting out new rules on the Italian national cyber security perimeter)[577] can help the data controller to assess or demonstrate the reliability and specialist skills of the

572. Luca Bolognini, Enrico Pelino & Camilla Bistolfi, *Il Regolamento privacy europeo* (2016).
573. Bolognini & Pelino, *Codice della disciplina Privacy* (Giuffré Francis Lefebvre, 2019).
574. Luca Antonetto & Francesco Pizzetti, Sulla qualificazione soggettiva dell'Organismo di Vigilanza ai fini privacy, in www.aodv231.it, 21 Mar. 2019.
575. Bolognini & Pelino, *Codice della disciplina Privacy* (Giuffré Francis Lefebvre, 2019).
576. GPDP, *supra* n. 558, para. 5.
577. *See* https://www.enisa.europa.eu/publications/minimum-security-measures-for-digital-service-providers/at_download/fullReport.

data processor. Furthermore, the data processor's adherence to a Code of Conduct (Article 40 GDPR) may be relevant in the assessment[578] as the adherence to a certification mechanism (Article 42 GDPR).[579] However, it is always necessary to take into account the 'state of the art'.

410. Regarding *culpa in vigilando,* vigilance takes the form of auditing activities. This concept is expressly reiterated in a number of recent measures taken by the GPDP, for example, in the noteworthy decision against TIM S.p.A., adopted on 15 January 2020.[580] At the end of the investigation, the GPDP found that TIM, as data controller, had not exercised sufficient control over the operations of its call centres, which carried out marketing activities on behalf of TIM, thereby acting as data processors.[581] In particular, the GPDP ascertained several systematic violations of the law by the call centres that TIM had failed to detect, given the lack of any actual supervision of the activities of the call centres. In particular, among the most important violations was the fact that the so-called blacklists – i.e., the list of contacts who had opted-out from being contacted by TIM for marketing purposes – leveraged by call centres for commercial campaigns were not kept up-to-date.

The GPDP, therefore, noted that TIM – as the data controller of the processing operations delegated to the data centres – did not have sufficient knowledge, let alone control, of the data flows and processing operations actually carried out by the data centres on TIM's behalf, and was therefore liable for *culpa in vigilando*.[582]

411. Another noteworthy Decision in this respect is the one against Sky Italia S.r.l.[583] In this Decision, the GPDP ascertained that Sky had failed to carry out the necessary compliance checks on contact lists acquired from third parties and to check the information notice given by the same suppliers – acting as data processors – to the data subjects upon first contact. Interestingly, the GPDP, in addition to outlining some of the distinctive features between third-party data controllers and data processors,[584] especially with reference to the outsourcing used to implement

578. *See* the Guide to the application of the European Data Protection GDPR available on the official website of the GPDP (at https://www.garanteprivacy.it/Regolamentoue/titolare-responsabile-incaricato-del-trattamento, in Italian only) which says that by adhering to Codes of Conduct or Certification Schemes, the data processor can demonstrate the 'sufficient guarantees' referred to in Art. 28, paras 1 and 4 GDPR. The GPDP is assessing the Codes of Conduct currently in force for some types of processing in the light of the requirements set out in the GDPR (Art. 40), while as regards Certification Schemes, we will have to wait for the intervention of the national legislator, who will have to establish some modalities of accreditation of the certifying bodies (if different from the GPDP: *see* Art. 43 GDPR).

579. Bolognini & Pelino, *Codice della disciplina Privacy* (Giuffré Francis Lefebvre, 2019).

580. GPDP, *Provvedimento correttivo e sanzionatorio nei confronti di TIM S.p.A.*, 15.01.2020, doc. web no. 9256486, https://www.garanteprivacy.it/home/docweb/-/docweb-display/docweb/9256486.

581. *Ibid.*, para. 2.1, where the GPDP noted a lack of control by the company over the actions of its partners during the conduct of commercial campaigns.

582. *Ibid.*

583. GPDP, *Ordinanza ingiunzione nei confronti di Sky Italia S.r.l.*, 16.9.2021, doc. web no. 9706389, https://www.garanteprivacy.it/home/docweb/-/docweb-display/docweb/9706389, para. 1.2.

584. *Ibid.*, para. 2.2.2. In particular, the GPDP clarified that – as already observed by the GPDP in past decisions (e.g., Tito*larità del trattamento di dati personali in capo ai soggetti che si avvalgono di agenti per attività promozionali*, 15.06.2011, doc. web no. 1821257, https://www.garanteprivacy.i

promotional campaigns, also expressly sets out the data controller's obligation to supervise its data processor activities. In the GPDP's view, the principles laid down in the GDPR frame the powers of the data controller in terms of accountability and impose on all those involved in the processing of personal data proactive and consistent behaviour with the aim of proving, at every stage, the lawfulness of the processing itself.

412. Another GPDP Decision in line with the jurisprudence above is the one against Eni Gas e Luce S.p.A.,[585] where the GPDP noted the significant negligent nature of the processing (Article 83, paragraph 2, letter b, GDPR), given that Eni as data controller, failed to adopt systems for monitoring the validity of consents relied on by Eni's external call centres, which acted as data processors on behalf of Eni.

t/web/guest/home/docweb/-/docweb-display/docweb/1821257) – outsourced agencies cannot be considered autonomous data controllers since, in concrete terms, they do not exercise the decisions which are typical of a data controller. In this case, the powers which are normally exercised by the data controller are: – taking decisions regarding the purpose of the processing, i.e., sending advertising material or direct sale or commercial research or commercial communication; – issuing instructions and binding directives to the outsourcers, substantially corresponding to the instructions that the data controller must give to the data processor; – controlling the activities of the outsourcers.

585. GPDP, *Provvedimento correttivo e sanzionatorio nei confronti di Eni Gas e luce S.p.A.*, 11.12.2019, doc. web no. 9244365, https://www.garanteprivacy.it/home/docweb/-/docweb-display/docweb/9244365.

Chapter 4. Data Protection Impact Assessment and Prior Consultation

§1. Introduction

413. Pursuant to Article 35 GDPR, where a processing activity will lead to a high risk to the rights and freedoms of the data subject, the data controller is required to carry out a data protection impact assessment (DPIA). Where the outcome of the DPIA shows that the risk continues to be high, the data controller must proceed with prior consultation under Article 36 GDPR, which consists of requesting the opinion from the competent supervisory authority, such as the GPDP.

414. The above-mentioned GDPR obligations recall, broadly speaking, the preliminary verification provided for in Article 17 of the Personal Data Protection Code, repealed by the 2018 reform, which always required prior authorization of the GPDP for high-risk processing. The preventive consultation provided for by Article 36 GDPR is, on the contrary, merely possible following the determination of the data controller in the context of the DPIA.[586]

It can therefore be maintained that the direct applicability of the GDPR and the subsequent 2018 reform replaced the intervention of the GPDP from being *ex ante* (Article 17 of the Personal Data Protection Code) to taking place *ex post*, that is, after the decision of the data controller to consult the GPDP (Article 36 GDPR). This appears to be in line with the accountability approach adopted by the GDPR, while the pre-2018 reform Personal Data Protection Code tended to be more bureaucratic.

§2. List of Types of Processing, to Be Subjected to a DPIA under Article 35, Paragraph 4, GDPR (So-called Blacklist)

415. The GPDP has adopted, as established under Article 35, paragraph 4, GDPR,[587,588] a general provision listing the types of processing activities that data controllers shall have to subject to a DPIA. The list incorporates the observations of

586. Bolognini & Pelino, *Codice Privacy: tutte le novità del D.lgs. 101/2018* 20 (Giuffrè Francis Lefebvre, 2019).

587. The GPDP has not adopted, to date, a list of processing activities exempted from the requirements to carry out a prior DPIA, under Art. 35, para. 5, GDPR ('The supervisory authority may also establish and make public a list of the kind of processing operations for which no data protection impact assessment is required. The supervisory authority shall communicate those lists to the Board').

588. 'The supervisory authority shall establish and make public a list of the kind of processing operations which are subject to the requirement for a data protection impact assessment pursuant to paragraph 1. The supervisory authority shall communicate those lists to the Board referred to in Article 68.'

the EDPB, pursuant to the consistency mechanism, as required by Article 35, paragraph 6, GDPR.[589] The list of processing activities for which it is necessary to carry out a DPIA is included in Annex 1 of the general provision adopted by GPDP and includes:[590]

(i) Large-scale evaluation or scoring processing, as well as processing that involves the profiling of data subjects as well as the performance of predictive activities also carried out online, relating to 'aspects concerning professional performance, economic situation, health, preferences or the personal interests, reliability or behaviour, location or movements of the data subject'.
(ii) Automated processing aimed at taking decisions that produce 'legal effects' or that affect the data subject 'in a similarly significant way', including decisions that prevent the person from exercising a right or making use of a good or service or continuing to be a party of an existing contract (e.g., screening of a bank's customers through the use of data recorded in a risk centre).
(iii) Processing that provides for the systematic use of data for the observation, monitoring or control of data subjects, including the collection of data through networks, also carried out online or through apps, as well as the processing of unique identifiers capable of identifying users of information society services including web services, interactive TV, etc. with respect to usage habits and viewing data for prolonged periods. The processing of metadata, e.g., in the field of telecommunications, banks, etc., also falls in this provision when carried out not only for profiling but more generally for organizational reasons, budget forecasts, technological upgrades, network improvement, offer of anti-fraud, anti-spam, security service etc.
(iv) Large-scale processing of data of an extremely personal nature (*see* WP248, rev.01),[591] for which reference is made, among others, to data related to family or private life (such as data relating to electronic communications for which it is necessary to preserve confidentiality), or which affect the exercise of a fundamental right (such as location data, the collection of which puts the freedom of movement at stake) or whose violation entails a serious impact on the life of the data subject (such as financial data which could be used to commit payment fraud).

---

589. 'Prior to the adoption of the lists referred to in paragraphs 4 and 5, the competent supervisory authority shall apply the consistency mechanism referred to in Article 63 where such lists involve processing activities which are related to the offering of goods or services to data subjects or to the monitoring of their behaviour in several Member States, or may substantially affect the free movement of personal data within the Union.' The EDPB has adopted its relevant opinion on 25 Sep. 2018: EDPB, *Opinion 12/2018 on the draft list of the competent supervisory authority of Italy regarding the processing operations subject to the requirement of a data protection impact assessment (Article 35.4 GDPR)*, 25.9.2018, https://www.garanteprivacy.it/web/guest/home/docweb/-/docweb-display/docweb/9058979.

590. GPDP, *Elenco delle tipologie di trattamenti soggetti al requisito di una valutazione d'impatto sulla protezione dei dati ai sensi dell'art. 35, comma 4, del Regolamento (UE) n. 2016/679*, 11.10.2018, doc. web no. 9058979, https://www.garanteprivacy.it/web/guest/home/docweb/-/docweb-display/docweb/9058979.

591. Article 29 Working Party, *Guidelines on Data Protection Impact Assessment (DPIA)* (wp248 rev.01) https://ec.europa.eu/newsroom/article29/items/611236/en.

(v) Processing carried out in the context of the employment relationship by means of technological systems (also with regard to video surveillance and geolocation systems) from which the possibility of carrying out a remote control of employee activity may derive (*see* the provisions of WP 248, rev. 01,[592] in relation to criteria 3, 7 and 8).

(vi) Non-occasional processing of data relating to vulnerable subjects (minors, disabled, elderly, mentally ill, patients, and asylum seekers).

(vii) Processing carried out through the use of innovative technologies, also with particular organizational measures (e.g., IoT, artificial intelligence systems, the use of online voice assistants through voice and text scanning, monitoring carried out by wearable devices, proximity tracking, for example, wi-fi tracking) whenever at least one of the other criteria identified in WP 248, rev. 01[593] are present.

(viii) Processing that involves the exchange between different data controllers on a large scale using telematic methods.

(ix) Processing of personal data carried out through interconnection, combination or comparison of information, including processing that involves the crossing of consumption data of digital goods with payment data (e.g., mobile payments).

(x) Processing of special categories of data pursuant to Article 9 GDPR or data relating to criminal convictions and the crimes referred to in Article 10 GDPR, interconnected with other personal data collected for different purposes.

(xi) Systematic processing of biometric data taking into account, in particular, the volume of data, the duration, or the persistence of the processing activity.

(xii) Systematic processing of genetic data taking into account, in particular, the volume of data, the duration, or the persistence of the processing activity.

§3. GPDP Decisions on DPIAs

416. The rules concerning DPIAs have been applied by the GPDP in several decisions.

417. In a noteworthy case,[594] the GPDP has provided its opinion to the data controller in reference to a request for prior consultation on the data protection impact assessment carried out by the Department for Youth Policies and Universal Civil Service of the Presidency of the Council of Ministers, concerning the processing of data in the context of the 'National Youth Card' ('*Carta Nazionale Giovani* or

592. *Ibid.* The wording of this provision seems to recall Art. 4 of the Workers' Statute, for which *see*, in this volume, Part IX, Ch. 4, *infra*.

593. *Ibid.*

594. GPDP, *Consultazione preventiva sulla valutazione d'impatto sulla protezione dei dati, predisposta dal Dipartimento per le politiche giovanili e il servizio civile universale presso Presidenza del Consiglio dei Ministri, concernenti il trattamento dei dati nell'ambito dell'iniziativa 'Carta giovani nazionale'*, 28.10.2021, doc. web no. 9722681, https://www.garanteprivacy.it/web/guest/home/docweb/-/docweb-display/docweb/9722681.

'CNG') initiative.[595] The CNG is a digital service accessible through a specific application, which allows young people between 18 and 35 years of age residing in Italy to obtain discounts on cultural and sporting events, career guidance, and access to the European Youth Card ('EYC'). Since the project involved the processing of personal data of millions of young people, a DPIA was carried out by the Department for Youth Policies pursuant to Article 35 GDPR, which was then sent to the GPDP for its formal approval.

The impact assessment was approved by the GPDP as it incorporated all relevant elements required by the law, including the identification of all the activities carried out as part of the processing, compliance with the principle of data minimization and privacy by design and by default, the methods of checking the different uses of the CNG by the beneficiaries, the methods of processing, the retention periods, and the subsequent deletion of the information of the CNG at the end of the retention period. The GPDP also paid attention to the definition and allocation of roles and relationships between the Department for Youth Policies and other entities involved in the processing, among which PagoPa S.p.A., that is, the company that manages the application through which it is possible to access the services provided by the card, thereby acting as a data processor.

Finally, with respect to the analysis of risks relating to data security, the GPDP acknowledged that the Department had adopted measures in accordance with the obligations established by Article 32 GDPR.

418. In another interesting case, already discussed *supra* in Part IV, Chapter 6, §2.II, the GPDP has fined the company Deliveroo Italy S.r.l. ('Deliveroo'), active in the field of the quick delivery of goods, of EUR 2.5 million for various non-conformities concerning the processing of personal data of its collaborators (so-called riders), among which the fact that they did not perform a DPIA.[596]

In this case, the GPDP considered that the personal data processing activity carried out by Deliveroo is characterized by the innovative use of a digital platform, which automatically collects a huge amount of personal data relating to order management, including geolocation and recording of communications via chat and e-mail between a large number of riders and the Deliveroo staff. This circumstance is also confirmed, as argued by the GPDP, by the data controller's Chamber of Commerce company registration, which includes the: 'organization and management of an online software platform (based on web and applications) to connect restaurants

---

595. It should be noted that, in this case, the request of the data controller toward the GPDP did not stem from Art. 36 GDPR, but was instead based on national rules (*'Disciplinare per il trattamento dei dati nell'ambito del progetto "Carta Giovani Nazionale"'*) adopted by the head of Department for Youth Policies and Universal Civil Service of the Presidency of the Council of Ministers, which mandated that the DPIA needed to be submitted to the GPDP in any case. The GPDP had already provided its favourable opinion on such rules, on July of the same year: GPDP, *Parere sullo schema di provvedimento del Capo del Dipartimento per le politiche giovanili e il servizio civile universale della Presidenza del Consiglio dei Ministri, recante il disciplinare tecnico per il trattamento dei dati nell'ambito dell'iniziativa 'Carta Giovani Nazionale'*, 22.7.2021, doc. web no. 9689751, https://www.garanteprivacy.it/web/guest/home/docweb/-/docweb-display/docweb/9689751.

596. GPDP, *Ordinanza ingiunzione nei confronti di Deliveroo Italy s.r.l,* 22.7.2021, doc. web no. 9685994, https://www.garanteprivacy.it/home/docweb/-/docweb-display/docweb/9685994.

and other partners with potential customers and facilitate the delivery of food and other goods through a network of independent transport service providers'.[597]

Furthermore, the processing included performance of profiling activities and automated processing of a large number of 'vulnerable' data subjects (the riders, as parties to an employment relationship, even if not legally *employed* from a labour law perspective) is of particular importance, in addition to the fact that the processing activity could cause discriminatory effects against the riders.

Taking into account these elements, the GPDP considered that the system envisaged the 'using [of] new technologies' and presented 'a high risk for the rights and freedoms of natural persons' with the consequent obligation to carry out, before the start of the processing, a DPIA pursuant to Article 35 of the GDPR, which, however, was not carried out by Deliveroo.

419. Moreover, in another recent case, the GPDP imposed a fine of EUR 100,000 on the Region of Lazio for unlawful monitoring of employees' e-mail metadata.[598] The data processing was deemed unlawful under several grounds, including the fact that a DPIA had not been carried out.

The Region of Lazio claimed that a DPIA regarding log management had been performed after the preliminary investigation had begun. Notwithstanding, the GPDP pointed out that the document in question does not expressly refer to the storage of metadata relating to the use of e-mail by employees.

In contrast, taking into account the guidance also provided at the European level on this point, it was argued by the GPDP that the data processing, consisting of the systematic collection of such metadata (including information about the sender/recipient and the subject of each e-mail), storage for 180 days and the possibility of extractions processing and verification of such metadata, entails specific risks to the rights and freedoms of data subjects in the work context, considering their status as vulnerable subjects, and that 'systematic monitoring' understood as 'processing used to observe, monitor or control data subjects, including data collected through networks'[599] was being carried out.

For all these reasons, the GPDP found that the data processing had been in breach of Article 35 of the GDPR.

---

597. Authors' translation.

598. GPDP, *Ordinanza ingiunzione nei confronti di Regione Lazio,* 01.12.2022, doc. web 9833530, https://www.garanteprivacy.it/web/guest/home/docweb/-/docweb-display/docweb/9833530.

599. Authors' translation.

Chapter 5. Data Protection Officer

420. This chapter analyses some aspects of interest pertaining to the Data Protection Officer ('DPO') in the Italian data protection legal framework. More specifically, it presents useful material made available by the GPDP, summarizes the provisions of the Italian Data Protection Code dedicated to the appointment of a DPO in connection with processing carried out by judicial authorities, examines the liability of the DPO under Italian civil law and, finally, analyses relevant decisions from the GPDP and from Italian Regional Administrative Courts.

§1. Guidance from the GPDP Regarding the Appointment and Role of the DPO

421. The official GPDP website contains an informational page specifically dedicated to the DPO.[600] This page provides very useful documents which help to clarify the activities of the DPO, as well as some operational material that can be used by DPOs to carry out their activities. This paragraph aims to provide an overview of such material, namely:

(i) The FAQs for DPOs in the private[601] and public[602] sectors.
(ii) A guideline document on the designation, role, and tasks of the DPO in the public sector.[603]
(iii) A DPO handbook[604] created in the context of a European H2020 project that aims to guide the DPO in the public and quasi-public sectors on how to ensure compliance with the GDPR.
(iv) An online procedure for communicating the DPO contact details to the GPDP.[605]
(v) A template which can be used for the appointment of the DPO.[606]

---

600. GPDP, *Il Responsabile della Protezione dei Dati (RPD)*, 7.6.2022, https://www.garanteprivacy.it/regolamentoue/rpd.
601. GPDP, *FAQ sul responsabile della protezione dei dati in ambito privato*, 7.6.2022, https://www.garanteprivacy.it/faq-sul-responsabile-della-protezione-dei-dati-rpd-in-ambito-privato.
602. *Ibid.*
603. GPDP, *Documento di indirizzo su designazione, posizione e compiti del Responsabile della protezione dei dati (RPD) in ambito pubblico*, 7.6.2022, https://www.garanteprivacy.it/web/guest/home/docweb/-/docweb-display/docweb/9589467.
604. GPDP, *T4DATA – The DPO Handbook*, 7.6.2022, https://www.garanteprivacy.it/web/guest/home/docweb/-/docweb-display/docweb/9127859.
605. GPDP, *Comunicazione dei dati di contatto del RPD*, 7.6.2022, https://servizi.gpdp.it/comunicazionerpd/s/.
606. GPDP, *Schema di atto di designazione del Responsabile della Protezione dei Dati*, 7.6.2022, https://www.garanteprivacy.it/web/guest/home/docweb/-/docweb-display/docweb/7322273.

I. FAQs for DPOs in the Private and Public Sector

422. The FAQs made available by the GDPD for DPOs in the private sector[607] contain interesting clarifications on the following aspects:

(i) *Internal or external DPO*: The DPO can be internal or external; in the first case, they should receive a letter of appointment, while the external DPO should enter into a service contract with the data controller; in both cases, the appointment should be made in writing and should regulate the resources made available to the DPO for the performance of their duties.
(ii) *Data processing roles*: The DPO should not be appointed as a data processor for their activities, since this would be in conflict with their autonomy.
(iii) *Other assignments*: The DPO can receive other assignments, provided that no conflict of interest arises from them; for instance, according to the GPDP, the DPO role is to be considered incompatible with top management functions and, more in general, with functions that require decision-making powers on data processing activities; this includes managing director, CEO, member of the Board of Directors, as well as manager of IT, audit and risk, HR, marketing or finance departments; concerning the head of legal department, according to the GPDP, the absence of conflict of interest with this function is not implicit, but it should be assessed on a case-by-case basis; concerning external DPOs, the GPDP clarifies that appointing an IT or software-house service provider as DPO might conflict with the independence requirement.
(iv) *Natural person or legal person*: In case of appointment of a natural person as DPO, the GPDP clarifies that this person can be supported by a specific office, whose members shall possess the necessary professional skills and expertise; in case of appointment of a legal person as DPO, it is necessary to define a single point of contact for the GPDP and it is also recommended to define an internal function of the data controller that should be the principal the point of contact for the external DPO, facilitating the interaction with the internal functions.
(v) *Group DPO*: In case of group DPO assignment, it is a best practice to provide for positions at the local level which could support the DPO activities with respect to the data subjects and the competent supervisory authorities; in case of several DPO appointments in the same group, the GPDP suggests setting up a network of DPOs and defining how they should be coordinated.

423. It should be noted that the FAQs for DPOs in the private sector were initially published in 2018 and were last updated in May 2021.

607. *See supra* n. 602.

II. Guidelines on Designation, Role and Tasks of the DPO in the Public Sector

424. After the entry into force of the GDPR, the GPDP had several occasions to interact with data controllers and DPOs from the public sector, and it was observed that there are still a lot of uncertainties in this respect, which impede the correct application of the GDPR. Consequently, with a view to resolving such uncertainties, in April 2021, the GPDP published the Guidelines on designation, role and tasks of the DPO in the public sector[608] (the 'Guidelines').

In the following paragraph, some of the most interesting topics examined in the Guidelines are presented.

(i) *Different DPOs for the same data controller*: The GPDP is often asked whether complex public organizations with structured entities active across the national territory (such as ministries) can appoint more than one DPO. According to the GPDP, there should be only one single DPO per organization; otherwise, this would create uncertainty or overlapping of liabilities among different subjects. It is intended that the DPO can be supported by different persons within the organization of the public body, but they should all refer to one single DPO.

(ii) *Appointment of an internal DPO* ad interim *while completing the public selection procedure of an external DPO*: In cases where the appointment of a DPO for a public body expires before a new one is designated, the GPDP clarified that the public body can appoint an internal DPO *ad interim*, pending the conclusion of the public selection for the new external DPO. The reason for this is that in such cases, the principle of continuity of the administrative activities of the public body should prevail.

(iii) *Appointment of the same DPO for different public bodies*: It might happen that the same natural or legal person acts as DPO for different data controllers; this could be the case of a natural person being appointed as DPO for different small public bodies (e.g., municipalities), that often have limited resources dedicated to data protection. The GPDP clarified that the appointment of the same DPO for different public bodies could be done provided that, pursuant to the principle of accountability, the data controllers have evaluated that the person appointed as DPO is able to adequately fulfil their duties. For example, such an evaluation could be motivated by the fact that the DPO is supported by a team and has defined how their activities should be divided among the different data controllers. The same principle also applies to big companies that act as DPOs for several data controllers. In this case, the data controller should consider the number of assignments obtained by the same company and evaluate whether the company can guarantee an adequate fulfilment of its duties, having taken into consideration its expertise and resources (e.g., its possibility to dedicate a team of experts to each data controller).

608. Author's translation. *See supra* n. 604.

(iv) *Duration of the assignment*: The GPDP clarifies that the duration of the DPO assignment should be evaluated by the data controller on a case-by-case basis, having taken into consideration the dimensions of the public bodies and the processing activities they carry out. Indeed, the duration of the assignment should be defined to allow the DPO to organize the activities necessary for compliance of the processing activities with the GDPR. According to the GPDP, three years could be an appropriate duration, since, in such a period, the DPO could have the time to understand the processing activities and the organization of the public body and suggest adequate data protection compliance activities.

(v) *Professional skills and qualifications*: The skills required to perform the duties of the DPO do not depend on specific qualifications, such as having a degree in law, being an attorney or having certain certifications. Consequently, access to the public selection for DPO appointment in the public sector should not require such qualifications as mandatory elements for applying for the position. Instead, when defining the professional skills and qualifications required for the appointment, the data controller should consider the relevance and proportionality of the requested skills and qualifications, as well as their connection with its data processing activities. The expertise of a candidate can be demonstrated by previous working experience in the same sector as well as documented training activities.

(vi) *Relevant certifications for DPOs*: The GPDP clarifies that even if there are different certifications available on the market which aim at demonstrating the qualification and skills of the DPO, none of them fall within the definition of the certification scheme provided under Article 42 of the GDPR. These available certifications can be used by controllers to assess the level of qualification and expertise of the DPO. However, alone, they are not sufficient by themselves to qualify for the DPO. This means that in appointing a DPO that possesses a certification, the public authorities still have the obligation to assess the fulfilment of the requirements necessary to perform the DPO's duties under the GDPR.

(vii) *Act of appointment*: The documents containing the appointment of the DPO by a public body should specify the reasons that led the data controller to appoint the DPO, also making the documents containing the results of the selection made by the public body publicly available. This is relevant for accountability purposes as well as to guarantee the principles of transparency and good administration of public bodies. Furthermore, for the same reason, in addition to the publication of the contact details of the DPO in the information notice, the latter can also be published in the section of the official website of the public body dedicated to transparency.

(viii) *Involvement of the DPO in the data processing activities and the DPO's tasks*: when interacting with public bodies, the GPDP has observed that, on the one hand, some DPOs did not adequately perform the tasks they were assigned, and on the other hand, data controllers often failed to involve the DPOs in the data processing activities. Consequently, the GPDP shared some examples of good practice:

(a) Having a person within the public body with adequate position and skills that could act as a point of contact with the DPO.
(b) Defining periodical meetings with the DPO and top management.
(c) The DPO may propose activities that aim at enhancing the compliance of the processing activities, such as: raising awareness on data protection among both top management and employees; supporting the data controller in the fulfilment of its obligations (information notices, data processing agreements, record of processing activities, etc.); proposing technical and security measures; providing procedures for data breach management.
(d) Regular reporting on the DPO's activities.
(e) Training authorized persons.

425. It should be noted that the GPDP explicitly points out that the DPO should be asked to carry out the first-person activities that, according to the GDPR, are up to the data controller. In this sense, the DPO should support the data controller in complying with its obligations, but they should not perform implementation tasks that rest with the data controller, nor should they be held liable for them:

(i) *Specific DPO Office*: The GPDP is often asked whether the DPO of a public body should have its own department. According to the GPDP, the need to have a specific department dedicated to data protection should be assessed on a case-by-case basis, taking into consideration the complexity of the data processing activities and the impossibility of one single person supporting the data controller. In any case, in case a specific data protection office is created, it is necessary to identify the natural person that, within this office, acts as DPO.
(ii) *Further assignments to the DPO*: In case of large public organizations that carry out complex data protection activities, it is unlikely that the DPO can receive further assignments without risking not being able to perform its duties in an adequate way. For what concerns conflicts of interest, the GPDP confirms the same principles detailed in the FAQs for the DPO of the private sector, specifying that the Information System Manager (who normally has decision-making powers on security measures) and the Head of the Statistical Department (who normally has decision-making powers on the means of data processing activities for statistical purposes) should not be appointed as DPO.

426. In conclusion, it should be noted that the GDPD does not seem to consider that the Guidelines at stake can always be applied to the activities of the DPOs in the private sector. As a matter of fact, the GPDP specifies that, in consideration of the differences between the public and the private sectors and of the fact that the appointment of the DPO is not always mandatory for private companies, the latter should rely on the clarifications provided by the GPDP in the FAQs for DPOs in the private sector.

III. Handbook for DPO in the Public and Quasi-Public Sector

427. The GPDP published its 'DPO Handbook: guidance for data protection officers in the public and quasi-public sectors on how to ensure compliance with the European Union General Data Protection Regulation' (hereinafter 'Handbook') on its official website.[609]

The Handbook was prepared as part of the training materials for an EU-funded project, in which the GPDP took part between 2018 and 2019, named 'Training for Data' or 'T4DATA'.[610] The document contains major contributions from the GPDP as well as from other EU Data Protection Authorities, with the support of European experts on fundamental rights. The aim of this project was to train the staff of EU data protection authorities in the training of DPOs, especially in the public sector, in their new duties under the GDPR.

The Handbook was made publicly available after the completion of the programme, hoping that it would guide the DPOs in the public sector in the correct application of the GDPR. Indeed, the Handbook – which is currently available in Italian,[611] English,[612] Croatian, Bulgarian, Polish and Spanish – contains a noteworthy section that 'provides practical guidance on how DPOs in the public sector can and should fulfil their numerous tasks, with real-life examples, relating in particular to the three focus areas: education, finance and health care, and exercises'.[613]

IV. Online Procedure for Communicating the DPO Contact Details to the GPDP

428. The GDPD dedicated a specific page[614] of its official website to the procedure for communicating the contact details of the DPO.

It is of high importance that data controllers take into consideration the content of this page because the DPO contact details can be communicated to the GPDP only by means of this online procedure. Communications sent via different means will not be accepted by the GPDP.

The page at stake contains all the relevant material necessary to guide the controller in the activity and, namely, provides:

(i) Instructions on how to send the communication via the online procedure.[615]

---

609. *See supra* n. 603.
610. For information on the program, *see*: GPDP, *T4Data*, 7 Jun. 2022, https://www.garanteprivacy.it/regolamentoue/formazione/t4data.
611. GPDP, *T4DATA – Manuale per gli RPD*, 7.6.2022, https://www.garanteprivacy.it/web/guest/home/docweb/-/docweb-display/docweb/9152344.
612. GPDP, *T4DATA – The DPO Handbook*, 7.6.2022, https://www.garanteprivacy.it/web/guest/home/docweb/-/docweb-display/docweb/9127859.
613. Douwe Korff & Marie Georges, *The DPO Handbook Guidance for data protection officers in the public and quasi-public sectors on how to ensure compliance with the European Union General Data Protection Regulation*, https://www.garanteprivacy.it/documents/10160/0/T4DATA-The+DPO+Handbook.pdf.
614. https://servizi.gpdp.it/comunicazionerpd/s/.
615. https://servizi.gpdp.it/comunicazionerpd/s/istruzioni.

(ii) FAQs which contain very useful information to guide the controller in case of problems with the completion of the online procedure.[616]

(iii) A facsimile of the document that results from the communication via the online procedure[617] that is embedded with relevant instructions that data controllers receive during the online procedure. It should be considered that this document is made available only in order to guide the data controller in the online procedure, but it cannot be used to send the communication to the GPDP.

429. Each communication sent via the online procedure is assigned a protocol number. At the conclusion of the procedure, the DPO and the data controller will receive a copy of the communication containing the related protocol number. It is of high importance that both the DPO and the data controller duly archive this communication because the protocol number assigned by the GPDP will be needed in case of future modifications to the communication.

§2. Appointment of a DPO in Connection with Processing Carried out by Judicial Authorities Acting in Their Capacity as Such

430. Pursuant to Article 2-*sexdecies* of the Personal Data Protection Code, 'A data protection officer shall also be appointed with regard to the processing of personal data that is carried out by judicial authorities acting in their capacity as such, pursuant to the provisions contained in Section 4 of Chapter IV of the Regulation.' The provision would seem to conflict with the purpose of Article 37, paragraph 1, letter a), GDPR, which – instead – provides for a specific exclusion/exception: 'The controller and the processor shall designate a data protection officer in any case where: (a) the processing is carried out by a public authority or body, except for courts acting in their judicial capacity', as well as with Recital 19 of the GDPR.[618]

---

616. https://www.garanteprivacy.it/regolamentoue/rpd/faq-relative-alla-procedura-telematica-per-la-comunicazione-dei-dati.
617. https://servizi.gpdp.it/comunicazionerpd/resource/1644225204000/RPD_facsimile.
618. According to Recital 19: The protection of natural persons with regard to the processing of personal data by competent authorities for the purposes of the prevention, investigation, detection or prosecution of criminal offences or the execution of criminal penalties, including the safeguarding against and the prevention of threats to public security and the free movement of such data, is the subject of a specific Union legal act. This Regulation should not, therefore, apply to processing activities for those purposes. However, personal data processed by public authorities under this Regulation should, when used for those purposes, be governed by a more specific Union legal act, namely Directive (EU) 2016/680 of the European Parliament and of the Council (1). Member States may entrust competent authorities within the meaning of Directive (EU) 2016/680 with tasks which are not necessarily carried out for the purposes of the prevention, investigation, detection or prosecution of criminal offences or the execution of criminal penalties, including the safeguarding against and prevention of threats to public security, so that the processing of personal data for those other purposes, in so far as it is within the scope of Union law, falls within the scope of this Regulation. With regard to the processing of personal data by those competent authorities for purposes falling within scope of this Regulation, Member States should be able to maintain or introduce more specific provisions to adapt the application of the rules of this Regulation. Such provisions may determine more precisely specific requirements for the processing of personal data by those

However, this provision must also be read in light of Articles 32–34 of Directive 680/2016/UE dealing with the obligation of judicial authorities to appoint the DPO in the exercise of their functions.[619] It may be argued that the difference between the above-mentioned Directive and Article 2-*sexdecies* may be as follows: The Directive refers to the tasks of the authorities in the prevention, investigation, detection and prosecution of crimes (criminal activities), while Article 2-*sexdecies* of the Personal Data Protection Code concerns the more generic obligation (as regards non-criminal activities) to appoint the DPO by judicial authorities. This latter Article, therefore, regulates the obligation to appoint the DPO for authorities in the exercise of judicial functions other than criminal ones; thus, it extends the obligation to appoint the DPO for judicial authorities. Arguably, it would have been better to specify that this obligation should apply to those who were not already subject to the obligation under the Directive.[620]

This was clarified by the GPDP on the Opinion on the draft legislative decree containing provisions for the adaptation of national legislation to the provisions of Regulation (EU) 2016/679 – 22 May 2018.[621]

§3. The Liability of the DPO

431. The GDPR is silent as to the nature of the civil liability of the DPO, i.e., whether it is of contractual or extra-contractual nature. Similarly, the Personal Data Protection Code does not have any specific provision dedicated to that. Therefore, Articles 37, 38, and 39 of the GDPR must be addressed together with principles applicable to the activities of the DPO under Italian civil law in order to qualify the

competent authorities for those other purposes, taking into account the constitutional, organizational and administrative structure of the respective Member State. When the processing of personal data by private bodies falls within the scope of this Regulation, this Regulation should provide for the possibility for Member States under specific conditions to restrict by law certain obligations and rights when such a restriction constitutes a necessary and proportionate measure in a democratic society to safeguard specific important interests including public security and the prevention, investigation, detection or prosecution of criminal offences or the execution of criminal penalties, including the safeguarding against and the prevention of threats to public security.

The protection of natural persons with regard to the processing of personal data by competent authorities for the purposes of the prevention, investigation, detection or prosecution of criminal offences or the execution of criminal penalties, including the safeguarding against and the prevention of threats to public security and the free movement of such data, is the subject of a specific Union legal act. This Regulation should not, therefore, apply to processing activities for those purposes. However, personal data processed by public authorities under this Regulation should, when used for those purposes, be governed by a more specific Union legal act, namely Directive (EU) 2016/680 of the European Parliament and of the Council (1). Member States may entrust competent authorities within the meaning of Directive (EU) 2016/680 with tasks which are not necessarily carried out for the purposes of the prevention, investigation, detection or prosecution of criminal offences or the execution of criminal penalties, including the safeguarding against and prevention of threats to public security, so that the processing of personal data for those other purposes, in so far as it is within the scope of Union law, falls within the scope of this Regulation.

619. Rocco Panetta et al., *Il Data Protection Officer tra regole e prassi* 20–22 (Giuffrè Francis Lefebvre 2021).

620. *Ibid.*

621. Please refer to https://www.garanteprivacy.it/home/docweb/-/docweb-display/docweb/9163359.

nature of the liability. In this respect, two categories of liability exist under Italian civil law, reflected in the Italian Civil Code: contractual liability and extra-contractual liability. Contractual liability is incurred, under Article 1218 of the Italian Civil Code, by the data controller or data processor for breach of contractual obligations, while extra-contractual or tort liability, under Article 2043 of the Italian Civil Code, is incurred in respect of damages that data subjects may suffer as a result of the actions of a person (who may also be the DPO) who has no contractual relationship with them.[622] In this latter case, there is, in fact, no contractual relationship and, therefore, no contractual liability in case of non-compliance.

I. The Contractual Liability of DPO

432. The act of designation of the DPO entrusts the latter with the tasks of Articles 38, paragraph 6, and 39 GDPR. The applicable civil law provisions are arguably those who regulate the provision of services of an intellectual nature, pursuant to Articles 2222 et seq. of the Italian Civil Code, and – in some other aspects – the mandate pursuant to Articles 1703 et seq. of the Italian Civil Code. With reference to the contractual nature of civil liability, it may be noted that under Italian law, such liability arises from the breach of a contractual obligation pursuant to Article 1218 of the Italian Civil Code. However, in order to determine liability, in addition to the breach of an obligation, there are further elements to be considered – in addition to the objective breach of an obligation – to determine liability:

(i) the breach must also be serious, so as to entail termination of the contract according to Article 1455 of the Italian Civil Code;
(ii) the DPO's liability shall not be incurred if she proves that non-performance (or delay in performance) has resulted from causes not attributable to them (pursuant to Article 1218 of the Italian Civil Code);
(iii) damage is attributable to the DPO if it is causally linked to the breach of the obligation or to the delay, pursuant to Articles 1223 and 1225 of the Italian Civil Code.

433. A further element to assess whether the DPO is liable is the nature of the obligation. In general, on the basis of the task entrusted to him by legislation, it is possible to argue that the DPO assumes obligations so-called of means,[623] not of results. In other words, the DPO would not be obliged to achieve a specific result,

622. Bolognini & Pelino, *Codice della disciplina Privacy* (Giuffrè Francis Lefebvre, 2019).

623. According to this type of obligation, in order to assess whether there has been proper performance, it is necessary to assess not the attainment of a specific result, but the diligence used in trying to attain it. If the diligence was in accordance with the nature of the obligation (e.g., it was qualified diligence under Art. 1176, para. 2, of the Italian Civil Code), the obligor can be said to have performed even if it did not achieve a specific result. Indeed, this distinction between obligations of means and of result was first attenuated (Supreme Court of Cassation no. 13533/2001, un. civ. sect.) by case law and then definitively overcome (Supreme Court of Cassation, no. 15781/2005, un. civ. sect., and Supreme Court of Cassation, no. 577/2008, un. civ. sect.). As a consequence, it may be said that in every obligation there is a need to achieve a result and the assessment as to whether

but he would be obliged to use a certain degree of diligence in the performance of his duties. In order to assess her performance, therefore, it would be necessary to verify whether she acted with qualified professional diligence pursuant to Article 1176, paragraph 2, of the Civil Code. This implies that for a breach of contract to be identified, it must be ascertained whether there has been a breach of the DPO's duty of care in fulfilling her obligations. The DPO's diligence must be considered a 'qualified diligence' under Article 1176, paragraph 2, of the Italian Civil Code, considering that, according to Article 37, paragraph 5, GDPR, the DPO shall have 'professional qualities and, in particular, expert knowledge of data protection law and practices and the ability to fulfil the tasks referred to in Article 39', while Article 39, paragraph 2, GDPR, requires that, in carrying out her activities, the DPO monitors the risks of processing, taking into account the state of art.

434. A limit to the DPO's liability can be found in Article 2236 of the Italian Civil Code, which provides that even in case of qualified professional diligence under Article 1176, paragraph 2, of the Italian Civil Code, if the service involves technical problems of particular difficulty, the DPO would be liable for damages only in case of fraud or gross negligence. Therefore, under Italian Civil Law, it would be possible to charge the responsibility directly against the DPO if the violation of the obligations imposed on the latter – via the act of appointment – under Article 39 GDPR stems from fraud or gross negligence attributable to the DPO and formally imposed through the act of appointment.[624]

435. It is possible that the tasks of the DPO can be conferred to a company (instead of a natural person), with the obligation for the company to have the task concretely carried out by natural persons who have the necessary requisites as established under law. In this case, on the one hand, the liability would fall on the company, while the company could then, in turn, claim damages towards the individual subjects who have concretely produced the damage. On the other hand, the company would be liable for *culpa in eligendo* in these cases. Possible liability for third parties' actions or omissions might arise, pursuant to Article 1228 of the Italian Civil Code, since the DPO is appointed by the data controller or data processor to carry out tasks that are necessary for the data controller in order to be compliant with the obligations of the GDPR. From this, it follows that the data controller could be liable for possible damages produced by the DPO if the result is that the data controller has violated a provision of the GDPR. This approach, in terms of responsibility, does not seem to be in conflict with Article 38, paragraph 3, GDPR, which guarantees the technical independence of the DPO. On the contrary, the scope of independence means that the DPO can (or must) also indicate to the data controller

this result is achieved may be stricter or milder depending on the type of obligation (e.g., for intellectual professions such as that of the DPO, it is necessary to value diligence in fulfilling one's duties rather than the achievement of a specific result).

624. It is important to note, however, that if this results in a violation of the GDPR that entails the application of administrative sanctions, such sanctions are imposed on the data controller or data processor, depending on the division of responsibility between the two, and not directly on the DPO. However, the DPO could be held directly liable if the damages result from a breach attributable to the DPO and these damages are causally related to the breach.

actions contrary to what the controller would like to do. If, however, the DPO suggests an action to the controller that proves to be contestable by the Authority, the sanction will be aimed at the data controller, who is liable precisely in his capacity as data controller. There may then be professional liability profiles for the DPO, but the sanction for the breach of law/provision of Authority will not be imposed on the DPO but on the data controller.

436. With reference to the recovery claims that the data controller or the data processor can pursue against the DPO if the latter is responsible for having negligently or intentionally breached its obligations and this breach has caused the violation of the GDPR, it should be considered that this civil principle is not in contrast with Article 38, paragraph 3, GDPR. The exercise of the right of recourse does not (or should not) automatically result in the removal of the DPO from their office as, indeed, the two actions remain on two separate levels. Moreover, in accordance with the principles of the Italian Civil Code, if the DPO has contributed to causing the damage or has refrained from limiting its consequences, the DPO and the data controller shall be liable pursuant to Article 1227 of the Italian Civil Code.

II. The Extra-Contractual Liability of DPO

437. As far as the extra-contractual liability of the DPO is concerned, in order for it to be raised, all the essential elements provided for by Article 2043 of the Italian Civil Code must be present. The unlawful processing of personal data, therefore, falls within the definition of 'unjust damage' referred to in Article 2043. Moreover, it should be considered that Article 15 of the Personal Data Protection Code, before being repealed by the 2018 reform, expressly stated that the legal nature of the liability arising from data protection activities fell within Article 2050 of the Italian Civil Code, i.e., liability arising from exercise of dangerous activities, which is considered a sub-set of extra-contractual liability.[625]

438. However, according to Article 82 GDPR, it is only the data controller or data processor that needs to compensate for the damage suffered by the data subject. Pursuant to Article 82 GDPR, therefore, the data controller or data processor shall be liable for the damage caused to data subjects by the actions of their DPO, while the DPO shall only be liable towards the data controller or processor for the damage caused if they have failed to fulfil the obligations imposed on them by the GDPR.

439. Concerning the burden of proof, Article 82 GDPR provides for an inversion of the burden of proof: the data controller or data processor will be held liable unless they prove that the damaging event was caused by a source outside their sphere of control or that they have prepared and implemented all appropriate measures to prevent the damage from occurring. Under Italian Civil law, the burden of

625. Bolognini & Pelino, *Codice Privacy: tutte le novità del D.lgs 101/2018* (Giuffrè Francis Lefebvre, 2019).

proof is generally ruled by the principle under which *onus probandi incumbit ei qui dicit,* that is, 'the one who claims a fact must prove it'; however, in this case, the burden of proof is reversed, which means that the burden of proof is exceptionally placed on the subjects who are claimed to have caused the damages and not on the plaintiff (i.e., the damaged party). The reason for this is that, in the Italian legal system, the processing of personal data is considered a 'dangerous activity'.[626] The legal system accepts a part of risk because of the social utility of the activity, but carrying out such activities requires the protection of data subjects and does so by reversing the burden of proof.[627]

§4. Decisions from the GPDP and from Italian Courts Concerning DPOs

440. Interesting decisions of the GPDP and some rulings of the Regional Administrative Tribunals ('*Tribunale Amministrativo Regionale*', commonly abbreviated as 'TAR') which help to identify the tasks and responsibilities of the DPO are explored below.

441. In a recent case against a Local Health Authority,[628] the GPDP found a violation of the rules on the processing of personal data. In particular, the consent of the data subject was wrongly indicated as the legal basis for processing personal data, and there were also several violations of the principle of fairness and transparency pursuant to Articles 13 and 14 of GDPR for failure to indicate the legal basis for each purpose indicated in the information notice, as well as the data retention period. In this context, the GPDP noted that it is not the DPO's task to draft the privacy notices to be given to data subjects. The GPDP also noted that the obligation (and the consequent responsibilities) to properly inform data subjects lies with the data controller, who may, for this purpose, leverage the advice of the DPO (Article 39, paragraph 1, letter a, GDPR), not on the DPO.

442. Another ruling worth mentioning is that of TAR Sicilia of 1 October 2018, no. 2020.[629] The judgment is interesting because it expressly confirms (in line which

---

626. *See*, for instance, Supreme Court of Cassation, no. 207/2019, civ. sect., and no. 14242/2018, civ. sect.; both rulings define data processing as a dangerous activity (in the same sense, *see also* Supreme Court of Cassation, no. 1931/2017, civ. sect.).

627. *See* Corte d'Appello di Potenza, no. 355/2020: 'Liability arising from the processing of personal data is of an objective nature, with the relative inversion of the burden of proof. it is whoever manages the processing of personal data that has the burden of proving that he has taken all measures suitable to avoid the damage, i.e. all measures that Art. 31 of Personal Data Protection Code (e.g., Art. 32 GDPR) prescribes to be taken for data security in order to minimise the risks of unauthorised access or unauthorised processing.' Author's translation.

628. GPDP, *Ordinanza ingiunzione nei confronti di Azienda Sanitaria Locale Frosinone – 13 gennaio 2022*, 13.01.2022, doc. web no. 9742959, https://www.garanteprivacy.it/web/guest/home/docweb/-/docweb-display/docweb/9742959.

629. Sicilian Regional Administrative Court, no. 02417/2019, 17.10.2019 available in Italian only in the GPDP website at the following URL: https://www.garanteprivacy.it/web/guest/home/docweb/-/docweb-display/docweb/9276747.

was expressed in the FAQ of the Italian Authority concerning the DPO)[630] that the role of a DPO may be fulfilled not only by a natural person but also by a company and that, in this latter case, a DPO team should be set up and a single point of contact for liaising with the GPDP should be established. The TAR observes that such an interpretation appears to be in line with the complex structure of organizations and the obligations connected with data protection legislation.

The decision at stake is interesting also to understand if, and in which terms, the qualifications and certifications can be evaluated in the public tenders set for DPO selection in the public sector can be evaluated in competitions. In this respect, the TAR clarified that the assessment of qualifications and the awarding of scores by the selection committee fall within the broad technical discretion granted to the public administration, and – therefore – the judge cannot replace the administration in assessing the requirements in its place but may ask the administration to carry out a new assessment.

443. Another interesting judgment relating to the professional skills that the DPO should have to perform his/her activities is the one issued by the Friuli Venezia-Giulia TAR shortly after the direct applicability of the GDPR.[631] This ruling has clarified that the ISO27001 certification cannot be placed as a mandatory requirement in the call for tenders for the appointment of a DPO in favour of a Health Care Agency. The TAR has also clarified that the DPO need to have a legal profile rather than a technical IT one. In any case, this judgment seems in line with Recital 97 of the GDPR, that states that the necessary level of expertise, skills and qualification should be determined, taking into consideration the peculiarities of the data processing carried out by the entity for whom the DPO has to be appointed.

630. Please, refer to the FAQ available at the following link: https://www.garanteprivacy.it/faq-sul-responsabile-della-protezione-dei-dati-rpd-in-ambito-privato.

631. Friuli Venezia Giulia Administrative Court, no. 287/2018, 13.09.2018, available at the following link in Italian only: https://www.giustizia-amministrativa.it/portale/pages/istituzionale/ucm?id=5LLMWH2MBE2JVPC536FUMJHNYU&q.

Part VI. Codes of Conduct and Certification (Left Open Attending Future Developments)

444. This Part will provide an overview of both the rules of conduct pursuant to Article 2-*quater* of the Italian Data Protection Code (§1), the codes of conduct pursuant to Articles 40 and 41 GDPR (§2) and the certification schemes (§3) in the context of Italian data protection law. Lastly, this Part will address other instruments and sets of rules relevant to the Italian legal framework (§4).

In this respect, the main difference between the rules of conduct and the codes of conduct is that compliance with the former is an essential condition to lawfully process personal data, while compliance with the latter depends on the data controller or processor voluntarily adhering to the code.[632] In other words, the rules of conduct apply *ex lege* to all data controllers and processors whose activities fall within the relevant scope of application, while codes of conduct apply only on a voluntary basis.

Moreover, the enforcement of the rules of conduct is carried out by the GPDP, while the body responsible for the enforcement of the codes of conduct is regulated by the code itself, to be determined in compliance with Article 40 GDPR.

§1. Rules of Conduct

445. Pursuant to Article 2-*quater* of the Personal Data Protection Code, the GPDP shall promote the adoption of rules of conduct for the processing activities referred to in Article 6, paragraph 1, letters c)[633] and e),[634] Article 9, paragraph 4,[635]

632. Except for the cases in which a legitimate interest is considered by the code of conduct, pursuant to Art. 40, para. 2, lett. b), GDPR. *See* Bolognini & Pelino, *Codice della Disciplina Privacy* (Giuffrè Francis Lefebvre, 2019, at 291.
633. Article 6, para. 1, lett. c), GDPR, 'Processing is necessary for compliance with a legal obligation to which the controller is subject'.
634. Article 6, para. 1, lett. e), GDPR, 'Processing is necessary for the performance of a task carried out in the public interest or in the exercise of official authority vested in the controller'.
635. Article 9, para. 4, GDPR, titled 'Processing of genetic data, biometric data or data concerning health'.

and Chapter IX[636] of the GDPR. In addition, in doing so, the GPDP shall take into account the recommendations by the Council of Europe on the processing of personal data, as well as verify that such rules are in compliance with the provisions in force by also evaluating the observations submitted by relevant stakeholders, and contribute to ensuring that such rules are disseminated and abided by.

446. As for the codes of ethics and conduct in force before the direct applicability of the GDPR,[637] the 2018 reform of the Data Protection Code carried out with Legislative Decree 10 August 2018, no. 101[638] confirmed a 'third generation' regulatory approach, which should imply the involvement and consultation of the relevant stakeholders when forming rules which may have an impact on specific sectors or domains.

However, some authors hoped for a different approach to this matter.[639] This is because, in the past, the initiative and the ownership of drafting and approving codes of ethics and conduct were quite exclusively in charge of the GPDP. Indeed, even if relevant stakeholders were formally involved in these activities, the effective contribution of third parties and trade representatives to this end was extremely reduced.

---

636. Chapter IX GDPR contains provisions relating to specific processing situations, such as: freedom of expression and information; public access to official documents; processing of the national identification number; processing in the context of employment; safeguards and derogations relating to processing for archiving purposes in the public interest, scientific or historical research purposes or statistical purposes; obligation of professional secrecy or other equivalent obligations of secrecy; data protection rules of churches and religious associations. *See infra*, Parts IX and X.
637. *See* Annexes A1-A7 of the Personal Data Protection Code previously in force, namely:

   - the 'Code of ethics for the processing of personal data in the exercise the profession of journalism' (Author's translation) (Annex A1);
   - the 'Code of ethics and conduct for the processing of personal data for historical purpose' (Author's translation) (Annex A2, https://www.garanteprivacy.it/web/guest/home/docweb/-/docweb-display/docweb/1556419);
   - the 'Code of ethics and conduct for the processing of personal data for statistics and scientific research purposes within the national statistical system' (Author's translation) (Annex A3, https://www.garanteprivacy.it/web/guest/home/docweb/-/docweb-display/docweb/1556573);
   - the 'Code of ethics and conduct for the processing of personal data for statistics and scientific purposes' (Author's translation) (Annex A4, https://www.garanteprivacy.it/web/guest/home/docweb/-/docweb-display/docweb/1556635);
   - the 'Code of conduct for credit reporting systems operated by private entities regarding consumer credit, creditworthiness and punctuality in payments' (Author's translation) (Annex A5, https://www.garanteprivacy.it/web/guest/home/docweb/-/docweb-display/docweb/1556693);
   - the 'Code of ethics and conduct for the processing of personal data for the performance of investigations by defence counsel' (Author's translation) (Annex A6, https://www.garanteprivacy.it/web/guest/home/docweb/-/docweb-display/docweb/1565171);
   - the 'Code of Ethics and Conduct in Processing Personal Data for Business Information Purposes' (Official translation) (Annex A7, https://www.garanteprivacy.it/web/guest/home/docweb/-/docweb-display/docweb/4298343).

638. Containing provisions for the alignment of the Italian legislation to the GDPR.
639. *See*, e.g., Bolognini & Pelino, *Codice della Disciplina Privacy* (Giuffrè Francis Lefebvre, 2019, at 289.

447. A public consultation of at least sixty-day duration shall be launched on the draft rules of conduct.[640] Upon finalization of the consultation phase, the rules of conduct shall be approved by the GPDP pursuant to Article 154-*bis*, paragraph 1, letter b) of the Personal Data Protection Code, then published in the Official Journal of the Italian Republic and included in Annex A of the Italian Data Protection Code by a decree of the Minister of Justice.[641]

As for the codes of ethics and conduct previously in force, compliance with the provisions set out in the rules of conduct referred to in Article 2-*quater* of the Italian Data Protection Code shall be a fundamental precondition for the processing of personal data to be lawful and fair.[642]

448. In this respect, it should be noted that in accordance with Article 20 of D.Lgs. 101/ 2018, the codes of ethics and conduct contained in the Personal Data Protection Code previously in force are allowed to continue producing their effects (to the extent that such effects can be considered compliant with the GDPR) provided that specific requirements have been respected. In particular, the GPDP was required to ascertain their conformity within ninety days from the entry into force of D.Lgs. 101/2018.

In line with the above, the GPDP published updated provisions for each of the codes of ethics and conduct previously in force by qualifying some of them (namely, Annexes A1, A2, A3, A4 and A6) as 'Rules of conduct' pursuant to Article 2-*quater* of the Italian Data Protection Code.

449. Therefore, the rules of conduct currently in force in Italy are the following:

(i) The 'Rules of conduct for the processing of personal data in the exercise the profession of journalism' (A1).[643]
(ii) The 'Rules of conduct for the processing of personal data for the performance of investigations by defence counsel or for the exercise or defence of a legal claim' (A2).[644]
(iii) The 'Rules of conduct for the processing for archiving purposes in the public interest or historical research purposes' (A3).[645]
(iv) The 'Rules of conduct for the processing for statistics and scientific research purposes within the national statistical system' (A4).[646]

640. Paragraph 2 of Art. 2-*quater* of the Personal Data Protection Code.
641. Paragraph 3 of Art. 2-*quater* of the Personal Data Protection Code.
642. Paragraph 4 of Art. 2-*quater* of the Personal Data Protection Code.
643. Author's translation. Published in the Official Journal of the Italian Republic no. 3 of 4 Jan. 2019, https://www.garanteprivacy.it/web/guest/home/docweb/-/docweb-display/docweb/9067692.
644. Author's translation. Published in the Official Journal of the Italian Republic no. 12 of 15 Jan. 2019, https://www.garanteprivacy.it/web/guest/home/docweb/-/docweb-display/docweb/9069653.
645. Author's translation. Published in the Official Journal of the Italian Republic no. 12 of 15 Jan. 2019, https://www.garanteprivacy.it/web/guest/home/docweb/-/docweb-display/docweb/9069661.
646. Author's translation. Published in the Official Journal of the Italian Republic no. 11 of 14 Jan. 2019, https://www.garanteprivacy.it/web/guest/home/docweb/-/docweb-display/docweb/9069677.

(v) The 'Rules of conduct for the processing for statistics and scientific purposes' (A5).[647]

450. Starting from the date of publication in the Official Journal of the Italian Republic of the above-mentioned rules of conduct, the corresponding codes of ethics and conduct ceased to be applicable. The new rules of conduct do not fundamentally alter the corresponding provisions contained in the codes of ethics and conduct, as they have basically been updated only from a formal perspective with the appropriate references to the new European regulatory framework provided with the GDPR. The GPDP, nevertheless, has made some further minor changes to the new rules (e.g., by deleting or rephrasing certain provisions) in light of the different approach required from data controllers under the GDPR, therefore taking into account the principles of accountability and data protection by design and by default.

451. According to Article 166, paragraphs 2 and 3, of the Personal Data Protection Code, the violation of the provisions of the rules of conduct shall entail the imposition of an administrative fine pursuant to Article 83(5) of the GDPR (up to 20,000,000 EUR, or in the case of an undertaking, up to 4% of the total worldwide annual turnover of the preceding financial year, whichever is higher).

§2. Codes of Conduct in Force under Italian Law

452. The 2018 reform carried out with D.Lgs. no. 101/2018 provided a different approach for Annex A5 ('Code of conduct for credit reporting systems operated by private entities regarding consumer credit, creditworthiness and punctuality in payments') and Annex A7 ('Code of Ethics and Conduct in Processing Personal Data for Business Information Purposes') of the Italian Personal Data Protection Code previously in force, by requiring their conversion in codes of conduct pursuant to Articles 40 and 41 of the GDPR.

453. Both for Annexes A5 and A7 of the Personal Data Protection Code in force prior to the 2018 reform, Article 20, paragraph 1, of D.Lgs. no. 101/2018 clarified that they are allowed to continue producing their effect, provided that:

(i) An amended or extended version of the existing code of conduct – drafted pursuant to Article 40, paragraph 2, GDPR – has been submitted by the trade associations and other bodies representing categories concerned to the GPDP within six months of the entry into force of the D.Lgs. no. 101/2018.
(ii) The approval process has been concluded within six months of the code of conduct first being brought to the attention of the GPDP.

647. Author's translation. Published in the Official Journal of the Italian Republic no. 11 of 14 Jan. 2019, https://www.garanteprivacy.it/web/guest/home/docweb/-/docweb-display/docweb/9069637.

454. Failure to comply with the above-mentioned requirements results – under Article 20, paragraph 2, of Legislative Decree 101/2018 – in the loss of effectiveness of these codes of conduct. However, the procedure required by Article 20, paragraph 11, of D.Lgs. no. 101/2018 has been duly and timely followed by all the parties involved. Therefore, the updated versions of both the 'Code of Conduct for Credit Reporting Systems Operated by Private Entities Regarding Consumer Credit, Creditworthiness and Punctuality in Payments'[648] (official translation) and the 'Code of Conduct in Processing Personal Data for Business Information Purposes'[649] (Author's translation) are now currently in force, as better explained below.

455. The 'Code of Conduct for Credit Reporting Systems Operated by Private Entities Regarding Consumer Credit, Creditworthiness and Punctuality in Payments' (hereinafter, the 'Code for Credit Reporting Systems') was approved and published on 12 September 2019. However, its effectiveness was subject to the conclusion of the accreditation process of the monitoring body, and the final version of the Code for Credit Reporting Systems was approved on 6 October 2022.[650] It applies to the processing of personal data carried out through credit reporting systems by private entities, used for the purpose of consumed credit or for the purpose of evaluating creditworthiness and punctuality in payments.

This can be the case, for example, of a company which acts as a data controller for the processing of personal data collected in the context of credit relationships or requests and which participates in a credit reporting system in order to be allowed to use the personal data contained in this system. Indeed, a mutual exchange of information between the participants can be identified in the credit reporting system, as each of them undertakes to systematically provide and feed the system with records and information on its credit relationships and requests.[651] Except for entities pursuing the activity of debt recovery, companies participating in a credit reporting system may include banks, financial intermediaries and other private entities.

The processing of personal data contained in a credit reporting system can be carried out by the participants only for purposes related to credit protection and its risk control, as well as for assessing the financial situation and the creditworthiness of the data subjects or for preventing the risk of fraud or identity theft (Article 3 of the

648. GPDP, *Codice di condotta per i sistemi informativi gestiti da soggetti privati in tema di crediti al consumo, affidabilità e puntualità nei pagamenti*, 12.9.2019, doc. web no. 9141941, https://www.gpdp.it/web/guest/home/docweb/-/docweb-display/docweb/9141941.

649. GPDP, *Deliberazione del 12 giugno 2019 – Codice di condotta per il trattamento dei dati personali in materia di informazioni commerciali*, 12.6.2019, doc. web no. 9119868, https://www.gpdp.it/web/guest/home/docweb/-/docweb-display/docweb/9119868.

650. GPDP, *Accreditamento dell'organismo di monitoraggio e approvazione del Codice di condotta per i sistemi di informazione creditizia in tema di credito al consumo, affidabilità e puntualità nei pagamenti*, doc. web no. 9818201, https://www.garanteprivacy.it/web/guest/home/docweb/-/docweb-display/docweb/9818201.

651. Bolognini & Pelino, *Codice della Disciplina Privacy* (Giuffrè Francis Lefebvre, 2019), at 51.

Code for Credit Reporting Systems). Any other purpose is not allowed. Only necessary, relevant data not exceeding those necessary for credit risk assessment purposes may be processed.

In order to facilitate the proper functioning of the financial and credit market, the records may be processed without the data subject's consent on the basis of the legitimate interest of the companies participating in the credit reporting systems (Article 6, paragraph 1, of the Code for Credit Reporting Systems).

456. Among the innovations laid down in the Code for Credit Reporting Systems, the institution of a monitoring body seems particularly relevant. This independent body oversees the work of credit reporting systems (cf. Annex 4 of the Code for Credit Reporting Systems). The accreditation of a monitoring body of the Code for Credit Reporting Systems was approved by the GPDP on 6 October 2022,[652] even if the trade associations which promoted the adoption of the Code for Credit Reporting Systems have undertaken to respect the rules and principles set out in the code from the date of its approval.

Another relevant innovation to the new Code for Credit Reporting Systems is the increase of transparency in decisions, as in the event of a denial of credit based on automated analysis; the data subject may request to know the logic underlying the operation of the algorithms (Article 10, paragraph 1, letter d, of the Code for Credit Reporting Systems).

Additional measures are also envisaged to protect data security, such as the pseudonymization of personal data for the training of algorithms and the periodic revision (at least every two years) of the statistical analysis models as well as the algorithms used.

457. The 'Code of Conduct in Processing Personal Data for Business Information Purposes' (hereinafter the 'Code for Business Information Purposes') was approved by the GPDP on 12 June 2019. However, as for the Code for Credit Reporting Systems, its effectiveness was subject to the conclusion of the accreditation *iter* requested by Article 41 GDPR for the corresponding monitoring body, and the final version of the Code for Business Information Purposes was published only on 29 April 2021.[653]

The Code for Business Information Purposes has been proposed by the relevant trade association (*Associazione Nazionale tra le Imprese di Informazioni Commerciali e di Gestione del Credito*, hereinafter 'ANCIC').

652. According to Annex 4 of the approved Code for Credit Reporting Systems, the monitoring body will be external and composed of three members, one of whom will be designated by the CNCU (*Consiglio nazionale consumatori e utenti*); another who will be unanimously designated by the operators adhering to this code of conduct and will act as vice-chairman of the monitoring body; the third one will be appointed by agreement between the latter and CNCU unanimously, and will hold the role of president of the monitoring body. The appointment, which is non-renewable, will last five years.

653. GPDP, *Provvedimento del 29 aprile 2021 – Approvazione del Codice di condotta per il trattamento dei dati personali effettuato a fini di informazione commerciale*, 19.4.2021, doc. web no. 9586215, https://www.gpdp.it/web/guest/home/docweb/-/docweb-display/docweb/9586215.

Under the Code for Business Information Purposes, companies offering information on the commercial reliability of entrepreneurs and managers are able to process personal data of registered persons (the persons to whom the business information service refers) on the basis of their legitimate interest, without requesting the consent of the data subject. The companies undertake, however, to guarantee greater protection to data subjects, adequately informing them about the processing carried out and ensuring that they can fully exercise their rights under applicable data protection legislation, such as objecting to the processing, correcting or updating their data. Pursuant to Article 4, paragraph 1, of the Code for Business Information Purposes, in order to provide information for commercial purposes, the business information service provider[654] may collect personal data from the registered person, from publicly and generally accessible sources or from other parties authorized by law to distribute and provide information.

Following the approval of the requirements for the accreditation of monitoring bodies published by the GPDP on 10 June 2020,[655] on 11 February 2021, the GPDP published the formal accreditation of a monitoring body arranged by ANCIC as the body in charge of verifying the observance of the Code for Business Information Purposes.[656]

The Code for Business Information Purposes entrusts the accredited monitoring body, among other things, with the task of verifying members' compliance with the code and handling the resolution of complaints. Pursuant to Article 12 of the Code for Business Information Purposes, the monitoring body consists of five members with a five-year non-renewable term of office. Each member of the monitoring body must guarantee an adequate level of competence and in-depth knowledge of business information and data protection, as well as ensure maximum impartiality and independence and avoid any situation of conflict of interest.

458. The third code of conduct approved by the GPDP since the GDPR entered into force is the 'Code of Conduct on the use of Health Data for Educational and Scientific Publication Purposes' proposed by the Veneto Region. This code of conduct was published on the website of the GPDP on 14 January 2021.[657] Its main purpose is to identify the modalities for the processing of health data of the data

654. A business information service provider is defined in Art. 2, para. 2, lett. f), of the Code of Conduct in Processing Personal Data for Business Information Purposes as the private entity which, pursuant to Art. 134 of the Italian Law on Public Security (R.D. 773/1931) and to Ministerial Decree 269/2010, provides the customer with a commercial information service.

655. GPDP, *Requisiti di accreditamento degli organismi di monitoraggio dei codici di condotta – 10 giugno 2020*, doc. web no. 9432569, https://www.gpdp.it/web/guest/home/docweb/-/docweb-display/docweb/9432569.

656. GPDP, *Accreditamento dell'organismo di monitoraggio del codice di condotta in materia di informazioni commerciali – 11 febbraio 2021*, doc. web no. 9565426, https://www.gpdp.it/web/guest/home/docweb/-/docweb-display/docweb/9565426. The monitoring body for the code of conduct at stake is 'ODM – Organismo di monitoraggio del Codice di condotta sulle informazioni commerciali'. Further information are available on the website https://www.odminformazionicommerciali.it/.

657. GPDP, *Regione Veneto – Codice di condotta per l'utilizzo di dati sulla salute a fini didattici e di pubblicazione scientifica*, doc. web no. 9535402 (14.01.2021), https://www.gpdp.it/web/guest/home/docweb/-/docweb-display/docweb/9535402.

subjects, also through anonymization or pseudonymization techniques, carried out by the data controllers and other participating entities in order for healthcare professionals to draft documents for educational or scientific purposes (e.g., theses, presentations for conferences, position papers, case studies for educational purposes, etc.).

459. Finally, on 5 May 2022, the GPDP announced the drafting of a new code of conduct for telemarketing against unsolicited commercial calls. Following a first meeting with representatives of the enterprises which promote their products via telemarketing campaigns and other stakeholders such as contact centres, list providers and consumers, an advisory committee was set up to provide a first draft of this code of conduct.[658] On 9 March 2023, the GPDP approved the Code of Conduct for telemarketing and teleselling activities promoted by the above-mentioned stakeholders, even if the Code will only become effective once the accreditation of the monitoring body has been completed.[659]

Companies adhering to the Code of Conduct for telemarketing and teleselling activities undertake to adopt specific measures in order to guarantee the correctness and legitimacy of data processing operations carried out throughout the telemarketing chain. They will have to collect specific consents for each relevant purpose (marketing, profiling, etc.), as well as duly inform the data subjects about the purposes for which their data are being processed, ensuring that they can fully exercise their rights according to privacy law. As stated by the GPDP in its press release announcing the approval of the Code of Conduct for telemarketing and teleselling activities, rules have also been introduced to counter the phenomenon of abusive call centres (since, according to the Code, the contracts entered into by the operator with the service provider must provide for a penalty or non-payment of commission for each sale of services made as a result of promotional contact without consent). Companies will also be required to carry out a data protection impact assessment if they carry out automated processing, including profiling, which involves a systematic and global analysis of personal data.

§3. Certification Schemes under Italian Law

460. The GDPR, pursuant to its Article 42, paragraph 1, provides that Member States and the Commission should encourage the establishment of certification mechanisms, seals and marks to demonstrate compliance with the GDPR. Pursuant to Article 43, paragraph 1, letter b), GDPR, if the accreditation is carried out by the national accreditation body in accordance with ISO/IEC 17065/2012, the additional requirements set by the competent supervisory authority – for Italy, the GPDP – shall also apply.

658. GPDP, *Telemarketing: al via i lavori per il codice di condotta*, 5.5.2022, doc. web no. 9767711, https://www.garanteprivacy.it/home/docweb/-/docweb-display/docweb/9767711.

659. GPDP, *Telemarketing: il Garante privacy approva il Codice di condotta. Le regole entreranno in vigore una volta costituito l'Organismo di monitoraggio*, doc. web no. 9868685, https://www.garanteprivacy.it/home/docweb/-/docweb-display/docweb/9868685.

461. Pursuant to Article 2-*septiesdecies* of the Personal Data Protection Code, in Italy, the national accreditation body referred to in Article 43, paragraph 1, letter b), GDPR is the single national accreditation body: in Italy, this body is Accredia.[660]

Accredia is set up in accordance with Regulation (EC) 765/2008[661] and is subject to the GPDP's power to directly take up the exercise of the relevant functions, following a resolution to be published in the Official Journal of the Italian Republic, also with regard to one or more types of processing, in case the single national accreditation body is deemed to be seriously in breach of its duties. Furthermore, without prejudice to what is stated in Article 2-*septiesdecies* of the Personal Data Protection Code, the GPDP and Accredia signed an agreement on 20 March 2019[662] aimed at facilitating the exchange of information regarding the accreditation and certification activities provided for by the GDPR, as also with the aim of enhancing their mutual competences.

462. On 29 July 2020, the GPDP approved the Additional Accreditation Requirements for Certification Bodies pursuant to Article 43, paragraph 1, letter b), GDPR,[663] after receiving a favourable opinion from the EDPB. The additional requirements state that Accredia shall verify that the certification bodies meet criteria of good reputation, independence and impartiality by certifying the absence of conflicts of interest with the subjects wishing to be certified. In addition, certification bodies must be equipped with qualified and constantly updated personnel and this can be ensured by adopting adequate processes for handling complaints which may occur, in addition to implementing periodic surveillance procedures on certified products, processes, and services.

463. For the time being, the GPDP has not recognized any certification scheme.[664]

However, the GPDP – together with Accredia – published FAQs regarding accreditation and certification under the GDPR.[665] The FAQs provide useful clarifications for data controllers and processors, both in the public and private sector,

660. Accredia official website may be found at the following URL: https://www.accredia.it/en.
661. Regulation (EC) no. 765/2008 of the European Parliament and of the Council of 9 Jul. 2008 setting out the requirements for accreditation and market surveillance relating to the marketing of products and repealing Regulation (EEC) no. 339/93, OJ L 218, 13.8.2008.
662. GPDP, *Convenzione Garante – Accredia 2019*, 20.3.2019, doc. web no. 9099622, https://www.garanteprivacy.it/web/guest/home/docweb/-/docweb-display/docweb/9099622.
663. Author's translation. Published in the Official Journal of the Italian Republic no. 201 of 12 Aug. 2020, https://www.garanteprivacy.it/web/guest/home/docweb/-/docweb-display/docweb/9445086.
664. Despite the fact that the GPDP has not yet recognized any certification scheme, Accredia clarifies on its official website that there are several privacy certifications issued by the accreditation bodies which are currently used in the market (i.e., certification for products and services according to the ISO/IEC 17065 standard, certification for management systems according to the ISO/IEC 17021-1 standard, certification for individuals according to the ISO/IEC 17024 standard). *See*: *Accredia – Certificazioni oggi*, https://www.accredia.it/certificazioni-oggi/.
665. GPDP, *FAQ – Certificazione e accreditamento ai sensi del GDPR – Booklet*, doc. web no. 9681327, https://www.garanteprivacy.it/web/guest/home/docweb/-/docweb-display/docweb/9681327.

wishing to obtain certification in order to demonstrate their commitment to data protection obligations and the compliance of the processing activities with the requirements of the GDPR.

§4. Other Instruments and Sets of Rules Relevant Within the Italian Legal Framework

464. Among the other instruments that are relevant within the Italian legal framework (and to the scope of the present Chapter), it is worth mentioning the Code of Conduct[666] and the Security, Trust, Assurance and Risk (STAR) programme developed by Cloud Security Alliance (CSA), which has acquired a central role in the Italian security landscape for cloud service providers (CSPs).

At the time of writing, the CSA Code of Conduct is undergoing Article 40 of the GDPR approval process with the '*Commission nationale de l'informatique et des libertés*' (i.e., the French Supervisory Authority, commonly known as 'CNIL'), that has been identified as the lead authority for the CSA Code of Conduct. Although the CSA Code of Conduct has not yet been assessed by the GPDP pursuant to Article 40 of the GDPR, the STAR programme developed by CSA has been recognized by the AgID[667] (and then by the Italian National Cybersecurity Agency – ACN) as the only alternative to ISO 27001 certification (integrated with ISO 27017 and 27018) as a means to certify the security of SaaS providers for the Italian public administration.

465. In greater detail, the Three-Year Plan for Information Technology in Public Administration 2017–2019 – which was approved by means of a D.P.C.M. of 31 May 2017 as part of the strategy for the development of cloud solutions for the Italian Public Administration – provides that specific rules and procedures need to be defined for the qualification of CSPs in the public sector. The strategic objectives of this Three-Year Plan in the context of physical infrastructures are the following:

(i) boosting the quality of the services offered in terms of security, resilience, energy efficiency and service continuity;
(ii) creating a cloud environment for the Italian Public Administration (by upgrading existing internal resources or by resorting to the resources offered by qualified external parties);

666. Cloud Security Alliance, *Code of Conduct for GDPR Compliance* (September 2020), https://cloudsecurityalliance.org/artifacts/cloud-security-alliance-code-of-conduct-for-gdpr-compliance/.

667. AgID is the technical agency of the Presidency of the Council of Ministers, that is entrusted with the task of ensuring the implementation of the objectives of the Italian Digital Agenda and of contributing to the fostering of digital innovation and economic growth, also in collaboration with international, national and local institutions and bodies. Additional information is available on AgID official website, https://www.agid.gov.it/it/agenzia. Concerning AgID, *see also supra* Introduction, Ch. 2, §2, as well as Introduction, Ch. 4, §1.

(iii) achieving efficiency and cost savings, thanks to data centre consolidation and the migration to cloud services.[668]

466. In this context (and in order to achieve the objectives identified above), on 9 April 2018, AgID set out two specific sets of requirements, one (circular no. 2) for the qualification of CSPs for the Public Administration (IaaS and PaaS services)[669] and the second one (circular no. 3) for the qualification of SaaS services.[670] All services that pass the qualification procedure defined by AgID are published in the so-called Cloud Marketplace, which collects the list of services and infrastructures that meet the prescribed security and reliability requirements (thereby supporting the Public Administration in identifying the services that meet the requirements defined by AgID).[671]

467. In particular, the second set of requirements for the qualification of SaaS services provides that, in order to successfully complete the qualification procedure, the SaaS provider needs to declare that it is certified according to the ISO/IEC 27001 standard (integrated with the controls of ISO/IEC 27017 and ISO/IEC 27018 standards). As an alternative, the SaaS provider needs to: (i) perform the CSA STAR Self-Assessment with reference to the service it intends to qualify (in the version known as CAIQ, which stands for 'Consensus Assessments Initiative Questionnaire'), (ii) produce the relevant documentation, and (iii) make it publicly available on its website.

The purpose of the above requirements is to demonstrate the SaaS provider's ability to deliver the proposed services while respecting some specific requirements in terms of security, privacy, and data protection.[672]

In this respect, it is worth recalling that the CSA STAR Self-Assessment is an instrument developed by CSA to document the security controls implemented by CSPs, thereby supporting their customers in assessing the level of security provided by the CSPs they currently use or that they are considering engaging. The CSA STAR provides several levels of assurance that CSPs may wish to provide. Under the version known as CAIQ (which, as mentioned above, is the relevant one in the qualification process developed by AgID for SaaS providers), CSPs submit the

668. These strategic objectives are set out at point 3.1.2. of the Three-Year Plan for Information Technology in Public Administration 2017–2019, https://docs.italia.it/italia/piano-triennale-ict/pianotriennale-ict-doc/it/2017-2019/doc/03_infrastrutture-fisiche.html#data-center-e-cloud.

669. AgID, *Circolare no. 2 del 9 aprile 2018*, 9.4.2018, https://cloud-italia.readthedocs.io/projects/cloud-italia-circolari/it/latest/circolari/CSP/circolare_qualificazione_CSP_v1.2.html.

670. AgID, *Circolare no. 3 del 9 aprile 2018*, 9.4.2018, https://cloud-italia.readthedocs.io/projects/cloud-italia-circolari/it/latest/circolari/SaaS/circolare_qualificazione_SaaS_v_4.12.27.html.

671. The 'Cloud Marketplace' is available at the following link: https://catalogocloud.agid.gov.it/.

672. This requirement can be consulted at the following page: https://cloud-italia.readthedocs.io/projects/cloud-italia-circolari/it/latest/circolari/SaaS/allegato_docs/sicurezza.html#.

CAIQ to document compliance with the Cloud Controls Matrix (i.e., a cybersecurity control framework for cloud computing). This information is then made publicly available, thereby providing users visibility over the security controls implemented by CSPs.[673]

468. Starting from January 2023, the ACN has undertaken the role of qualifying cloud services for the Public Administration, therefore taking over from AgID (although the qualifications already obtained pursuant to circulars no. 2 and 3 are still valid for a transitional period). By means of Resolution no. 307 of 18 January 2022,[674] the ACN (in agreement with the Department of Digital Transformation) has defined the minimum requirements and characteristics that digital infrastructures and cloud services used by Public Administrations need to ensure, in addition to defining the new qualification process for the provision of cloud services to the Public Administration. Attachment 1 of the said Resolution defines the requirements for the qualification of cloud service providers for the Public Administration based on four different levels of qualification (from 1 to 4). The CSA STAR Self-Assessment retains its importance under this new set of requirements since it is listed as one of the certifications to be presented by cloud service providers in order to achieve levels 1 and 3.

673. Additional information on the CSA STAR Self-Assessment is available on CSA official website, https://cloudsecurityalliance.org/star/#tab_levelOne.

674. ACN, *Resolution 307 n.2022*, 18.1.2022, https://assets.innovazione.gov.it/1642694131-det_307_cloud_ulteriorilerqc_20220118.pdf. Attachment 1 of the said Resolution is available at the following link: https://assets.innovazione.gov.it/1642754054-all1det307acn.pdf.

Part VII. International Transfers

Chapter 1. General Principles (Refer to the GDPR Provisions + Add National DPA Opinions, etc.)

§1. DATA TRANSFERS IN GENERAL

469. The Italian normative framework in relation to international data transfers is essentially aligned with the EU framework. Data transfers are indeed not subject to (additional) specific restrictions beyond those set out under the GDPR.

At the same time, it may be worth recalling that the transfer of personal data to third countries in violation of Articles 45, 46 or 49 of the GDPR may, under certain circumstances, amount to a criminal offence pursuant to Article 167, paragraph 3 of the Personal Data Protection Code. The said Article indeed provides that 'any person who, with a view to gain for themselves or another or with intent to cause harm to the data subject, causes harm to the data subject by transferring the personal data to a third country or a [sic] international organization in cases other than those permitted under Articles 45, 46 or 49 GDPR shall be punished by imprisonment for one to three years, unless the offence is more serious'.

470. Moreover, as outlined in Part IX, Chapter 1, *infra*, Article 137 of the Personal Data Protection Code provides that the requirements set out in Chapter V of the GDPR concerning transfers of personal data to third countries or international organizations do not apply to the processing activities conducted for journalistic purposes and other intellectual work referred to in Article 136 of the Personal Data Protection Code. Article 137 of the Personal Data Protection Code, therefore, provides a derogation from the applicability of the provisions on international data transfers set out under the GDPR since those provisions and the limitations established therein would not be compatible with the exercise of journalistic activities and the other activities that fall under the scope of Article 136 of the Personal Data Protection Code.[675]

675. Bolognini & Pelino, *Codice della Disciplina Privacy* (Giuffrè Francis Lefebvre, 2019), at 475.

§2. Decisions Adopted by the GPDP Concerning Data Transfers

I. Pre-Schrems II

471. Moving to the position adopted by the GPDP in relation to international transfers, it is worth recalling that, in 2019, the GPDP ruled that Mybestoption S.r.l. (i.e., a company engaged by another entity acting as data controller in relation to the provision of telemarketing services) failed to comply with the data controller's instructions, since Mybestoption S.r.l. had outsourced some of the activities that had been entrusted to it by the data controller to another entity established in Albania (Europe Service Group S.r.l.) in the absence of the data controller's authorization.[676] According to the GPDP, this not only led to the unauthorized (and therefore unlawful) sharing of personal data with Europe Service Group S.r.l. but also to a transfer of personal data to a third-country entity in the absence of appropriate safeguards. In reaching this conclusion, the GPDP noted that the country of destination (i.e., Albania) had not received an adequacy decision from the European Commission and that no appropriate safeguards had been identified since the transfer in question was carried out in the absence of the data controller's authorization. Moreover, none of the derogations that apply in specific situations (and to which data controllers can resort in the absence of adequacy decisions and appropriate safeguards) was found to be applicable in the case in question, considering that:

(i) data subjects were not aware of the said transfer and were therefore unable to express their specific and informed consent to have their personal data shared with a third-party entity established outside the European Economic Area;
(ii) the transfer in question was also not *necessary* for the performance of the contract between the data controller (which did not authorize such transfer) and the data subjects (which were not aware of the transfer) since the outsourcing of that activity to Europe Service Group S.r.l was a mere business choice taken by Mybestoption S.r.l.

II. Post-Schrems II

472. Moving to the so-called post-Schrems II[677] landscape, the GPDP fined Luigi Bocconi University of Milan for the violation of several provisions, including provisions on international data transfer, for the use of a proctoring software provided by a company based in the United States (Respondus, Inc.) which had been implemented by the University in order to monitor students when taking remote

676. GPDP, decision no. 223 of 18 Dec. 2019, https://www.garanteprivacy.it/web/guest/home/docweb/-/docweb-display/docweb/9220727.

677. Case C-311/18, *Data Protection Commissioner v. Facebook Ireland Ltd., Maximilian Schrems*, 17.7.2020, ECLI:EU:C:2020:559.

exams during the COVID-19 pandemic.[678] Among the several violations found in the aforementioned decision, the GPDP concluded that Bocconi University had unlawfully transferred students' personal data to the United States by using the software, in violation of Articles 44 and 46 GDPR. The GPDP quoted the Schrems II decision in recalling that when implementing the Standard Contractual Clauses, the data exporter is required to verify whether the law of the third country of destination guarantees adequate protection of the transferred personal data on a case-by-case basis, implementing (where necessary) supplementary measures.

In the case in question, the GPDP first detected a non-conformity in the content of the Standard Contractual Clauses[679] signed between the parties since the technical and organizational measures implemented by the software provider were not listed in Appendix 2 of the Standard Contractual Clauses but were only made available upon request (to be submitted by the data controller via a specific online form). According to the GPDP, the description of the technical and organizational measures carried out in this manner led to uncertainties around the technical measures implemented by the software provider, which may be subject to changes over time without the knowledge of the data controller.

Moreover, the GPDP concluded that there was no evidence that the exporter had carried out an assessment as to the effectiveness of the Standard Contractual Clauses in guaranteeing compliance with the obligations undertaken by the data importer in light of the legislation of the third country to which the data were transferred. In particular, considering that the personal data in question were transferred to the United States (i.e., a third country whose national law, as established by the Court of Justice in Schrems II, does not guarantee a level of protection essentially equivalent to that offered in the EU), Bocconi University should have assessed and implemented, where necessary, additional measures in order to bring the level of protection of the data transferred up to the EU standard of 'essential equivalence'. In this respect, the GPDP also noted that the encryption system to which the personal data in question were subject was unable to provide an adequate level of protection since the encryption of the personal data in question took place *after* the processing of such data by the software provider, which needed to access the data in clear text in order to be able to examine the videos relating to the exams. The encryption system was, therefore, only implemented at the end of the processing activity conducted by the software provider.

Along the same lines, the pseudonymization of the personal data transferred abroad was not considered by the GPDP to be an effective measure in filling the gaps in the protection of personal data, since pseudonymization differs from anonymization and still amounts to a processing of personal data.

---

678. GPDP, *Ordinanza ingiunzione nei confronti di Università Commerciale 'Luigi Bocconi' di Milano – 16 settembre 2021*, 16.9.2021, doc. web no. 9703988, https://www.garanteprivacy.it/home/docweb/-/docweb-display/docweb/9703988.

679. In the case in question, the Standard Contractual Clauses were those set out in 2010 by the European Commission: Commission Decision of 5 Feb. 2010 on standard contractual clauses for the transfer of personal data to processors established in third countries under Directive 95/46/EC of the European Parliament and of the Council (notified under document C(2010) 593), OJ L 39, 12.2.2010.

Based on the above, the GPDP concluded that Bocconi University had transferred personal data to a third country (i.e., the United States) without having proven that it had verified and ensured that the transfer in question was carried out in compliance with the conditions set forth in Chapter V of the GDPR. This violation was deemed by the GPDP to be particularly serious, especially considering that the data transferred also included special categories of personal data (in particular, biometric data).[680] It is worth mentioning that, in determining the amount of the administrative fine, the GPDP took into consideration the fact that the Schrems II judgment was issued when the processing operations in question were already in place, that the principles set out in the said judgment may, in some cases, be complex to implement and, more generally, that the legal framework for international transfers is still evolving.[681]

473. Similar considerations were expressed by the GPDP on 9 June 2021[682] in relation to the application for mobile devices 'IO' ('App IO', i.e., one of the digital tools identified by the Italian Government for obtaining the digital Covid Certificate or 'Green Pass') managed by PagoPA. After having assessed the functionalities and the compliance posture offered by the App IO, the GPDP ordered – pursuant to Article 58, paragraph 2, letter f), GDPR – the provisional limitation of certain data processing activities performed by means of the said app since they entailed an interaction with services offered by Google LLC and Mixpanel Inc. and therefore resulted in the transfer of personal data to third parties.

In particular, the GPDP noted that the transfer of personal data that was triggered using the services offered by those providers (which in turn make use of other third-party providers located outside the EU) was not sufficiently regulated since no evidence was produced in relation to the implementation of adequate safeguards pursuant to Articles 44 and following of the GDPR.

In this decision, the GPDP went further in stating that the aforementioned consideration applies regardless of the specific location of the IT systems on which the personal data of IO App users are located since, as noted by the European Data Protection Board in its Recommendations 01/2020 on measures that supplement transfer tools to ensure compliance with the level of protection of personal data offered in the EU,[683] remote access to such systems by entities outside the EU is also considered to be a transfer.

The limitation to the processing of personal data was later lifted by the GPDP,[684] following the implementation by the data controller of several technical measures

---

680. GPDP, *supra* n. 679, para. 3.7.

681. *Ibid.*, para. 6.

682. GPDP, *Provvedimento correttivo nei confronti di PagoPA sul funzionamento dell'App IO – 9 giugno 2021*, 9.6.2021, doc. web no. 9668051, https://www.garanteprivacy.it/web/guest/home/docweb/-/docweb-display/docweb/9668051.

683. European Data Protection Board, Recommendations 01/2020 on measures that supplement transfer tools to ensure compliance with the EU level of protection of personal data, 18.6.2021), https://edpb.europa.eu/our-work-tools/our-documents/recommendations/recommendations-012020-measures-supplement-transfer_en.

684. GPDP, *Provvedimento del 16 giugno 2021*, 6.6.2021, doc. web no. 9670061, https://www.garanteprivacy.it/web/guest/home/docweb/-/docweb-display/docweb/9670061; GPDP, *Provvedimento*

that had been identified in order to protect the privacy of users of the IO App. In particular, PagoPA deactivated a number of unnecessary services powered by Google LLC and committed to minimizing the amount of user data that was transmitted to Mixpanel Inc. In lifting the said limitation, the GPDP also took into account the fact that the data controller specified that they were in the process of stipulating the new set of Standard Contractual Clauses issued by the European Commission on 4 June 2021[685] and that they were expected to be signed shortly. On this latter point, the GPDP recalled that the implementation of the new Standard Contractual Clauses does not exempt the data exporter from assessing the effectiveness of such measure, nor does it exempt them from the requirement to adopt supplementary measures that may be deemed necessary if the data exporter concludes that the laws of the third country in question prevent the data importer from complying with the guarantees enshrined in those clauses.

The GPDP has also issued different decisions concerning the international data transfers triggered by the use of Google Analytics, declaring the unlawfulness of such transfers. In particular, on 9 June 2022, the GPDP reprimanded a website operator (Caffeina Media S.r.l.) for the unlawful transfer put in place by means of Google Analytics (specifically, from Google Ireland acting as processor on behalf of the website operator to Google LLC, acting as sub-processor, based in the US) and ordered the company to implement appropriate safeguards pursuant to Chapter V of the GDPR (within ninety days) or otherwise suspend the transfer.[686]

In reaching this conclusion, the GPDP first noted that the use of Google Analytics does involve the collection (and consequent transfer) of personal information. The GPDP, in fact, pointed out that the IP address qualifies as 'personal data' under the GDPR to the extent that this can be used to indirectly identify a specific user (through the identification of the electronic device used by the latter). Moreover, so-called IP-Anonymisation (whereby a part of users' IP address is truncated so as to limit identification capabilities) was deemed by the GPDP to be a form a pseudonymisation (rather than anonymisation) since the truncated IP address could still be used by Google to re-identify a specific user by combing such IP address with other pieces of information in its possession.

The GPDP also refused the application of a risk-based approach and noted that the exporter is not exempted from its obligation to ensure adequate protection to the transferred personal data (where necessary, by implementing supplementary measures) based on the (allegedly) low and residual probability of receiving access requests from US public authorities. In this respect, the GPDP also noted that, based on the White Paper released by the US Government in September 2020 (titled 'Information on U.S. Privacy Safeguards Relevant to SCCs and Other EU Legal Bases for EU-U.S. data Transfers after Schrems II') and on the 'Transparency report

---

recante garanzie per l'utilizzo dell'App IO per recuperare le certificazioni verdi Covid-19 – 17 giugno 2021, 17.6.2021, doc. web no. 9670670, https://www.garanteprivacy.it/web/guest/home/docweb/-/docweb-display/docweb/9670670.

685. Commission Implementing Decision (EU) 2021/914 of 4 Jun. 2021 on standard contractual clauses for the transfer of personal data to third countries pursuant to Regulation (EU) 2016/679 of the European Parliament and of the Council, C/2021/3972, OJ L 199, 7.6.2021.

686. GPDP, *Provvedimento del 9 giugno 2022*, doc. web no. 9782890, https://www.garanteprivacy.it/web/guest/home/docweb/-/docweb-display/docweb/9782890.

on United States national security requests for user information' published by Google on its website,[687] it appears that also 'non-content metadata', such as IP addresses, may be subject to disclosure requests by US public authorities.

As for the supplementary measures implemented by the data controller, the GPDP concluded that the encryption solution adopted by Google was an insufficient technical measure since Google LLC (as the relevant importer) was in possession of the encryption key. This entails that US authorities could request Google LLC to disclose such encryption key together with the encrypted data, thereby eliminating the effectiveness of the encryption in safeguarding data from similar requests.

Lastly, the GPDP noted that the asymmetry in bargaining power faced by the company *vis-à-vis* the contractual and technical measures unilaterally determined and 'imposed' by Google to the company does not relieve the website operator, as data controller, from its obligations under the GDPR pursuant to the accountability principle. The responsibility to autonomously determine the safeguards to be implemented on its processing operations and make the relevant determinations in relation to the transfer of personal data to third countries, therefore, lies on the part of the data controller.

474. Similar considerations were also expressed by the GPDP in relation to the use of Google Analytics made by Il Meteo S.r.l. (in its decision of 7 July 2022)[688] and by Fastweb S.p.A. (in its decision of 21 July 2022).[689]

§3. TRANSFERS CARRIED OUT BY COMPETENT AUTHORITIES IN THE CONTEXT OF THE PREVENTION, INVESTIGATION, DETECTION AND PROSECUTION OF CRIMINAL OFFENCES OR THE EXECUTION OF CRIMINAL PENALTIES

475. With Legislative Decree 18 May 2018, no. 51 (within this Chapter referred to as the 'Decree'), Italy transposed Directive (EU) 2016/680[690] (within this Chapter referred to as the 'Directive').

The Decree lays down, *inter alia*, the methods for processing and storing personal data, the rights of the data subject and the procedure for the exercise of such rights, obligations in terms of data security and imposes administrative and criminal sanctions, as better detailed in Part X, Chapter 3, of this volume. It furthermore regulates the transfer of personal data to third countries or international organizations.

---

687. The Transparency Report is available at the following link: https://transparencyreport.google.com/user-data/us-national-security?hl=en.

688. GPDP, *Provvedimento del 7 luglio 2022*, doc. web no. 9806053, https://www.garanteprivacy.it/web/guest/home/docweb/-/docweb-display/docweb/9806053.

689. GPDP, *Provvedimento del 21 luglio 2022*, doc. web no. https://www.garanteprivacy.it/home/docweb/-/docweb-display/docweb/9808698.

690. Directive (EU) 2016/680 of the European Parliament and of the Council of 27 Apr. 2016 on the protection of natural persons with regard to the processing of personal data by competent authorities for the purposes of the prevention, investigation, detection or prosecution of criminal offences or the execution of criminal penalties, and on the free movement of such data, and repealing Council Framework Decision 2008/977/JHA, OJ L 119, 4.5.2016.

476. Chapter IV of the Decree lays down the prerequisites, the legitimate grounds and the requirements that the data controller must take into account when carrying out a personal data transfer to third countries or international organizations while guaranteeing a high level of protection of personal data and the protection of the fundamental rights and freedoms of data subjects. In particular, Article 31, paragraph 1, of the Decree defines the general criteria for a lawful cross-border transfer of personal data within the scope of the Decree, providing that the transfer of personal data processed or to be processed after the transfer to a third country or international organization (including onward transfers to an additional third country or international organization) is only allowed when the following conditions are met:

(i) The transfer is necessary[691] for the purposes set out in Article 1, paragraph 2, of the Decree, i.e., for the prevention, investigation, detection and prosecution of criminal offences or the execution of criminal penalties, including the protection against and prevention of threats to public safety.
(ii) Personal data are transferred to the data controller in a third country or to an international organization[692] that is a competent authority for the purposes set out in Article 1, paragraph 2, of the Decree.
(iii) Where personal data are transmitted or made available by a Member State, that Member State has given its prior authorization to the transfer in accordance with its national law.
(iv) The European Commission has adopted an adequacy decision pursuant to Article 32 of the Decree or, in the absence of an adequacy decision, adequate safeguards have been provided or are in place pursuant to Article 33 of the Decree; in the absence of an adequacy decision and appropriate safeguards, derogations for specific situations shall apply pursuant to Article 34 of the Decree.
(v) In the event of an onward transfer to another third country or to another international organization, the competent authority that carried out the initial transfer or another competent authority of the same Member State authorizes the onward transfer after having assessed all relevant factors, including the gravity of the offence, the purpose for which personal data have been transferred, and the level of protection of personal data provided for in the third country or international organization to which the personal data are subsequently transferred.

477. While all the conditions set forth in Article 31, paragraph 1, of the Decree shall generally be met, Article 31, paragraph 2, provides for an exception to the need to obtain a prior authorization under Article 31, paragraph 1, letter c), above, specifying that the transfer can also be carried out without such prior authorization where

691. The onus is on the data controller to ascertain and prove the existence of the requirement of necessity, which must be interpreted in strict and restrictive terms.

692. Article 2, lett. t), of the Decree defines 'international organization' as 'an organization and bodies governed by public international law subordinate to it, or any other body established by or on the basis of an agreement between two or more States.' For instance, the International Criminal Police Organization (commonly known as Interpol) is an international organization for the purposes of the Decree.

this is necessary to prevent an immediate and serious threat to the public security of a Member State or a third country or to the vital interests of a Member State, and the prior authorization cannot be obtained in a timely manner. In any case, where this exception applies, the authority competent to issue the prior authorization shall be informed of the transfer without delay.

I. Transfer Based on Adequacy Decisions

478. Pursuant to Article 32 of the Decree, where the transfer of personal data is based on an adequacy decision issued by the European Commission, no specific authorizations are required for a lawful transfer of personal data. It should be noted that as opposed to Article 45, paragraph 2, GDPR, Article 32 of the Decree does not specify the elements which shall be taken into account by the European Commission when issuing an adequacy decision.[693] However, such elements may be found in Recital 67 of the Directive, which – in particular – specifies that the European Commission should:

> [T]ake into account how a particular third country respects the rule of law, access to justice as well as international human rights norms and standards and its general and sectoral law, including legislation concerning public security, defence and national security, as well as public order and criminal law. The adoption of an adequacy decision with regard to a territory or a specified sector in a third country should take into account clear and objective criteria, such as specific processing activities and the scope of applicable legal standards and legislation in force in the third country.

479. Recital 68 of the Directive also specifies that in considering the adequacy of a third country or international organization:

> [T]he Commission should also take account of obligations arising from the third country's or international organization's participation in multilateral or regional systems, in particular in relation to the protection of personal data, as well as the implementation of such obligations. In particular the third country's accession to the Council of Europe Convention of 28 January 1981 for the Protection of Individuals with regard to the Automatic Processing of Personal Data and its Additional Protocol should be taken into account.

II. Transfers Subject to Adequate Safeguards

480. In cases where an adequacy decision has not been made, has been suspended, modified or revoked, Article 33 of the Decree provides for two exceptions under which the transfer of personal data to a third country or international organization is still permitted. Before analysing the exceptions laid down in Article 33

693. Bolognini & Pelino, *Codice della Disciplina Privacy* (Giuffrè Francis Lefebvre, 2019), at 799.

of the Decree, it is first of all worth noting that, with its Decision no. 99 of 22 February 2018,[694] the GPDP clarified, on the one hand, that the reference to a modification of the adequacy decision seems to be unnecessary, considering that, in case of modification, the adequacy decision would still exist and, as such, personal data could still be lawfully transferred on that basis. On the other hand, where an adequacy decision is revoked or suspended, the transfer should be considered falling in the case where a (valid) adequacy decision is missing.[695]

481. Pursuant to Article 33(1)(a) of the Decree, the transfer of personal data to a third country or international organization is still permitted where appropriate safeguards are provided for the protection of personal data through a legally binding instrument. As concerns which instrument shall be considered 'legally binding', Recital 71 of the Directive specifies that 'Such legally binding instruments could, for example, be legally binding bilateral agreements which have been concluded by the Member States and implemented in their legal order and which could be enforced by their data subjects, ensuring compliance with data protection requirements and the rights of the data subjects, including the right to obtain effective administrative or judicial redress.'

Even where there is no legally binding instrument in place, Article 33, paragraph 1, letter b) of the Decree specifies that the transfer of personal data may be deemed admissible if the data controller has assessed all the circumstances surrounding the data transfer and, on the basis of such assessment, considers that adequate safeguards exist with regard to the protection of personal data.

Recital 71 of the Directive also helps to understand the conditions which must be met to rely on this second exception, and in particular, what is to be intended by having assessed 'all the circumstances surrounding the data transfer'. In this regard, Recital 71 of the Directive not only states that 'The controller should be able to take into account cooperation agreements concluded between Europol or Eurojust and third countries which allow for the exchange of personal data when carrying out the assessment of all the circumstances surrounding the data transfer', but also clarifies that the controller should take into account the fact that the transfer of personal data will be subject to confidentiality obligations and to the principle of specificity (thus ensuring that personal data will not be processed for purposes other than that of the transfer), as well as that the personal data will not be used to request, hand down or execute a death penalty or any form of cruel and inhuman treatment.

Although the existence of the above-mentioned conditions may be considered to provide adequate safeguards and, as such, allow the transfer of personal data, Recital 71 of the Directive states that it is, in any case, possible for the data controller to require additional safeguards for the transfer.

694. GPDP, *Parere sullo schema di decreto legislativo recante Attuazione della direttiva (UE) 2016/680 del Parlamento europeo e del Consiglio – 22 febbraio 2018*, 22.2.2018, doc. web no. 8005333, https://www.garanteprivacy.it/web/guest/home/docweb/-/docweb-display/docweb/8005333.

695. Bolognini & Pelino, *Codice della Disciplina Privacy* (Giuffrè Francis Lefebvre, 2019), at 801.

482. Whenever the data controller bases the transfer of personal data on the exemption set forth in Article 33, paragraph 1, letter b) of the Decree, the data controller is required to inform the GPDP of the transfer carried out, as well as to keep documentation related to the transfer (and to its circumstances) and make such information available to the GPDP upon request. Such documentation shall contain the date and time of the transfer, the receiving competent authority, and the reason for the transfer, as well as indicate the personal data transferred.

III. Derogations in Specific Situations

483. Where the conditions under Articles 32 and 33 of the Decree do not apply (i.e., where there is no adequacy decision or where adequate safeguards are not in place), data controllers can still rely on one of the specific derogations laid down in Article 34 of the Decree to carry out a lawful transfer of personal data under the scope of the Decree.

In particular, data transfers are still allowed where they are necessary for one of the following purposes:

(i) to protect a vital interest[696] of the data subject or of another person;
(ii) to safeguard the data subject's legitimate interests when provided for by the law of the Member State transferring the personal data;
(iii) to prevent an immediate and serious threat to public security of a Member State or of a third country;
(iv) in individual cases, for the purposes referred to in Article 1, paragraph 2, of the Decree (i.e., for the purposes of the prevention, investigation, detection or prosecution of criminal offences or the execution of criminal penalties, including the safeguarding against and the prevention of threats to public safety);
(v) in individual cases, where it is necessary to ascertain, exercise or defend a legal claim in connection with the purposes referred to in Article 1, paragraph 2, of the Decree.

484. With specific reference to the purpose referred to under point (v) above, it should be noted that this assumption may not be limited to court litigation but may be extended to similar hypotheses of 'establishment of a right' in extrajudicial settings.[697]

---

696. The concept of 'vital interest' is to be interpreted in a particularly restrictive way, also taking into account the interpretation of Art. 29 Working Party (now European Data Protection Board), according to which 'the phrase "vital interest" appears to limit the application of this ground to questions of life and death, or at the very least, threats that pose a risk of injury or other damage to the health of the data subject'. *See* to this end, *Opinion 06/2014 on the notion of legitimate interests of the data controller under Article 7 of Directive 95/46/EC*, (9 Apr. 2014), 20, https://ec.europa.eu/justice/article-29/documentation/opinion-recommendation/files/2014/wp217_en.pdf.

697. Bolognini & Pelino, *Codice della Disciplina Privacy* (Giuffrè Francis Lefebvre, 2019), at 803.

485. In cases where the transfer is based on points (iv) and (v) above, Article 34, paragraph 2, of the Directive specifies that the competent authority intending to carry out the transfer has the burden of weighing the fundamental rights and freedoms of the data subject against the public interest in the transfer.

486. As also provided in Article 33 of the Decree, Article 34, paragraph 3, specifies that the data controller must document the transfer made, indicating the date and the time of the transfer, the receiving competent authority, the reason for the transfer and the personal data transferred, and shall make this documentation available to the GPDP upon request. However, unlike the provisions of Article 33 of the Decree, there is no obligation to inform the GPDP.

IV. Transfers to Recipients Established in Third Countries

487. While, as specified in Article 31, paragraph 1, letter b) of the Decree, the recipient of personal data is typically an international authority or organization competent for the purposes of preventing, investigating, detecting and prosecuting criminal offences or executing criminal penalties, Article 35 of the Decree provides that, without prejudice to any international agreements,[698] competent authorities have the possibility to transfer directly to recipients established in third countries. However, this possibility is exclusively provided for in individual and specific cases provided for by national laws or regulations and European Union law, and where the:

(i) transfer is strictly necessary for the performance of a task prescribed by European Union law or domestic law for the purposes referred to in Article 1, paragraph 2, of the Decree (i.e., for the purposes of the prevention, investigation, detection or prosecution of criminal offences or the execution of criminal penalties, including the safeguarding against and the prevention of threats to public safety);
(ii) competent authority carrying out the transfer concludes that the fundamental rights and freedoms of the data subject do not outweigh the public interest necessitating the transfer;
(iii) transferring competent authority considers that the transfer to an authority in the third country for the purposes referred to in Article 1, paragraph 2, of the Decree is ineffective[699] or inappropriate,[700] in particular because it cannot be carried out in a timely manner;

698. As specified in Art. 35, para. 2, of the Decree, international agreement means any bilateral or multilateral international agreement in force between Member States and third countries in the field of judicial cooperation in criminal matters and police cooperation.

699. According to Recital 71 of the Directive, 'This may be the case where there is an urgent need to transfer personal data to save the life of a person who is in danger of becoming a victim of a criminal offence or in the interest of preventing an imminent perpetration of a crime, including terrorism'.

(iv) competent authority in the third country is informed without undue delay, unless this prejudices the purpose for which the transfer is carried out;[701]

(v) competent authority carrying out the transfer informs the recipient of the specific purpose(s) for which the personal data shall be processed, provided that such processing is necessary.

488. The competent authority is also required to inform the GPDP of the transfers carried out (similarly to what is provided under Article 33 of the Decree), as well as to document the transfer (as also provided under Articles 33 and 34 of the Decree).

V. International Cooperation for the Protection of Personal Data and Previously Concluded International Agreements

489. Article 36 of the Decree provides that, in relation to transfers to third countries and international organizations, appropriate measures must be taken for the purposes of international cooperation for the protection of personal data, pursuant to Article 50 GDPR.

Such a requirement arises from the fact that, as specified in Recital 74 of the Directive, cross-border data transfers may give rise to the risk of data subjects being prevented from exercising their data protection rights to protect themselves from the unlawful use of disclosure of data referring to them, or for supervisory authorities not to be able to pursue complaints or conduct investigations relating to the activities outside their borders.

Supervisory authorities' efforts to work together in the cross-border context may also be hampered by insufficient preventative or remedial powers and inconsistent legal regimes. Therefore, the Decree aims to encourage closer cooperation among data protection supervisory authorities and to help them exchange information with their foreign counterparts.[702]

700. Transfer to a competent authority in the third country may be considered inappropriate, for instance, where such authority in the third country does not respect the rule of law or international human rights norms and standards, as specified in Recital 71 of the Directive.

701. This may be the case, for instance, where the data transferred relates to allegations of corruption or irregularities in the authority of the third country and there is the risk that the transfer may inform the relevant personnel within that authority of an ongoing investigation.

702. Bolognini & Pelino, *Codice della Disciplina Privacy* (Giuffrè Francis Lefebvre, 2019), at 806.

Chapter 2. Transfers in the Context of International Agreements (e.g., Mutual Legal Assistance Treaties)

§1. Transfer in the Context of Mutual Legal Assistance Treaties

490. The transfer of personal data may take place in the context of multilateral and bilateral international agreements which Italy has entered into with third countries or international organizations in several fields. Examples of international agreements involving the transfer of personal data are mutual legal assistance agreements. In particular, within the framework of the Council of Europe, the main multilateral agreements on mutual legal assistance ratified by Italy which may involve a transfer of personal data to third countries or international organizations are the:

(i) 1957 Council of Europe Convention on Extradiction.[703]
(ii) Second Additional Protocol to the European Convention on Extradiction.[704]
(iii) 1959 European Convention on Mutual Legal Assistance in Criminal Matters[705] and the 1978 Additional Protocol.[706]

491. Italy is also a party in several bilateral agreements on judicial cooperation in criminal matters with countries located outside the EEA, such as Algeria, Argentina, Australia, Bolivia, Brazil, Canada, Chile, El Salvador, Japan, Hong Kong, Lebanon, Morocco, Montenegro, Paraguay, Peru, China, Mexico, US, Switzerland, Tunisia, and Venezuela.[707]

§2. Transfer in the Context of the EU-PNR Directive

492. With Legislative Decree 21 May 2018, no. 53 (the 'PNR Decree'), Italy transposed Directive (EU) 2016/681 (the 'EU-PNR Directive').[708]

The PNR Decree lays down, *inter alia*, the methods for processing and storing personal data, the purpose for which PNR data[709] can be processed, the information

703. European Covention on Extradiction, Paris, 13.XII.1957.
704. Second Additional Protocol to the European Convention on Extradition, Strasbourg, 17.III.1978.
705. European Convention on Mutual Assistance in Criminal Matters, Strasbourg, 20.IV.1959.
706. Additional Protocol to the European Convention on Mutual Assistance in Criminal Matters, Strasbourg, 17.III.1978.
707. The full list of multilateral and bilateral agreements in force between Italy and other countries is available at: https://www.giustizia.it/giustizia/it/mg_1_3.page?tabaip=y.
708. Directive (EU) 2016/681 of the European Parliament and of the Council of 27 Apr. 2016 on the use of passenger name record (PNR) data for the prevention, detection, investigation and prosecution of terrorist offences and serious crime, OJ L 119, 4.5.2016.
709. PNR data are collected by air carriers during the flight reservation process and are defined under Art. 2, lett. a), of the PNR Decree as the information relating to each passenger flight consisting in those data referred to in Annex I of the EU-PNR Directive, necessary to enable reservations to be processed and controlled by air carriers and contained in the passenger name record. Such data include, among others, the names, addresses, credit card details, and seat numbers of air passengers, as well as the complete travel itinerary for specific PNR and travel status of passenger.

system to be used for the collection, processing and sharing of PNR data, the retention periods of PNR data within the information system, as well as the transfer of such data both within the EEA and to third countries.

493. As concerns the transfer of personal data to third countries, the PNR Decree first of all specifies, in Article 1, paragraph 3, that the provisions on personal data transfers to third countries laid down in the PNR Decree are without prejudice to the application of bilateral or multilateral agreements regulating the share of information between competent authorities entered into between Member States before 24 May 2016. The same Article also specifies the application of the obligations arising out from bilateral or multilateral agreements entered into with third countries outside the EU.

494. Chapter III of the PNR Decree regulates the information flows of PNR data and the results of their processing. In more detail, Chapter III regulates, on the one hand, the procedure for internal information communication, i.e., the methods of cooperation between the national Passenger Information Unit (PIU)[710] and the competent national authorities and, on the other hand, the international communication mechanisms (i.e., the information exchange between the Italian PIU and the PIUs or the competent authorities of other Member States, the transfer of PNR data to Europol, and the transfer of PNR data to third countries).

495. The transfer of PNR data to third countries is regulated by Article 19 of the PNR Decree, according to which, save specific conditions set forth in any international agreements, PNR transfers to third-country competent authorities are only allowed:

(i) On a case-by-case basis.
(ii) Where the transfer is carried out in compliance with the PNR Decree and Legislative Decree 18 May 2021, no. 51.[711]
(iii) Where the conditions set forth in Article 19 of the PNR Decree are met.

496. Specifically, the transfer of PNR data to a third country can only be carried out as per Article 19, paragraph 1, of the PNR Decree, where the:

710. The PIU is defined under Art. 2, para. 2, lett. s), of the PNR Decree as the authority competent for the prevention, detection, investigation or prosecution of terrorist offences and of serious crime or a branch of such an authority.

711. Legislative Decree no. 51 of 18 May 2021, implementing the Directive (EU) 2016/680 of the European Parliament and of the Council of 27 Apr. 2016 on the protection of natural persons with regard to the processing of personal data by competent authorities for the purposes of the prevention, investigation, detection or prosecution of criminal offences or the execution of criminal penalties, and on the free movement of such data, and repealing Council Framework Decision 2008/977/JHA. For an overview of this Legislative Decree, *see infra* Part X, Ch. 3.

(i) Request is made in compliance with the provisions of Article 13, paragraphs 2[712] and 3[713] of the PNR Decree.
(ii) Transfer is necessary for the purposes laid down in Article 3, paragraph 1, of the PNR Decree (i.e., for the prevention and prosecution of terrorist offences and serious crimes).
(iii) Third country commits to process personal data in compliance with the guarantees laid down in the PNR Decree and to carry out an onward transfer to another third country only for the prevention and prosecution of terrorist offences and serious crimes and subject to a prior authorization from the Italian government.

497. While the general principle for the transfer of PNR data to a third country requires the prior consent of the Member State from which such data have been obtained, Article 19, paragraph 2, of the PNR Decree provides for an exception where the:

(i) Transfer is essential to respond to a specific and actual threat related to terrorist offences or serious crime in a Member State or in a third country.
(ii) Prior consent cannot be obtained in a timely manner.

498. In order to rely on the exception from gathering the prior Member State consent for transferring PNR data to a third country under Article 19, paragraph 2, of the PNR Decree, both of the above conditions must be met. Additionally, the transfer of PNR data without prior consent must, in any case, be communicated to the PIU of the Member State which has transmitted such data and shall be noted in a dedicated record for the data protection officer assessments.

§3. Transfers in the Context of Automated Processing under the Convention 108 and the Convention 108+

499. International data transfers from Italy to a third country may also take place on the basis of the data protection framework provided by the Council of Europe's 'Convention 108',[714] which was signed by Italy in February 1983 and came into force in July 1997. Convention 108 applies to automated personal data files and the automated processing of personal data in the public and private sectors.

712. Pursuant to Art. 13, para. 2, of the PNR Decree, PNR data and the results of their processing (where already carried out) are transferred to the PIU of another Member State on the basis of a duly motivated request (which may also only partially concern PNR data) relating to a specific case of prevention and prosecution of terrorist offences and serious crimes.

713. Pursuant to Art. 13, para. 3, of the PNR Decree, where the requested data have pseudonymised in compliance with Art. 10, para. 2, of the PNR Decree, the Italian PIU transmits complete PNR data to the PIU of another Member State only where necessary to respond to a request made under Art. 6, para. 2, lett. c), of the PNR Decree (i.e., a duly motivated request), prior to the authorization of the competent authorities mentioned in Art. 10, para. 3, of the PNR Decree.

714. Convention for the Protection of Individuals with regard to Automatic Processing of Personal Data, Strasbourg, 28.I.1981.

500. In 2018, the Convention was subject to a revision procedure aimed at better facing the challenges deriving from the use of new information and communication technologies. Such revision resulted in a Protocol,[715] the purpose of which was to amend and modernize Convention 108 in order to provide a flexible multilateral legal framework to facilitate the transborder flows of personal data. The Protocol was signed by Italy in March 2019 – marking the conclusion of the modernization process of Convention 108 – and subsequently ratified and executed with Law 22 April 2021, no. 60.

The main innovations of the modernized Convention 108 (commonly known as 'Convention 108+') concern, among others, the extension of the special categories of personal data so as to cover genetic data, biometric data, and personal data that may reveal information relating to ethnic origin or trade-union membership, the implementation of the obligation to make data breach notifications, the creation of further data subject rights in relation to automated decision-making, and provisions concerning the transfer of personal data to countries that are non-signatory parties of Convention 108+.

501. In particular, as concerns the transfers of personal data to recipients subject to the jurisdiction of a State or international organization which is not party to Convention 108+, Article 14, paragraph 2, of Convention 108+ specifies, similarly to the principles laid down in Article 45 GDPR, that such a transfer is considered lawful only to the extent that an appropriate level of protection based on the standards established by Convention 108+ is ensured. According to Article 14, paragraph 3, of Convention 108+, an appropriate level of protection can be secured by:

(i) The law of that State or international organization, including the applicable international treaties or agreements.
(ii) Ad hoc or approved standardized safeguards provided by legally binding and enforceable instruments adopted and implemented by the persons involved in the transfer and further processing.

502. While the above-mentioned Article 14, paragraph 3, lays down the general principles to be taken into account for the transfer of personal data to non-signatory parties of Convention 108+, Article 14, paragraph 4, of the Convention provides for some exceptions, stating that a transborder transfer of personal data may still take place where:

(i) The data subject has given explicit, specific and free consent after being informed of the risks arising in the absence of appropriate safeguards.
(ii) The specific interests of the data subject require it in the particular case.
(iii) There are prevailing legitimate interests, in particular, important public interests which are provided for by law, and such transfer constitutes a necessary and proportionate measure in a democratic society.

715. Protocol amending the Convention for the Protection of Individuals with regard to Automatic Processing of Personal Data, Strasbourg, 10.X.2018.

(iv) It constitutes a necessary and proportionate measure in a democratic society for freedom of expression.

§4. Transfers Between Financial Supervisory Authorities for the Purpose of Suppressing Unlawful Conducts in the Financial Markets

503. In 2019, after an authorization was received by the GPDP,[716] the Italian authority responsible for regulating the Italian financial markets (the '*Commissione Nazionale per le Società e la Borsa*' or 'CONSOB') entered into an administrative arrangement for the transfer of personal data between EEA financial authorities and non-EEA financial authorities (the 'Arrangement').[717] The Arrangement – defined by the European Securities and Markets Authority ('ESMA') and the International Organization of Securities ('IOSCO') – aims to facilitate the transfer of information in the framework of international cooperation activities in order to ensure mutual assistance for the repression of illegal conducts in the markets and for the compliance of operators with transparency obligations towards the market and investors.

504. The authorization issued by the GPDP is the first case of a data transfer authorization under Article 46, paragraph 3, letter b), GDPR, according to which, in the absence of an adequacy decision issued by the European Commission, appropriate safeguards for the transfer of personal data may also be inserted into administrative arrangements between public authorities or bodies which include enforceable and effective data subject, provided that such arrangements have been subject to the prior authorization of the national supervisory authority.

In issuing its authorization, the GPDP – in line with the opinion provided by the EDPB on this matter[718] – considered that the safeguards set out in the Arrangement ensure an adequate level of data protection. In particular, the GPDP noted that the Arrangement contains the following safeguards necessary to comply with Article 46, paragraph 3, letter b), GDPR, including:

(i) Definitions of key concepts (such as personal data, data breach, processing, etc.) and data subject rights as defined by the GDPR.

---

716. GPDP, *Autorizzazione alla CONSOB per sottoscrivere un accordo amministrativo per il trasferimento di dati personali tra le autorità di vigilanza finanziaria dello Spazio economico europeo (SEE) e le autorità di vigilanza finanziaria al di fuori del SEE – 23 maggio 2019*, 23.5.2019, doc. web no. 9119857, https://www.garanteprivacy.it/web/guest/home/docweb/-/docweb-display/docweb/9119857.

717. The Arrangement is available at https://www.esma.europa.eu/sites/default/files/administrative_arrangement_aa_for_the_transfer_of_personal_data_between_eea_and_non-eea_authorities.pdf.

718. EDPB, Opinion 4/2019on the draft Administrative Arrangement for the transfer of personal data between European Economic Area (EEA) Financial Supervisory Authorities and non-EEA Financial Supervisory Authorities, 12.2.2019, https://edpb.europa.eu/our-work-tools/our-documents/opinion-board-art-64/opinion-42019-draft-aa-between-eea-and-non-eea_en.

(ii) The principle of purpose limitation and the prohibition of any further processing of personal data, according to which the data transfer can only be carried out within the framework of the mandates and responsibilities assigned to the authorities which are party to the Arrangement (i.e., insofar as the transfer is necessary to support the institutional tasks of such authorities), and the receiving authority is not authorized to further process personal data in a way which is incompatible with those purposes.

(iii) The principle of data quality and proportionality, according to which the transferring authority shall only transfer accurate and up-to-date personal data which are adequate, relevant, and limited to what is necessary for the purposes for which they are transferred and further processed.

(iv) The principle of transparency, according to which each authority shall provide data subjects with a general information notice on the processing carried out indicating, *inter alia*, the transfer, the types of entities to which personal data may be transferred, the rights data subjects can exercise along with the modalities for exercising those rights, information on any deferral or restriction of the exercise of those rights, and contact information for lodging a complaint. Each authority shall provide data subjects with a general information notice on the processing carried out, indicating, *inter alia*, the transfer, the types of entities to which personal data may be transferred, the rights data subjects can exercise along with the modalities for exercising those rights, information on any deferral or restriction of the exercise of those rights, and contact information for lodging a complaint. Such information notice shall be provided by means of publication, together with the Arrangement, on the website of each authority. In addition, EEA authorities will provide data subjects with an individual notice in accordance with the GDPR and, in the case of the ESMA, in accordance with Regulation (EU) 2018/1725.[719]

(v) The principle of data retention, according to which the authorities shall retain personal data for no longer than necessary to achieve the purpose for which personal data are processed.

(vi) The implementation of security measures, according to which each authority shall implement appropriate technical and organizational security measures to protect personal data transferred to it from a data breach, e.g., by marking information as 'personal data' and restricting access to it.

(vii) Guarantees for data subjects rights, according to which the data subject may obtain confirmation of any transfer of their data to a financial supervisory authority outside the EEA and, upon request, can have access to their personal data. In addition, the data subject may directly ask the financial supervisory authority concerned or the financial supervisory authority outside the EEA to rectify, erase, restrict or block their data. Information regarding these safeguards shall be provided on the website of the financial supervisory authority/ non-EEA financial supervisory authority. Any restriction to these

719. Regulation (EU) 2018/1725 of the European Parliament and of the Council of 23 Oct. 2018 on the protection of natural persons with regard to the processing of personal data by the Union institutions, bodies, offices and agencies and on the free movement of such data, and repealing Regulation (EC) no. 45/2001 and Decision no. 1247/2002/EC, OJ L 295, 21.11.2018.

rights shall be provided for by law, and such restriction is only permitted to the extent and for the time period necessary to protect confidentiality or to meet important objectives of general public interest which, when the transferring authority is an EEA financial supervisory authority, shall be recognized by the Member State to which that authority belongs.

(viii) Restrictions on onward transfers, according to which any onward transfer to a third party which is not an authority party to the Arrangement, to another country that is not the subject of an adequacy decision issued by the European Commission, will only take place with the prior written consent of the transferring authority and provided that the third party provides adequate safeguards that are consistent with those provided for in the Arrangement. The same guarantees are provided in case of communication of personal data to a third party in the same country of the receiving authority unless, in exceptional cases, that third party cannot provide such guarantees. In such a case, the transfer may only take place if the communication is necessary 'for important reasons of public interest'. When the transferring authority is an EEA financial supervisory authority, the public interest shall be recognized by the Member State to which that authority belongs. Personal data may only be disclosed to a third party in the same country as the receiving authority (such as public bodies, courts, self-regulatory bodies and entities involved in enforcement proceedings) without the consent of the transferring authority or without safeguards where alternatively:

(a) The sharing is for purposes that are consistent with the purpose for which the data were initially transferred or with the general framework of the use stated in the specific initial request of the receiving authority and is necessary to fulfil the mandate and responsibilities of the receiving authority and/or the third party.

(b) The sharing of personal data follows a legally enforceable demand or is required by law, in which case the receiving authority shall notify the transferring authority prior to the sharing and include information about the data requested, the requesting body, and the legal basis for sharing.

(ix) Redress, according to which data subjects who believe that an authority has failed to comply with the safeguards as set forth in the Arrangement, or who believe that their personal data have been subject to a data breach, may seek redress (which may include monetary compensation for damages) against that authority to the extent permitted by applicable legal requirements.

(x) Provision of an oversight mechanism aimed at ensuring the implementation of the guarantees set out in the Arrangement, whereby each authority shall conduct periodic reviews of its own policies and procedures that implement the Arrangement and of their effectiveness and, upon reasonable request by another authority, the requested authority shall review its personal data processing policies and procedures to ascertain and confirm that the safeguards included in the Arrangement are being implemented effectively. This internal oversight is complemented by an external oversight carried out by an assessment group established as a sub-committee of IOSCO (the Assessment Group), which shall conduct periodic reviews of the implementation of the safeguards included in the Arrangement and shall consider best practices with a view to continuing to enhance the protection of personal data where appropriate.

505. The GPDP has, however, made the validity of the Arrangement subject to certain conditions. In particular, CONSOB shall inform the GPDP of any suspension of data transfers and any revision or suspension of participation in the Arrangement. Additionally, the Assessment Group is required to conduct adequate oversight of compliance with the arrangement. Finally, in accordance with the principle of accountability, CONSOB (like the other financial supervisory authorities and ESMA) will have to keep records documenting compliance with the Arrangement. The documentation shall include:

(i) The number of requests and complaints of infringements submitted by data subjects at the EU level.
(ii) Details on cases not resolved through the dispute resolution mechanisms envisaged by the Arrangements and the respective findings.
(iii) The notifications received concerning the disclosure of information to third parties by financial supervisory authorities outside the EEA, following a legally binding request or as a result of a legal obligation.

506. Such documentation shall be made available to the GPDP upon request, and for the first two years of application of the Agreement, CONSOB has transmitted to the GPDP an annual report drawn up on the basis of the aforementioned documentation.

507. The GPDP has the task of monitoring compliance with the safeguards included in the Arrangement and, in the event of non-compliance, will provide for the suspension of personal data transfers by CONSOB.

Chapter 3. Transfers from Public Registers

508. Article 49, paragraph 1, letter g), GDPR, allows transfer of personal data to a third country or international organization, even in the absence of an adequacy decision pursuant to Article 45, paragraph 3, GDPR, or of appropriate safeguards pursuant to Article 46, if:

> [T]he transfer is made from a register which according to Union or Member State law is intended to provide information to the public and which is open to consultation either by the public in general or by any person who can demonstrate a legitimate interest, but only to the extent that the conditions laid down by Union or Member State law for consultation are fulfilled in the particular case.

509. Paragraph 2 of Article 49 further specifies that:

> A transfer pursuant to point (g) of the first subparagraph of paragraph 1 shall not involve the entirety of the personal data or entire categories of the personal data contained in the register. Where the register is intended for consultation by persons having a legitimate interest, the transfer shall be made only at the request of those persons or if they are to be the recipients.

510. At the time of writing this Chapter, Italian law does not provide particular specifications as to this derogation, while the GPDP does not seem to have adopted relevant decisions concerning this provision yet. In line with the foregoing, on the institutional website of the GPDP,[720] regarding the derogations referred to in Article 49 of the GDPR, the GPDP refers directly to the EDPB Guidelines 2/2018.[721]

---

720. GDPD, *Trasferimenti di dati personali all'estero*, https://www.garanteprivacy.it/temi/trasferimento-di-dati-all-estero.
721. EDPB, Guidelines 2/2018 on derogations of Article 49 under Regulation 2016/679, 25.5.2018, https://edpb.europa.eu/our-work-tools/our-documents/guidelines/guidelines-22018-derogations-article-49-under-regulation_en.

Chapter 4. Transfers for Reasons of Public Interest

511. Article 49, paragraph 1, letter d), GDPR, allows transfer of personal data to a third country or international organization, even in the absence of an adequacy decision pursuant to Article 45, paragraph 3, GDPR, or of appropriate safeguards pursuant to Article 46, if 'the transfer is 'necessary for important reasons of public interest'.

Paragraph 4 of Article 49 further specifies that 'The public interest referred to in point (d) of the first subparagraph of paragraph 1 shall be recognised in Union law or in the law of the Member State to which the controller is subject.'

512. At the time of writing this Chapter, Italian law does not provide particular specifications as to this derogation, while the GPDP does not seem to have adopted relevant decisions concerning this provision yet.

In line with the above, on the institutional website of the GPDP,[722] regarding the derogations referred to in Article 49 of the GDPR, the GPDP refers directly to the EDPB Guidelines 2/2018.[723]

722. GDPD, *Trasferimenti di dati personali all'estero* https://www.garanteprivacy.it/temi/trasferimento-di-dati-all-estero.

723. EDPB, Guidelines 2/2018 on derogations of Article 49 under Regulation 2016/679 (25 May 2018), https://edpb.europa.eu/our-work-tools/our-documents/guidelines/guidelines-22018-derogations-article-49-under-regulation_en.

Part VIII. Enforcement

Chapter 1. Supervisory Authorities

§1. The GPDP at a Glance

513. The Italian Supervisory Authority is the *Garante per la protezione dei dati personali*, or 'GPDP'.

The GPDP is an independent administrative authority established by Law 31 December 1996, no. 675, and regulated by the Personal Data Protection Code. The 2018 reform confirmed that the GPDP is the designated supervisory authority also for the purposes of implementing the GDPR under Article 51 of the latter.[724] The GPDP, located in Rome, is a collegiate body composed of the Panel of Commissioners with four members elected by the Italian Parliament[725] for a seven-year mandate and the Bureau.

514. The organization and operation of the GPDP are governed by its own rules of procedure 1/2000[726] which contain, *inter alia*, provisions governing the President and members of the Panel of Commissioner, the carrying out of meetings, the tasks of the Bureau and the secretary general, the general organization of the Bureau, etc.

515. The GPDP carries out the tasks provided in Article 154 of the Personal Data Protection Code in addition to the provisions set out in Article 57 GDPR. Its main function is to ensure that, in all public and private sector organizations, data are processed as required by the applicable law, and the rights of individuals are respected whenever their personal data are processed.

---

724. *See* Art. 2-*bis* (Supervisory Authority) of the Personal Data Protection Code: '1. The supervisory authority referred to in Article 51 of the Regulation shall be the Garante per la protezione dei dati personali, hereinafter the "Garante", as per Section 153 hereof'.
725. The current College was elected by the Italian Parliament in July 2020. The members are indicated on the GPDP's website, at this webpage: https://www.garanteprivacy.it/home/autorita/collegio.
726. Rules of procedure 1/2000, https://www.garanteprivacy.it/home/docweb/-/docweb-display/docweb/1098801.

§2. The Relationship with Other Authorities

516. According to Article 156, paragraph 4, of the Personal Data Protection Code, the GPDP cooperates with other national independent administrative authorities. In practice, the GPDP cooperates mostly with the Agency for Digital Italy (*'Agenzia per l'Italia Digitale'*, or 'AgID'), the AgCM (*'Autorità per la Concorrenza e il Mercato'*, or 'AgCM') and the Italian Telecommunication Authority (*'Autorità per le Garanzie nelle Comunicazioni'*, or 'AgCom'), given that these authorities operate in fields connected to ICT technologies and, therefore, to the processing of personal data.[727]

517. Moreover, the GPDP cooperates with the Italian financial police (*'Guardia di Finanza'*, or 'GdF'), especially as regards the enforcement of data protection law.

To this aim, the GPDP periodically signs protocol agreements with the GdF.[728] On the basis of this protocol agreement, the GdF collaborates in inspection activities, obtaining data and information on subjects to be inspected, accessing databases, performing online audits, and providing assistance in collaboration with the judicial authorities. In the context of data protection enforcement, the GdF generally operates with its Special Unit for the Protection of Privacy and Technological Fraud and through its Privacy Group.

518. The GPDP is represented in judicial proceedings by the State legal service (*'Avvocatura dello Stato'*, *see* Article 154-*ter*, paragraph 2 of the Personal Data Protection Code).

519. Finally, the staff of the Bureau in charge of the investigations referred to in Article 158 of the Personal Data Protection Code and in Article 57, paragraph 1, letter h, Article 58, paragraph 1, letter b, and Article 62 GDPR shall act in the capacity of judicial police officers or staff with respect to the duties they are required to fulfil in accordance with the powers respectively conferred on them.

---

727. For example, the GPDP, AgCM and AgCom have drafted and published a joint survey on Big Data in 2018, available in the AgCM website: https://www.agcm.it/dotcmsdoc/allegati-news/IC_Big%20data_imp.pdf.

728. The most recent protocol agreement has been signed in 2021, https://www.garanteprivacy.it/web/guest/home/docweb/-/docweb-display/docweb/9570071.

Chapter 2. Composition

520. The GPDP is comprised of a collegiate body known as the Panel of Commissioners, consisting of four elected members,[729] and the Bureau, which is under the authority of the GPDP.[730] Pursuant to Article 153, paragraph 1 of the Personal Data Protection Code, the Panel of Commissioners heads the Bureau.

521. The members of the GPDP's Panel of Commissioners are elected by the Italian parliament for seven-year non-renewable terms.[731] At least sixty days before their appointment, a public notice is published on the Italian Data Protection Authority Website, the Chamber of Deputies website, and the Senate website, calling upon qualified members of the public to put forth their applications in the context of the selection procedure.[732]

According to the procedure laid out in Article 153, paragraph 1 of the Personal Data Protection Code, individual applications must be submitted at the very latest, thirty days before the appointment takes place. Furthermore, the CVs of the applications are to be posted on the aforementioned websites. In order to be considered for the position, successful candidates are required to have 'proven experience in the field of personal data protection with particular regard to law or computer science'[733] and must be independent.

522. Pursuant to paragraph 2 of Article 153 of the Personal Data Protection Code, once the Panel is elected, the members elect their President, who has a casting vote in cases of a tie. A Vice President, who replaces the President in cases of absence or inability to carry out their official functions, is also elected. In order to safeguard the members of the Panel's independence, Article 153, paragraph 3, of the Code prohibits them from carrying out any advisory or professional activities, even of a voluntary and non-remunerated nature, nor may they hold other elected offices, or be managers or employees of public or private entities; failure to comply with this requirement is punishable by disqualification.

523. Under Article 153, paragraph 4, both during and following their seven-year term, the members are required to abide by professional secrecy obligations and to

729. GPDP, *The Italian Data Protection Authority: Who We Are*, https://www.garanteprivacy.it/web/garante-privacy-en/the-italian-data-protection-authority-who-we-are#:~:text=The%20DPA%20was%20set%20up,has%20an%20office%20in%20Rome.&text=and%20in%20other%20national%20and%20EU%20regulatory%20instruments.

730. *See* Art. 153, para. 7, Personal Data Protection Code. *See also* Art. 155 of the Personal Data Protection Code.

731. *Collegio*, Garante per la protezone dei dati personali, https://www.garanteprivacy.it/home/autorita/collegio. Also *see* the text of Art. 153, para. 3 of the Italian Personal Data Protection Code and note that 'This paragraph was amended by section 47-c of Law No 31/2008, which brought about amendments to the term of office of the commissioners appointed to certain independent authorities (seven years) including the members making up the Italian data protection authority. The previous term of office was four years and was renewable once'.

732. *See* Art. 153, para. 1, of the Italian Personal Data Protection Code.

733. *Ibid.*

keep any information they come to be aware of in the course of exercising the powers vested in them during their term. Upon acceptance of the appointment, the members of the Panel and the President who were previously employed by the public administration or who are members of the judiciary are removed from the list of permanent employees and cannot be replaced; university professors are put on an unpaid leave of absence pursuant to Article 13 of DPR no. 382 of 11.07.1980.[734]

524. With respect to remuneration, both the President and the members of the panel are paid an amount which must not exceed the salary which is paid to the President of the Supreme Court of Cassation.[735] Under Article 153, paragraph 6, the amount paid is also regulated by the legal restrictions governing the income of public employees.

This so-called allowance is intended to 'cover all the relevant expenses except for the reimbursement of documented costs that have been actually incurred in connection with activities related to official duties'. This has been recently amended by Law Decree 8 October 2021, no. 139, converted into law with amendments by Law 3 December 2021, no. 205.

525. Lastly, paragraph 8 of Article 153 establishes that the GPDP's members, including the President, members of the Panel, the secretary general, and, more generally, staff, are not permitted to handle proceedings before the same authority. Such prohibition lasts for a period of two years following the end of their mandate or service. This prohibition also includes complaints, inquiries, and requests for opinions.

526. The current Panel of Commissioners was elected by the Italian Parliament (pursuant to Article 153, paragraph 1, of the Personal Data Protection Code) on 14 July 2020. The members took office approximately two weeks later, on 29 July 2020.[736] The Panel is presently comprised of Pasquale Stanzione (President), Ginevra Cerrina Feroni (Vice President), and members Agostino Ghiglia and Guido Scorza.[737] In 2027, after seven years from the previous appointment, a new Panel of Commissioners will be appointed following the procedure referred to above.

527. Finally, Article 155, paragraph 1 of the Italian Personal Data Protection Code mandates that, with the aim of promoting both autonomy and accountability as required under Law no. 241/1990 and Legislative Decree 3 February 1993, no. 29, each as subsequently amended, the Bureau is required to 'implement the principles concerning appointment and tasks of officials responsible for handling the individual cases and separation between guidance and supervisory tasks as committed to the heads of the authority and managerial tasks as committed to the heads of

734. *See* Art. 153, para. 5, of the Italian Personal Data Protection Code.
735. *See* Art. 153, para. 6, Italian Personal Data Protection Code.
736. *Collegio*, Garante per la protezone dei dati personali, https://www.garanteprivacy.it/home/autorita/collegio.
737. The official appointments of Ginevra Cerrina Feroni and Guido Scorza were communicated by the Italian Chamber of Deputies to the GPDP on 14 Jul. 2020 and the appointments of Pasquale Stanzione and Agostino Ghiglia were communicated by the Senate of the Italian to the same authority on 15 Jul. 2020.

departments or units'. Additionally, it should be noted that what is established by D.Lgs. 165/2001, which provides for 'General provisions concerning employment at public entities', also applies where specifically referenced in the Personal Data Protection Code.

Chapter 3. Competence, Tasks and Powers

528. The investigations, tasks and powers of the GPDP are provided for in Articles 154, 154-bis, 154-ter, 157, 158, 159 and 160 of the Personal Data Protection Code.

§1. Competence

529. Article 51, paragraph 1, GDPR, provides for the institution of a Supervisory Authority for each Member State. In Italy, the Supervisory Authority is called GPDP. Each Member State Supervisory Authority is competent in the local territory of their State, and therefore, the GPDP is competent for the Italian territory.

530. However, the competence of the GPDP is not limited to the application of GDPR and the Personal Data Protection Code. Instead, it is also competent for the application of the e-Privacy Directive and, according to the provision of Article 154 of the Personal Data Protection Code, also for Regulation (EC) 1987/2006[738] (so-called as SIS II), Regulation (EU) 2016/794[739] (about the European Union Agency for Law Enforcement Cooperation 'Europol'), Regulation (EU) 2015/1525[740] (on mutual assistance between the administrative authorities of the Member States and cooperation between the latter and the Commission to ensure the correct application of the law on customs and agricultural matters), Regulation (EU) 604/2013[741] (establishing the criteria and mechanisms for determining the Member State responsible for examining an application for international protection lodged in one of the Member States by a third-country national or a stateless person 'recast'), Regulation (EC) 767/2008[742] (concerning the Visa Information System 'VIS' and the exchange of data between Member States on short-stay visas 'VIS Regulation'),

---

738. Regulation (EC) no. 1987/2006 of the European Parliament and of the Council of 20 Dec. 2006 on the establishment, operation and use of the second-generation Schengen Information System (SIS II), OJ L 381, 28.12.2006.
739. Regulation (EU) 2016/794 of the European Parliament and of the Council of 11 May 2016 on the European Union Agency for Law Enforcement Cooperation (Europol) and replacing and repealing Council Decisions 2009/371/JHA, 2009/934/JHA, 2009/935/JHA, 2009/936/JHA and 2009/968/JHA, OJ L 135, 24.5.2016.
740. Regulation (EU) 2015/1525 of the European Parliament and of the Council of 9 Sep. 2015 amending Council Regulation (EC) no. 515/97 on mutual assistance between the administrative authorities of the Member States and cooperation between the latter and the Commission to ensure the correct application of the law on customs and agricultural matters, OJ L 243, 18.9.2015.
741. Regulation (EU) no. 604/2013 of the European Parliament and of the Council of 26 Jun. 2013 establishing the criteria and mechanisms for determining the Member State responsible for examining an application for international protection lodged in one of the Member States by a third-country national or a stateless person, OJ L 180, 29.6.2013.
742. Regulation (EC) no. 767/2008 of the European Parliament and of the Council of 9 Jul. 2008 concerning the Visa Information System (VIS) and the exchange of data between Member States on short-stay visas (VIS Regulation), OJ L 218, 13.8.2008.

Regulation (EU) 1024/2012[743] (on administrative cooperation through the Internal Market Information System and repealing Commission Decision 2008/49/EC 'the IMI Regulation'), as well as L. 98/1989, which has ratified and transposed in the Italian legal framework the Strasbourg Convention no. 108 of 1981 ('Convention for the Protection of Individuals with Regard to Automatic Processing of Personal Data').

§2. Tasks

531. In addition to the provisions set out in the GDPR, under Article 154 of the Personal Data Protection Code, the GPDP shall, also of its own motion and by relying on the Bureau:

(a) verify whether data processing operations are carried out in compliance with applicable laws and regulations, also in case of termination of processing and with regard to the storage of traffic data;
(b) handle the complaints lodged with it in pursuance of the Regulation and the provisions of this Code by also laying down specific arrangements in that respect through its rules of procedure and setting the priority issues as resulting annually from such complaints, which issues may then become the subject of investigations in the course of the relevant year;
(c) encourage the adoption of rules of conduct in the cases mentioned under section 2-c;
(d) report facts and/or circumstances amounting to offences to be prosecuted ex officio, which it has come to know either in carrying out or on account of its functions;
(e) transmit the annual report as drawn up pursuant to Article 59 of the Regulation to Parliament and Government by the 31 May of the year following that to which the report refers;
(f) ensure the protection of the fundamental rights and freedoms of the individuals by implementing the Regulation and this Code as appropriate;
(g) discharge such tasks as are committed to it by EU or State law and carry out such additional functions as are laid down in domestic law.

532. Taking into account the complaints lodged by individuals, the GPDP determines the priority issues on an annual basis, taking from such complaints issues that may then become the subject of investigations in the course of the relevant year. Every six months, the GPDP approves its semestral inspection plan, which is published on its website. The inspection activities may also be carried out by means of the GdF's Special Unit for the Protection of Privacy and Technological Fraud.[744]

743. Regulation (EU) no. 1024/2012 of the European Parliament and of the Council of 25 Oct. 2012 on administrative cooperation through the Internal Market Information System and repealing Commission Decision 2008/49/EC ('the IMI Regulation'), OJ L 316, 14.11.2012.

744. *See* Part VIII, Ch. 1, §1, *supra*.

533. The GPDP is also required to discharge supervisory or assistance tasks concerning personal data processing as provided for by laws ratifying international agreements and conventions or else by EU regulations,[745] such as the Council of Europe's Convention no. 108 on the protection of individuals with regard to the automated processing of personal data, implemented by L. 98/1989, being the GPDP designated as the relevant authority for the purpose of inter-State cooperation pursuant to Article 13 of said Convention.

534. However, the GPDP's tasks do not include the supervision over processing that is carried out by judicial authorities acting in their judicial capacity.

535. In order to carry out its tasks under Article 158 of the Personal Data Protection Code, the GPDP may request the controller, the processor, or their representative, the data subject or a third party to provide information and produce documents regarding the content of databases. The GPDP may order those databases and filing systems to be accessed and other inspections or checks to be carried out at the premises where the processing takes place or where investigations are to be performed that are instrumental on whatever ground to check compliance with personal data protection law. In addition, pursuant to paragraph 4 of Article 158, inquiries can be carried out at a person's home or in other private dwelling place and/or the relevant appurtenances, but only on the basis of the informed consent of the data controller or processor or, alternatively, on the basis of an authorization from the judge presiding over the court that is competent geographically for the place where the inquiries are to be carried out; such authorization shall be granted by a reasoned decree without delay and anyhow within three days of receiving the relevant request from the GPDP, if it can be proven that the inquiries cannot be postponed.

Pursuant to paragraph 5 of Article 158, inquiries may also concern publicly available communications networks and entail the online acquisition of data and information, subject to the safeguards referred to in paragraph 4. Moreover, specific minutes shall be drawn while ensuring the right of every party to be heard if the said inquiries are carried out at the controller's.

§3. Powers

536. According to the provision of Article 154-*bis* of the Personal Data Protection Code, the GPDP has the power to:

(i) Adopt necessary guidelines concerning organizational measures according to the principles of the GDPR, especially with respect to Article 25 GDPR on data protection by design and by default. This provision should be interpreted as being limited to specific national provisions to avoid compromising the

745. *See*, for a general overview, Part II, Ch. 1, *supra*.

uniformity of interpretation of GDPR.[746] The GPDP may also prescribe simplifications in the application of the provisions of the GDPR for small or medium-sized companies which act as data controllers,[747] which is in line with Recital 13 GDPR.

(ii) Approve rules of conduct according to Article 2-*quater* of the Personal Data Protection Code.[748]

537. In addition, the GPDP may invite representatives of other national independent administrative authorities to attend its meetings or be invited to the meetings held by other national independent administrative authorities and take part in discussing issues of shared interest; the GPDP may also request the cooperation of specialized staff from any other national independent administrative authority.

538. Moreover, the GPDP shall publish its decisions based on the provisions made in a decision of general application regulating the duration of such publication, the publication in the Official Journal of the Italian Republic and on the GPDP's own website, and the cases where it is empowered to blank certain items in its decisions.[749]

539. Article 166 of the Personal Data Protection Code provides the power of the Supervisory Authority to start civil proceedings against data controllers and processors in the case of violations of data protection legislation according to Article 58, paragraph 4, GDPR.[750]

540. The GPDP may also request information and/or order the exhibition of documents from any data controller or processor or from the appointed representative of the data controller under Article 27 GDPR.

According to Article 158 of the Personal Data Protection Code, the GPDP can also have direct access to databases and files and may carry out in-person inspections and checks directly in the places where the processing is taking place or in other places where it is possible to find information concerning the processing performed.

---

746. Bolognini & Pelino, *Codice della Disciplina Privacy* (Giuffrè Francis Lefebvre, 2019).
747. To determine the concept of the small or medium enterprise *see* Art. 2 of the attachment at the Recommendation 2003/361/CE of the Commission.
748. For more information, *see* Part VI, §1 of this volume, *supra*.
749. *See*, in particular, GPDP's internal Regulation 1/2019: GPDP, Deliberazione del 4 aprile 2019 – Regolamento n. 1/2019 concernente le procedure interne aventi rilevanza esterna, finalizzate allo svolgimento dei compiti e all'esercizio dei poteri demandati al Garante per la protezione dei dati personali, 4.4.2019, doc. web no. 9107633, https://www.garanteprivacy.it/web/guest/home/docweb/-/docweb-display/docweb/9107633 and Art. 154-*bis*, para. 3, of the Personal Data Protection Code.
750. This provision, even if arguably not in contrast with the GDPR, is unclear, because the GPDP may sanction directly the data controller who acts in violation of the GDPR, so it is not clear why it should start a civil proceeding in front of another authority. For more insights, *see* Giulia Milizia, *Il Garante della privacy può agire contro le violazioni transfrontaliere di Facebook. Ecco le 'linee guida' della CGUE*, 116 Diritto e Giustizia 2 (2021).

541. Under Article 159 of the Personal Data Protection Code, before starting the inspection, the GPDP must show an identification document and the President's decree if the inspection takes place in a private space. A consultant of the Authority may also participate in the operation, who must maintain the secrecy of what was found during the investigation.

If the Supervisory Authority carries out an inspection requiring access to the premises of an organization, it may inform the data controller or processor before the inspection commences. A person appointed by the data controller or processor may also be present to assist in the verification activities.

If the inspection is going to take place in a place of private residence or in its appurtenances, the GPDP needs to obtain the prior consent of the data controller or the processor or, in case of their absence, the preventive authorization of the President of the Civil Court of the place in which the inspection is being carried out. In case of urgency, the President of the Tribunal shall act without delay by reasoned decree within three days following the requests.

542. The inspection is carried out by the personnel of the GPDP's Office with the participation, if necessary, of the personnel of the Data Protection Authorities of other Member States. The GPDP, in the performance of its tasks, can also request the collaboration of other State bodies and authorities. Inspections are carried out by a member of the *Collegio* appointed by the GPDP. This person may not delegate the inspection to others in cases where the investigation involves a body acting for the defence or security of the State. In those cases, specific safeguards are provided to guarantee the necessary secrecy of the information collected as well as the result of the investigations.

During the inspection, the personnel of the GPDP can copy any document, act, or personal data, also by sample and by way of informatic or telematic means. After the checks have been carried out, minutes are taken in which any statements made by those present are also recorded.

All persons involved in inspection activities must provide the necessary collaboration with the GPDP. If those present refuse to provide the necessary cooperation to the GPDP and/or do not consent to the conduct of the inspection, the GPDP may still proceed with the inspection activities, and the resulting additional expenses will be charged to the data controller or processor with the final GPDP's decision. This part of the decision constitutes an enforcement order under Articles 474 and 475 of the Civil Code.

543. Unless the GPDP's President's decree provides otherwise, inspections cannot commence before 7:00 am and may not go on after 8:00 pm. In addition, prior to the start of the inspection, the parties can be notified if this would be helpful to the successful completion of the operations.

The GPDP may also transmit e-mail requests for information or documents, checklists and any other information useful for the inspection.

544. If, during the inspection, the GPDP suspects that a crime has been committed, all provisions of the Code of Criminal Procedure shall be observed.

545. Once the inspection is concluded, the GPDP is required to draft a minute of all operations carried out in an adversarial manner between the parties.

Following an investigation, the Supervisory Authority may order the adoption of the necessary measures to restore compliance with applicable legislation. If the inspection commences following the receipt of a request from a data subject, the Authority shall inform him or her about the outcome of the proceedings, except in cases where such information may prejudice public security or if there are reasons for national security defence or for the prevention of crimes.

Chapter 4. Remedies

§1. Introduction

546. Before the 2018 reform, in Italy, there were three types of administrative remediations which the GPDP could take against infringements of personal data protection legislation: appeals, complaints, and reporting. The latter remedy (reporting) was akin to a less formal complaint to the GPDP.

One of the most important modifications seen with the 2018 reform has arguably been the elimination of the appeal as a remedy. There are now only two types of administrative remedies: complaints, under Article 77 GDPR and further regulated by Italian law under Articles 140-*bis* to 143 of the Personal Data Protection Code, and reporting under Article 144 of the Personal Data Protection Code.

547. More specifically, according to Article 140-*bis* of the Personal Data Protection Code, if the data subject believes that their rights have been infringed because of a violation of applicable data protection legislation, they may lodge a complaint with the GPDP or file an appeal before the Judicial Authority. Judicial and administrative remedies (i.e., those in front of the GPDP) are alternatives to each other.

Claims to the GPDP cannot be proposed if, for the same object and between the same parties, the judicial proceeding has already been started. At the same time, a complaint to the GPDP renders an action brought before the judicial authority between the same parties and for the same subject matter inadmissible, except in the case provided for in Article 10, paragraph 4, of Legislative Decree 1 September 2011, no. 150. This provision has been amended from the pre-2018 version, which only provided one type of remedy (the appeal) exclusively for the infringement of Article 7 of the Personal Data Protection Code (repealed by the 2018 Reform), which concerned data subject's rights.

548. The circumstance that the remedies are alternative to each other could be problematic for data subjects who want to enforce their data protection rights because of the fact that they should decide, in advance, which remedy to choose, possibly without having appropriate knowledge or expertise for their decision.

In addition, the proceedings in front of the GPDP proceeding are less procedurally burdensome than judicial proceedings. As a result, the proceedings in front of the GPDP do not have the same strict rules of civil proceedings, and as a result, the adversarial process between the parties risk being not adequately guaranteed.[751]

It should finally be noted that this alternativity of remedies is not foreseen under the GDPR which, in accordance with its Articles 77 and 79, clearly provide that both remedies can be initiated by a data subject without prejudice to the possibility of undergoing both of them.

751. *See* Bolognini & Pelino, Codice privacy: tutte le novità del d.lgs. 101/2018 (Giuffrè Francis Lefebvre, 2019), at 87–89.

§2. Remedies in Front of the GPDP

I. The Complaint to the GPDP

549. The Personal Data Protection Code (Articles 140-bis to 143) regulate the complaint to the GPDP in actuation of the provision of Article 77 GDPR.

With the complaint, a data subject may represent a possible violation of the data protection legislation to the GPDP, but, unlike recourse to the judicial authority, it is not possible to advance a request for compensation for any damages suffered as a result of the violation for the proceedings are being carried out.

550. Complaints can be personally submitted by the data subject or by a lawyer or with the assistance of a non-profit association or other similar body. In these cases, if the data subject does not act on their own behalf, they should give the power of attorney to the lawyer or to the association, and such power of attorney must be attached to the complaint together with the other relevant documents.

The complaint and the power of attorney must be signed with an authenticated signature, with a digital signature, or with a handwritten signature. In the latter case, a copy of a valid identification document of the party must also be attached to the complaint.

The complaint can be delivered personally by hand to the GPDP's office, by registered letter with a return receipt, or via certified electronic mail.

551. After receiving the complaint, the GPDP initiates a preliminary investigation. If the complaint is not manifestly unfounded and it is possible to immediately adopt corrective measures the GPDP, also before the conclusion of the procedure, may order the data controller to adopt measures as provided for by Article 58 GDPR.

The complaint should be decided within nine months from the starting date, and in any case, within three months, the GPDP may inform the data subject about the status of the proceedings. Otherwise, if the GPDP does not inform the data subject at the end of three months, they could act before the Civil Court.

Only for motivated reasons related to the investigation, the GPDP may define the claim in twelve months. Where it is necessary to initiate the cooperation procedure provided by Article 60 GDPR, the term for the decision is suspended for the entire duration of that procedure.

552. The decision, once adopted, may be appealed in accordance with Article 152 of the Personal Data Protection Code in front of the Civil Court. Possible claims for damages suffered by the data subject as a result of infringement of applicable law may be requested by referring to the Civil Court.[752]

---

752. As indicated *supra* in this Ch. 2, the GPDP is competent for the adoption of corrective measures (Art. 58, para. 2, GDPR) and for imposing sanctions (Art. 83 GDPR and Art. 166 of the Personal Data Protection Code), but not for restoring damages suffered by the data subject.

553. Concerning costs, there is no compensation for the litigation costs even for the winning party; these costs may be asked to the Civil Court as a part of the pecuniary damage suffered by the data subject.[753]

554. In light of the GDPR (Articles 57, paragraph 1, letter f), and 57, paragraph 3, GDPR) complaints are now free of charge. Before, the cost of filing a complaint with the GPDP was EUR 150.00, except in special cases such as with regard to persons entitled to legal aid. The new provision introduced with the 2018 reform has therefore provided further safeguards to data subjects, especially in the case of less severe violations that are, however, perpetrated against multiple individuals.

II. The Reporting to the GPDP

555. The reporting to the GPDP was provided by Italian data protection law also before the direct applicability of the GDPR, but the 2018 reform of the Personal Data Protection Code has introduced some new provisions. In particular, this remedy, differently than a complaint, is not an alternative remediation to the civil judicial proceeding and may be presented by anyone (Article 144, paragraph 2, of the Personal Data Protection Code) even if the person does not qualify as a data subject. Before the 2018 reform, this remedy was available only to data subjects (Article 141, paragraph 1, of the pre-2018 Personal Data Protection Code).

556. In addition to this provision, there is another type of reporting introduced by Article 9, paragraph 1, letter g), of Law Decree 8 October 2021, no. 139, converted into law with amendments by Law 3 December 2021, no. 205, with a view to combat the so-called revenge porn. In particular, according to Article 144-*bis* of the Personal Data Protection Code, anyone who suspects that videos, photos or other digital documents with sexual content of themselves that should have remained restricted and are sent, given to, or published on a digital platform without their consent, may be reported to the GPDP, which shall decide within the following forty-eight hours to adopt the remedies provided by Articles 143 or 144 of the Personal Data Protection Code.

If the images belong to minors, this reporting can be done by the parents or by those exercising parental responsibility. Service providers should maintain those contents for twelve months after receiving the GPDP's order, with a view to guarantee the preservation of the proof of the crime.

The GPDP should report, without any delay, to the competent public prosecutor, the notice of facts punishable under Article 615-*ter* of the Criminal Code.

753. *See* Bolognini & Pelino, Codice privacy: tutte le novità del d.lgs. 101/2018 (Giuffrè Francis Lefebvre, 2019), at 87–89.

§3. Judicial Remedies

I. Civil Court

557. The Italian civil courts are competent for all the disputes that have as their object judicial appeals in relation to Articles 78 and 79 GDPR and for all matters relating to data protection legislation or the compensation for damages under Article 82 GDPR.

558. It follows that data subjects wishing to act before the Civil Court can file an appeal.

The appeal against a decision of the Supervisory Authority, should start within thirty days following receipt of the notice of the contested decision, or the tacit rejection, except where it involves foreign people, as in that case the appeal should start within sixty days. The execution of the decision could also be suspended if there is a risk of prejudice for the party.

559. The decision of the Court cannot be appealed, with the exception of the recourse to the Supreme Court of Cassation in case one of the parties contests a violation or wrong application of the law by the Court. At the end of the proceeding, the Court may condemn the defendant to restore the damages suffered by the recurrent. The timeline for these remedies is equal to the one applicable in civil proceedings, while the proceeding follows the same rules of proceedings concerning labour law, which are faster than ordinary proceedings. The Court decides in monocratic composition.

II. Criminal Court

560. If the violation of data protection legislation constitutes a crime (Articles 167–171 of the Personal Data Protection Code), the victim may file a petition before the Criminal Court.

561. The GPDP can also send the public prosecutor a motivated report if, during the inspection activities, it detects the commission of a crime.

The transmission of the acts to the Public Prosecutor's Office takes place, at the latest, at the end of the activity of verification of the violations of the provisions of the Personal Data Protection Code. This is because both authorities, the public prosecutor and the GPDP, should adjust their sanctions in compliance with Recital 149 GDPR and in observance of the principle of *ne bis in idem* (prohibition of double jeopardy), also foreseeing a reduction of the criminal sanction if an administrative sanction has already been levied.[754]

Conversely, if the prosecutor detects an unlawful processing in the context of its activities, it shall notify this fact to the GPDP without delay.

754. *Ibid.*, at 93–99.

Chapter 5. Liability of Controllers and Processors

§1. Criminal Liability

562. The Personal Data Protection Code also provides for criminal penalties within its Title III – Penalties, Chapter 2 – Criminal Offences.

563. In particular, under Article 167, paragraph 1, of the Personal Data Protection Code, anyone who, for profit or to cause other damages, violates the prescriptions specified by Article 123 ('Traffic Data'), Article 126 ('Location data'), Article 130 ('Unsolicited communication') or Article 129 ('Directories of contracting parties'),[755] the violation has caused harm to the data subject, shall be punished by imprisonment for between six months and one year, unless the offence is more serious.

Moreover, according to the second paragraph of Article 167 of the Personal Data Protection Code, anyone who, with a view to gain for themselves or another or with intent to cause harm to the data subject, causes harm to the data subject by processing the personal data mentioned in Articles 9 and 10 of the GDPR in breach of the provisions set out in Article 2-*sexies* ('Processing of special categories of personal data that is necessary for reasons of substantial public interest') and 2-*octies* ('Principles relating to the processing of data relating to criminal convictions and offences') or the safeguards referred to in section 2-*nonies* ('Safeguards applying to the processing of genetic data, biometric data, and data relating to health') shall be punished by imprisonment for one to three years, unless the offence is more serious.

According to paragraph 3 of Article 167, the same penalty shall also apply to any person who, with a view to gain for themselves or another or with the intent to cause harm to the data subject, causes harm to the data subject by transferring the personal data to a third country or an international organization in cases other than those permitted under Articles 45, 46 or 49 of the GDPR, unless the offence is more serious.

564. Article 167 provides for so-called blank criminal law provisions because it does not state an exhaustive description of the prohibited conduct but rather refers to other rules that establish the criteria of lawfulness of certain processing of personal data whose violation integrates precisely the case in question.

In other cases, the conduct that integrates the crime is even contained in other provisions of secondary rank and future issuance or in general provisions of the Supervisory Authority.

565. The jurisprudence that was formed on this Article has always interpreted the 'harm' in terms of the objective condition of punishability, i.e., as an external element to the case that in itself is already perfect in terms of compliance with the

---

755. The mentioned provisions stem from the transposition of the ePrivacy Directive within the Italian legal system and are addressed *supra* in this volume in Part I, Ch. 3.

hypothesis provided in the abstract by the legislature, which, however, was punishable only at the occurrence of actual damage to the person concerned.[756] This made it necessary to interpret the conduct in terms of concrete danger. More specifically:

> [T]he crime of unlawful processing of personal data, as per Article 167 of Legislative Decree no. 196/03, is a crime of actual threat and not merely presumed; consequently, the unlawful use of personal data is punishable, not in itself, but insofar as it is likely to produce damage to the person concerned and/or his/her assets. The damage does not only have to be economic, but can also be more immediately personal, such as, for example, the loss of time in sifting through unwanted emails and in the procedures to be followed to avoid further mailings.[757]

566. However, the Supreme Court of Cassation more recently changed its interpretation, thereby holding that:

> [I]n order for such conduct to assume criminal relevance, it is necessary that there is an actual 'harm' for each recipient, which certainly cannot be the simple annoyance of having to delete from time to time unwanted mail, but must result in a concrete injury, even if not patrimonial, but in any case susceptible to be legally appreciated, requiring in this sense an adequate factual verification aimed at ascertaining, for example, whether the user has indicated to the sender that he does not want to receive a certain type of message and whether, despite this initiative, the agent has persisted in a non-occasional manner to send unwanted messages, thus creating a real inconvenience to the recipient. 'Harm' cannot be the mere discomfort of having to delete a few occasional unwanted messages, requiring, in order to give criminal relevance to the fact, *a quid pluris*, consisting of an actual injury, which proves to be proportionate to the invasiveness of the behaviour of those who send unwanted content, perhaps remaining indifferent to any requests to put an end to high delivery of a certain type of messages.[758]

567. The new interpretation of the concept of harm was, therefore, changed by the Supreme Court, becoming a constituent element of the typical action punished by the provision. In the grounds of the judgment, in fact, the Court stated that 'the notion of harm, ultimately, consistently with the etymology of the term (derived from the verb to harm, or cause damage even moral), evokes the existence of a concrete injury to the personal or property, which, in view of the case for which we proceed, must be considered directly attributable to an operation of unlawful processing'.[759]

756. *See* Supreme Court of Cassation, no. 7504/2013, crim. sect. and no. 44940/2011, crim. sect.
757. *Ibid.* Author's translation.
758. *See* Supreme Court of Cassation, no. 40103/2015, crim. sect. Author's translation.
759. *See* Supreme Court of Cassation, no. 41604/2019, crim. sect., para. 2. Author's translation.

This interpretative change is found in terms of the existence of the criminal relevance of conduct since, without the harm, the crime cannot be punished. In addition, the new interpretation means that the offender also has to voluntarily cause harm to their victim.[760]

In other words, according to this new interpretation, in order to be liable for unlawful processing of personal data, the data controller is required to act with the consciousness and willingness to carry out an unlawful processing, not only for the purpose of profit, but also with the awareness of causing harm to others (or, at least, anticipating and accepting that there is such harm).[761]

Another important ruling of the Supreme Court of Cassation concerns the failure to remove the news of the incrimination of a person not criminally relevant under Article 167 of the Personal Data Protection Code if the initial processing was lawful and carried out according to the rules of the right to report the news.

568. The Personal Data Protection Code also establishes new criminal provisions on unlawful disclosure and dissemination of personal data undergoing large-scale processing (Article 167-*bis* of the Personal Data Protection Code) and on the fraudulent acquisition of personal data processed on a large scale[762] (Article 167-*ter* of the Personal Data Protection Code) were introduced.

Article 167-*bis*, paragraph 1, is aimed at punishing the illegal communication or diffusion of a database or a substantial part of it to gain profit or cause damage. The second paragraph punishes the communication or dissemination of an automated filing system or of a substantial part of it containing personal data undergoing large-scale processing without consent of the data subject(s) when the processing activity is based on consent. This new provision is aimed at repressing those behaviours which, due to their vastness, are not limited to the mere violation of the rules on processing and is aimed at combating the practice of creating private databases, also used for commercial purposes, in defiance of the rules on the lawfulness of processing. Unlike the unlawful processing of personal data, which can only be committed by the data controller and processor, in this case, the crime can be committed by anyone.

Article 167-*ter* of the Personal Data Protection Code represents a new and additional incriminating case that punishes the fraudulent acquisition of an automated filing system or a substantial part of it containing personal data in order to gain profit for oneself or others. This is a new criminal provision aimed at punishing the fraudulent acquisition of personal data. The essential elements of this crime are the same as those found in Article 167-*bis* of the Personal Data Protection Code.

---

760. The Supreme Court of Cassation, in some points of the judgment, shows that it accepts an opposite address that was formed on the point and that required that 'the harm to the person to whom the illegally processed data relate is, for its homogeneity with respect to the interest affected, and its direct causal derivation from the typical conduct, a constituent element of the crime, and not an objective condition of punishability, with the result that it must be expected and desired or otherwise accepted by the agent as an effect of his action, regardless of whether it constitutes or is identified with the purpose of the action (*see* Supreme Court of Cassation, no. 40103/2015)'. Author's translation.

761. *See* Supreme Court of Cassation, no. 7504/2013, crim. sect., and no. 44940/2011, crim. sect.

762. For the concept of 'large scale' *see* Recital 91 GDPR.

569. The offence in question has elements of commonality with computer crimes and, above all, with abusive access to a computer system (Article 615-*ter* of the Criminal Code) which protects against unauthorized intrusions aimed at infringing the confidentiality of personal data contained in computer systems protected by passwords. As pointed out by the doctrine: 'There is no doubt, in fact, that also the crime of abusive access to computer system, although it does not expressly regulate computer systems containing personal data, is aimed at protecting individual privacy, consistently with its placement in the Criminal Code among the crimes against individual freedom.'[763]

Since access to a computer system does not presuppose the acquisition of the data contained in the computer system, it must be considered that the two provisions may be applied cumulatively, since Article 167-*ter* punishes a further and consequential conduct to abusive access.[764]

570. According to Article 168 of the Personal Data Protection Code, false declarations to the GPDP during a proceeding or during an investigation are punished. Additionally, interruptions or disturbances of the regularity of a procedure before the Supervisory Authority or of the investigations carried out by the same are punishable.

However, the violation of minimum security measures provided by Annex B of the Personal Data Protection Code, now repealed by the 2018 reform, is no longer a crime. This choice is probably motivated by the fact that a list of measures that should be implemented no longer exists, and the risk-based approach under Article 32 GDPR is incompatible with the constitutional principle of determinateness of criminal provision.

571. According to Article 170 of the Personal Data Protection Code, anyone who, being obliged to do so, does not observe the measure adopted by the GPDP pursuant to Article 58, paragraph 2, letter f), GDPR, of Article 2-f(1), as well as the general measures referred to in Article 21, paragraph 1, of the Legislative Decree implementing Article 13 of Law 25 October 2017, no. 163, is punished with imprisonment for between three months and two years. This provision was introduced to ensure the effectiveness of the GPDP decision, but the manner in which the conduct is punished under this provision is indeterminate and refers its content to another

763. *See* Irene Gasparini, *La tutela penale della 'privacy sanitaria' nell'era del GDPR*, 3 Rivista Italiana di Medicina Legale (e del Diritto in campo sanitario) 863, (2019). Author's translation.

764. *See* Supreme Court of Cassation no. 1761/2021, crime sect., according to which there would be no relationship referable to the provision of Art. 15 of the Criminal Code between the Art. 615-*ter* of the Criminal Code, which punishes the abusive access to a computer system, and the Art. 167 of the Personal Data Protection Code, which punishes the unlawful processing of personal data, since these are totally different provisions in terms of their finalistic conduct and material activity which exclude the uniqueness and homogeneity necessary to be qualified as a special crime. Author's translation.

provision. For this reason, some authors maintain that this provision amounts to a violation of the constitutional principle of legality.[765]

572. Under the provisions of Article 171 of the Personal Data Protection Code, the violations of Article 4 of the Law 20 May 1970, no. 300 (so-called *Statuto dei Lavoratori*, i.e., 'Workers' Statute'), i.e., those conducts that could determine am unlawful remote control of workers, are punished. By way of example, all the cases relating to the violation of the rules on the installation of video surveillance systems fall within the scope of this Article.

§2. Civil Liability

573. For some time now, there has been a tendency to recognize the patrimonial value of personal data: this element seems to bring the processing of personal data from a 'moral' dimension and the protection of a fundamental right to a 'negotiation' and marketing of data dimension, where personal data are understood as a possible object of a sale, put in place both between market operators and between the data subjects.[766]

574. This theory is confirmed by the relevant Italian jurisprudence. In particular, the AgCM, with measure no. 27432 adopted on 29 November 2018,[767] intended to sanction the practice of Facebook Inc. and Facebook Ireland Ltd. which constituted an undue conditioning of the consumer-user through the request for the insertion of their personal data on the platform, then using such data for commercial profiling for marketing purposes, as a binding step to be able to access the membership, which was nonetheless marketed as being 'free of charge'.

The decision of the AgCM has been upheld by the Council of State[768] which affirmed that the reproach addressed to Facebook consists of not having fairly informed the user, who in this case is technically a 'consumer' pursuant to consumer protection law, at the moment in which he makes available his personal data in order to be able to use the services offered by Facebook companies free of charge. In fact, in those cases, the user remains convinced that the achievement of the benefits associated with access to the platform is free and is not able to recognize and realize that, in exchange for the advantage of membership, an automatic profiling for commercial use takes place, not clearly and immediately perceived, at the time of the first access, as an inevitable consequence of the provision of data.

---

765. *See* Matteo Solinas, *Tutela penale della privacy dopo il GDPR: la frettolosa giustapposizione delle fonti è scaturigine di un sistema farraginoso, che crea confusione*, 1 Responsabilità civile e previdenza sociale 336, (2020).
766. Mariafrancesca Cocuccio, *Dimensione 'patrimoniale' del dato personale e tutele risarcitorie*, 1 Diritto di Famiglia e delle Persone 230, (2022).
767. Available at: http://www.agcm.it/dotcmsCustom/tc/2023/12/getDominoAttach?urlStr=192.168.14.10:8080/C12560D000291394/0/5A1EFA963A109B64C125835F00542FE2/%24File/p27432.pdf.
768. *See* Council of State: no. 2631 of 29.3.2021, Diritto di Famiglia e delle Persone, 965, (2021). Author's translation.

According to the AgCM, it is not possible to agree with the argument of Facebook, according to which personal data constitutes a *res extra commercium* (i.e., a non-marketable object). The monetization of personal data, which in the case in point occurs unconsciously, constitutes the consequence of the intervention of the companies through the making available of the data and the profiling of the user for commercial purposes.

575. Of the same opinion is the Council of State, which underlined:

> [T]he absence of an adequate alert informing users, with immediacy and effectiveness, about the importance of the commercial value of their data with respect to the social networking service offered, Facebook merely emphasizing how membership is free forever. The incompleteness of the information provided on the Facebook login page is not diminished even by the recent introduction, from April 2018, of the 'cookie banner' in that its display is only eventual and not necessarily linked to registration in the Facebook Platform. In fact, the banner does not appear during the creation of the account if the user has already 'clicked and navigated' on the site. Moreover, it is, in any case, generic and placed in a position not adjacent to the indication of the free service.[769]

576. This new concept of commercialization of personal data has also been confirmed by other bodies, not only at the Italian level.[770] For example, Opinion 4/2017 of the European Data Protection Supervisor ('EDPS') published on 17 March 2017 regarding the proposal for a directive of the European Parliament and of the council on certain aspects of contracts for the supply of digital content COM/2015/0634 final – 2015/0287 (COD) underlines one aspect of the Proposal that is deemed problematic, i.e., that it 'would apply to "any contract where the supplier supplies digital content to the consumer or undertakes to do so" in exchange of a price but also when "the consumer actively provides counter-performance other than money in the form of personal data or any other data"'.[771] In relation to this provision, the EDPS warns against the adoption of new provisions such as the one set out in Article 3 of the aforementioned proposal, which introduces the idea that people can pay for goods or services with their data in the same way as money, since a fundamental right such as the right to the protection of personal data cannot be considered a commodity and reduced to simple consumer interest.[772]

---

769. *Ibid.*, para. 10.
770. *See also* https://www.garanteprivacy.it/home/docweb/-/docweb-display/docweb/9569905 in which the Italian Supervisory Authority underlines the concepts mentioned above.
771. *See* EDPS, *Opinion 4/2017 on the Proposal for a Directive on certain aspects concerning contracts for the supply of digital content*, https://edps.europa.eu/sites/edp/files/publication/17-03-14_opinion_digital_content_en.pdf.
772. *See* Vincenzo Ricciuto, La patrimonializzazione dei dati personali. Contratto e mercato nella ricostruzione del fenomeno, 4 Diritto dell'Informazione e dell'Informatica (Il) 689, (2018).

577. In the EDPS Opinion, the above-mentioned is underlined as one of the aspects most problematic of the Proposal. In particular, the following passage seems particularly relevant:

> [S]ince it will be applicable to situations where a price is paid for the digital content, but also where digital content is supplied in exchange for a counter-performance other than money in the form of personal data or any other data. The EDPS warns against any new provision introducing the idea that people can pay with their data the same way as they do with money. Fundamental rights such as the right to the protection of personal data cannot be reduced to simple consumer interests, and personal data cannot be considered as a mere commodity. The recently adopted data protection framework (the 'GDPR') is not yet fully applicable and the proposal for new e-Privacy legislation is currently under discussion. The EU should avoid therefore any new proposals that upset the careful balance negotiated by the EU legislator on data protection rules. Overlapping initiatives could inadvertently put at risk the coherence of the Digital Single Market, resulting in regulatory fragmentation and legal uncertainty. The EDPS recommends that the EU apply the GDPR as the means for regulating use of personal data in the digital economy. The notion of 'data as counter-performance' – left undefined in the proposal – could cause confusion as to the precise function of the data in a given transaction. The lack of clear information from the suppliers in this regard may add further difficulties. We therefore suggest considering, as a way of resolving this problem, using the definition of services under the TFEU or the provision used by the GDPR to define its territorial scope.[773]

578. The idea of personal data having a monetary value is strictly connected with the restoration of damages suffered in case of illicit processing. Before the entry into force of the GDPR in the Italian system, the subject of civil liability arising from the unlawful processing of personal data found its discipline in Article 15 of the Personal Data Protection Code, which established that 'Whoever causes damage to others as a result of the processing of personal data is required to pay compensation pursuant to Article 2050 of the Civil Code. Non-asset damage is also compensable in case of violation of article 11.'[774]

579. Article 82 GDPR, with a view to standardize the rules of liability in case of unlawful processing of personal data, states that 'Anyone who suffers material or immaterial damage caused by a breach of this Regulation has the right to obtain compensation from the controller or processor', who may be exempt from liability if they prove that the damaging event is not 'in any way attributable' to them.

More precisely, the controller is liable for the damage caused by the processing in violation of the GDPR, while the processor is only liable for the damage caused by failure to correctly fulfil its specific obligations or if it acted in a manner which is inconsistent with the instructions of the data controller. Sub-processors, instead,

773. *See* the executive summary of the Opinion 4/2017 (*supra* n. 772) available at www.edps.europa.eu.
774. Author's translation.

are liable for damages only 'internally' towards the processor, not towards the data subject. In summary, the data controller (and any processor) is strictly liable for non-compliance with the precepts of the GDPR.

The people who suffered some damages for the illicit processing shall have the *onus* of demonstrating their occurrence.

580. In some jurisprudential rulings of lower courts, the compensation for damages is considered to be *in re ipsa*, i.e., stemming from the violation itself.[775] If the damage were to be compensated *in re ipsa*, it would mean that the conduct, simply because it was unlawful, that is, in breach of data protection provisions, would by itself give rise to a right to compensation, irrespective of the actual damage, the proof of it, and its gravity.

However, this jurisprudential orientation has never been accepted by the Supreme Court of Cassation, as it unhinges the now consolidated elements of compensation for non-material damage introduced by the 'San Martino' Supreme Court of Cassation decision in 2008[776] which have instead affirmed that simple discomfort and annoyance cannot be compensated, but it must be assessed whether the illicit conduct carried out in violation of the legal precept has effectively produced serious and not trivial damage ('damage-consequence'), so as to overcome the threshold of minimum seriousness required by Article 2 of Italian Constitution to grant compensation (the so-called *bagatellare* clause).

In order to be compensated, the damage must therefore derive from the violation of the rule of law, but next to the 'damaging-event' (the event which amounts to a violation of the data protection provision), the actual 'damage-consequence' must be assessed in practice. It follows that compensation cannot arise from unlawful processing itself, but only once it has been verified that cumulatively:

(i) damage to an interest protected by the law has taken place, in this case, the fundamental rights of the individual under Articles 2 and 21 of the Constitution and Article 8 ECHR, such as a violation of the right to privacy and the protection of personal data; and
(ii) that such damage is serious and non-tolerable.

581. Unlawful processing would, therefore, be compensable at the civil law level, according to constant case law, only where this causes inconvenience, suffering, anxiety and concern, all of which must be proven by the plaintiff, even through simple assumptions, demonstrating that a certain threshold of 'tolerability' and therefore seriousness has been exceeded.[777]

There is, therefore, a presumption of guilt on the part of the entity that carries out the processing, and this implies that instead of being the injured party who must prove that damage has been suffered, it will be the entity which carried out the

775. *See*, for example: Tribunal of Siena, case no. 1244 of 29.10.2018.
776. *See* Italian Supreme Court United Division: no. 26972 11/11/2008, https://www.altalex.com/documents/news/2010/02/19/il-danno-esistenziale-esiste-la-posizione-delle-sezioni-unite.
777. *See*, e.g., Supreme Court of Cassation, no. 207/2019, civ. sect.; Supreme Court of Cassation, no. 16402/2021.

(allegedly, illicit) processing who must overcome the presumption that such damage has occurred, providing proof to the contrary (e.g., by demonstrating that it has acquired consent, or that the behaviour does not reach a certain threshold of gravity).[778] That gravity of damage should not necessarily be read in quantitative terms.

778. *See*, for the contrary interpretation, Supreme Court of Cassation no. 14618/2021 according to which it is the injured party who must prove the damages occurred under the Art. 2050 of the Civil Code. The offender should demonstrate that it has put in place all measures necessary to avoid such damages.

Chapter 6. Penalties

§1. Criteria for the Application of Administrative Fines

582. The criteria for the application of administrative fines and the relevant procedure to be followed by the GPDP when it issues sanctions and adopts corrective measures are found in Article 166 of the Personal Data Protection Code. Paragraph 1 of Article 166 of the Code, which was amended by Law Decree 8 October 2021, no. 139, converted into law with amendments by Law 3 December 2021, no. 205, on urgent provisions for access to cultural, sports and recreational activities, as well as for the organization of public administrations and on the protection of personal data,[779] references the violations which may lead to the application of administrative fines under Article 83, paragraph 4, GDPR.

To this end, it is useful to recall that under Article 83, paragraph 4, GDPR, violations are subject to the application of administrative fines up to EUR 10,000,000, or for undertakings, up to a maximum of 2% of the total worldwide annual turnover of the entity in the preceding financial year (whichever is higher).[780] Under Italian data protection law, violations subject to such penalties include infringements of the following articles of the Personal Data Protection Code:

(i) Article 2-*quinquies,* paragraph 2 in relation to the consent of children in the context of the provision of information society services and the necessity to provide adequate information to the concerned data subjects through the use of clear and plain language, exhaustive but concise, easily intelligible and accessible so as to render the provision of consent meaningful.

(ii) Article 92, paragraph 1, concerning clinical records and, more specifically, in relation to the requirement to adopt specific measures that allow for data to be understandable, distinct in that data concerning a patient is separate from data that concerns other patients, also with respect to unborn children, and that such data are kept up-to-date.

(iii) Article 93, paragraph 1, concerning birth certificates, and more specifically, that the 'certificate of attendance at birth shall be replaced by a declaration only containing the data that must be entered into the register of births'.

(iv) Article 123, paragraph 4, concerning traffic data and, more specifically, violations concerning the provision of information to be provided to data subjects under Articles 13 and 14 GDPR, insofar as service providers are required to inform contracting parties of both the duration of the processing and the nature of the traffic data processed for the purposes laid down in Article 123, paragraphs 2 and 3.

(v) Article 128 on automatic call forwarding, insofar as contracting parties should be facilitated in stopping automatic call forwarding to their own device.

779. Paragraph as amended by D.L. 139/2021, converted, with amendments, by L. 205/2021, on urgent provisions for access to cultural, sports and recreational activities, as well as for the organization of public administrations and on the protection of personal data.

780. Article 83, para. 4, GDPR.

(vi) Article 129, paragraph 2, on directories of contracting parties and the use of personal data contained in publicly available electronic and paper directories.
(vii) Article 132-*ter* on the security of processing by providers of publicly available electronic communications services.
(viii) Article 110, paragraph 1, covering exceptions to the requirement to collect the consent of data subjects where, in the context of medical, biomedical and epidemiological research, an organization fails to either: (i) carry out and publish a data protection impact assessment,[781] or (ii) consult the GPDP prior to such processing in the case where such consultation is required under the GDPR.[782]

583. Article 166, paragraph 2 of the Personal Data Protection Code, instead, deals with administrative fines issued under Article 83, paragraph 5, GDPR. Under the aforementioned GDPR Article, infringements are punishable with administrative fines of up to a maximum of EUR 20,000,000, 'or in the case of an undertaking, up to 4% of the total worldwide annual turnover of the preceding financial year, whichever is higher'.[783]

584. Under Part I of the Personal Data Protection Code titled 'Principles', violations which may lead to the application of administrative fines under Article 83(5) GDPR include:

(i) Title I – Principles and General Provisions, Chapter II – Principles: Article 2-*ter;* Article 2-*quinquies,* paragraph 1; Article 2-*sexies;* Article 2-*septies,* paragraph 8; Article 2-*octies.*
(ii) Title I – Principles and General Provisions, Chapter III – Provisions on the Rights of Data Subjects: Article 2-*duodecies,* paragraphs 1 to 4.

585. Other violations which may lead to the application of administrative fines under Article 83, paragraph 5, GDPR, include violations found in Part II of the Personal Data Protection Code titled 'Provisions applying to processing that is necessary for compliance with a legal obligation or for the performance of a task carried out in the public interest or in the exercise of official authority and to processing referred to in Chapter IX of the Regulation.' These provisions include:

781. The first sentence of Art. 110, para. 1, reads, 'The data subject's consent shall not be required to process data relating to health for scientific research purposes in the medical, bio-medical or epidemiological sectors if the said research is carried out in accordance with laws or regulations or EU law pursuant to Article 9(2), letter i), of the Regulation, including research that is part of a biomedical or health care research programme pursuant to Section 12-a of legislative decree No 502 of 30.12.92, and if a data protection impact assessment is carried out and published in accordance with Articles 35 and 36 of the Regulation.'

782. *See* Art. 110, para. 1, third sentence which reads, 'In such cases, the controller shall take appropriate measures to protect the rights, freedoms and legitimate interests of the data subjects and the research programme shall be the subject of a reasoned, favourable opinion by the geographically competent ethics committee as well as being submitted to the Garante for prior consultation in accordance with Article 36 of the Regulation.'

783. Article 83, para. 5, GDPR.

(i) Title I – Processing Operations in the Judicial Sector, Chapter III – Legal Information Services: Article 52, paragraphs 4 and 5.
(ii) Title V – Processing of Personal Data in the Health Care Sector, Chapter I – In General: Article 75.
(iii) Title V – Processing of Personal Data in the Health Care Sector, Chapter II – Specific Arrangements to Inform the Data Subject and Process Personal Data: Article 78; Article 79, Article 80, Article 82.
(iv) Title V – Processing of Personal Data in the Health Care Sector, Chapter VI – Miscellaneous Provisions: Article 92, paragraph 2; Article 93, paragraphs 2 and 3.
(v) Title VI – Education, Chapter I – In General: Article 96.
(vi) Title VII – Processing for Archiving Purposes in the Public Interest, Scientific or Historical Research Purposes or Statistical Purposes, Chapter I – In General: Article 99; Article 100, paragraphs 1, 2 and 4.
(vii) Title VII – Processing for Archiving Purposes in the Public Interest, Scientific or Historical Research Purposes or Statistical Purposes, Chapter II – Processing for Archiving Purposes in the Public Interest or for Historical Research Purposes: Article 101.
(viii) Title VII – Processing for Archiving Purposes in the Public Interest, Scientific or Historical Research Purposes or Statistical Purposes, Chapter III – Processing for Statistical Purposes or Scientific Research Purposes: Article 105, paragraphs 1, 2 and 4; Article 110-a, paragraphs 2 and 3.
(ix) Title VIII – Processing Activities in Employer-Employee Relations, Chapter I – In General: Article 111; Article 111-*bis*.
(x) Title VIII – Processing Activities in Employer-Employee Relations, Chapter IV – Assistance Boards and Welfare Boards: Article 116, paragraph 1.
(xi) Title IX – Other Processing Activities in the Public Sector or in the Public Interest, Chapter I – Insurance Companies: Article 120, paragraph 2.
(xii) Title X – Electronic Communications, Chapter I – Electronic Communications services: Article 122; Article 123, paragraphs 1, 2, 3 and 5; Article 124; Article 125; Article 126; Article 130, paragraphs 1 to 5; Article 131; Article 132; Article 132-a, paragraph 2; Article 132-*quater*.

586. Part III of the Personal Data Protection Code, titled 'Remedies and Sanctions' provides for the application of administrative fines under Article 83, paragraph 5, GDPR, for violations of Article 157 of the Personal Data Protection Code[784] on the 'Request for Information and Provision of Documents' as well as for violations of the safeguards and rules of conduct referred to in Articles 2-*quater* and 2-*sexies*, respectively titled 'Rules of conduct' and 'Safeguards applying to the processing of genetic data, biometric data, and data relating to health.'

587. Other sanctions are provided by Article 42 of Legislative Decree 18 May 2018, no. 51, in the context of the processing of personal data by law enforcement

784. *See* Title II – Independent Supervisory Authority, Ch. III – Inquiries and Controls, Personal Data Protection Code.

agencies, in the context of Italy's transposition of Directive 2018/680. Such sanctions shall be examined within Part X, Chapter 3, VII.

§2. Procedural Rules for the Adoption and Quantification of Administrative Fines and Other Corrective Measures

588. Paragraph 3, Article 166 of the Personal Data Protection Code, recalls that the GPDP is empowered under Article 58, paragraph 2, GDPR, to adopt corrective measures and issue administrative sanctions as referred to in Article 83 GDPR and in paragraphs 1 and 2 of Article 166 of the Personal Data Protection Code. Paragraph 4 of the same Article provides that the GPDP may issue fines and adopt measures against public and private bodies and authorities either following a complaint which can be lodged with the authority under Article 77 GDPR or carry out investigations on its own volition or otherwise exercise the powers it is vested with under Article 58, paragraph 1, GDPR to, e.g., carry out audits and inspections and to gain access.[785]

Additionally, Article 166, paragraph 5, of the Code establishes that in cases where the Bureau deems that the aforementioned investigatory activities (i.e., those referred to in paragraph 4) ascertain violations of applicable data protection law, i.e., those which are referred to in the relevant Title and in Article 83, numbers 4 to 6 GDPR), the GPDP shall commence the adoption of measures and administrative sanctions as referred to in paragraph 3 of Article 166 of the Personal Data Protection Code. This is accomplished by notifying the controller or processor which violated the provisions cited above.

589. In terms of the notification to the violating entity, the GPDP shall carry out such act in accordance with what is mentioned in paragraph 9 of Article 166. This shall be done with the exception of cases where providing such notification may be 'incompatible with the nature and objective of the measures to be adopted', and in cases included in Articles 2-*quater* and 58 of the Code and Article 1, paragraph 1, of D.Lgs. 51/2018, 'exclusively if the Garante has established that the alleged violations have already caused and continue to cause effective, factual, current and substantial harm to the data subjects concerned by the said processing'.[786]

590. Concerned controllers and processers which have allegedly violated the legal data protection provisions have the possibility to send documentation and

785. Article 166, para. 4 of the Personal Data Protection Code reads, 'The proceeding to adopt the measures and fines referred to in para. 3 may be initiated against both private and public bodies or public authorities following a complaint lodged in accordance with Art. 77 of the Regulation or else following inquiries carried out by the Garante of its own motion, within the framework of the exercise of the investigative powers referred to in Art. 58(1) of the Regulation as well as in connection with accesses, inspections and audits that are carried out on the basis of either autonomous powers to carry out controls or of powers delegated by the Garante.'

786. Article 166, para. 5, of the Personal Data Protection Code.

pleadings to the GPDP in a period which does not exceed thirty days of receipt of the communication.[787] Additionally, such entities may request to be heard by the GPDP.[788]

591. Under paragraph 7, Article 166, certain provisions of Law 24 November 1981, no. 689, where applicable, must be followed in the context of imposing the administrative sanctions included in paragraph 3 of Article 166 of the Personal Data Protection Code.

More specifically, Articles 1 to 9, 18 to 22, and 24 of L. 689/1981 which concern the application of administrative fines and calls, e.g., with respect to the notions that administrative penalties can only be imposed after a law violating such activities was in force (Article 1), establish rules for applying orders and injunctions (Article 18), for seizures of property (Article 19), ancillary administrative penalties (Article 20), and the rules for opposing orders and injunctions (Article 22).

Paragraph 7 of Article 166 of the Code also establishes that in such cases, the GPDP may impose an ancillary administrative sanction upon the offending entity. Such a sanction may consist in the publication of the injunctive order on the GPDP's website (either in full or in part) or by way of carrying out 'official communication campaigns to raise awareness of the right to the protection of personal data on the basis of projects that shall be approved beforehand by the Garante and take account of the gravity of the infringement'.

592. When determining the amount of the administrative fine to be imposed on the offending entity pursuant to Article 83, paragraph 2, GDPR, the GPDP is, under paragraph 7, required to also take into consideration efforts by the offending entity to 'raise awareness of the right to the protection of personal data and were implemented by the offender prior to the commission of the infringement at issue'.[789] This notion is particularly relevant insofar as one of the main missions of supervisory authorities such as the GPDP is that of raising awareness among the public.

Further proof of the fundamental nature of raising awareness is furthermore seen in the requirement of the GPDP, under paragraph 7, to allocate half (50%) of the

787. Article 166, para. 6, of the Personal Data Protection Code.

788. *Ibid.*

789. Along these lines, it is interesting to note that in the context of the Italian DPA's initial investigation into TikTok in 2021 and its subsequent order to stop processing the personal data of users whose age could not be verified (triggered by the death of a young Italian girl after participating in a so-called challenge on the social network), the company both implemented AI-based age verification systems and launched an information campaign to raise awareness among both children and parents about the use of social networks. The GPDP itself also launched an 'awareness-raising campaign on national TV channels, in cooperation with a child protection charity ("*Telefono Azzurro*"), to foster safeguards for children'. The campaign was 'aimed at calling upon parents to actively supervise and pay special attention to the situations where their children are requested to enter their age in order to access TikTok.' More information can be found in the GPDP's press release. *See*: GPDP, *Tik Tok si adeguerà alle richieste del Garante privacy. Ma l'Autorità vigilerà sull'effettiva efficacia delle misure che verranno adottate*, Garante per la protezione dei dati personali, 3.2.2021, doc. web no. 9533424, https://www.garanteprivacy.it/home/docweb/-/docweb-display/docweb/9533424#english_version.

total proceeds gained by the administration of sanctions into the so-called appropriations which are referred to in Article 156, paragraph 8, of the Personal Data Protection Code which are, in fact, destined to the very cause of organizing awareness-raising and investigatory activities of the GPDP in addition to ensuing the implementation of the GDPR.

§3. Appeal Against GPDP Decisions

593. Entities which have been accused of violating applicable data protection legislation have the opportunity to challenge orders of the GPDP. As referred to in paragraph 8, Article 166, of D.Lgs. 150/2011, in its Article 10, paragraph 3 (providing additional provisions to the Code of Civil Procedure with respect to the reduction and simplification of civil proceedings), establishes that 'The appeal against the orders of the GPDP, including those issued as a result of a complaint of the data subject, shall be lodged, under penalty of inadmissibility, within thirty days from the date of communication of the measure or within sixty days if the complainant resides abroad.'[790]

594. Entities which have violated data protection law, as well as other parties which may be jointly and severally liable, are also entitled to 'settle the litigation by complying with the measures imposed by the GPDP, if any, and paying half of the amount of the administrative fine imposed by the GPDP'.[791]

595. Paragraph 9 of Article 166 furthermore requires the GPDP to establish a procedure for the adoption of administrative sanctions and measures (*see* paragraph 3) and to establish its own regulations for the establishment of deadlines. Such regulations are to be made public by way of their publication in the Official Gazette of the Italian Republic pursuant to Article 58, paragraph 4, GDPR, in an effort to adhere to the 'principles of full disclosure of procedural documents, equality of arms, full reporting, and separation between preparatory and decision-making phase in imposing any administrative fine'.[792] To this end, following the applicability of the GDPR, the GPDP published its 'Deliberation of 4 April 2019 – Regulation no. 1/2019 concerning internal procedures having external relevance, aimed at carrying out the tasks and exercising the powers delegated to the Data Protection Supervisor' in April 2019.[793] The Regulation was first published in the Italian Official Gazette on 8 May 2019.[794] Regulation no. 1/2019 specifically concerns procedures which are 'aimed at carrying out the tasks and exercising the powers delegated to

790. Author's translation.
791. Article 166, para. 8, of the Personal Data Protection Code.
792. Article 166, para. 9, of the Personal Data Protection Code.
793. Author's translation. GPDP, Deliberazione del 4 aprile 2019 – Regolamento n. 1/2019 concernente le procedure interne aventi rilevanza esterna, finalizzate allo svolgimento dei compiti e all'esercizio dei poteri demandati al Garante per la protezione dei dati personali, 4.4.2019, doc. web no. 9107633, https://www.garanteprivacy.it/home/docweb/-/docweb-display/docweb/9107633.
794. *Ibid.* Also note that, as the Deliberation states, 'The regulation is attached to this resolution, of which it forms an integral part, and orders its publication in the Official Gazette of the Italian

the GPDP for the protection of personal data, in particular as regards the adoption of the corrective measures referred to in Article 58, paragraph 2, of the GDPR, and of the sanctions referred to in Articles 83 of the same Regulation and 166, paragraphs 1 and 2, of the Code'.

The text was later amended on 17 February 2022, following the Resolution of 27 January 2022, to include provisions on revenge porn.[795]

596. Under its Chapter I, 'General Provisions', Regulation no. 1/2019 requires the GPDP to carry out its duties in accordance with principles including, e.g., transparency, proportionality, reasonableness, non-discrimination, the criteria of good administration, impartiality, etc. Article 4 of the aforementioned Regulation establishes that at least every six months, the GPDP must schedule the work of the Panel, the priorities of the Bureau, and its inspection activities. The Regulation also governs the initiation of procedures and the individual responsible for them (Article 6), as well as the handling of business and proceedings (Article 7). Chapter II instead deals with 'Procedures concerning protection before the Supervisor' such as complaints (Article 8) and how to handle them (Article 9); preliminary investigations (Article 10) and their closure (Article 11); the initiation of the procedure for the adoption of corrective measures and sanctions (Article 12); and the right of defence (Article 13). Chapter III of Regulation no. 1/2019 deals with Control and inspection activities, while Chapter IV details rules of ethics, Chapter V Codes of Conduct, and Chapter VI concerns other relevant activities of the GPDP.

Paragraph 10 of Article 166 finally establishes that the application of administrative sanctions under both the Code and Article 83 GDPR does not apply to the judicial sector.

Republic, pursuant to articles 142, paragraph 5, 154, paragraphs 1, letter b) and 3, 156, paragraph 3, letter a), and 166, paragraph 9, of the Code' (author's translation).

795. The GPDP adopted its general provision titled 'Amendments to Regulation No. 1/2019 regarding revenge porn ' (author's translation) on 27 Jan. 2022, and it was published in the Official Gazette of the Italian Republic on 17 Feb. 2022: GPDP, *Deliberazione del 27 gennaio 2022 – Modifiche al regolamento n. 1/2019 in materia di revenge porn*, 27.1.2022, doc. web no. 9744477, https://www.garanteprivacy.it/web/guest/home/docweb/-/docweb-display/docweb/9744477 The provisions on revenge porn can be found in Art. 33-*bis* of the Regulation titled 'Revenge porn'.

Part IX. Specific Processing Situations

Chapter 1. Processing for Journalism, Academic or Artistic Expression

§1. The Constitutional Protection of Journalistic, Academic, Artistic and Literary Activities

597. Article 21, paragraph 1 of the Italian Constitution provides that 'anyone has the right to freely express their thoughts in speech, writing, or any other form of communication', while the second paragraph provides that 'the press may not be subjected to any authorization or censorship'.[796] This Article expressly lays down the right to freedom of expression within the Italian constitutional order while also granting specific constitutional protection to the journalistic profession. Overtime, the Italian Constitutional Court has also recognized the right to be informed as being protected by the Constitution.[797]

598. In turn, Article 33 of the Italian Constitution guarantees the freedom of the arts and sciences, thereby including their free teaching.

§2. Derogations to Some Provisions of the Personal Data Protection Code

599. In order to balance the aforementioned rights and freedoms, as well as the constitutional status of the journalistic profession, the Personal Data Protection Code lays down some derogations aimed at balancing those rights and freedoms with the right to personal data protection[798] within its 'Title XII – Journalism, Freedom of Expression and Information' (Articles 136 et seq.). Such derogations have

796. Author's translation. Paragraphs 3 et seq. of Art. 21 subject the possibility of seizure and censorship of journals to procedural guarantees, while also stating that publications offensive to public morality are prohibited and that the law may require the disclosure of financial information regarding periodical publications; these provisions do not seem relevant from a data protection perspective.

797. The leading case in this respect is judgment no. 420/1994.

798. In line with the obligation for Member States to provide for derogations to data protection law in order to balance the right to the protection of personal data with the right to freedom of expression and information, including processing for journalistic purposes and the purposes of academic, artistic or literary expression, set forth by Art. 85, paras 1 and 2 GDPR.

been included in the Personal Data Protection Code well before the 2018 reform, which has provided for – mostly – formal amendments to this part of the Code, in particular with a view to updating the references in light of the direct applicability of the GDPR.[799]

600. Concerning the subjective scope of the derogations, Article 136 of the Italian Data Protection Code provides that they apply not only to processing operations that are carried out in the exercise of, and for the purpose of exercising the journalistic profession but also to those that are carried out by persons included either in the list of free-lance journalists or in the roll of trainee journalists,[800] and even to processing operations that are aimed exclusively at publishing or circulating, also occasionally, articles, essays and other intellectual works, also in terms of academic, artistic or literary expression.

601. Concerning the legal bases for processing personal data in the case of the processing operations referred to above, Article 137, paragraph 1, of the Personal Data Protection Code, provides that in case of processing special categories of personal data under Article 9 GDPR, as well as data relating to criminal convictions and offences under Article 10 GDPR, the data may be processed even without the data subject's consent.

However, it has rightly been observed that the reference to the possibility of processing special category and judicial data *even* without data subject's consent is ill-formulated and seems to be an 'inheritance' from the pre-2018 'consent-centric' approach of Italian data protection law,[801] given that Article 10 GDPR does not require consent to be used as a legal basis for processing data on criminal convictions and offences, but rather mandates that such processing is authorized by national or European law. In this respect, the correct interpretation of Article 137, paragraph 1, of the Personal Data Protection Code is that its effect consists in derogating the applicability of Articles 9 and 10 GDPR.[802] As a result, where special category and/or data relating to criminal convictions and offences are processed in the context of the processing operations referred to in Article 136, the data controller is required to ground the processing activity only on one of the legal bases set forth under Article 6 GDPR; typically, such legal basis would either be Article 6, paragraph 1, letter f) (legitimate interest – *rectius*, exercise of the fundamental right of freedom of expression and the right to be informed – of the data controller or a third party), or Article 6, paragraph 1, letter e) (performance of a task carried out in the public interest, especially relevant for the journalistic activity).

602. Paragraph 2 of Article 137 provides for more derogations. In particular, letter a) of this paragraph derogates the applicability of Article 2-*septies* of the Data

799. Bolognini & Pelino, *Codice privacy: tutte le novità del D.lgs. 101/2018* (Giuffré Francis Lefebvre, 2019), at 65.
800. As per Arts 26 and 33 of L. 69/1963.
801. *See supra* Part III, Ch. 2.
802. Bolognini & Pelino, *Codice privacy: tutte le novità del D.lgs. 101/2018* (Giuffré Francis Lefebvre, 2019), at 65–66.

Protection Code,[803] which implements Article 9, paragraph 4, GDPR, thereby establishing that the data controller need not abide by the safeguards laid down by the GPDP when processing health, genetic and biometric data.

In turn, letter b) provides that the provisions contained in Chapter V of the Regulation concerning transfers of personal data to third countries or international organizations do not apply.

603. Finally, paragraph 3 of Article 137 specifically addresses the communication and/or disclosure of personal data in the context of the journalistic profession, where the provision codifies the 'limitations imposed on freedom of the press' as an inherent limit to those processing activities. The expression refers to the so-called journalist's decalogue, i.e., the three criteria enucleated by the Italian jurisprudence in order to assess the legitimacy of the journalistic activity vis-à-vis other fundamental rights and freedoms recognized by the Constitution and, particularly, the right to privacy.[804] Such criteria are:

(i) Truthfulness of the news, even putative, as long as it is the product of diligent and serious research on the part of the journalist.
(ii) Social usefulness of the news.
(iii) Self-restraint, i.e., non-offensive exposition of the facts or opinions.[805]

604. The same paragraph 3 sets forth a further criterion for assessing the legitimacy of the processing operations referred to above, i.e., 'the essential nature of the information with regard to facts of public interest', which is generally interpreted as translating the data minimization principle within the context of the journalistic activity.[806]

605. Article 138 of the Data Protection Code, titled 'professional secrecy' closes Title XII by establishing that: 'the provisions concerning professional secrecy in the journalistic profession shall be left unprejudiced as related to the source of the information if a data subject requests to be informed of the source of the personal data in accordance with Article 15(1), letter g), of the Regulation'. This Article, therefore, partially derogates the right of access in order to protect the professional secrecy of the journalist concerning the sources used.

606. In the context of criminal procedural law, another provision aimed at protection the professional secrecy of the journalist is set forth by Article 200 of the

803. *See supra*, Part III, Ch. 3, §2.
804. This decalogue has been upheld multiple times by the Italian Supreme Court. *Ex multis*: Cass. Civ., sez III, 5 Dec. 2014, no. 25739.
805. Bolognini & Pelino, *Codice privacy: tutte le novità del D.lgs. 101/2018* (Giuffré Francis Lefebvre, 2019), at 67–68.
806. *Ibid.*, at 68.

Code of Criminal Procedure, which recognizes that journalists are generally not under an obligation to testify on what they have known by reason of their profession.[807]

§3. Other Italian Law Provisions Which Are Relevant to Processing Operations Carried Out for Journalistic Purposes

607. Italian law lays down further provisions aimed at protecting the right to privacy of individuals, which may impact processing activities carried out for journalistic purposes. Such provisions usually consist of the prohibition from disclosing or publishing certain information. The most notable are in the context of legal proceedings (especially criminal ones):

(i) Article 13 of the Code of Criminal Procedure for Minors, Article 114, paragraph 6, of the Code of Criminal Procedure and Article 50 of the Personal Data Protection Code, which prohibits the publication and dissemination of images and news which may identify a minor involved in legal proceedings, even indirectly, except where the hearing is public or the minor over sixteen years of age has consented to the publication.
(ii) Article 114, paragraphs 1 and 2, and Article 329 of the Code of Criminal Procedure, which prohibit the publication of documents covered by the secrecy of ongoing investigations and even of documents not covered by such secrecy, up until the end of the investigations or of the preliminary hearing.[808] The Code expressly allows, however, the publication of the content of judicial acts (i.e., not the publication of the act itself) not covered by such secrecy (Article 114, paragraph 7, of the Code of Criminal Procedure) and considers the investigative acts carried out by the public prosecutor and the judicial police no longer covered by secrecy when the suspect may legally have knowledge of such acts (Article 329 of the Code of Criminal Procedure and Article 268, paragraph 6, of the Criminal Code, relating to the filing of documents after the interception operations have been completed).
(iii) Article 114, paragraph 6-*bis*, of the Code of Criminal Procedure prohibits the publication of images depicting a person with handcuffs or subject to other means of physical coercion, except where the person has consented to such publication.
(iv) Articles 732 and 114, paragraph 6, of the Code of Criminal Procedure, which prohibit the publication of the identity of victims of sexual violence, as well as the disclosure of elements which may lead, even indirectly, to their identification.

807. However, if the information in question is strictly necessary for the purpose of ascertaining the commission of a crime and its truthfulness can only be ascertained by identifying the source of the information, the judge may order the journalist to disclose the source.

808. Except for the judge's decision which establishes precautionary measures (Art. 292 of the Code of Criminal Procedure).

§4. Deontological Rules Relating to the Processing of Personal Data in the Exercise of the Journalistic Activity

608. On 29 November 2018, the GPDP adopted the 'Deontological Rules Relating to the Processing of Personal Data in the Exercise of Journalistic Activity' ('Deontological Rules').[809] The Deontological Rules set out the main principles that should guide the exercise of the journalistic profession and that aim to reconcile the fundamental rights of individuals with the right to information and freedom of press. The Deontological Rules are composed of several articles which set out both specific obligations that should be followed when performing journalistic activity, as well as exceptions from some of the requirements set out under the Regulation.

The Deontological Rules have been published pursuant to Article 20, paragraph 4, of Legislative Decree 10 August 2018, no. 101, under which the GPDP was entrusted with the task of verifying compliance with the Regulation of the provisions of the deontological codes indicated therein (and adopted before the entry into force of the Regulation). Pursuant to the same Article, the provisions deemed to be compatible with the Regulation shall be set out as Annex A to the Personal Data Protection Code.[810]

609. Among others, Article 2 of the Deontological Rules provides that journalists who collect information in the context of their processing activities shall disclose their identity, their profession, and the purpose of their collection, unless this would pose a risk to their safety or otherwise make it impossible for them to perform their functions. At the same time, journalists are not obliged to provide the other elements of information pursuant to Articles 13 and 14 GDPR.

As for the principle of storage limitation, the same Article provides that journalists may keep the data collected for as long as necessary to achieve the purposes of their profession. As an additional obligation that applies to the journalistic profession, Article 4 provides that journalists shall rectify errors and inaccuracies without undue delay, while Article 5 prescribes that, when collecting special categories of personal data, journalists shall guarantee the right to information about facts of public interest, while respecting the essential nature of the information and avoiding references to individuals which are not involved in those facts.

610. Article 6 sets out a key principle which clarifies that the disclosure of pieces of news of major public or social interest is not in conflict with the protection of the private sphere when the information is essential, considering the originality of the facts in question, the description of how those facts have occurred, and the qualifications of the main individuals involved. Moreover, the privacy of publicly known persons or of those performing public functions should be respected if the news or information has no bearing on their role or public life. The same Article

809. GPDP, *Regole deontologiche relative al trattamento di dati personali nell'esercizio dell'attività giornalistica pubblicate ai sensi dell'art. 20, comma 4, del d.lgs. 10 agosto 2018*, no. 101, 29.11.2018, doc. web no. 9067692, https://www.garanteprivacy.it/web/guest/home/docweb/-/docweb-display/docweb/9067692.

810. *See supra* Part VI, §1.

also stresses that comments and opinions expressed by journalists belong to the freedom of information and to the freedom of speech and thought, which are guaranteed to all individuals under the Italian Constitution.

611. The Deontological Rules also afford specific protection to the rights and/or aspects of the personal sphere with which the exercise of journalistic activities is more likely to interfere. Article 3 provides that the protection of home and other places of private residence shall be extended to places of care, detention, and rehabilitation.

Special protection shall also be granted to minors, whose names (or other details that could lead to their identification) shall not be published in news items, as prescribed under Article 7 of the Deontological Rules. At the same time, if journalists choose to disseminate news or images concerning minors for important reasons of public interest and in compliance with the law, they shall assess whether this is in the objective interests of the child and in compliance with the principles set out under the Treviso Charter (which provides, among others, that minors shall not be subjected to arbitrary or unlawful interference in their privacy sphere nor be subjected to offences to their honour or reputation).

612. Human dignity shall also be protected. In this respect, Article 8 of the Deontological Rules provides that journalists shall not publish news, images or photographs of persons involved in events that may offend their dignity. To the same aim, journalists shall not take or publish photos of persons in custody without the consent of the person concerned, unless there are important reasons of public interest or for well-grounded purposes of police and justice. Moreover, individuals shall not be photographed with handcuffs around their wrists, unless this is necessary to report abuses. Article 10 is devoted to the protection of the dignity of sick people, especially in case of serious and terminal illness (in which case journalists shall refrain from publishing analytic details of strictly clinical interest).

613. Journalists shall also respect the rights of individuals not to be discriminated against on grounds of race, religion, political opinion, sex, personal, physical or mental conditions (Article 9), as well as the sexual sphere of individuals whose sexual habits shall not be described unless this is permitted in pursuit of the essentiality of the information and without infringing their dignity in case the person in question holds a position of particular social and public importance (Article 11). Lastly, Article 12 provides that the processing of personal data relating to criminal proceedings is not subject to the limitations set out under Article 10 of the Regulation and under Article 2-*octies* of the Personal Data Protection Code.

614. As for the scope of application of the Deontological Rules, Article 13 clarifies that the Deontological Rules apply to professional journalists, freelancers, trainees, and anybody else conducting, even occasionally, publishing activities. In terms of disciplinary sanctions, the same Article provides that the disciplinary sanctions referred to in Title III of Law 3 February 1963, no. 69 (i.e., the Italian normative act that disciplines the organization and the exercise of the journalist profession) only applies to the persons registered in the official register of journalists.

615. Before concluding, it is worth mentioning that, in March 2022, the GPDP announced the beginning of a dialogue with the National Council of the Order of Journalists aimed at discussing the respect by the media of the current ethical rules on privacy, the responsibilities of journalists when facing new forms of digital communication and social media, and the need to update the Deontological Rules and the Treviso Charter.[811]

§5. GPDP Decisions on Processing Operations Carried Out in the Context of Journalistic Activities

616. The principles summarized above have been clarified and applied by the GPDP in several decisions.

617. The GPDP has, for example, imposed the provisional limitation of any further dissemination of personal data on a number of newspapers in a case concerning the alleged intimate relationship between the head of a high school (which was identified with her full name and with some pictures) and a student. Since the stories published by the newspapers also included the transcript of some messages allegedly exchanged between the two parties involved, the GPDP recalled that Article 137(3) of the Personal Data Protection Code provides that, in the communication and dissemination of personal data for journalistic purposes, the limitations imposed on the freedom of press in order to protect human dignity and the rights and fundamental freedoms of the individuals concerned and the essential nature of the information with regards to the facts of public interest shall always be respected (as also set out under Articles 5 and 6 of the Deontological Rules).

In light of this, the GPDP noted that the content of the private conversations and messages reported in the articles in question were not necessary to shed light on the matter and on the legitimacy of the behaviour of the head of the school, on which investigations on the part of the competent authorities were in progress. In order to protect the confidentiality and dignity of the persons involved, the GPDP imposed on the newspapers – pursuant to Article 58, paragraph 2, letter f), GDPR – the provisional limitation of the data processing in question and, specifically, of the further dissemination of the content of the private messages between the parties involved.[812]

618. Several decisions have also been issued by the GPDP in cases pertaining to the processing of judicial data in the context of journalistic activities. In this respect,

811. GPDP, *Protezione dati e media: incontro Garante privacy e Consiglio Nazionale dell'Ordine dei Giornalisti*, 24.3.2022, doc. web no. 9755685, https://www.garanteprivacy.it/web/guest/home/docweb/-/docweb-display/docweb/9755685.

812. Among others, GPDP, *Provvedimento del 1 aprile 2022*, 01.04.2022, doc. web no. 9759762, https://www.garanteprivacy.it/web/guest/home/docweb/-/docweb-display/docweb/9759762; GPDP, *Provvedimento del 1 aprile 2022*, 01.4.2022, doc. web no. 9759716, https://www.garanteprivacy.it/web/guest/home/docweb/-/docweb-display/docweb/9759716; GPDP, *Provvedimento del 31 marzo 2022*, 31.3.2022, doc. web no. 9759899, https://www.garanteprivacy.it/web/guest/home/docweb/-/docweb-display/docweb/9759899.

the GPDP has stressed the importance of ensuring that updated news is conveyed to the public, considering the significant impacts that the disclosure of information pertaining to the involvement of a person in judicial events may have on their personal and social identity.

Among others, it is worth recalling a case where the complainant lamented the fact that the news related to a criminal proceeding in which she was involved was not updated in light of the further development of the case. The data controller argued in its defence that it had ensured the accuracy of the information in question through the publication – within its own website – of more recent articles, which were correlated to the previous ones through appropriate reference. The GPDP, however, noted that such a system was not suitable to guarantee compliance with the principle of lawfulness since the latter requires the creation of a system capable of indicating, in the body or in the margin of the article, the existence of follow-ups and developments of the same news.[813]

619. Conversely, in a case pertaining to the right to be forgotten, the GPDP dismissed a complaint raised against '*Laboratorio Abruzzo Giovani*' (the publisher of an online newspaper) concerning an article which described a legal matter in which the complainant was involved a few years earlier. In the case in question, the GPDP concluded that, even if the legal matter had been initiated years before, the article in question referred to further developments that had occurred more recently and that concerned the conclusion of the said matter. Moreover, the GPDP noted that the processing activity in question took place in the exercise of the freedom of press and in compliance with the principle of the essentiality of the information, considering (among others) that no personal data suitable for the identification of the complainant was included in the article in question (since the complainant was identified with her initials). In dismissing the complaint, the GPDP also recalled that Article 17, paragraph 3, letter d), GDPR, provides for an exception to the possibility for data subjects to exercise their right of erasure, where the processing is necessary for exercising the right of freedom of expression and information.[814]

620. The GPDP has also often highlighted the importance of protecting human dignity when it comes to the publication of news that may offend the dignity of the persons involved. In decision 85 of 25 February 2021, the GPDP has, for example, concluded that the fact of 'pixelating' the image of the handcuffs of an arrested person (whose face was still clearly visible) was an insufficient measure to ensure compliance with the prohibitions set out under Article 8 of the Deontological Rules and under Article 114, paragraph 6-*bis*, of the Italian Criminal Procedure Code[815]

813. GPDP, *Provvedimento del 9 aprile 2020*, 9.4.2020, doc. web no. 9426173, https://www.garanteprivacy.it/home/docweb/-/docweb-display/docweb/9426173.

814. GPDP, *Provvedimento del 27 gennaio 2022*, 27.1.2022, doc. web no. 9747522, https://www.garanteprivacy.it/web/guest/home/docweb/-/docweb-display/docweb/9747522.

815. GPDP, *Ordinanza ingiunzione nei confronti di Gedi Gruppo Editoriale S.p.A. – 25 febbraio 2021*, 25.2.2021, doc. web no. 9568244, https://www.garanteprivacy.it/home/docweb/-/docweb-display/docweb/9568244.

621. These principles have also been reiterated and applied by the GPDP in relation to the processing of special categories of personal data in the context of journalist activities. Among others, the GPDP has issued a decision in relation to the publication by an online newspaper of information on the pathology of which an individual was affected, together with a full copy of the results of the laboratory test undertaken by the latter. In this respect, the GPDP recalled the provisions set out under Article 137 of the Personal Data Protection Code (that provides that special categories of personal data may be processed even without data subject's consent subject to compliance with the Deontological Rules and with the principle of essentiality of information) and Article 10 of the Deontological Rules under which journalists shall refrain from publishing analytic details of strictly clinical interest. The GPDP concluded that the above-mentioned principles were not respected in the case in question, where detailed information on the data subject's health status has been disseminated. In light of the above, the GPDP has disposed of the temporary limitation on the processing activity in question (pursuant to Article 58, paragraph 2, letter f) of the GDPR) in relation to the further dissemination of the health information that had been reported in the article in question.[816]

§6. GPDP Decisions on the Dissemination of Personal Data on Social Networks

622. The GPDP has also adopted several decisions in the context of the dissemination of personal information on social networks. These decisions stem from complaints concerning the publication of personal data (e.g., by means of comments or photographs) on social networks, in particular, on Facebook, Instagram, and YouTube. In this respect, the GPDP has clarified that the provisions that apply to the publication of personal information on social networks are those set out under Article 136 and following the Personal Data Protection Code, since the broad wording of those provisions allows for the extension of the guarantees and derogations established therein regarding the protection of personal data to the data published on the network.

623. For the personal data published through social media, similarly to what happens in the case of the dissemination for journalistic purposes, it is therefore not necessary to collect the consent of the person concerned, provided that the publication of such information is supported by adequate purposes of public interest.[817] In applying the principle of the essentiality of information in the context of social media, the GPDP has, for example, imposed a fine of EUR 50,000 on the Mayor of the city of Messina for publishing on his Facebook page videos and images of minors and individuals undergoing social and economic difficulties, and portraying

816. GPDP, *Provvedimento del 18 gennaio 2023, 18.1.2023*, doc. web no. 9860487, https://www.garanteprivacy.it/web/guest/home/docweb/-/docweb-display/docweb/9860487.

817. GPDP, *Relazione annuale 2020* (Annual Report for 2020), 2.7.2021, doc. web no. 9676435, at 133 (a summary of the 2020 GPDP report is available at this URL: https://www.garanteprivacy.it/web/guest/home/docweb/-/docweb-display/docweb/9701041).

those individuals as alleged perpetrators of crimes, thereby exposing them to the harmful comments of the other social network users. In the case in question, the GPDP concluded that such publication was not justified by reasons of public and social interest (and thereby violated the principles of lawfulness and accuracy), went beyond the limitations set out under Article 137, paragraph 3, of the Personal Data Protection Code, and represented a violation of the principles set out under Articles 7, 8, 9, and 10 of the Deontological Rules.[818]

§7. GPDP Decisions and Recommendations on the Dissemination of Personal Data in Relation to the COVID-19 Outbreak

624. In the context of the health emergency related to the COVID-19 outbreak, the GPDP also dealt with several complaints generated from the spread of the virus – both through newspaper articles and through social networks – of an excessive amount of information about individuals who tested positive for COVID-19. In this context, a press release was published by the GPDP,[819] where it stressed that the guarantees set forth in the Deontological Rules aimed at protecting the dignity and confidentiality of individuals should always be preserved even in emergency situations and that this obligation applies not only to professional journalists but also to the users of social networks.

A violation of the applicable data protection principles was, however, not found in a case concerning the publication of an article that reported that a council member of a municipality had tested positive for COVID-19 and that he was in home isolation (even if it was not known whether he had been infected by the Delta variant). In the case in question, the GPDP dismissed the complaint on the alleged unlawfulness of the publication of such information in consideration (among others) of the following: the article in question was published in the context of the general information in the public interest related to the pandemic and its containment measures; the public role played by the person in question in the local community and the fact that his health status had an impact on the regular functioning of the public administration of the municipality; the details provided in the article were not detrimental to his dignity and that the print version of the journal was only circulated in the relevant local area; the picture of the complainant that was published in the article was not 'excessive' in nature considering that the same picture was also published on the institutional website of the municipality; overall, the publication of the information in the article in question was an expression of the freedom of press and has occurred in compliance with the principle of essentiality of information.[820]

---

818. GPDP, *Ordinanza ingiunzione – 13 maggio 2021*, 13.5.2021, doc. web no. 9670001, https://www.garanteprivacy.it/web/guest/home/docweb/-/docweb-display/docweb/9670001.
819. GPDP, *Coronavirus: Garante privacy, su social e media troppi dettagli sui malati*, 31.03.2020, doc. web no. 9303613, https://www.garanteprivacy.it/home/docweb/-/docweb-display/docweb/9303613.
820. GPDP, *Provvedimento del 2 marzo 2023*, 2.3.2023, doc. web no. 9874436, https://www.garanteprivacy.it/web/guest/home/docweb/-/docweb-display/docweb/9874436.

§8. GPDP Jurisprudence on Requests of Delisting from Search Engine Results

625. The GPDP has also examined a great number of delisting requests in relation to personal data processed through search engines, such as delisting requests concerning judicial information still available online but referred to past events considered by the person concerned as no longer corresponding to their current social identity, or in relation to the continued availability of information pertaining to judicial events for which subsequent favourable developments have occurred that were however not represented online.

626. In its decision 417 of 25 November 2021, the GPDP ordered Google to comply with the complainant's request to remove the search results to articles referring to legal matters in which the complainant was involved since those articles contained outdated information which was considered damaging for the complainant's reputation.[821] However, in decision no. 51 of 10 February 2022, the GPDP concluded that Google's refusal to remove URLs linked to articles relating to criminal proceedings in which the complainant was involved was justified on the basis that (among others) there was a public interest in knowing the relevant facts concerning the criminal proceeding in question.[822] In the same context, specific importance has been attributed by the GPDP to some institutions of the Italian criminal system, with specific reference to 'rehabilitation' (which aims to facilitate the social integration of the offender) and the right not to disclose a criminal conviction in criminal records (which aims to limit the knowledge of the conviction suffered by a specific individual), whose intended legal effects would be nullified if a search engine would be allowed to disseminate judicial information pertaining to the data subjects concerned.[823]

821. GPDP, *Provvedimento del 25 novembre 2021*, 25.11.2021, doc. web no. 9732385, https://www.garanteprivacy.it/web/guest/home/docweb/-/docweb-display/docweb/9732385.

822. GPDP, *Provvedimento del 10 febbraio 2022*, 10.2.2022, doc. web no. 9751169, https://www.garanteprivacy.it/web/guest/home/docweb/-/docweb-display/docweb/9751169.

823. Among others, GPDP, *Provvedimento del 28 febbraio 2019*, 28.2.2019, doc. web no. 9103108, https://www.garanteprivacy.it/home/docweb/-/docweb-display/docweb/9103108; GPDP, *Provvedimento del 30 aprile 2020*, 30.4.2020, doc. web no. 9426491 https://www.garanteprivacy.it/home/docweb/-/docweb-display/docweb/9426491.

Chapter 2. Data Protection Versus Public Access to Documents

§1. INTRODUCTION: THE VARIOUS RIGHTS OF ACCESS IN THE ITALIAN LEGAL SYSTEMS

627. In 2016, the National Anticorruption Authority, together with the GPDP, published a document[824] to clarify the difference between the right of access to the information granted by several Italian provisions (hereinafter the 'Guidelines').

In particular, in the Guidelines, we can *see* a first type of right to access called 'generalized Civic Access' (hereinafter, 'Civic Access') provided by Articles 5 and 5-*bis* of Legislative Decree 14 March 2013, no. 33 (so-called Transparency Decree).

Those provisions establish that 'anyone has the right to access data and documents held by public administrations, in addition to those subject to publication pursuant to this decree, in compliance with the limits related to the protection of public and private interests legally relevant, as provided for by Article 5-*bis*'.[825]

This translates, in a nutshell, into a right of access not conditioned by the ownership of legally relevant situations and concerning all data, documents and information held by public administrations, in addition to those for which a publication obligation is established. This provision wants to favour the control by the general public on the correctness of government's management of the public function and, in particular, on the spending of public finance. Furthermore, the provision also wants to increase civil participation in public matters. Civic Access need not be motivated, and it can be qualified as a right that any citizen may exercise against the government.

628. There is also another type of Civic Access limited to when the public administration must publish a document. In this case, any person can act with this access request to force the public administration to comply. This second type of access is provided by Articles 22 et seq. of the Law 7 August 1990, no. 241, and is called 'documental access'.[826] This access is a specific remedy granted in case of a violation that the person would need to demonstrate and is related to the document being accessed. Indeed, this type of access can be exercised only by the person who can be qualified as an 'interested person'.

The main difference with Civic Access is that documental access is not generally granted to any individual in order to verify the exercise of public function but can only be activated if there is a specific and relevant interest related to the specific document to which the person is requesting access.

629. A third type of access right is the right of access to personal data provided by the GDPR in its Article 15. In light of that provision, the person who can be

824. GPDP & National Anticorruption Authority, *Linee Guida Recanti Indicazioni Operative ai Fini della Definizione delle Esclusioni e dei Limiti all'accesso Civico di cui All'art. 5 Co. 2 Del D.Lgs. 33/2013*, 28.12.2016, https://www.anticorruzione.it/portal/rest/jcr/repository/collaboration/Digital%20Assets/anacdocs/Attivita/Atti/determinazioni/2016/1309/del.1309.2016.det.LNfoia.pdf.

825. *Ibid.*, at 5. Author's translation.

826. *See also* the information sheet on this right, published by the GPDP in its website: https://www.garanteprivacy.it/web/guest/home/docweb/-/docweb-display/docweb/9517732.

qualified as a data subject under the GDPR is entitled to obtain from the data controller access to the personal data processed concerning them.

In this Chapter, we focus only on the first two types of access (Civic Access and documental access), as the right of access to personal data under Italian legislation has been examined in Part IV, Chapter 2, *supra*.

§2. Safeguards and Limitations to the Rights of Civic Access and Documental Access

630. The first limit to Civic Access is provided by the Article 5-*bis* of the Transparency Decree. Specifically, in case the request for Civic Access may undermine the protection of the personal data of the person concerned by the request, the request may be refused.

A finding of such prejudice will result in the rejection of the request, unless it may be determined that the request can be granted by obscuring any personal data that may be present and other information that may allow the identification, even indirectly, of the person(s) concerned. In this context, an account must be taken of the reasons given by the interested party, which must be mandatorily questioned by the entity receiving the request for generalized access, pursuant to Article 5, paragraph 5, of the Transparency Decree.

The prejudice to the protection of personal data included in the document subject to the access request amounts to an indication of the existence of a concrete prejudice, the assessment of which, however, is the responsibility of the public administration and must be conducted even in the case of silence on the part of the data subject, taking, also, into consideration the other elements illustrated below.

The fact that Article 5, paragraph 5, of the Transparency Decree, mentioned above recalls the respect of GDPR provisions and means that when the entity evaluates the Civic Access request, it should also consider the respect of the principle of minimization and proportionally provided by Articles 5 and 6 GDPR.

631. In this sense, the public administration should limit Civic Access (i.e., erasing personal data) if the document contains personal data whose ostension is not necessary and proportionate to the respect of duty of transparency, which all provisions strive to protect.[827] The prejudice to the data subject (the person whose personal data is contained in the document being accessed) should be taken into account, based on the fact that after the Civic Access, the document being accessed will be 'public' and, as such, also the personal data contained therein. For example, it can be considered a possible prejudice that personal data can be an object of identity theft or can be a prejudice against the diffusion of the notice that some person is an inspector. The reasonable expectation that the data subject had at the time of processing must also be considered when assessing prejudice.[828]

In this respect, according to the Guidelines, in order to verify the unfavourable impact that could derive to the data subject from the acquaintance by anyone of the

827. GPDP & National Anticorruption Authority, *supra* n. 825, at 22 et seq.
828. *Ibid.*, at 23.

requested information, the entity receiving the request for Civic Access must refer to several parameters, among which, the nature of the personal data that are contained in the documents to which access is requested, as well as the role held in public life, the public function exercised or the activity of public interest carried out by the person to whom the said data refer.

With regard to the nature of the personal data included in the document subject to the access request, the presence of special categories data under Article 9 GDPR and/or data concerning criminal conviction and security measures under Article 10 GDPR may be symptomatic of the existence of the aforementioned prejudice, where the knowledge by anyone that would result from the display of such information – even in different contexts (family and/or social) – may be a source of discrimination or harbinger of specific risks for the person concerned.

Other elements which might be considered in the assessment are, for example, that the data subject is a minor or that the personal data disclosed, while not falling into the judicial or special categories, are nevertheless likely to cause harm to the data subject, such as in the case of localization data.

632. From the procedural perspective, pursuant to Articles 5, paragraph 7, and 5-*bis*, paragraph 2, letter a), of D.Lgs. 33/2013, the Anticorruption Authority shall seek the opinion of the GPDP if the request for access is denied for reasons of prejudice to the right to personal data protection.

633. In addition, according to the most recent jurisprudence of the Court of Strasbourg, Article 10 of the ECHR does not confer, as a general rule, on the individual the right of access to information held by public authorities in general. Such a right, or such an obligation, can, in fact, be traced back to the broader freedom of expression protected by Article 10 of the ECHR, only in particular situations and under specific conditions. For example, if the information subject to access relates to matters of public interest and, therefore, access to information held by public authorities may be deemed instrumental to the exercise of the applicant's freedom to receive and disseminate the same information to the public, such that the denial of access would constitute an infringement of this freedom.[829]

634. The picture might be different in case of documental access; in this case, as explained above, the person seeking access needs to have in place a relevant interest that justifies its request. Indeed, according to Article 24, paragraph 6, letter d), of L. 241/1990, access can be excluded:

> [W]hen the documents concern the privacy or confidentiality of natural persons, legal persons, groups, enterprises and associations, with particular reference to the epistolary, health, professional, financial, industrial and commercial interests of which they are concretely holders, even if the relevant data are provided to the administration by the same persons to whom they refer' but the access should be guaranteed in any case if 'is necessary to take care of or

829. *See* on this point most recently, *Magyar Helsinki Bizottság v. Hungary*, 8.11.2016, Eur. Ct. H.R., paras 156 and 160–163.

defend their legal interests. In the case of documents containing sensitive and judicial data, access shall be granted to the extent strictly necessary and within the terms provided for in Article 60 of Legislative Decree No. 196 of June 30, 2003, in the case of data disclosing health and sex life.[830]

635. These provisions mean that documental access (protected by Article 97 of the Constitution) can be denied for the sake of safeguarding the interest in data protection (according to Article 2 Constitution). However, the protection of privacy and data protection yields the right to defence in court of the person concerned (according to Article 24 Constitution).

In the 1990s, a jurisprudential strand began demarcating the boundary between the right of documental access and the right of defence. The first decision was pronounced by the Council of State (Plenary Assembly), with judgment no. 5/1997, according to which the right to documental access can generally be excluded and, therefore, yields to confidentiality (exception to the right of access); on the other hand, the right to access must prevail over confidentiality, even where sensitive data are present in the document, in case where the applicant's (proven) need for ostension is aimed at establishing or defending legal claims (exception of the exception, or 'counter-exception,' according to the scheme above); however, where sensitive data are present, access must be granted only as a mere 'viewing' (without retaining a copy).[831]

636. Administrative jurisprudence initially conformed to this ruling. However, in the following years, a *revirement* of this jurisprudence began to take place: in particular, it was asserted that the presence of sensitive data within the relevant documents must yield against privacy, even if the right to access is functional to defence of legally relevant interests in court, in the absence of specific legislative authorization: in other words, the 'privacy' exception does not tolerate 'counter-exceptions' of any kind that are not rooted in precise legislative choices.[832]

637. The legislator followed up this ruling by introducing Article 16, paragraph 2, of Legislative Decree 11 May 1999, no. 135, where it was held that access to sensitive data may be allowed only if the right of defence is at least equal in rank to that of the person concerned with regard to the confidentiality of his or her own health.

638. In 2001,[833] another overruling took place, where it was held that the exception to privacy is not absolute and does not always override the right of defence, but such prevalence must be evaluated on a concrete case-by-case basis. This case law

830. *See* Art. 24, para. 7, of L. 241/1990. Author's translation.

831. *See* Giulio Bacosi, Accesso e Privacy: prima e dopo la riforma della l. 241/90: l'emblematico caso INAIL. Spunti su un fantomatico 'diritto' e su un esercizio negletto, 2 Diritto Procedura Amministrativa 360, (2007).

832. *Ibid*, at 365.

833. *See* Council of State, s. VI, 30.03.2001, no. 1882, *Massimario giuriurisprudenza del lavoro* 912, (2001).

would later be incorporated into Articles 59 and 60 of the Personal Data Protection Code,[834] according to which documental access and its limits are governed by L. 241/1990.

639. In particular, according to Article 60 of the Personal Data Protection Code, if the personal data within the document are in a so-called super-sensitive category (i.e., data relating to health, sex life or sexual orientation), the access is permitted in two exclusive cases:

(i) The legal interest intended to be protected by access (counter-exception) is of at least equal rank to that of the data subject (exception): *ceteris paribus*, access therefore prevails.
(ii) The legal interest sought to be protected by access (counter-exception) involves a personality right or other inviolable fundamental right or freedom, as such, capable of prevailing over privacy (exception).

640. Under this provision, if the public administration denies the legitimate request for access, it can be ordered to compensate the damage caused to the party for such denial.

641. In summary, where documental access concerns documents which present special categories of data or judicial data, access is permitted under the following limits:

(i) Generic limit: the access need to be strictly necessary to achieve the purposes for which access is sought.
(ii) Specific limit: in the case of 'super-sensitive' data, in the terms provided for by Article 60 of the Personal Data Protection Code, and thus:
   (a) the access is necessary to protect interests 'of at least equal rank' to those connected with the aforementioned 'super sensitive' data; and
   (b) the access is necessary for the care or protection of fundamental rights.[835]

642. Procedurally, in accordance with Article 25 of L. 241/1990, in the case where access is denied, the applicant may appeal to the Regional Administrative Court, the Ombudsman or the Access Commission. If access is denied or deferred because personal data concerning third parties is present, the Access Commission shall hear the GPDP, who shall rule within ten days of the request.

643. The GPDP has received a number of queries on access to acts and documents containing personal data which held health status data to ascertain within what limits persons other than the data subjects may view and take copies of such

---

834. These provisions were introduced in the previous version of the Personal Data Protection Code and now maintained after the latest reform of the Personal Data Protection Code in light of the 2018 reform carried out by means of D.Lgs. 110/20018, which adapted the internal provisions to those of the GDPR.

835. *See* Bacosi, *supra* n. 832, at 370.

documents. As a result, in 2003, the GPDP issued a general decision[836] to clarify the application requirements and scope limits of access to documents. In particular, the decision addresses:

(i) The case in which the request for access is made to a public administration under the regulations on access to administrative documents (L. 241/1990 and other regulations on transparency).
(ii) Access to medical records held at healthcare facilities.
(iii) The casc in which the request is made by a defence attorney in accordance with the provisions of the Code of Criminal Procedure on so-called defensive investigations (Article 391-quater of the Code of Criminal Procedure).

644. In particular, according to the GPDP, in light of Article 60 of the Personal Data Protection Code and the balancing required by that norm, it must be considered that in case 'super sensitive' data is present in the document to which access is sought, it is not possible to satisfy the request for access even if the applicant endeavours to protect in court a legitimate interest or a subjective right, in case the latter does not override the competing need to protect the privacy, dignity and other fundamental rights and freedoms of the person to whom the 'super sensitive' data belong: access would need to be denied, for example, in case the request is aimed at satisfying generic and merely eventual rights, not effectively at issue at the time.[837]

645. The normative reference to personality rights and other fundamental rights and freedoms is linked to an 'open list' of subjective positions identifiable in a historical-evolutionary key and presupposes an assessment in concrete terms so as to avoid public administration, other recipients of the requests and for the judge himself in case of appeal, 'the risk of preconstituted solutions resting on an abstract hierarchical scale of the rights in dispute'.[838]

According to the Council of State, the assessment of the request for access or communication must not be limited to the comparison between the rights involved but must also be based on further verification aimed at ascertaining – even for the purposes of only partial acceptance of the request – whether the data or all the personal data suitable for revealing the state of health or sexual life that are the subject of the request are actually 'necessary' for the purpose of asserting or defending the equivalent rights in litigation.[839]

---

836. GPDP, *Dati sanitari. Provvedimento generale sui diritti di 'pari rango'*, 9.7.2003, doc. web no. 29832, https://www.garanteprivacy.it/home/docweb/-/docweb-display/docweb/29832.
837. *See* Council of State, s. VI, 9.5.2002, no. 2542.
838. *See* Council of State, s. VI, 30.3.2001, no. 1882 and s. VI, 9.5.2002, no. 2542.
839. *See* Art. 16, para. 1, lett. b), of D.Lgs. 135/1999; Council of State, s. VI, 09/05/2002, no. 2542, mentioned above and Regional Administrative Court of Emilia Romagna-Bologna 16.12.2001, no. 1207.

646. According to the Council of State, similar conclusions to those indicated above must be reached in the case in which the request for access or communication of data is formulated by the defence attorney pursuant to Article 391-*quater* of the Code of Criminal Procedure.

§3. GPDP Decisions

647. Over the years, the GPDP has been called upon to give its opinion when the Anticorruption Authority has refused a request for Civic Access on data protection grounds.

648. So, for example, in 2018, the Civic Access request was about a note connected to a criminal proceeding. That note also contained the Prosecutor's indictment request and, consequently, some personal data referring to various people and also judicial data under Article 10 GDPR.[840]

The GPDP, in ruling on this request, analysed the relevant normative basis on which the request was grounded. Indeed, after access to documents was granted under Article 5 of D.Lgs. 33/2013, the documents became public. Consequently, it is also in the light of this amplified regime of public disclosure in the context of Civic Access that the existence of a possible concrete prejudice to the protection of personal data of the counter-interested parties must be assessed, on the basis of which a decision should be made whether or not to refuse access to the requested.

649. According to the Guidelines mentioned above and the consistent opinion of the GPDP in its pronouncements 'the presence of [...] judicial data may be an indication of the existence of the aforementioned prejudice, where the knowledge by anyone that would result from the ostension of such information-even in different contexts (family and/or social) may be a source of discrimination or harbinger of specific risks for the person concerned,' and that 'In principle, therefore, generalized access to such information should be refused.'[841]

Moreover, the GPDP has clarified that 'Excluded [...] from generalized access are judicial acts, i.e., procedural acts or acts that are an expression of the jurisdictional function, even if not immediately related to measures that are an expression of "*ius dicere*" provided that they are intimately and instrumentally connected to the latter. Access to and limits on the knowledge of judicial acts, i.e., all acts that are expressions of the jurisdictional function, even if they are acquired in administrative proceedings, are in fact governed by autonomous rules provided for in the respective codes of procedure.'[842]

840. GPDP, *Parere su una istanza di accesso civico*, 15.11.2018, doc. web no. 9063993, https://www.garanteprivacy.it/web/guest/home/docweb/-/docweb-display/docweb/9063993.

841. GPDP, *Parere su una istanza di accesso civico*, 16.5.2018, doc. web no. 8997258, https://www.garanteprivacy.it/web/guest/home/docweb/-/docweb-display/docweb/8997258; *see also*: GPDP, *Parere su una istanza di accesso civico*, 15.1.2018, doc. web no. 7828631, https://www.garanteprivacy.it/web/guest/home/docweb/-/docweb-display/docweb/7828631.

842. *Ibid.*, at 2. Author's translation.

650. In another opinion, the GPDP also noted that Civic Access is aimed at granting the general public knowledge of data and documents held by the public administration in order to promote widespread forms of control over the pursuit of institutional functions and the use of public resources and to promote participation in public debate (Article 5, paragraph 2, of D.Lgs. 33/2013). Accordingly, when the subject of the request for access concerns documents containing information relating to natural persons (and as such 'personal data') that is not necessary to achieve the aforementioned purpose or detailed personal information that is in any case disproportionate, excessive and irrelevant, the entity receiving the request, in responding to the request for generalized access, should generally choose the manner least prejudicial to the rights of the interested party.[843]

651. With reference to the request of Civic Access connected with disciplinary proceedings against employees, the GPDP in its pronouncements has affirmed the principle according to which the knowledge of the information contained in the acts relating to the disciplinary sanction imposed on an employee, combined with the aforementioned regime of publicity of the acts subject to Civic Access – considering the disciplinary nature of the proceedings – meets the limit provided by Article 5-*bis,* paragraph 2, letter a), of D.Lgs. 33/2013, with reference to the protection of personal data.[844]

652. In all those opinions, the GDPD has had the occasion to specify the difference existing between Civic Access provided by Articles 5 and 5-*bis* of the D.Lgs. 33/2013 and the access provided by Article 22 of the L. 241/1990. Notably, the latter provision, being linked to a qualified interest of the access seeker, is not subject to the same limitations as Civic Access, which is generally focused on the transparency of public activities and functions. For this reason, when the applicant for Civic Access can be qualified as an 'interested party' under Article 22 of L. 241/1990, he or she will be able to obtain copies of the documents for which Civic Access has been denied.

---

843. GPDP, *Parere su una istanza di accesso civico*, 31.5.2017, doc. web no. 6495493, https://www.garanteprivacy.it/home/docweb/-/docweb-display/docweb/6495493. Author's translation.

844. GPDP, *Parere su una istanza di accesso civico*, 7.12.2017, doc. web. no. 7316830, https://www.garanteprivacy.it/web/guest/home/docweb/-/docweb-display/docweb/7316830, *see also* GPDP, *Parere su una istanza di accesso civico* 9.2.2017, doc. web no. 6057812, https://www.garanteprivacy.it/home/docweb/-/docweb-display/docweb/6057812, *see also* GPDP, *Parere su un'istanza di accesso civico*, 31.05.2017, doc. web no. 6495493, https://www.garanteprivacy.it/home/docweb/-/docweb-display/docweb/6495493, and, recently, GPDP, *Parere su un'istanza di accesso civico,* 16.08.2019, doc. web no. 9161714, https://www.garanteprivacy.it/web/guest/home/docweb/-/docweb-display/docweb/9161714 and *see*, GPDP *Parere su un'istanza di accesso civico,* 21.11.2018, doc. web no. 9065404, https://www.garanteprivacy.it/web/guest/home/docweb/-/docweb-display/docweb/9065404, *see,* GPDP, *Parere su un'istanza di accesso civico*, 05.03.2020, doc. web no. 9309491, https://www.garanteprivacy.it/home/docweb/-/docweb-display/docweb/9309491.

§4. Other Specific Cases

653. There are other specific cases, different to those mentioned above, in which the data subject – also through their lawyer – acts to access some information, for example, in the case of the banking sector, and those requests could not be qualified as requests made under the right to access (or civic access) but should be satisfied by the controller.

These cases are governed by different provisions, and the duty to fulfil them responds to a kind of public legitimate interest.

The first group of these cases is regulated by Article 24 of Legislative Decree no. 11/2010 which provides that if someone sends money to the incorrect individual, the receiving bank may disclose the personal data of the person who receives the wrong payment to the sending bank if the sending bank requests it and if the incorrect payment was made by mistake. A broad interpretation of this provision, which allows for communication-based processing activities to be based on legitimate interest, may effectively reveal the same information to be disclosed to the payer and even to the recipients if the erroneous payment is caused by fraud rather than error.

A second group of provisions concerns the case where information is requested by a lawyer acting during defensive investigations. In those cases, Article 391-*quarter* of the Italian Code of Criminal Procedure provides that a lawyer – even before commencement of criminal proceeding – if they receive a specific mandate from their client, may act as a Prosecutor and request the public institution to have access to documents and information necessary for their client's defence. In the author's opinion, an extensive interpretation of this rule is also possible, according to which the request for documents could also be made to private institutions.

The same consideration should also be made if the request for personal data and information is made by public or judicial authority.

654. Finally, Article 533 and the following of the Civil Procedure Code provides that, during the executive procedure, personal data of the third interested party may be disclosed to the claimant creditor.

Chapter 3. Processing of the National Identification Number

655. Pursuant to Article 87 GDPR, the national legislator may provide for additional conditions for the processing of a national identification number, provided that such conditions do not conflict with the GDPR.

656. The main national identification number in Italy is the tax code (‘*codice fiscale*’). For natural persons, the code consists of a formula based on the data subject’s name, surname, date and place of birth, while for legal entities, the code is a random number assigned by the Italian Revenue Agency (‘*Agenzia delle Entrate*’).

In its Opinion dated 9 July 2003, the GPDP clarified that the tax code qualifies as personal data and its use should, therefore, be regulated in order to ensure that it is processed on the basis of adequate guarantees, in line with applicable data protection law.[845] Consequently, as the tax code is recognized as personal data, its unlawful publication is prohibited.[846]

845. GPDP, *Il parere del Garante sull’uso e la diffusione della Carta nazionale dei servizi*, 9.7.2013, doc. web no. 1054823, para. 3, https://www.garanteprivacy.it/web/guest/home/docweb/-/docweb-display/docweb/1054823.

846. GPDP, *Assicurazioni auto: trattamento di dati personali nell’ambito di servizi di preventivazione tramite call center*, 2.12.2010, doc. web no. 1780277, https://www.garanteprivacy.it/web/guest/home/docweb/-/docweb-display/docweb/1780277; GPDP, *Diffusione sul sito web istituzionale di un istituto scolastico di dati personali, contenuti in graduatorie, eccedenti rispetto a quelli necessari*, 6.6.2013, doc. web no. 2536184, https://www.garanteprivacy.it/web/guest/home/docweb/-/docweb-display/docweb/2536184. *See also* Bolognini & Pelino, *Codice della disciplina privacy* (Giuffrè Francis Lefebvre, 2019), at 482.

Chapter 4. Processing in the Context of Employment

§1. General Rules for Processing in the Context of Employment

657. The legal bases for the processing of data on employment relations are those stipulated in Article 6 (in particular, Articles 6, paragraph 1, letter b), 6, paragraph 1, letter c) and 6, paragraph 1, letter f), GDPR) and for the processing of special categories of personal data, the legal bases listed in Article 9 and, in particular, Article 9, paragraph 2, letter b), f) and h) of the GDPR.

According to Article 2-*sexies*, paragraph 2, of the Personal Data Protection Code, it is possible to also use the legal basis of processing that is necessary for reasons of substantial public interest (Article 9, paragraph 2, letter g) for the processing of special category data of employees, where the data controller processes such data to carry out tasks in the public interest or in the exercise of official authority.[847]

In general, consent is not considered to be a valid legal basis for the processing of personal data of employees.[848] This is because such consent is not considered, in general, to be *freely given* by the employee in light of the type of relationship existing between the parties, as there usually is a power imbalance between the employee and their employer.

658. After the entry into force of the 2018 reform, Article 21 of Legislative Decree 10 August 2018, no. 101, provides that the General Authorizations of the GPDP are maintained into force only if they are compatible with the new provisions, as determined by the GPDP. In particular, in 2018, the GPDP provided a general decision[849] in which it established that the General Authorization no. 7/2016

847. More precisely, where the processing is aimed at 'Establishing, managing and terminating labour relations of any kind whatsoever, including unpaid, honorary, and other types of employment, trade union-related matters, implementing the provisions concerning mandatory employment of disabled persons, handling welfare and social security policies, protecting minorities and ensuring equal opportunity policies in employer-employee relations, fulfilling obligations concerning wages, taxation or accounting in respect of staff, or concerning occupational hygiene and safety, population health and safety, and carrying out activities aimed at establishing civil, disciplinary and accounting liability and performing inspection activities.'

848. *See Provvedimento del 19 luglio 2018*, 19.7.2018, doc. web no. 9039945, https://www.garanteprivacy.it/web/guest/home/docweb/-/docweb-display/docweb/9039945; *see* Arts 6–7 and Recitals 42–43 of GDPR; *see also*, in the same sense, EDPB, *Guidelines 05/2020 on consent under Regulation 2016/679*, 4.5.2020, https://edpb.europa.eu/sites/default/files/files/file1/edpb_guidelines_202005_consent_en.pdf, spec. para. 3.1.1.; Article 29 Working Party, *Opinion No. 2/2017 on data processing in the workplace*, WP 249, https://ec.europa.eu/newsroom/article29/items/610169/en, spec. paras 3.1.1 and 6.2; Article 29 Working Party, 26.6.2017, Opinion 8/2001 on the processing of personal data in the context of employment, https://ec.europa.eu/justice/article-29/documentation/opinion-recommendation/files/2001/wp48_en.pdf, WP 48, 13.9.2001, at 3, 23 and 26; European Commission, *Communication of November 6, 2015*, COM(2015) 566, 6.11.2015, https://eur-lex.europa.eu/legal-content/EN/TXT/PDF/?uri=CELEX:52015DC0566&rid=3, at 12–13; Article 29 Working Party, *Working paper on a common interpretation of Article 26(1) of Directive 95/46/EC of October 24, 1995*, 25.11.2005, WP 114, at 11–12.

849. GPDP, *Provvedimento che individua le prescrizioni contenute nelle Autorizzazioni generali nn. 1/2016, 3/2016, 6/2016, 8/2016 e 9/2016 che risultano compatibili con il Regolamento e con il d.lgs. n. 101/2018 di adeguamento del Codice*, 13.12.2018, doc. web no. 9068972, https://www.garanteprivacy.it/web/guest/home/docweb/-/docweb-display/docweb/9068972.

Concerning Processing of Judicial Data by Private Entities, Profit-Seeking Public Bodies and Public Entities is repealed, as it is not compatible with the GDPR. Indeed, according to the combined provisions of Articles 10 of the GDPR and 2-*octies* of the Personal Data Protection Code, as amended by the 2018 reform, the processing of judicial data is lawful – *inter alia* – only if authorized by a specific law provision.[850]

659. According to Article 111 of the Personal Data Protection Code, the GPDP is entitled to provide deontological rules for the personal data processed during working activities according to Article 88 of GDPR.[851] Until now, however, the GPDP has not issued such rules.

660. With reference to the processing of personal data of candidates who voluntarily apply for an employment position, Article 111-*bis* of the Personal Data Protection Code provides that the information referred to in Article 13 GDPR may be provided when the respective data subject is first contacted thereafter. Moreover, the provision states that it is not necessary for the candidate to provide their consent for the processing of their personal data,[852] nor must they provide their consent for the processing of their special category personal data (which can be processed thanks to the General Authorization no. 1/2016 of the GPDP).[853]

661. According to Article 113 of the Personal Data Protection Code and Article 8 of Law 20 May 1970, no. 300 (so-called *Statuto dei Lavoratori*, i.e., 'Workers' Statute'), it is forbidden for the purpose of recruitment, as during the course of the employment relationship, to make inquiries, including through third parties, into the employee's political, religious or trade union views, as well as facts not relevant to the assessment of the employee's professional aptitude.

662. Article 114 of the Data Protection Code also recalls that the employer shall comply with Article 4 of the Workers Statute. This provision is particularly relevant because it establishes that in case where video surveillance devices or IT tools – aside from those which are necessary for the employee to provide its activity or for the employer to manage attendance – are leveraged by the employer, such tools may only be used for purposes related to organization and production in the workplace,[854] for purposes of workplace safety, as well as to secure company assets. Moreover, before starting to use the tool, the employer shall request and obtain

850. For example, according to Art. 80 of D.Lgs. 50/2016, if a company participates in a public tender, the criminal records of top management must also be submitted as a part of the tender documents. At the same time, also Art. 25-*bis* of the D.P.R. no. 313/2002 provides that if an employer wants to hire an employee who will work in contact with minors, the employer must verify that the person has no criminal convictions for crimes committed against minors.

851. For an overview of the deontological rules currently in force, *see supra* Part VI.

852. It may be argued that this provision has no legal effect, as it simply reiterates the content of Art. 6, para. 1, letter b), GDPR.

853. *See* Part III, Ch. 3, *supra*.

854. *See* GPDP, *Ordinanza ingiunzione nei confronti di Proma S.S.A. s.r.l. – 15 aprile 2021*, 15.4.2021, doc. web no. 9586936, https://www.garanteprivacy.it/web/guest/home/docweb/-/docweb-display/docweb/9586936.

authorization for its use from the labour inspectorate or must enter into a collective agreement with company's union representatives, if any. It should be noted that this violation can be subject to criminal liability provided by Article 171 of the Personal Data Protection Code.[855]

663. Article 115 concerns smart and remote working and provides that employers shall be required to ensure that the employees' personality and moral freedom are respected. Moreover, it mandates that home-based workers are required to ensure confidentiality as necessary with regard to all family-related matters.

664. Other important provisions regarding data processing in the context of employment are found within two important opinions of the GPDP. In particular, these are the 'Guidelines Applying to the Use of E-Mails and the Internet in the Employment Context'[856] which shall be examined in the next paragraph, and the 'Guiding principles applying to the processing of employee's personal data for the purposes of managing employment relations in private sector' (the 'Guidelines').[857]

665. The Guidelines are aimed at providing guidance to the employer regarding processing activities carried out during the employment relationship. In particular, referring to the individuation of the data controller, the Guidelines clarify that it is always necessary to identify who is the centre of imputation of the employment relationship, especially when there is a group of companies. The Guidelines, which are mostly outdated due to them being adopted in 2006, interestingly clarify that the data controller is always the employer even if, in a group of companies, the holding carries out some of the processing activities for the management of employees. In those cases, the latter acts as the processor of the employer which remains the sole data controller of the personal data of its employees.

666. Additional considerations must be made in relation to certain specific processing activities that may or must be carried out in accordance with occupational safety and hygiene regulations. Similar regulations, which also implement some EU directives and are part of the more general framework of measures necessary to protect the psycho-physical integrity of workers (as also required under Article 2087 of the Civil Code), place hygiene and safety in the workplace for the mandatory health surveillance according to Legislative Decree no. 9 April 2008, no. 81, directly under the responsibility of the employment medical doctor.

Concerning this specific processing activity, the GPDP published an opinion[858] which analyses the role of the medical doctor responsible for hygiene and safety in

855. For an overview of the criminal provisions established by the Personal Data Protection Code, *see infra* Part X, Ch. 5.

856. GPDP, *Guidelines Applying to the Use of E-mail and Internet in the Employment Context*, *supra* n. 253.

857. GPDP, *Guiding Principles Applying to the Processing of Employees' Personal Data for the Purpose of Managing Employment Relations in the Private Sector*, 23.11.2006, doc. web no. 1364939, https://www.garanteprivacy.it/web/guest/home/docweb/-/docweb-display/docweb/1427027.

858. *See* GPDP, *Il ruolo del 'medico competente' in materia di sicurezza sul luogo di lavoro, anche con riferimento al contesto emergenziale*, https://www.garanteprivacy.it/documents/10160/0/Protezione

the workplace. This opinion – even if published during the COVID-19 emergency period – contains some indications which can be applied more generally. According to that opinion, the doctor acts as an autonomous data controller[859] of the processing of employee's personal data collected for pre-employment health checks and, during the course of the working activities, for health surveillance activities.

Moreover, the GPDP clarifies that the competent doctor is the sole entity who may have knowledge of the health information concerning employees contained in their health records. The health records are kept by the competent doctor as an autonomous data controller during the employment relationship, and at the end of such relationship, the file is provided to the employee, and a copy is then maintained by the employer for ten years. Starting from the beginning of the retention period of ten years, the employer acts as an autonomous data controller, even if it is unable to access the content of the health records.

In the words of the GPDP:

> Although the assessments aimed at verifying the suitability for the 'specific task' of the employee are mandatory by law and are carried out 'at the expense' and 'by the care' of the employer …, they must be put in place exclusively through the competent doctor. In this way, although the regulatory framework makes the employer assume the costs and resources instrumental to the activity put in place by the competent doctor (on the economic level but, in some cases and for some profiles, also on the organizational level), nevertheless this does not result in controllership over the processing of personal data carried out by the doctor.[860]

667. With reference to the publication of employee data on the company bulletin board, it is considered permissible to publish only those data that are necessary and consistent with the performance of the job/task (e.g., work shifts), but it is disproportionate to disseminate information related to health status[861] or disciplinary measures imposed on an employee.[862]

+dei+dati+-+Il+ruolo+del+medico+competente+in+materia+di+sicurezza+sul+luogo+di+lavoro%2C+anche+con+riferimento+al+contesto+emergenziale.pdf/768bfc74-31c0-6ded-be3b-f1e2644ccce5?version=1.0, para. 3.

859. *See also* EDPB, *Guidelines 7/2020 on the concepts of controller and processor in the GDPR*, esp. para. 2.1.2. (paras 21 and 22 on ownership arising from explicit legal competence or specific legal provisions).

860. *See* GPDP, *supra* n. 846, para. 4. Author's translation.

861. In particular, the GPDP has considered unlawful the publication in tables of the reason, even if briefly stated, of the worker's absence, even if such tables were available only to the absent person's colleagues being published on the intranet and only in the specific space where the workers activities interested by the absence are carried out (GPDP, *Comunicazione di dati personali relative ai motivi dell'assenza dal lavoro*, 3.7.2014, doc. web no. 3325317, https://www.garanteprivacy.it/web/guest/home/docweb/-/docweb-display/docweb/3325317, author's translation).

862. *See* GPDP, *Pubblicazione in bacheca di dati relativi a contestazioni disciplinari e valutazioni dei soci lavoratori*, 13.12.2018, doc. web no. 9068983, https://www.garanteprivacy.it/home/docweb/-/docweb-display/docweb/9068983, and GPDP, *Ordinanza ingiunzione nei confronti di TB s.r.l.*, 2.7.2020, doc. web no. 9445567, https://www.garanteprivacy.it/home/docweb/-/docweb-display/docweb/9445567.

668. With regard to the information contained inside physical identification tags, even if justified due to the necessity to guarantee adequate interactions with the public, the GPDP has clarified that nametags should respect the data minimization principle and, therefore, illustrate only necessary information (e.g., name and job title).[863]

669. The above guidelines prescribe that before each processing of employee personal data, the worker should be adequately informed. Particular attention is also prescribed to the adoption of adequate safeguards and measures to protect the personal data of the employees and, in particular, their health data.

I. Specific Transparency Obligations for Automated Decision-Making and Monitoring Systems

670. In the context of employment law, the topic of transparency obligations for monitoring and decision-making systems was interesting in a relevant national legislative update.

On 29 June 2022, Legislative Decree no. 104/2022 (also known as the 'Transparency Decree') was published in the Italian Official Journal,[864] entering into force on 13 August 2022.

This decree transposes Directive (EU) 2019/1152[865] and amends Legislative Decree no. 152/1997, providing for additional information requirements for employers in drafting public and private subordinate employment contracts. Among the new obligations set forth by the decree is the same obligation provided for by Articles 13 and 14 GDPR, i.e., the right to inform the data subject.

More specifically, Article 4 of the Decree introduces an Article 1-bis to Legislative Decree no. 152/ 1997 according to which:

The public and private employer is required to inform the employee of the use of automated decision-making or monitoring systems that aim at providing indications relevant to the recruitment or assignment, management or termination of employment, assignment of tasks or duties, as well as indications affecting the supervision, evaluation, performance and fulfilment of contractual obligations of employees.[866]

671. Paragraph 2 of Article 1-bis further clarifies such obligation, stating that the employer shall disclose the following information:

863. *See* GPDP, *supra* n. 846, para. 54. *See also* GPDP, *Lavoro e previdenza sociale – Cartellini identificativi dei lavoratori*, 11.12.2000, doc. web no. 30991, https://www.garanteprivacy.it/web/guest/home/docweb/-/docweb-display/docweb/30991.

864. D. Lgs. no. 152/1997, https://www.gazzettaufficiale.it/eli/id/2022/07/29/22G00113/sg.

865. Directive (EU) 2019/1152 of the European Parliament and of the Council of 20 Jun. 2019 on transparent and predictable working conditions in the European Union. OJ L 186, 11.7.2019.

866. Author's translation.

(i) the aspects of the employment relationship which are affected by the use of such systems: for example, the employer shall clarify if the system is likely to impact decisions pertaining to the duration of the employment relationship;[867]
(ii) the purposes of such systems, i.e., why the employer implemented them;
(iii) the logic of such systems and how they function;
(iv) the categories of data and the main parameters used to programme or train such systems, including the performance evaluation mechanisms, e.g., the employer shall clarify if the system assigns benefits taking into consideration the comments of clients on the activities of the employee;
(v) the control measures adopted for the automated decisions, any correction processes, and the person in charge of the quality management system;
(vi) the level of accuracy, robustness and cybersecurity of such systems, the metrics used to measure these parameters, and the potentially discriminatory impacts of the metrics themselves.

672. In addition to this, the third paragraph of Article 1-bis specifies that the employee has the right to access the information described above. Such disposition is coherent with Article 15 of the GDPR, but it is not completely aligned with the latter. In fact, the decree also allows the union representative to exercise such right of access on behalf of the employee and requires that the employer replies within thirty days, not specifying that the term can be extended for two months, as provided for by Article 12, paragraph 3, GDPR.

Furthermore, the fourth paragraph provides for an obligation for the employer to provide the employee with 'instructions' regarding data security and the updating of the record of processing concerning the activities referred to in paragraph 1, including the activities of surveillance and monitoring.[868] The same paragraph also provides for an obligation to perform a risk analysis and a Data Protection Impact Assessment, pursuant to Article 35 GDPR, and (where necessary) a prior consultation, under Article 36 GDPR, on the processing activities carried out through these systems.

The Transparency Decree further specifies that in case of any modification in the processing activities described above that might impact the condition of work, the employees should be notified in writing at least twenty-four hours in advance. In addition to the information obligations set forth in Articles 13 and 14 GDPR, the decree specifies that the information on the processing activities carried out through these systems shall be communicated to the employees and the union representative in a transparent way, using a structured, commonly used and machine-readable format.

---

867. Luca Iadecola, *Adempimenti privacy e prime indicazioni operative dopo il decreto trasparenza*, Altalex (23 Aug. 2022), https://www.altalex.com/documents/news/2022/08/23/adempimenti-privacy-prime-indicazioni-operative-dopo-decreto-trasparenza.
868. Author's translation.

673. In terms of penalties, the failure, delay, or incomplete fulfilment of the information obligations set forth in the Transparency Decree can cause the application of an administrative sanction of between EUR 250 and EUR 1,500 for each worker concerned, subject to a complaint by the worker and an inspection.

674. In August 2022, some clarifications on the interpretation of the Transparency Decree were provided by the National Labour Inspectorate (Circular no. 4, dated 10 August 2022)[869] and the Ministry of Labour (Circular no. 19, dated 20 September 2022).[870] In particular, the first circular better clarified the information to be provided with reference to the use of automated decision-making or monitoring systems and divided them into two categories:

(i) systems that aim at generating a decision-making process capable of affecting the employment relationship, such as algorithm/artificial intelligence from which automated decisions are derived or with respect to which the human factor is merely ancillary. This category may include hiring, assignment of tasks through chatbots, automated profiling of candidates, automated assignment of work shifts, definition of working hours, determination of remuneration, and so on;

(ii) systems that monitor and evaluate workers, as well as systems incident to performance and fulfilment of bargaining obligations, such as tablets, digital or facial recognition devices, GPS, and the like.

675. According to the Circular from the National Labour Inspectorate, the use of automated means of recording employee attendance on entry or exit (so-called badges) would be outside the scope of the information requirement set forth by the Transparency Decree, unless such tools are included in an automated procedure generating an employer decision.[871]

676. After this, the GPDP intervened as well, publishing a document[872] that aimed at coordinating the different interpretations of the Transparency Decree shared by different institutions and giving a systematic interpretation of its dispositions that took into consideration the European data protection framework.

First, the GPDP clarified that the Transparency Decree, pursuant to Article 88 GDPR, provides for additional further and more specific information requirements

869. Circular no. 4/2022 of the National Labor Inspectorate, 10.8.2022, https://www.ispettorato.gov.it/files/2023/01/INL-circolare-4-2022-chiarimenti-decreto-trasparenza.pdf.

870. Circular no. 19/2022 of the Ministry of Labor, 20.11.2022) https://www.lavoro.gov.it/notizie/Pagine/Pubblicata-la-circolare-sulle-novita-introdotte-dal-DLgs-n104-2022-in-materia-di-condizioni-di-lavoro-trasparenti.aspx#:~:text=%E2%80%8BLa%20Circolare%20n,di%20lavoro%20trasparenti%20e%20prevedibili.

871. *La circolare ministeriale sul cd. Decreto Trasparenza,* Bollettino ADAPT no. 32, 27.11.2022 https://www.bollettinoadapt.it/la-circolare-ministeriale-sul-cd-decreto-trasparenza/.

872. GPDP, *Questioni interpretative e applicative in materia di protezione dei dati connesse all'entrata in vigore del d. lgs. 27 giugno 2022, n. 104 in materia di condizioni di lavoro trasparenti e prevedibili (c.d. 'Decreto trasparenza'),* doc web no. 9844960, 13.12.2022), https://www.garanteprivacy.it/web/guest/home/docweb/-/docweb-display/docweb/9844960.

for employers that use monitoring and decision-making systems in the recruitment phase or during the employment, but that the dispositions of the GDPR as well as those of the Personal Data Protection Code and of the Workers' Statute still remain applicable and shall be complied with by the employers. Therefore, the adoption of monitoring systems in the work context must always be grounded on an adequate legal basis and be subject to prior verification by the employer of the conditions of lawfulness established by the regulations on remote controls (Article 80 of the Workers' Statute, Article 10 of Legislative Decree 10 September 2003, no. 276, and Articles 113 and 114 of the Personal Data Protection Code), as well as risk assessment and Data Protection Impact Assessment to verify their impact on the rights and freedoms of the data subjects. In addition to this, with reference to some dispositions which raised doubts on their alignment with the GDPR, the GPDP clarified that:

(i) With reference to the right of access to data, Article 15 of the GDPR still remains applicable.
(ii) With reference to the moment in which the employer has to share the information: the Transparency Decree requires that such information be shared before the beginning of the employment, but that Articles 13 and 14 GDPR that provide for different timings remain applicable (e.g., Article 13, paragraph 1 and Article 14, paragraph 3, GDPR).
(iii) With reference to Article 22 GDPR, the GPDP recommends that employers verify whether the use of automated decision-making or monitoring systems integrates a uniquely automated decision-making process, including profiling, that produces legal effects or significantly affects the data subject. If so, the data subject must be guaranteed human intervention on the part of the data controller, as well as the right to express their opinion and challenge the decision. Thus, the view of the GPDP is that the decree applies even in cases where the automated decision-maker is not autonomous but is accompanied by a human operator.[873]

677. Finally, with regard to particularly intrusive systems, such as machine learning, rating and ranking tools, the GPDP pointed out that their use might entail critical issues in terms of proportionality and risks that conflict with data protection principles and national dispositions protecting the freedom, dignity and privacy of the employee.

678. In conclusion, based on the changes introduced by the Transparency Decree, from a data protection point of view, it would be necessary for data controllers to carry out the following activities:

(i) mapping of the company systems in use to verify whether they fall within the perimeter of application of the Transparency Decree;

873. Riccardo Berti & Franco Zumerle, *Decreto Trasparenza: ecco le indicazioni operative del Garante privacy*, Cybersecurity360 (30 Jan. 2023), https://www.cybersecurity360.it/legal/privacy-dati-personali/decreto-trasparenza-ecco-le-indicazioni-operative-del-garante-privacy/.

(ii) in case of a positive outcome of the verification referred to in the point above, it would be necessary to carry out a risk analysis and impact assessment in accordance with Articles 35 and 36 GDPR;
(iii) review and, if necessary, update the relevant information notices (e.g., candidates, employees), verifying that the information required by the Transparency Decree is also present. In this regard, it should be made sure that information is provided in a structured, commonly used and machine-readable format, both for employees and trade union representatives, and that any changes to the information notice are communicated to workers at least twenty-four hours in advance;
(iv) guarantee the employee's right of access to the information referred to in the Transparency Decree, allowing the data subject the possibility of submitting the request for access also through trade union representatives, with the need for the employer to reply within thirty days from the request;
(v) verify appointment letters provided to authorized persons, pursuant to Articles 29 GDPR and 2-quaterdecies Personal Data Protection Code, which must contain written instructions regarding personal data processing activities carried out in the performance of work duties assigned to employees; it should be taken into consideration that the Transparency Decree requires that the instructions be rendered in writing and in a structured, commonly used and machine-readable format;
(vi) verify the mapping of such automated decision-making or monitoring systems within the company's policy on the use of IT tools;
(vii) verify and, if necessary, update the record of processing activities pursuant to Article 30 of the GDPR.

§2. Management of E-mails in the Context of Employment: The GPDP Guidelines Applying to the Use of E-mail (and Internet) and the Relevant GPDP's Decisions

679. Regarding the management of the employee's e-mail account and the detention of the related e-mail messages, the GPDP has adopted a highly restrictive approach, which can be found in the analysis of the GPDP's decision-making practices.[874] With reference to the management of e-mail during the employment relationship, it is necessary to refer to the provisions and recommendations set out by

874. *See*, *inter alia*: GPDP, *Trattamento di dati personali effettuato sugli account di posta elettronica aziendale*, 1.2.2018, doc. web no. 8159221, https://www.garanteprivacy.it/web/guest/home/docweb/-/docweb-display/docweb/8159221; GPDP, *Ordinanza ingiunzione nei confronti di Gaypa s.r.l.*, 29.10.2020, doc. web no. 9518890, https://www.garanteprivacy.it/web/guest/home/docweb/-/docweb-display/docweb/9518890; GPDP, *Provvedimento del 4 dicembre 2019*, 4.12.2019, doc. web no. 9215890, https://www.garanteprivacy.it/web/guest/home/docweb/-/docweb-display/docweb/9215890; GPDP, *Ordinanza ingiunzione nei confronti di Palumbo Superyacht Ancona S.r.l.*, 7.4.2022, doc. web no. 9771545, https://www.garanteprivacy.it/web/guest/home/docweb/-/docweb-display/docweb/9771545: GPDP, *Ordinanza ingiunzione nei confronti di Consorzio Concessioni Reti Gas S.c.a.r.l., 9.3.2023, doc. web no. 9877754, https://www.garanteprivacy.it/web/guest/home/docweb/*

the GPDP with its *Guidelines Applying to the Use of E-mail and Internet in the Employment Context*[875] (hereinafter referred to as the 'Guidelines' within this Chapter). Instead, for the management of the e-mail box at the end of the employment relationship, the indications contained in various decisions issued by the GPDP after complaints and disputes brought forth by the ex-employees of individual organizations should be taken into consideration.

680. The 2007 Guidelines were issued by the GPDP after the analysis of several claims and questions which were brought to its attention. The Guidelines aim to ensure that the processing of personal data performed by employers to verify that e-mails and the Internet are used appropriately in the employment context is brought fully into line with Italian data protection legislation. The Guidelines state the need to process personal data in line with the general data protection principles, such as transparency, purpose limitation, and data minimization (today set out in Article 5 GDPR).

681. In addition, employers shall also take into consideration the provisions provided by the Workers Statute (L. 300/1970), more specifically, its Article 4 as a specific rule under Article 88 GDPR.[876] Under this Article, the company network equipment used to provide Internet connection and the company e-mail are understood as instruments used to carry out work and may be installed without a prior trade union agreement or authorization from the territorial inspectorate.

In any case, employers cannot remotely control employees' activities or use such tools to monitor the performance of workers. Therefore, the information collected through the instruments used by employees to carry out their duties is usable for all purposes related to the employment relationship on condition that the worker is given adequate information on how to use the tools and how the organization can carry out the controls and in compliance with the provisions of the Personal Data Protection Code.

682. According to these principles, under the Guidelines, the data controller shall indicate, in a clear and detailed manner, how work tools can be used and whether and to what extent controls are or may be carried out. To this end, the Guidelines suggest issuing internal guidelines and policies, which should be adequately publicized (e.g., by sharing them on the company's intranet) and will have to be regularly updated. In these internal policies, the following should be specified at least:

-/docweb-display/docweb/9877754. GPDP, *Ordinanza ingiunzione nei confronti di Reweb S.r.l.*, 11.01.2023, doc. web no. 9861827, https://www.garanteprivacy.it/web/guest/home/docweb/-/docweb-display/docweb/9861827.

875. *See* GPDP, *Guidelines Applying to the Use of E-mail and Internet in the Employment Context, supra* n. 253.

876. *See also* Art. 8 of the Workers' Statute, which prohibits the employer from carrying out investigations, including through third parties, on the political, religious or trade union opinions of the worker, as well as on facts not relevant for the purpose of evaluating the professional attitude of the worker.

(i) If and how the employee can use the Internet and other relevant information (such as prohibited usage, information and files kept by the organization).
(ii) If and how the employee can use their professional e-mail address for personal purposes.
(iii) What information generated using work tools is retained (such as log files, browsing history, backup copies, etc.), who is lawfully entitled to access such information and why.
(iv) Whether (and if so, what) information is kept for longer periods of time.
(v) Whether and to what extent the employer reserves the right to carry out controls in pursuance of applicable laws, also on an occasional and/or non-regular basis. In particular, it should be specified whether the occurrence of individual and/or repeated cases of misuse results in the issuing of prior collective and/or individual warnings and the performance of controls on individual employees and/or individual devices and workstations.
(vi) Which consequences, also of a disciplinary nature, may be drawn by the employer where the latter establishes that e-mail and Internet services are misused.
(vii) The procedure to access the worker's inbox during their absence – access may be permitted, for instance, if it is necessary to guarantee business continuity.
(viii) Which solutions are envisaged to ensure, with the employees' collaboration, that work can continue in the employees' absence – especially in case of planned leaves – with particular regard to the use of out-of-office auto-reply messages.
(ix) The security measures that the employee must put in place.

683. With specific reference to the use of e-mail, considering the Guidelines, the following may be possible depending on the specific circumstances:

(i) Use group e-mail addresses shared by several employees (e.g., info@company.it; salesoffice@company.it) which might be added to individual e-mail accounts (e.g., name.surname@company.it).
(ii) Assign a different e-mail account to employees, to be used for personal and professional purposes.
(iii) Assign specific functions to allow automatically sending out-of-office reply messages in case an employee is absent (e.g., during their holidays), whereby such messages contain details of colleagues or other contact details to contact the organization.
(iv) Allow for the designation of another employee (so-called trusted party) to access the inbox to search and send relevant e-mails to the data controller for the purpose of business continuity during the employee's absence.

684. Detailed information must also be given in the privacy notice, which must contain, *inter alia*, and in addition to the information provided by Article 13 GDPR, the main features of the processing operations carried out by the data controller, the person/unit the employees may contact in order to exercise their rights, as well as how to know the identity of the system administrators who can process their personal information.[877]

685. Regarding the topic of data retention, according to the Guidelines:

> Software systems must be configured and programmed so as to regularly and automatically delete – for instance via the so-called log file rotation – the personal data related to Internet accesses and network traffic, where their retention is unnecessary. In the absence of specific technical and/or security requirements, the provisional retention of the data related to the use of electronic tools must be accounted for on the basis of specific, proven purposes; additionally, the data retention period should not be in excess of the time required – as set out in advance – for achieving such purposes.[878]

686. Only on an exceptional basis may the retention period be extended.[879]

687. With reference to metadata relating to the use of e-mail, the GPDP has recently stated that:

> The retention of this information for a period of 180 days for generic security purposes did not appear to be justified because, where necessary, any security incidents can and should be promptly detected and mitigated, in order to protect the integrity and proper functionality of information systems, by implementing appropriate measures and, where appropriate, by using metadata related to the use of e-mail, in any case within much tighter time limits.[880] The generalized collection and storage for a time frame of 180 days of metadata related to employees' e-mail usage, are also contrary to the principles of storage limitation as well as data protection by design and by default, in violation of Articles 5(1)(e) and 25 GDPR.[881]

---

877. *See* GPDP, *Measures and arrangements applying to the controllers of processing operations performed with the help of electronic tools in view of committing the task of system administrator*, 27.11.2008, doc. web no. 1628774, https://www.garanteprivacy.it/web/guest/home/docweb/-/docweb-display/docweb/1628774, para. 4.3: 'To that end, they may rely on the information notice they are to provide to their employees – i.e. the data subjects – under s. 13 of the DP Code; alternatively, they may avail themselves of the technical specifications that are to be adopted pursuant to the DPA's decision no. 13 dated 1 Mar. 2007 … or else make use of internal communication tools such as the corporate intranet, circular letters and/or bulletins … '.
878. GPDP, *Guidelines Applying to the Use of E-mail and Internet in the Employment Context*, *supra* n. 253, para. 6.2.
879. *Ibid.* '[…] The retention period may only be extended on an exceptional basis in connection with the following: highly specific technical and/or security requirements; the circumstance that a data is indispensable to establish or defend a judicial claim; the obligation to keep and/or surrender the data in order to comply with a specific request lodged by either judicial authorities or the judicial police.'
880. *See* GPDP, *Ordinanza di ingiunzione nei confronti di Regione Lazio*, 1.12.2022, doc web no. 9833530, https://www.garanteprivacy.it/home/docweb/-/docweb-display/docweb/9833530.
881. Author's translation.

688. In addition, with regard to employees' e-mails, the GPDP, in the context of its practice and decisions, does not identify a specific term, although it has clarified that:

> The systematic storage of external data and the content of all electronic communications exchanged by employees through company accounts, in order to be able to reconstruct the exchange of communications between internal offices as well as all relationships with external stakeholders (customers, suppliers, insurance companies, tour operators), also in view of possible litigation, carried out by persons other than the owner of the specific mailbox for the entire duration of the employment relationship and after the interruption of the same, does not [...] comply with the principles of lawfulness and transparency, necessity and proportionality of the processing.[882]

689. In addition, the GPDP has decided that the practice implemented by an employer consisting of the storage of e-mail for 'respectively one and twelve months after the termination of the relationship for employees and managers' was unlawful.[883]

690. Regarding the management of the e-mail inbox of the employee (e.g., name.surname@company.it) at the time of termination of the employment relationship, the GPDP's decisions show that such personal mailbox must be disabled to prevent the sending and receiving of other e-mails. The opinion of the GPDP aims to balance the interests of the employer in accessing necessary information for carrying out its activities with the expectations of privacy and confidentiality of correspondence of employees, collaborators, and third parties. Furthermore: 'the exchange of email with other employees with people inside or outside the company allows one to become aware of personal information about the data subject, even if only by viewing external communications data (date, time, subject, names of senders and recipients)'.[884]

691. In several decisions, the GPDP holds that:

> With reference to processing carried out on e-mail after termination of employment, in accordance with the principles of protection of personal data, accounts attributable to identified or identifiable persons must be removed after deactivation of the same and contextual adoption of automatic systems designed to inform third parties and to provide them alternative addresses related to the professional activity of the data controller. The interest of the data controller to access the information necessary for the efficient management of its business,

882. *Ibid.*

883. *Ibid. See* GPDP, *Trattamento effettuato sugli account di posta elettronica aziendale*, 1.2.2018, doc. web no. 8159221, https://www.garanteprivacy.it/web/guest/home/docweb/-/docweb-display/docweb/8159221.

884. *See* GPDP, *Provvedimento del 4 dicembre 2019*, 4.12.2019, doc. web no. 9215890, https://www.garanteprivacy.it/web/guest/home/docweb/-/docweb-display/docweb/9215890. Author's translation.

therefore, must be balanced with the legitimate expectation of confidentiality on correspondence by employees as well as third parties.[885]

692. Internal procedures which implement an automatic redirection to the manager or to other colleagues of the ex-worker's e-mail are also prohibited.

Therefore, a single organization must define a retention period of electronic mail, both during and after the work relationship, taking into consideration the GPDP's decisions outlined above and the Workers' Statute as specific rules under Article 88 GDPR.

§3. GPS SYSTEMS

693. In Italy, before the direct application of the GDPR, public or private data controllers could only initiate processing of data revealing the geographical location of individuals by means of an electronic communication, with the prior authorization of the GPDP (called 'preliminary verification'),[886] unless specific exemptions applied.[887]

The principle of accountability introduced by the 2018 reform significantly changed the approach to be taken by data controllers, who no longer have to comply with the minimum security measures provided by the previous legislation and the instructions provided by GPDP with the preliminary verifications but must perform a risk analysis independently, and implement certain organizational and security measures aimed at ensuring compliance with the GDPR.[888]

694. With specific reference to the use of GPS (i.e., global positioning system) in the context of employment, the same considerations mentioned above apply.[889]

885. *See* GPDP, *Trattamento effettuato sulle e-mail di dipendenti ed ex dipendenti – 30 luglio 2015*, 30.7.2015, doc. web no. 4298277, https://www.garanteprivacy.it/web/guest/home/docweb/-/docweb-display/docweb/4298277; GPDP, *Provvedimento del 5 marzo 2015*, 5.3.2015, doc. web no. 3985524, https://www.garanteprivacy.it/web/guest/home/docweb/-/docweb-display/docweb/3985524; GPDP, *Provvedimento del 27 novembre 2014*, doc. web no. 3718714, https://www.garanteprivacy.it/web/guest/home/docweb/-/docweb-display/docweb/3718714.

886. Author's translation.

887. *See* Art. 37, para. 1, lett. a), of the Personal Data Protection Code, in the text prior to the amendments of D.Lgs. no. 101/2018.

888. Some provisions and decisions provided by the GPDP prior to the direct application of the GDPR can be considered guidance when using GPS tools to process workers' data. *See, inter alia*, GPDP, *Sistemi di localizzazione dei veicoli nell'ambito del rapporto di lavoro*, 4.10.2011, doc. web no. 1850581, https://www.gpdp.it/web/guest/home/docweb/-/docweb-display/docweb/2444921, which, among the other instructions, provides 'that data controller relying on location systems that are installed on vehicles used for the performance of work shall also have to place stickers bearing the notice "VEICOLO SOTTOPOSTO A LOCALIZZAZIONE" [GEO-LOCATED VEHICLE] inside such vehicles'; GPDP, *Verifica preliminare. Trattamento dei dati personali derivanti dalla rilevazione di coordinate satellitari relative alla geolocalizzazione di apparati elettronici di tipo radio mobili e veicolari*, 24.05.2017, doc. web no. 6495708, https://www.garanteprivacy.it/home/docweb/-/docweb-display/docweb/6495708, which provides that the collection of geolocation data should not be constant but limited in scope when necessary to achieve the specific purposes legitimately pursued.

889. *See* §1, *supra* in this Ch. 4.

Specifically, the collection of workers' location data through geolocation tools may result in potential remote monitoring of their activities which falls within the scope of Article 4 of the Workers Statute.[890] The employer may use such tools only for organizational and production needs, work safety and protection of company assets and must obtain a specific authorization from the competent Labour Inspector Office or enter into a collective agreement with the company trade union representatives, except when such tools are necessary to perform the work.

695. Guidance on whether GPS equipment is to be considered tools used by the worker to render work performance – to which Article 4, paragraph 1 of the Workers Statute does not apply – has been provided by National Labour Inspectorate circular no. 2/2016, with specific regard to tools installed in corporate vehicles.[891]

According to the National Labour Inspectorate, in general, geolocation systems should be considered an 'additional' work tool, not essential for the performance of work activities but rather to meet insurance, organizational and production needs or work safety. In very specific cases, the use of GPS on vehicles is to be considered necessary to enable the concrete and effective performance of the work, for example, when the equipment is required by specific legislative or regulatory provisions (e.g., the transport of carriers with a value exceeding EUR 1,500,000.00). In such cases, GPS can be considered an essential tool which does not require authorization from the competent Labour Inspector Office or the collective agreement with the company trade union representatives.

696. The GPDP, in an important decision issued against the delivery company Foodinho, already discussed *supra* in Part IV, Chapter 6, §2.II, also remarked that the use of GPS must be closely related to the performance of work, otherwise Article 4, paragraph 1 of the Workers Statute applies. More specifically, in that decision, the GPDP established that the tracking of riders' location every fifteen seconds and the storage of their routes for ten months entailed a processing not proportional to the purpose declared by the company, namely the allocation of orders to riders based on distance from the pickup and delivery point.[892]

697. In several decisions, the GPDP also clarified that data collected via GPS may fall within the definition of 'personal data' under Article 4, paragraph 1, letter a), GDPR, even when the tool is not univocally associated with the worker.[893] For

890. *Ibid.*

891. *See* https://www.lavoro.gov.it/documenti-e-norme/normative/Documents/2016/Circolare-INL-n-2-indicazioni-operative-utilizzazione-impianti-GPS-signed.pdf.

892. *See* GPDP, *Ordinanza ingiunzione nei confronti di Foodinho s.r.l.*, 10.6.2021, doc. web no. 9675440, https://www.garanteprivacy.it/home/docweb/-/docweb-display/docweb/9675440. However the decision was later annulled by the Milan Court on grounds of the excessiveness of penalties imposed by the GPDP.

893. *See, inter alia*: GPDP, *Localizzazione di veicoli aziendali*, 28.06.2018, doc. web no. 9023246, https://www.garanteprivacy.it/home/docweb/-/docweb-display/docweb/9023246; GPDP, *Verifica preliminare. Trattamento dei dati personali derivanti dalla rilevazione di coordinate satellitari relative alla geolocalizzazione di apparati elettronici di tipo radio mobili e veicolari*, 24.05.2017, doc. web no. 6495708, https://www.garanteprivacy.it/home/docweb/-/docweb-display/docweb/6495708; GPDP, *Trattamento di dati personali dei dipendenti mediante dispositivi indossabili*, 28.02.2018,

instance, data collected by GPS installed on a vehicle used by several workers can be combined with other information held by the employer – such as shift records – indirectly allowing a specific worker to be identified.

698. Before the GPS system is activated and data processing starts, workers need to be provided with a privacy information notice under Article 13 GDPR. In several decisions, the GPDP has emphasized the need to provide workers with clear and detailed information on how their data are processed through geolocation systems, for instance, providing details about the characteristics of the tool used, the type of data collected, the purposes of the data processing, the frequency of the detection and the retention period.[894]

699. In addition, the GPDP has included in the list of data processing activities that require a data protection impact assessment under Article 35, GDPR, those carried out with IT tools, including geolocation systems, from which the possibility of remote monitoring of employees' activities arises.[895]

§4. Video Surveillance

700. The use of video surveillance systems by the employer could determine a potential remote control of the workers' activities and, for that reason, fall under the provisions of Article 4 of the Workers Statute (and its violation under the criminal provision set forth by Article 171 of the Personal Data Protection Code).[896]

In particular, video surveillance systems can be installed by the employer only to pursue one of the aims set forth by Article 4 of the Workers Statute and never with the purpose of remotely controlling the employee. The legal basis for this processing is, therefore, the legitimate interest of the employer as data controller, as also recognized by the GPDP in its 2010 provision on video-surveillance.[897] In addition,

---

doc. web no. 9094427, https://www.gpdp.it/web/guest/home/docweb/-/docweb-display/docweb/90 94427; GPDP, *Ordinanza ingiunzione nei confronti di Giessegi Industria Mobili S.p.A.*, 15.12.2022, doc. web no. 9861249, https://www.garanteprivacy.it/web/guest/home/docweb/-/docweb-display/d ocweb/9861249.

894. *See, inter alia*: GPDP, *Trattamento dei dati personali derivanti dalla rilevazione di coordinate satellitari relative alla geolocalizzazione di apparati elettronici di tipo radio mobili e veicolari*, 24.05.2017, doc. web no. 6495708, https://www.garanteprivacy.it/home/docweb/-/docweb-display /docweb/6495708; GPDP, *Ordinanza ingiunzione nei confronti di Foodinho s.r.l.*, 10.6.2021, doc. web no. 9675440, https://www.garanteprivacy.it/home/docweb/-/docweb-display/docweb/96754 40; GPDP, *Ordinanza ingiunzione nei confronti di Giessegi Industria Mobili S.p.A.*, 15.12.2022, doc. web no. 9861249, https://www.garanteprivacy.it/web/guest/home/docweb/-/docweb-display/d ocweb/9861249.

895. *See* GPDP, *Elenco delle tipologie di trattamenti soggetti al requisito di una valutazione d'impatto sulla protezione dei dati ai sensi dell'art. 35, comma 4, del Regolamento (UE) n. 2016/679*, 11.10.2023, doc. web no. 9058979, https://www.garanteprivacy.it/home/docweb/-/docweb-display /docweb/9058979.

896. *See* §1, *supra* in this Ch. 4.

897. GPDP, *Provvedimento in materia di videosorveglianza*, 8.10.2010, doc. web no. 1712680, https:/ /www.garanteprivacy.it/home/docweb/-/docweb-display/docweb/1712680, para. 6.2.2. This provision is usually considered outdated, in light of the entry into force of the GDPR, the 2018 reform,

before the activation of the system, it is mandatory to obtain the authorization of the territorial competent Labour Inspector Office or enter into a collective agreement with the company trade union representatives, if any.[898]

The GPDP, within the 2010 provision referred to above, also prescribes installation of the cameras in a way that limits the visual of the camera and using technical measures (e.g., masking parts of the captured field where not relevant) to ensure the respect of the rights of the data subjects.

701. Before the start of the processing, it is also necessary to inform data subjects according to Article 13 GDPR. The privacy notice shall be provided with a layered approach, first in a concise manner, through signage summarizing the most important information, and with which reference will be made to the extended privacy policy to be made available to data subjects. The signage should be displayed in the vicinity of the cameras. After 2019, reference should be made to the layered approach suggested by the EDPB within the relevant guidelines on video-surveillance.[899]

Referring to the application of Article 4 of the Workers Statute to video surveillance systems, an important decision of the Supreme Court of Cassation reiterated that:

> [A]re excluded from the scope of application of Article 4 of the Workers Statute, and not require compliance with the guarantees provided therein, the defensive controls performed by the employer if they are aimed at ascertaining unlawful conduct detrimental to the company's assets and image, all the more so when they are arranged *ex post*, that is, after the fraudulent or conduct by the employee has already taken place, so as to disregard mere supervision of the performance of work.[900]

702. In other words, Article 4 of the Workers Statute does not apply where the employer uses video surveillance (also by means of covert surveillance) in order to obtain proof of a grave misconduct of the employee, such as stealing company's property.

In some cases, in the presence of concrete indications of wrongdoing by employees to the detriment of the company's assets, covert surveillance by the employer in the workplace to dispel doubt as to whether or not such conduct had taken place was deemed permissible, even without having first carried out the necessary steps imposed by Article 4 of the Workers Statute.

---

and the adoption of the EDPB Guidelines 3/2019 on processing of personal data through video devices; however, some of the indications are still sound and may serve as guidance for employers. *See also* FAQ of the GPDP http://www.lavorosi.it/fileadmin/user_upload/PRASSI_2020/garante-privacy-FAQ-Videosorveglianza-aggiornate-reg-ue-2016-679.pdf.

898. The new guidelines of the National Labour Institute (no. 2572/23) specify that for the companies which have different production units or sites on the same territory do not need to request different authorizations, instead, it is enough to request one for all the locations.

899. *Ibid.*, paras 108 et seq.

900. Supreme Court of Cassation, no. 3255/2020, crim. sect. Author's translation.

703. When considering the compliance of the system, the prescription provided by the National Labour Inspectorate circular no. 5/2018[901] that contains some practical indications about the content of the request of authorization should also considered. In particular, according to the circular, access to the images captured by video surveillance systems should be properly logged (and the log must be kept for at least six months).

I. Other Monitoring Systems: The Case of Call Centres

704. The same considerations above can be applied to the tools used by call centres to track the activities carried out by operators in real time, as these can imply a potential remote controlling of workers' activities. The above interpretation is the same as that expressed by the Italian GPDP in similar cases.

705. Among the most recent is the one relating to the processing carried out by Sky Italia S.p.A., in which the GPDP confirmed the application of Article 4, paragraph 1, of the Workers Statute if the system:

> Does not merely allow the association between the call and the customer's personal data in order to facilitate the call handling activity [...] but allows 'further processing' (e.g., storage of personal data, including of operators, and extractions of reports) relating to telephone activity in general by different business functions. This makes it possible to reconstruct, even indirectly, the activity carried out by the operators and represents a system suitable for realizing a control, even if only potential and indirectly, of the work activity. Therefore, when the characteristics of the system and the range of processing operations made possible by it are not exclusively functional to the mere management of the contact with the customer and, therefore, 'to the mere execution of work performance … the system thus configured cannot be considered an "instrument used by the worker to render work performance" (pursuant to and for the purposes of Article 4, paragraph 2, Law no. 300/1970), but rather falls among those organizational tools, from which the remote control of workers' activities may indirectly results, with the consequent need to activate the procedures provided therein (Article 4, Paragraph 1, Law no. 300/70).[902]

901. *See,* https://www.lavorosi.it/vigilanza-e-accertamenti-ispettivi/organi-e-attivita-di-vigilanza/inl-circ-n-5-del-19022018-indicazioni-sulla-sorveglianza-biometrica-e-audiovisiva/#:~:text=5%20del%2019.02.2018%3A%20Indicazioni%20sulla%20sorveglianza%20biometrica%20e%20audiovisiva,-20%2F02%2F2018&text=L'Ispettorato%20nazionale%20del%20Lavoro,l'utilizzazione%20di%20dati%20biometrici.

902. GPDP, *Trattamento dei dati personali dei dipendenti di un call center*, 8.3.2018, doc. web no. 8163433. https://www.garanteprivacy.it/home/docweb/-/docweb-display/docweb/8163433. Author's translation.

§5. Biometric Data as a Means of Physical or Logical Access to the Workplace

706. Article 2-*septies*, paragraph 7, of the Personal Data Protection Code, allows biometric processing to be used as a means of secure access, but only when this is necessary under Article 32 GDPR (e.g., in order to enable access to data centres), as better detailed in Part III, Chapter 3, § 3, *supra*. This also applies in the context of employee access to the workplace or to some specific parts of the workplace which require biometric access controls pursuant to Article 32 GDPR.

707. Before the direct application of the GDPR, biometric data were not considered 'sensitive,' yet in view of their close and stable relationship with the individual and their identity, public or private data controllers could initiate processing, subject to specific exemption hypotheses, only after prior authorization by the GPDP.[903]

Since 2007, the GPDP has emphasized that data protection principles require prior consideration of other less intrusive systems that can provide reliable verification of attendance without resorting to the processing of biometric data.[904] These principles are also found at the international level and in the positions taken by other supervisory authorities.[905]

708. Against this background, with regard to some cases of generalized use of biometric systems in the work context, grounded on alleged generic prevention needs about the possible distorted use of attendance detection tools in common use (such as badges), the GPDP has assessed the relevant processing as disproportionate.[906] In other cases, the GPDP admitted the uses of biometric systems in the work

903. *See* Arts 17 and 37, para. 1, lett. a), of the Personal Data Protection Code, in the text prior to the amendments of D.Lgs. no. 101/2018; GPDP, *Provvedimento generale prescrittivo in tema di biometria*, 12.11.2014, doc. web no. 3556992, https://www.garanteprivacy.it/home/docweb/-/docweb-display/docweb/3556992, item no. 4); GPDP, *Linee guida in materia di trattamento di dati personali di lavoratori per finalità di gestione del rapporto di lavoro in ambito pubblico*, 14.6.2007, doc. web no. 1417809, https://www.garanteprivacy.it/home/docweb/-/docweb-display/docweb/1417809; GDPD, *Sistema biometrico basato sul trattamento di impronte digitali per finalità di rilevazione delle presenze dei dipendenti di un Comune*, 17.03.2016, doc. web no. 4948405, https://www.garanteprivacy.it/web/guest/home/docweb/-/docweb-display/docweb/4948405; more recently, the obligation for the data controller to carefully assess the actual need to implement biometric access systems has been expressed in GPDP, *Ordinanza ingiunzione nei confronti di Azienda sanitaria provinciale di Enna*, 14.1.2021, doc. web no. 9542071, https://www.garanteprivacy.it/home/docweb/-/docweb-display/docweb/9542071.

904. *See* the decisions outlined in the previous note.

905. *See* Committee of Ministers to Member States, Processing of Personal Data in the Employment Context, Recommendation CM/Rec(2015)5, para. 18; A29WP, Data Processing in the Workplace, Opinion no. 2/2017, para. 5; CNIL, Resolution no. 10.1.2019 https://www.cnil.fr/fr/biometrie-sur-les-lieux-de-travail-publication-dun-reglement-type and the FAQs published on 28 Mar. 2019 '*Question-réponses sur le règlement type biométrie as well as the previous guidelines "Travail & données personnells"*'.

906. *See*, GDPD, *Videosorveglianza e biometria all'interno di un istituto scolastico per la rilevazione delle presenze dei dipendenti,* 30.5.2013, doc. web no. 2502951, https://www.garanteprivacy.it/web/guest/home/docweb/-/docweb-display/docweb/2502951; GDPD, *Installazione in un istituto scolastico di un dispositivo a riconoscimento biometrico (impronta digitale) per finalità di controllo*

context, but in limited circumstances and in the presence of objective and documented needs that made the adoption of such systems indispensable, taking into account the specificity of the concrete case, the socio-economic context of reference and the characteristics of the technology used.[907]

709. In a recent opinion, the GPDP affirmed that 'at present, therefore, there is no suitable legal basis that can meet the requirements of the GDPR and the Personal Data Protection Code to legitimize public administrations to implement the processing of biometric data for purposes of employee attendance records under Article 9, paragraph 2, letter b), GDPR'.[908] The same consideration should also be made in the private sector.[909]

---

*del rispetto dell'orario di se*rvizio, 30.5.2013, doc. web. no. 2503101, https://www.garanteprivacy.it/web/guest/home/docweb/-/docweb-display/docweb/2503101; GDPD, *Sistema biometrico di rilevazione delle presenze dei dipendenti in una scuola*, 1.8.2013, doc. web n. 2578547, https://www.garanteprivacy.it/web/guest/home/docweb/-/docweb-display/docweb/2578547; but also GDPD *Trattamento di dati biometrici per finalità di rilevazione delle presenze dei dipendenti: verifica preliminare richiesta dal Comune di Boscoreale*, 31.1.2013, doc. web no. 2304669, https://www.garanteprivacy.it/web/guest/home/docweb/-/docweb-display/docweb/2304669; GPDP, *Raccolta di dati biometrici in occasione del rilascio della Carta Multiservizi della Difesa,* 24.5.2017, doc. web no. 6531525, https://www.garanteprivacy.it/web/guest/home/docweb/-/docweb-display/docweb/6531525.

907. *See*, for example, GPDP, *Verifica preliminare. Sistema di lettura di dati biometrici mediante parziale identificazione dell'impronta digitale per la rilevazione della presenza in servizio*, 15.09.2016, doc. web no. 5505689, https://www.garanteprivacy.it/home/docweb/-/docweb-display/docweb/5505689.

908. *See* GPDP, *Ordinanza ingiunzione nei confronti di Azienda sanitaria provinciale di Enna*, *supra* n. 904, *supra*.

909. *See* GPDP, *Ordinanza ingiunzione nei confronti di Sportitalia*, società sportiva dilettantistica a responsabilità limitata, 10.11.2022, doc. web n. 9832838, www.garanteprivacy.it/web/guest/home/docweb/-/docweb-display/docweb/9832838.

Chapter 5. Processing for Scientific Research, Public Archiving and Statistical Purposes

§1. Applicable Normative Framework

710. Under the Italian normative framework, the processing of personal data for archiving purposes in the public interest, scientific or historical research purposes or statistical purposes shall be performed not only pursuant to the provisions set out under the GDPR but also (as applicable depending on the specific purpose) in compliance with the rules and principles set out hereunder:

(i) Title VII of the Personal Data Protection Code.
(ii) The Rules of conduct annexed to the Personal Data Protection Code[910] and, in particular, the 'Rules of conduct on the processing for archiving purposes in the public interest or historical research purposes' (Annex A.3),[911] the 'Rules of conduct on the processing for statistics and scientific research purposes within the National Statistical System' (Annex A.4),[912] and the 'Rules of conduct on the processing for statistics and scientific purposes' (Annex A.5).[913]
(iii) The requirements set out under the decision adopted by the GPDP on 5 June 2019 pursuant to Article 21, paragraph 1, of Legislative Decree 10 August 2018, no. 101, pertaining to the processing of special categories of personal data carried out for purposes of scientific research.[914]

711. Title VII of the Personal Data Protection Code is meant to regulate the processing of personal data for archiving purposes in the public interest, scientific or historical research purposes or statistical purposes pursuant to Article 89 GDPR. The Title is divided into three different Chapters: Chapter I includes general provisions, Chapter II regulates the processing for archiving purposes in the public

910. On the Rules of conduct and the procedure that has led to their adoption *see also* Part VI. In Part VI, §2, *see also* the 'Code of Conduct on the use of Health Data for Educational and Scientific Publication Purposes' proposed by the Veneto Region.

911. Author's translation. GPDP, *Regole deontologiche per il trattamento a fini di archiviazione nel pubblico interesse o per scopi di ricerca storica pubblicate ai sensi dell'art. 20, comma 4, del d.lgs. 10 agosto 2018*, n. 101, 19.12.2018, doc. web no. 9069661, https://www.garanteprivacy.it/web/guest/home/docweb/-/docweb-display/docweb/9069661.

912. Author's translation. GPDP, *Regole deontologiche per trattamenti a fini statistici o di ricerca scientifica effettuati nell'ambito del Sistema Statistico nazionale pubblicate ai sensi dell'art. 20, comma 4, del d.lgs. 10 agosto 2018*, n. 101 – 19 dicembre 2018, 19.12.2018, doc. web n. 9069677, https://www.garanteprivacy.it/web/guest/home/docweb/-/docweb-display/docweb/9069677.

913. Author's translation. GPDP, *Regole deontologiche per trattamenti a fini statistici o di ricerca scientifica pubblicate ai sensi dell'art. 20, comma 4, del d.lgs. 10 agosto 2018*, n. 101 – 19 dicembre 2018, 19.12.2018, doc. web no. 9069637, https://www.garanteprivacy.it/web/guest/home/docweb/-/docweb-display/docweb/9069637.

914. GPDP, *Provvedimento recante le prescrizioni relative al trattamento di categorie particolari di dati, ai sensi dell'art. 21, comma 1 del d.lgs. 10 agosto 2018*, n. 101, 5.6.2019, doc. web no. 9124510, https://www.garanteprivacy.it/web/guest/home/docweb/-/docweb-display/docweb/9124510#5.

interest or for historical research purposes, while Chapter III regulates the processing for statistical purposes or scientific research purposes.

712. Chapter I (which includes Articles from 97 to 100 of the Personal Data Protection Code) includes a provision (set out under Article 99) pertaining to the duration of the processing activity, which specifies that the processing 'of personal data for archiving purposes in the public interest, scientific or historical research purposes or statistical purposes may be carried out also for longer than is necessary for achieving the individual purposes for which the data had been previously collected or processed'. Moreover, Article 99, paragraph 2, provides that, where the processing of personal data is terminated, such data may be retained or transferred to another data controller in order to achieve purposes in the public interest, scientific or historical research purposes or statistical purposes, in compliance with the safeguards set out under Article 89, paragraph 1, GDPR.

713. Article 100, which is titled 'Data Concerning Studies and Researches', provides that public bodies (including universities and research institutions) may determine – by means of autonomous decisions – to communicate and disseminate, also to private bodies and by telematic instruments, 'data concerning studies and researches, graduates, post-graduates, technicians and engineers, researchers, professors, experts and scholars', with the exclusion of the categories of personal data falling under Articles 9 and 10 GDPR. The same Article also clarifies that the above provision shall be without prejudice to the rights to which data subjects are entitled under the GDPR (in particular, rights of rectification, erasure, restriction, and objection).

§2. Processing for Archiving Purposes in the Public Interest or for Historical Research Purposes

I. Chapter II of Title VII of the Personal Data Protection Code

714. As mentioned above, Chapter II of Title VII of the Personal Data Protection Code (which includes Articles 101 to 103) regulates the processing for archiving purposes in the public interest or for historical research purposes.

715. In particular, Article 101 provides that 'personal data that has been collected for archiving purposes in the public interest or for historical research purposes' shall not be used 'for taking measures or issuing provisions against the data subject in administrative matters, unless said data are also used for other purposes in compliance with Article 5 GDPR'. Moreover, documents containing personal data that are processed for archiving purposes in the public interest or for historical research purposes may only be used if they are 'relevant and indispensable' for achieving the aforementioned purposes.

716. Article 102, paragraph 1, provides that the GPDP shall encourage the adoption of rules of conduct (pursuant to Article 2-*quater* of the Personal Data Protection Code) addressed to both private and public entities that are involved in the processing of personal data for archiving purposes in the public interest or historical research purposes. In this respect, Article 102, paragraph 2, specifies that such rules of conduct shall set out appropriate safeguards for the rights and freedoms of the data subjects, including: rules aimed at ensuring fairness and non-discrimination; the safeguards that should be implemented in the context of the collection, access to, and dissemination of documents concerning 'data disclosing health, sex life or confidential family-related matters'; and the modalities under which the rules on the processing of data for archiving purposes in the public interest or historical research purposes should apply to private archives.

717. Lastly, Article 103 provides that access 'to documents kept in State archives, historical archives of public bodies and private archives that have been declared to be of especially substantial historical interest shall be regulated by legislative decree no. 42 of 22 January 2004' (which sets out the Italian national code for the protection of the cultural and landscape heritage) and the relevant rules of conduct.

II. Rules of Conduct on the Processing for Archiving Purposes in the Public Interest or Historical Research Purpose (A.3)

718. As mentioned above, the 'Rules of conduct on the processing for archiving purposes in the public interest or historical research purpose', adopted by the GPDP, set out some additional conditions for the lawfulness and the fairness of the processing activities performed for the purposes in question.

The infringement of these Rules of conduct (as well as of the other Rules of conduct annexed to the Personal Data Protection Code) may therefore lead to sanctions pursuant to Article 83, paragraph 5, GDPR.

719. In particular, Article 1 of the Rules of conduct clarifies that the purpose of such rules is to ensure that the processing of personal data collected in the context of historical research and in the exercise of the right to study and right to information and the access to acts and documents is performed in compliance with the rights, fundamental freedoms, and dignity of the individuals concerned, in particular, the right to privacy and personal identity. The same Article further states that the rules are meant to regulate the processing of personal data carried out for historical purposes in relation to documents kept in the archives of public administrations, public bodies, and private archives declared to be of considerable historical interest.

It is also worth noting that the rules in question set out guiding principles directed at both 'archivists'[915] (in relation to which the rules aim to ensure fairness and non-discrimination towards users) and 'users'[916] (in relation to which the rules aim to identify precautions for the collection, use and dissemination of the data contained in the documents). Among the rules directed at archivists, it is worth recalling that, under Article 3 of the said Rules of conduct, when processing documents containing personal data, archivists shall adopt the most appropriate procedures to promote the respect for the rights, fundamental freedoms, and dignity of the persons to which the personal data refer to. Moreover, Article 3, paragraph 4, provides that personal data processed for historical purposes can be further processed for these purposes, and are subject to the same provisions, regardless of the document in which they are contained and of the place of storage.

720. In relation to the exercise of data subjects' rights, Article 7 provides that archivists shall favour the exercise of data subjects' right to rectification. Moreover, for the purpose of the application of Article 15 GDPR, when faced with a generalized request for access to a wide range of data or documents, the archivist should make available the relevant research tools and sources and provide the person exercising their right to access with all suitable indications for their easy consultation.

721. Among the rules directed at users, Article 9 provides that, when their research and study activities involve the processing of personal data, users shall adopt the most appropriate methods to favour the respect for the rights, fundamental freedoms and dignity of the persons concerned. Pursuant to this principle, users shall use the documents to which they have access under their own responsibility and in accordance with the purpose of their research project, and only to the extent the personal data involved are relevant and indispensable for the said purpose.

722. Article 11 on the dissemination of research results provides, among others, the following principles:

(i) User's interpretation falls under their freedom of speech and expression, as long as it does not infringe upon the right to privacy and the dignity of other parties.
(ii) When referring to the health status of other individuals, users shall refrain from publishing analytical data of strictly clinical interest and from describing sexual habits referring to a specific identified or identifiable person.

915. 'Archivist' is defined under Art. 2 of the 'Rules of conduct on the processing for archiving purposes in the public interest or historical research purpose' as anyone, natural or legal person, responsible for managing and preserving archives of the public administration, as well as private archives declared to be of considerable historical interest.

916. 'User' is defined under Art. 2 of the 'Rules of conduct on the processing for archiving purposes in the public interest or historical research purpose' as 'any person requesting access or accessing for historical purposes documents containing personal data, including for journalistic purposes or for the occasional publication of articles, essays and other expressions of thought' (Author's translation).

(iii) When disclosing data, users shall assess the extent to which those data are relevant by taking into account the individual personal data contained in the documents in question rather than the documents as a whole. Users may also disclose personal data only if they are relevant and indispensable for their research purposes, and if such disclosure does not violate the dignity and privacy of individuals.

723. Lastly, under Article 12, both public and private entities which are required to apply these rules must undertake to promote their maximum dissemination while, pursuant to Article 13, the competent administrations (in the context of public archives) as well as the companies and associations required to apply the rules can report violations of the rules to the GPDP, which may then adopt measures and sanctions within its sphere of competence.

§3. Processing for Statistical Purposes or Scientific Research Purposes

I. Chapter III of the Personal Data Protection Code

724. Chapter III of the Personal Data Protection Code (which includes Articles 104 to 110-*bis*) is devoted to the regulation of the processing activities for statistical purposes or, to the extent that they are compatible, for scientific research purposes (as clarified under Article 104).

725. In particular, Article 105 provides that personal data that is processed for statistical purposes or scientific research purposes shall not 'be used for taking decisions or measures with regard to the data subject or else with a view to processing data for different purposes'.

Moreover, pursuant to the same Article, data subjects shall be informed of statistical and scientific research purposes in compliance with Articles 13 and 14 GDPR. At the same time, an exception to the requirement of informing data subjects of the processing activities in question is set out under Article 105, paragraph 4, which provides that, as 'for processing operations for statistical purposes or scientific research purposes concerning data collected for other purposes, no information shall have to be provided to data subjects if it entails a disproportionate effort compared with the right to be protected'. This 'exception' is, however, subject to the requirement that appropriate forms of publicity are adopted, in compliance with the rules of conduct referred to in Article 106 of the Personal Data Protection Code.

726. This latter Article indeed provides that the GPDP shall encourage the adoption of rules of conduct (pursuant to Article 2-*quater* of the Personal Data Protection Code) 'by the private and public entities, including scientific societies and professional associations, that are involved in processing data for statistical purposes or scientific research purposes with a view to determining appropriate safeguards for the rights and freedoms of the data subject pursuant to Article 89' GDPR.

Taking into account the requirements already set out under D.Lgs. no. 322/1989, which has established and organized the National Statistical System (*Sistema Statistico Nazionale* – SISTAN),[917] such rules of conduct shall specify (among others) the following:

(i) The conditions and procedures for documenting and verifying that the processing activities are performed for appropriate and effective statistical or scientific research purposes.
(ii) Further requirements and safeguards to be taken into account (in addition to those already set out under the Personal Data Protection Code) with reference (among others) to the duration of the processing activities, to the information to be provided to data subjects in relation to data also collected from third parties, and to 'the specific security measures and the mechanisms to amend the data as a result of the exercise of data subjects' rights'.
(iii) Simplified modalities that can be used by data subjects to provide their consent in relation to the processing of special categories of personal data falling under the scope of Article 9 GDPR.
(iv) The circumstances under which the data subjects' rights provided under Articles 15, 16, 18 and 21 GDPR may be restricted in accordance with Article 89, paragraph 2, GDPR.

727. Article 107 of the Personal Data Protection Code is specifically devoted to the processing of special categories of personal data and provides that the data subjects' consent to the processing of their personal data pursuant to Article 9 GDPR may be given in a simplified manner[918] (as further specified under the rules of conduct referred to under Article 106 or following the measures set out under Article 2-*septies* of the Personal Data Protection Code).

728. Moving forward with the provisions set out under Chapter III of the Personal Data Protection Code, Article 108 includes a specific reference to other applicable normative requirements that complement the data protection provisions in the context of the SISTAN.

In particular, Article 108 clarifies that, besides the provisions set out under the rules of conduct referred to under Article 106 of the Personal Data Protection Code,

917. The SISTAN is the network of public and private entities that provides official statistical information in Italy, and includes the National Statistical Institute (*Istituto nazionale di statistica* – ISTAT), the National Institute for the Analysis of Public Policies (*Istituto nazionale per l'analisi delle politiche pubbliche* – INAPP), and the statistics offices of several state administrations and public bodies, as well as of other public and private institutions that perform functions in public interest. Additional information is available on the SISTAN official website, https://www.sistan.it/index.php?id=422.

918. This applies without prejudice to the requirements set out under Art. 2-*sexies* of the Personal Data Protection Code and 'except for specific investigations or studies for statistical purposes or scientific research purposes that are provided for by law'.

the processing of personal data by entities included in the National Statistical System shall be further regulated by D.Lgs. 322/1989. In this respect, it is worth recalling that Article 6-*bis*[919] of the said D.Lgs. (as amended by D.L. no. 4/2019, which has inserted the new paragraph 1-*bis*) details the information to be included in the national statistical programme (*Programma Statistico Nazionale* – PSN)[920] in relation to the processing of personal data.

In particular, Article 6-*bis*, paragraph 1-*bis*, of D.Lgs. no. 322/1989 provides that the PSN shall specify:

(i) The categories of personal data.
(ii) The operations that can be performed.
(iii) The measures taken to protect the fundamental rights and freedoms of data subjects and the appropriate technical and organizational measures to ensure the lawfulness and fairness of the processing activities in question, with particular reference to the principle of data minimization.

729. Moreover, for each processing operation, the following information shall be indicated in the PSN: the methods, the categories of data subjects, the objectives pursued, the sources used, the main variables acquired, the retention periods, and the categories of the recipients. Article 6-*bis* of D.Lgs. 322/1989 also provides that the PSN shall be adopted after having consulted the GPDP.

730. References to additional normative requirements to be taken into account together with the provisions set out under the data protection normative framework are also provided under Article 109 concerning the processing of 'Statistical Data Concerning Births'. This Article provides that the 'collection of statistical data concerning births including malformed new-borns and stillborns and the data flows also by healthcare managers shall be regulated by the technical specifications determined by the National Statistics Institute after hearing the Minister of Health, the

919. Article 6-*bis*, para. 1-*bis*, of D.Lgs. no. 322/1989, states the following (author's translation): 'As for the processing of personal data, including the processing of personal data that fall [under Article 9 GDPR], carried out for statistical purposes of substantial public interest within the meaning of Article 2-*sexies*, paragraph 2, letter cc), of the Personal Data Protection Code, as set out under Legislative Decree no. 196 of 30 June 2003, in accordance with article 108 of the said Personal Data Protection Code, the national statistical programme shall specify the types of data, the operations that can be performed and the measures adopted to protect the fundamental rights and freedoms of the data subjects concerned, where these elements are not identified by statutory or regulatory provisions. The national statistical programme, which shall be adopted after consulting the [GPDP], specifies the technical and organisational measures suitable to guarantee the lawfulness and fairness of the processing activity, with specific reference to the principle of data minimisation, and, for each processing operation, the methods, the categories of data subjects concerned, the objectives pursued, the sources of data, the main variables acquired, the retention periods and the categories of data recipients. For the processing of personal data referred to in Article 10 of the [GDPR] carried out for statistical purposes of public interest relevant within the purposes of the aforementioned Article 2-*sexies*, paragraph 2, letter (cc) of the [Personal Data Protection Code], Article 2-*octies* of the Personal Data Protection Code shall apply.'

920. The PSN is the regulatory act adopted pursuant to Art. 13 of D.Lgs. 322/989 which establishes the statistical surveys of public interest entrusted to the SISTAN and the related objectives. Additional information is available on the SISTAN official website: https://www.sistan.it/?id=52.

Minister of Justice' and the GPDP, as well as by the provisions laid down in Decree 16 July 2001, no. 349, of the Ministry of Health, which includes 'Amendments to the birth certificate, for the collection of public health and basic statistical data on birth events, stillbirths and births with malformations.'[921]

731. Article 110 of the Personal Data Protection Code concerning the processing of personal data for medical, biological and epidemiological research provides for some exceptions to the obligation of requiring data subject's consent. In particular, the said Article provides that 'data subject's consent shall not be required to process data relating to health for scientific research purposes in the medical, biomedical or epidemiological sectors' if:

(i) The said research is performed in accordance with laws and regulations or EU law pursuant to Article 9, paragraph 2, letter j), GDPR and a data protection impact assessment is carried out and published pursuant to Articles 35 and 36 GDPR.
(ii) '[I]f informing the data subjects proves impossible or entails a disproportionate effort on specific grounds, or if it is likely to render impossible or seriously impair the achievement of the research purpose.'

732. When the above-mentioned cases apply, the data controller shall take the appropriate measures to protect the rights, freedoms, and legitimate interests of the data subjects concerned. Moreover, the research programme shall be subject to the favourable opinion of the competent ethics committee and be submitted to the GPDP for prior consultation pursuant to Article 36 GDPR.[922]

In addition to this, where data subjects exercise their right to rectification pursuant to Article 16 GDPR in relation to the processing operations that fall under the scope of Article 110 of the Personal Data Protection Code, paragraph 2 of the latter Article specifies that 'any rectification or completion of the data shall be recorded without modifying the data if the rectified or completed data do not produce significant effects on the outcome of the research'.

---

921. Author's translation.

922. Among the decisions adopted by the GPDP pursuant to Art. 110 of the Personal Data Protection Code, it is worth mentioning the following: GPDP, *Parere in ordine al trattamento dei dati personali, anche inerenti a particolari categorie di dati, per finalità di ricerca medica, biomedica e epidemiologica, riferiti alla coorte di pazienti arruolati nello studio 'MATTERHORN' – 20 giugno 2019*, 20.6.2019, doc. web no. 9123447, https://www.garanteprivacy.it/home/docweb/-/docweb-display/docweb/9123447; GPDP, *Provvedimento del 29 ottobre 2020*, 29.10.2020, doc. web no. 9517401, https://www.garanteprivacy.it/web/guest/home/docweb/-/docweb-display/docweb/9517401; GPDP, *Provvedimento del 10 dicembre 2020*, 10.12.2020, doc. web no. 9520597, https://www.garanteprivacy.it/web/guest/home/docweb/-/docweb-display/docweb/9520597; GPDP, *Provvedimento dell'11 novembre 2021*, 11.11.2021, doc. web ni. 9736936, https://www.garanteprivacy.it/web/guest/home/docweb/-/docweb-display/docweb/9736936; GPDP, *Provvedimento del 1° novembre 2021*, 1.11.2021, doc. web no. 9731827, https://www.garanteprivacy.it/web/guest/home/docweb/-/docweb-display/docweb/9731827; GPDP, *Provvedimento del 7 aprile 2022*, 7.4.2022, doc. web no. 9772545, https://www.garanteprivacy.it/web/guest/home/docweb/-/docweb-display/docweb/9772545.

733. Lastly, Article 110-*bis* of the Personal Data Protection Code pertaining to the 'Further processing of personal data by third parties for scientific research or statistical purposes' provides that the GPDP may authorize the further processing of personal data, including special categories of personal data referred to in Article 9 GDPR, for the purposes of scientific research or for statistical purposes by third parties who carry out such activities 'to a prevailing extent' when, due to particular reasons, informing data subjects proves impossible or involves a disproportionate effort, or risks rendering impossible or seriously impairing the achievement of the purposes of the research activities in question. At the same time, Article 110-*bis* also specifies that, in similar cases, appropriate measures shall be adopted in order to protect the rights, freedoms and legitimate interests of the data subjects in compliance with Article 89 GDPR, including measures aimed at ensuring the prior minimization and anonymization of the data concerned.

Moreover, Article 110-*bis*, paragraph 4, of the Personal Data Protection Code also specifies that the 'processing for scientific purposes of the personal data collected in the course of clinical activities by public and private *Istituti di ricovero e cura a carattere scientifico*[923] shall not be' considered further processing by third parties considering the 'instrumental nature of the health care activities carried out by such *Istituti* vis-à-vis research activities', subject to compliance with the requirements set out under Article 89 GDPR.

II. Rules of Conduct on the Processing for Statistics and Scientific Research Purposes Within the National Statistical System (A.4)

734. The second set of Rules of Conduct that is relevant for the purposes described in the present chapter is the 'Rules of conduct on the processing for statistics and scientific research purposes within the National Statistical System.'

735. First of all, Article 1 specifies the scope of application of the rules by clarifying that the rules apply to the bodies and offices which are part of or participate in the SISTAN for the purpose of implementing the national statistical programme or for the creation of statistical information, in accordance with their respective institutional areas. Moreover, the rules also apply to bodies different from those identified above but that belong to the same administration/entity, where the relevant processing operations are set out under the national statistical programme and the competent statistical offices certify the methodologies adopted in compliance with the provisions set out in D.Lgs. 322/1989, the GDPR, the Personal Data Protection Code, as well as these Rules of conduct.

736. Among the provisions set out under these Rules of Conduct, it is worth mentioning that Article 3 sets out the criteria that should be taken into account in order to determine whether a data subject is identifiable or not. In particular, said

923. In Italy, *Istituti di ricovero e cura a carattere scientifico* are hospitals that, besides managing health services, also conduct clinical research activities and that receive public funding in support of their contribution to research.

Article clarifies that, for the purposes of the Rules of Conduct, 'a data subject shall be deemed to be identifiable when, with the use of reasonable means, it is possible to establish a significantly likely association between the combination of the modalities of the variables relating to a statistical unit and the data identifying that unit'.[924] The same Article also lists the 'reasonable means' that may be used in order to identify a data subject, which includes resources both in economic terms and in terms of time, archives which provide further information in addition to those subject to communication or dissemination, and hardware and software resources that allow to carry out the processing activities necessary to link non-nominative information to an identified person.

737. Article 4-*bis* concerns the processing of special categories of personal data and the processing of personal data relating to criminal convictions and offences in the context of the national statistical programme. In particular, the Article provides that the national statistical programme shall set out the objectives pursued and the guarantees provided for by D.Lgs. 322/1989 and by the Personal Data Protection Code. The national statistical programme shall also identify personal data that fall under the scope of Articles 9 and 10 GDPR and the purposes and means of their processing.

Moreover, the national statistical programme shall be adopted, with reference to the personal data referred to in Articles 9 and 10 GDPR, after consulting the GPDP, pursuant to Article 58, paragraph 3, letter b),e GDPR.

738. The Rules of Conduct also specify the information that should be provided to data subjects whose personal data are collected and processed for statistical purposes.

In particular, Article 6 provides that, where personal data are collected from the data subject, besides the information to be provided under Article 13 GDPR, the data subjects shall also be informed of the possibility that their personal data may be processed for additional statistical purposes, pursuant to D.Lgs. 322/1989, the GDPR and the Personal Data Protection Code. However hand, where personal data are *not* collected from the data subject and the provision of such information to the data subjects concerned would require a disproportionate effort vis-à-vis the right protected (as envisaged under Article 14, paragraph 5, letter b), GDPR), Article 6, paragraph 2, specifies that the requirement of informing data subjects is considered satisfied if the processing activity in question is included in the national statistical programme or is otherwise advertised in appropriate manners.

739. Article 10 of the Rules of Conduct pertains to the retention of personal data and confirms that personal data may be kept beyond the time strictly necessary to achieve the purpose for which they have been collected and subsequently processed, in compliance with the principle of purpose limitation set out under Article 5, paragraph 1, letter e). GDPR.

---

924. Article 3, para. 1, 'Rules of conduct on the processing for statistics and scientific research purposes within the National Statistical System'. Author's translation.

740. The last provision that is worth mentioning is set out under Article 11, pertaining to the exercise of data subjects' rights. The said Article indeed provides that the data controller (or the data processor) shall record, in appropriate spaces and registers, the amendments requested by the data subjects, without changing the personal data originally entered in the relevant files, as long as those operations do not have a significant effect on the statistical analysis or on the statistical results related to the processing in question. In particular, changes should not be made if these would conflict with the categorizations and the statistical methodologies adopted pursuant to the applicable national and international standards.

741. The provisions described above are, however, undergoing a revision on the part of the GPDP. Indeed, on 15 April 2021, the GPDP announced its intention to elaborate new rules on the processing for statistical or scientific research purposes carried out within the SISTAN in order to respond to changes that have occurred (since the adoption of such Rules of conduct in 2018) in the way official statistics are produced, thanks to the evolution of technology and advancements inherent to the data-driven economy.[925]

742. Before concluding, it is worth mentioning that the GPDP has adopted several decisions in the context of official statistics, starting from its opinions on the PSN. These opinions are adopted pursuant to Article 4-*bis* of the Rules of conduct and pursuant to Article 6-*bis* of D.Lgs. 322/1989 (as amended in 2019, as mentioned in I *supra*). As noted by the GPDP on several occasions, the publication of the PSN is particularly important since it serves the purpose of providing data subjects with information on the processing activities that concern them (where personal information has been collected from third parties), as prescribed under Article 6, paragraph 2, of the Rules of conduct. Moreover, the PSN also serves as the legal basis for the processing of personal data for statistical purposes (pursuant to Articles 6, paragraph 3, letter b) and 9, paragraph 2, letter g) GDPR; Articles 2-*ter* and 2-*sexies* of the Personal Data Protection Code; and Articles 6-*bis*, paragraph 1-*bis* and 13 of D.Lgs. 322/1989), including for special categories of data and data relating to criminal convictions and offences.

743. Among the (numerous) considerations expressed by the GPDP when investigating the statistical work(s) envisaged in the context of PSNs, it may worth mentioning that, in its opinion on the PSN for the triennium 2020–2022 issued on 10 December 2020,[926] the GPDP noted the importance of ensuring that data subjects are informed of the fact that, by participating in a survey included in the PSN, they will not be granted to the right to object since the exception provided under Article

---

925. GPDP, *Nuove regole deontologiche per trattamenti a fini statistici o di ricerca scientifica effettuati nell'ambito del Sistema Statistico nazionale*, 15.4.2021, doc. web no. 9582086, https://www.garanteprivacy.it/home/docweb/-/docweb-display/docweb/9582086.

926. GPDP, *Parere sullo schema di Programma statistico nazionale 2020–2022*, 10.12.2020, doc. web no. 9520567, https://www.garanteprivacy.it/web/guest/home/docweb/-/docweb-display/docweb/9520567.

21, paragraph 6, GDPR, will apply.[927] The processing of personal data carried out by SISTAN for the purpose of carrying out the statistical works included in the PSN is indeed conducted for reasons of public interest, in order to create official statistical information in relation to which data subjects are not entitled to exercise their right to object.

As another example, in its opinion of 16 September 2021 on the PSN for triennium 2020–2022 – Update 2021–2022,[928] the GPDP specifically recalled the importance of ensuring compliance with Article 105 of the Personal Data Protection Code in relation to the survey on anti-violence centres and on centres and services for the victims of trafficking. The GPDP indeed noted that the description of the statistical work in question indicated that the (ultimate) aim of this work was to build exit strategies from violence. In this respect, the GPDP noted that even if the results of this statistical work can certainly support anti-violence centres in identifying better strategies to ensure that victims do not suffer from future abuses, the objectives pursued by ISTAT[929] can only be purely statistical. This derives from Article 105 of the Personal Data Protection Code under which, as noted *supra* (I.), personal data processed for statistical or scientific research purposes shall not be used to take decisions or measures relating to the data subjects concerned. For this reason, the GPDP concluded that the description of the statistical work in question needed to be modified by deleting the reference to the purpose (i.e., building exit strategies from violence) which cannot be directly pursued by ISTAT as the relevant controller for the processing activities in question.

744. Lastly, it is worth mentioning that an essential role was accorded to official statistics by the Italian legislator in the context of the SARS-CoV-2 pandemic. Taking into account the urgent need to collect timely, reliable, and complete official statistics on the economic and productive national system as well as on social, epidemiological, and environmental phenomena, Article 13 of D.Lgs. 19 May 2020, no. 34 (which was adopted to put in place urgent measures in various fields, including in the health sector, in the context of the pandemic), specifically authorized ISTAT to process personal data, including special categories of personal data and personal data relating to criminal convictions and offences, until the end of the state of health emergency (and the following twelve months). The same Article also provides that the President of ISTAT shall adopt one or more directives, subject to the GPDP opinion, which shall indicate (among others) the objectives pursued, the categories of personal data involved, the processing operations that can be performed,

927. Article 21, para. 6, GDPR, provides the following: 'Where personal data are processed for scientific or historical research purposes or statistical purposes pursuant to Article 89(1), the data subject, on grounds relating to his or her particular situation, shall have the right to object to processing of personal data concerning him or her, unless the processing is necessary for the performance of a task carried out for reasons of public interest'.

928. GPDP, *Parere sullo schema di Programma statistico nazionale 2020–2022, aggiornamento 2021–2022*, 16.9.2021, doc. web. no. 9717477, https://www.garanteprivacy.it/web/guest/home/docweb/-/docweb-display/docweb/9717477.

929. ISTAT is one of the bodies that compose the SISTAN (*see supra* n. 918) and the main producer of official statistics in support of both citizens and public decision-makers.

the measures and safeguards implemented to protect the fundamental rights and freedoms of the data subjects, and the relative retention periods.

In this context, on 24 June 2021, the GPDP expressed its positive opinion in relation to a draft directive of the President of ISTAT, which identified the processing activities of personal data referred to in Articles 9 and 10 GDPR within the scope of the so-called Alert-Cov statistical work (i.e., a project carried out by ISTAT with the purpose of studying and analysing the spread of the SARS-CoV-2 infection and elaborate a system, based on statistical methods, for the early detection of epidemic outbreaks).[930]

III. Rules of Conduct on the Processing for Statistics and Scientific Purposes (A.5)

745. In addition to the provisions set out under the Personal Data Protection Code and summarized above, all processing operations carried out for statistical and scientific purposes which are carried out by universities, research bodies or institutes and scientific societies, as well as by researchers that work within the aforementioned bodies, shall be conducted (also) in compliance with the 'Rules of conduct on the processing for statistics and scientific purposes' (*see* Article 2, paragraph 1, of the said Rules which sets out their scope of application).[931]

Among the provisions set out under the said Rules of conduct, it is worth recalling that, pursuant to Article 3, research activities shall be conducted on the basis of a project drafted in accordance with the methodological standards of the relevant subject area and establish where the statistical or scientific purposes should be documented. The research project must also specify:

(i) the measures to be adopted in the processing of personal data in order to ensure compliance with the Rules of conduct and with the applicable legislation;
(ii) the data processors involved (if any); and
(iii) provide a declaration of commitment to comply with the Rules of conduct.

746. The research project must then be kept by the relevant university or research body or scientific company for five years after the planned conclusion of the project. Article 4 sets out the criteria that should be taken into account to determine whether a data subject is identifiable or not, along the lines of Article 3 of the

930. GPDP, *Parere sullo schema di Direttiva del presidente dell'Istat recante* 'Individuazione dei trattamenti dei dati personali di cui agli articoli 9 e 10 del regolamento (ue) 2016/679 nell'ambito del lavoro statistico alert-cov – 24 giugno 2021', 24.6.2021, doc. web no. 9681795, https://www.garanteprivacy.it/web/guest/home/docweb/-/docweb-display/docweb/9681795.

931. As clarified under Art. 2, para. 2, of the 'Rules of conduct on the processing for statistics and scientific purposes', the rules do not apply to the processing of personal data for statistical and scientific purposes conducted in the context of activities aimed at the protection of human health and carried out by health professionals or health organizations, or in the context of similar activities in terms of the impact they may have on individuals, which remain governed by the relevant provisions.

'Rules of conduct on the processing for statistics and scientific research purposes within the National Statistical System', summarized *supra* (II).

747. Article 6 of the Rules of conduct specifies that, when collecting information for a statistical purpose, data subjects shall be informed, pursuant to Article 13 GDPR, of the fact that their personal data may be stored and processed for other statistical or scientific purposes. At the same time, pursuant to Article 6, paragraph 3, when data is collected from third parties or the processing carried out for statistical or scientific purposes concerns data that have been (originally) collected for other purposes, and the provision of the information to data subjects involves a disproportionate effort, the data controller shall adopt appropriate forms of publicity, for example, by inserting information on the project in national/regional (depending on the scale of the project) newspapers with wide circulation.

For example, in its decision (adopted pursuant to Article 110 of the Personal Data Protection Code) issued on 10 December 2020[932] in relation to a study initiated by *Fondazione per la Ricerca Ospedale di Bergamo*, the GPDP found a violation of the principle of transparency pursuant to Article 6, paragraph 3, of the Rules of conduct (as well as of Article 5, paragraph 1, letter a) and 14, paragraph 5, letter b), GDPR). In the said decision, the GPDP indeed concluded that the data controller, which had collected health data – albeit in a pseudonymized form – from a third party for the purpose of scientific research, failed to make information on the processing activities performed for scientific purposes publicly available, as prescribed under Article 6, paragraph 3, of the Rules of conduct.

Compliance with the requirements set out under Article 6, paragraph 3, of the Rules of conduct was instead found by the GPDP in its decision of 7 April 2022[933] in relation to a non-profit study aimed at describing the effect of the SARS-CoV-2 pandemic on the occurrence of hospitalizations and on the admissions in emergency rooms in the hospitals of the *Emilia-Romagna* Region of individuals aged less than 18 years old. In the said decision, the GPDP acknowledged the impossibility of the data controller (i.e., *Azienda Ospedaliero Universitaria di Parma*) to collect consent from the individuals concerned. This impossibility was due to organizational reasons (since it was not possible to contact all parents of all individuals who have been hospitalized in the last five years in the hospitals where the study was conducted), the limited resources available to the study (which was non-profit), and in consideration of the time that would be required to collect consent from all interested parties (around 30,000), which would have jeopardized the objectives of the study. Taking into account the above, the GPDP concluded that the transparency requirements set out under Article 6, paragraph 3, of the Rules of conduct were satisfied by the fact that information pursuant to Articles 13 and 14 GDPR were going to be published on the websites of all centres participating to the study.

---

932. GPDP, *Provvedimento del 10 dicembre 2020*, 10.12.2020, doc. web no. 9520597, https://www.garanteprivacy.it/web/guest/home/docweb/-/docweb-display/docweb/9520597.

933. GPDP, *Provvedimento del 7 aprile 2022*, 7.4.2022, doc. web no. 9772545, https://www.garanteprivacy.it/web/guest/home/docweb/-/docweb-display/docweb/9772545.

748. Moving to Article 7 of the Rules of conduct, this Article provides that special categories of personal data that fall under the scope of Article 9 GDPR, as well as personal data relating to criminal convictions and offences pursuant to Article 10 GDPR that are processed for statistical and scientific purposes must, as a rule, be anonymized. The same Article also specifies that the entities identified in Article 2, paragraph 1 of the Rules of Conduct may process special categories of personal data for statistical and scientific purposes when the data subject has freely expressed their consent on the basis of the information provided, and where such consent is given in writing (or at least, if this would be particularly burdensome, documented in writing). Article 8 includes specific provisions for medical, biomedical, and epidemiological research. Among others, this Article recalls the international guidelines and recommendations to be followed in the field (such as the Convention for the Protection of Human Rights and Dignity of the Human Being with regard to the Application of Biology and Medicine of 4 April 1997) and provides that information on the processing of personal data shall allow data subjects to distinguish research activities from activities related to the protection of their health.

749. Moving to Article 11, personal data may be stored for statistical or scientific purposes even beyond the period necessary to achieve the purposes for which they were collected or subsequently processed, in accordance with Article 5, paragraph 1, letter e), GDPR. Lastly, it is worth mentioning that, under Article 12 of the Rules of conduct, when changes to personal data are necessary in response to the exercise of data subject's rights pursuant to Article 15 and following the GDPR, the data controller must record the changes requested by the data subject concerned in appropriate spaces or registers, without changing the data originally entered in the file/archive.

§4. GPDP Decision of 5 June 2019 Adopted Pursuant to Article 21, Paragraph 1, of D.Lgs. 101/2018, Pertaining to the Processing of Special Categories of Personal Data Carried out for Purposes of Scientific Research

750. Some additional requirements that apply to the processing of special categories of personal data carried out for purposes of scientific research are set out in the decision adopted by the GPDP on 5 June 2019 pursuant to Article 21, paragraph 1, D.Lgs. 101/2018. The said Article of D.Lgs. 101/2018 provides that the GPDP shall identify the provisions set out under the general authorizations adopted by the GPDP before the direct applicability of the GDPR relating to the processing situations referred to in Article 6, paragraph 1, letters c) and e) and Article 9, paragraph 2, letters b) and paragraph 4, GDPR, as well as in Chapter IX of the GDPR, which are compatible with the provisions set out under the GDPR and under D.Lgs. 101/2018 (the GPDP must also update them where necessary).

Article 21, paragraph 5, of D.Lgs. 101/2018 also provides that the infringement of the provisions identified by the GPDP by means of the decision adopted pursuant to paragraph 1 of the same Article is subject to the administrative sanctions set out under Article 83, paragraph 5, GDPR.

751. After having reviewed the general authorizations adopted pursuant to the previous legislation (in compliance with Article 21, paragraph 1, of D.Lgs. 101/2018), by means of its decision of 5 June 2019,[934] the GPDP identified the obligations that need to be complied with by a large number of public and private entities in different sectors in order to process special categories of personal data, such as those related to health, political opinions, ethnicity, and sexual orientation. For the purpose of the present Chapter, it is worth recalling some of the provisions that apply to the processing of personal data for scientific research purposes, as set out under Attachment 1, point 5 ('*Prescrizioni relative al trattamento dei dati personali effettuato per scopi di ricerca scientifica (aut. gen. n. 9/2016)*') to the said GPDP decision.[935] In particular, point 5.1 specifies that the requirements set out under the said decision apply to the processing activities performed by:

(i) universities, other research bodies or institutes and scientific societies, as well as researchers working within those universities, bodies, research institutes, and members of those scientific societies;
(ii) health professionals and health care organizations;
(iii) natural or legal persons, entities, associations and private bodies, as well as persons that have been specifically authorized to carry out processing activities on behalf of the data controller, such as researchers or committees of experts (pursuant to Article 2-*quaterdecies* of the Personal Data Protection Code and Article 28 GDPR).

752. Point 5.2 further specifies that the provisions in question apply to the processing of personal data for medical, biomedical and epidemiological research purposes when the 'processing is necessary in order to conduct studies carried out with data previously collected for health care purposes or for the performance of previous research projects or obtained from biological samples previously collected for health care purposes or for the performance of previous research projects' or when 'the processing is necessary in order to conduct studies by using data relating to persons who, due to the severity of their clinical condition, are not in a position to understand the indications given in the information notice and to express their valid consent'.[936] In the above situations, the research activity in question can only be conducted on the basis of a project that has received a favourable opinion from the competent ethics committee.

753. Point 5.3 lists the conditions under which the consent of data subject is not required. In particular, consent is not required when research activities are performed on the basis of statutory or regulatory provisions or on the basis of European Union law. In all other cases where it is not possible to obtain consent from

---

934. *See supra* Part III, Ch. 3, §3.
935. GPDP, *Provvedimento recante le prescrizioni relative al trattamento di categorie particolari di dati, ai sensi dell'art. 21, comma 1 del d.lgs. 10 agosto 2018*, n. 101, n. 902, *supra*, Allegato 1 – 5. Prescrizioni relative al trattamento dei dati personali effettuato per scopi di ricerca scientifica (aut. gen. n. 9/2016).
936. Author's translation.

the data subjects involved, in the research project, data controllers shall document the specific reasons (that should be limited to very special or exceptional situations) why informing data subjects proves impossible or involves a disproportionate effort, or risks making the purposes of the project impossible or jeopardizes the achievement of the purposes of the project. This impossibility may derive from ethical reasons,[937] organizational reasons (e.g., where a large number of stakeholders cannot be contacted), or the severity of the clinical conditions of the persons concerned, which makes those persons unable to understand the information provided in the information notice and therefore unable to provide their valid consent.

754. Point 5.6, which pertains to the storage of data and samples, provides that biological data and samples used to carry out research activities must be stored by means (such as encryption) that do not make data subjects directly identifiable and for no longer than is necessary for the purposes for which data were collected or subsequently processed.

755. Lastly, it is worth mentioning that point 5.7 specifies some of the measures that need to be adopted in order to increase the level of security applied to the data processed for the purposes of the study. This may include, among others, appropriate measures to protect the data in question from the risk of abusive access, secure transmission channels when data needs to be communicated in the context of the study, and appropriate authentication and authorization systems for the personnel in charge of processing data stored in centralized databases.

756. Before concluding, it is worth mentioning that the GPDP decision of 5 June 2019 sets out some additional provisions (under Attachment 1, point 4 – *Prescrizioni relative al trattamento dei dati genetici (aut. gen. n. 8/2016)*) for the processing of genetic data for scientific and statistical research purposes.[938]

---

937. For example, where the provision of the information notice would lead to the disclosure to the persons concerned of information that may cause material or psychological harm to those data subjects, such as the case of epidemiological studies on factors that may predict the development of a morbid state for which no treatment exists.

938. GPDP, *Provvedimento recante le prescrizioni relative al trattamento di categorie particolari di dati, ai sensi dell'art. 21, comma 1 del d.lgs. 10 agosto 2018*, n. 101, n. 902 *supra*, Allegato 1 – 4. Prescrizioni relative al trattamento dei dati genetici (aut. gen. n. 8/2016) (*see*, in particular, para. 4.11). *See supra* Part III, Ch. 3, III.

Part X. Specific Data Protection Regimes

Chapter 1. Obligations of Professional Secrecy (Incl. Equivalent Obligations of Secrecy)

§1. Introduction

757. The right to privacy, elaborated at the end of the nineteenth century in the common law context in terms of the 'right to be let alone' was, in the beginning, placed on a similar level to that of the right to property and, therefore, was understood in the limited sense of the right to exclude others from knowledge of anything pertaining to one's own person.[939]

With technological development, privacy has acquired a new dimension, one that can be understood as going 'from secrecy to control'.[940]

§2. Overview of the Main Types of Secrecy

758. The only provision of the Personal Data Protection Code which directly concerns professional secrecy is Article 138, titled 'Professional secrecy'. This provision is limited to journalistic activities and mandates that in the event of a request by the data subject to know the origin of personal data pursuant to Article 15, paragraph 1, letter g, GDPR, the rules on professional secrecy of journalists shall remain unaffected, limited to the source of the news. Such provision means that the right to confidentiality, instrumental to the journalistic profession, prevails over the right of access. In fact, in the case of journalistic activities, the data subject does not have the right to know the origin of their personal data that could remain secret, i.e., exclusive to the knowledge of the journalist.[941]

759. This provision is an expression of a major principle that can be found in Article 622 of the Italian Criminal Code. According to this provision, those who reveal without any reason or employ such information for their own or others' profit, confidential information that they have come to know because of their state or

939. Raffaella Miranda, *Accesso e riservatezza dopo la legge 15/2005: un conflitto non ancora sopito*, 3 Diritto Informatica 571 (2005). For the development of the right to privacy under the Italian Constitution, *see* in this volume: Part I, Ch. 1.

940. *Ibid.*

941. For a more detailed overview of this matter *see supra*: Part IX, Ch. 1.

office, profession, or art, are punished with reclusion up to a year, or with a fine from EUR 30 up to EUR 516. This crime can be committed only by the person who is under a legal obligation of secrecy, which may derive:

(i) From their status, that is, from their personal situation resulting from the permanent exercise of a certain activity such as, for example, the clergymen.
(ii) From their office, to be understood as the exercise of certain functions of a social nature, as in the case of a guardian.
(iii) Or, finally, from their profession or art, that is, from a continuous activity aimed at offering services carried out with a view to economic gain, as in the case of lawyers or medical doctors.

760. These are, in all cases, situations in which a person, by reason of their profession, status or office, acquires confidential information of others and comes to know the secrets of others. They are, in this sense, 'burdened' with an obligation of secrecy to be ascertained by the court from time to time.

The Criminal Code merely refers to certain personal situations that can give rise to an obligation of secrecy. In particular, Article 622 of the Criminal Code refers to 'status', which is to be understood as the legal status arising from kinship or marital relations or the condition in which the person is performing a certain activity vis-à-vis the applicant, such as that of a trainee or secretary.

The reference to the 'office' refers to the performance of public or private activities from which rights and duties derive, including functions performed by guardians, consultants or employees. 'Profession or art', instead, means any form of activity, generally remunerated, of an intellectual or manual nature, carried out in the provision of the service to other persons. At the same time, public officials or persons in charge of public services who reveal secret information gained in the context of their office are punished under Article 326 of the Criminal Code with up to five years of imprisonment, if certain aggravating circumstances are met.

761. The difference between the crimes punished by Article 622 of the Criminal Code and those punished by Article 326 of the Criminal Code is in the type of secret protected, which, according to the latter, concerns the office itself and, therefore, includes only an act or fact of the public administration. The less serious offence laid down in Article 622 of the Criminal Code, conversely, protects all secret information as long as they are learned within the scope of one's private office, thus including private facts if learned by reason of professional status.

762. The preservation of secrecy is, moreover, ensured by prohibiting the person obliged to secrecy from assuming the role of witness concerning information or facts that they have learned on the basis of their ministry, office or profession, except in the cases where they are obliged to report such information to the Judicial Authorities, under Article 200 of the Code of Criminal Procedure.

The jurisprudence of the Supreme Court of Cassation has consolidated the idea that, on the subject of disclosure and use of official secrecy, office news that must remain secret include not only information that is withheld from disclosure at all times and to anyone but also information which dissemination is prohibited by the rules on the right of access, when, for example, the dissemination of the information is carried in breach of the procedures laid down by the rules on access, or where disclosure takes place towards persons who do not hold a relevant right to know the information.[942]

942. *See inter alia* Supreme Court of Cassation, no. 19216/2016, crim. sect.

Chapter 2. Churches and Religious Associations

§1. Introduction

763. The protection of special categories of personal data also directly involves religious beliefs, as the mere fact of belonging to religious groups or the participation of the faithful in the exercise of religious activities makes the relative personal data subject to the forms and modalities of processing laid down by applicable data protection law for special category data.

764. The direct applicability of the GDPR has superseded the approach of the Personal Data Protection Code previously in force, i.e., Article 4, paragraph 1, letter d) – now repealed by the 2018 reform – which laid down a specific categorization of 'sensitive' data (including personal data related to religious beliefs), by dedicating to this type of data a peculiar discipline that allowed processing only with the written consent of the data subject and the prior authorization of the GPDP, as mandated by Article 26, paragraph 1, of the Personal Data Protection Code in force before the 2018 reform, now repealed.

Today, Article 9, paragraph 1, GDPR, prohibits the processing of special categories of personal data, while paragraph 2 sets out a list of exceptions applicable to this set of data. These exceptions include the processing:

> [C]arried out in the course of its legitimate activities with appropriate safeguards by a foundation, association or any other not-for-profit body with a political, philosophical, religious or trade union aim and on condition that the processing relates solely to the members or to former members of the body or to persons who have regular contact with it in connection with its purposes and that the personal data are not disclosed outside that body without the consent of the data subjects.[943]

765. In addition, the GDPR provides the possibility for the Member State to maintain a special data protection regime for churches and religious associations, stipulating that:

> (1) Where in a Member State, churches and religious associations or communities apply, at the time of entry into force of this Regulation, comprehensive rules relating to the protection of natural persons with regard to processing, such rules may continue to apply, provided that they are brought into line with this Regulation.

943. Article 9, para. 2, lett. d), GDPR.

(2) Churches and religious associations which apply comprehensive rules in accordance with paragraph 1 of this Article shall be subject to the supervision of an independent supervisory authority, which may be specific, provided that it fulfils the conditions laid down in Chapter VI of this Regulation.[944]

766. It seems possible to maintain, therefore, that the processing of data concerning religious beliefs is part of the broader general system, even by indicating some peculiarities that may have to be modulated according to the structure that each Member State reserves for relations with churches and religious associations or communities. The above can be partly confirmed following the 2018 reform of the Personal Data Protection Code as, for example, in the case of Article 22, paragraph 2, of Legislative Decree 10 August 2018, no. 101, which establishes a correspondence between the expressions 'sensitive data' used pursuant to the former Article 4, paragraph 1, letter d), wherever they occur, and the 'special categories of personal data' referred to in Article 9 GDPR.

According to some authors, this correspondence can be seen as an appropriate coordination tool or – from another point of view – as an attempt to maintain a peculiar area (about the nature of this data) that the European legislator wanted to overcome. Such ambiguity seems to be present also with reference to the provision contained in Article 21 of D.Lgs. 101/2018, which deals with the general authorizations to process 'sensitive' data issued by the GPDP until the GDPR becomes directly applicable.[945]

§2. The General Authorization Issued by the GPDP

767. In this respect, starting in 1997, the GPDP has issued general authorizations for the processing of 'sensitive' data. These authorizations were periodically renewed until the GDPR became directly applicable. Members of religious communities were allowed to operate on the basis of Authorization no. 3 concerning the 'Processing of Sensitive Data by Associations and Foundations'[946] which authorized the processing of 'sensitive' data – among others – of members, supporters or subscribers and any person applying for membership in or accession to, or having regular contacts with, an association, foundation or other entity.

Against this background, Article 21 of D.Lgs. 101/2018 required a revision of all general authorizations by submitting them to public consultation in order to verify if the requirements contained therein (including Authorization no. 3) could be considered compatible with the GDPR and if necessary, update them accordingly. In

944. Article 91 GDPR, named 'Existing data protection rules of churches and religious associations'.

945. Enrico Vitali, Antonio G. Chizzoniti, *Manuale breve diritto ecclesiastico* 298 (Giuffrè Francis Lefebvre, 2019).

946. GPDP, *Autorizzazione n. 3/2016 – Autorizzazione al trattamento dei dati sensibili da parte degli organismi di tipo associativo e delle fondazioni*, 15.12.2016, doc. web no. 5803310, https://www.garanteprivacy.it/home/docweb/-/docweb-display/docweb/5803310, which is the last renewed version of the Authorization no. 3 published by the GPDP in 2016 before the direct applicability of the GDPR.

accordance with this requirement, on 13 December 2018, the GPDP published the 'Provisions relating to the processing of special categories of data by association-type bodies, foundations, churches and religious associations or communities (General Authorization No 3/2016)'[947] and, on 5 June 2019, further amended the conclusion of the public consultation period, which contained significant amendments of the previous version of Authorization no. 3.[948]

In fact, only Article 2 of the previous Authorization no. 3 passed the compatibility screening of the GPDP, while the other articles were repealed. The personal scope of Authorization no. 3 currently in force includes – among others – churches, religious associations or communities (Article 2, paragraph 1, letter e)) and educational institutions (with regard to the processing of data disclosing religious beliefs as well as to the activities that are absolutely necessary in order to implement Article 310 of Legislative Decree 16 April 1994, no. 297, and Articles 3 and 10 of Legislative Decree 19 February 2004, no. 59).

768. The data subjects to whom personal data may refer are indicated in Article 2, paragraph 2, of Authorization no. 3 and include members, supporters or subscribers, and any person applying for membership in, or accession to, or having regular contacts with, associations, foundations, churches and religious communities, as well as students registered and/or applying for registration with the institutions mentioned in Article 2, paragraph 1, letter d), and, as for underage persons, their parents or any other person having parental authority over them.

Pursuant to paragraph 3 of said Article, Authorization no. 3 shall be granted for religious and educational purposes, including the freedom to choose one's religious education.

The processing of data included in the scope of the Authorization may also concern the keeping of accounting books and records, lists, mailing lists, and any other documents required with a view to managing administrative matters in respect of associations, foundations, churches and religious associations or communities, complying with tax requirements, or circulating journals, bulletins and similar publications. It is worth pointing out that the above-mentioned Article, by identifying the purpose of the processing, places great attention not only to the legitimate purposes identified by law but also as set out in the relevant internal articles and/or memorandums of association or collective agreements.[949]

769. The specific previsions set out in Article 2, paragraph 4, of Authorization no. 3 state that personal data relating to members/adherents may be communicated to other members/adherents of the entity involved without the consent of the data

947. GPDP, *Provvedimento che individua le prescrizioni contenute nelle Autorizzazioni generali nn. 1/2016, 3/2016, 6/2016, 8/2016 e 9/2016 che risultano compatibili con il Regolamento e con il d.lgs. n. 101/2018 di adeguamento del Codice*, 13.12.2018, doc. web no. 9068972, https://www.garanteprivacy.it/home/docweb/-/docweb-display/docweb/9068972.

948. GPDP, *Provvedimento recante le prescrizioni relative al trattamento di categorie particolari di dati, ai sensi dell'art. 21, comma 1 del d.lgs. 10 agosto 2018*, n. 101, 5.6.2019, doc. web no. 9124510, https://www.garanteprivacy.it/web/guest/home/docweb/-/docweb-display/docweb/9124510#2.

949. Bolognini & Pelino, *Codice della disciplina privacy* (Giuffré Francis Lefebvre, 2019), at 937–938.

subject (while communication to persons outside the entity always requires the consent of the data subject), provided that the communication is set out in the relevant internal articles and/or memorandums of the association and it is provided for legitimate purposes. Moreover, the data subject shall be provided with an appropriate information notice pursuant to Article 13 GDPR.

§3. The Catholic Church: CEI General Decree No. 389/2018

770. For the time being, among the various religious organizations present in Italy, only the Catholic Church has provided for the drafting of a complete body of internal data protection rules by means of General Decree no. 389/2018 of the Italian Conference of Bishops ('*Conferenza Episcopale Italiana*', abbreviated as '*CEI*'),[950] which replaced the previous General Decree no. 1285 of 20 October 1999 and which aims to apply Article 91 GDPR.

With this Decree, the Catholic Church claims, as an independent and autonomous legal order, 'the native and proper right to acquire, store and use for its institutional purposes data relating to faithfuls, ecclesiastical entities and aggregations'[951] by ensuring the respect of the individual's right to good fame and confidentiality. The CEI Decree is characterized by a strong symmetry to the GDPR, thereby mirroring many parts of the rules established by EU data protection legislation in the canonical sphere.

However, for the time being, as the General Decree does not identify a specific independent authority tasked with supervising and enforcing data protection rules,[952] it also extends the powers of the GPDP to the Catholic Church.

771. Of particular relevance is Article 8 of the General Decree, which defines 'register' as the volume containing – in chronological order – the records related to the celebration of the sacraments or other facts concerning membership or participation in the Church so that the canonical status of each member of the faithful can be identified. Furthermore, paragraphs 6, 7 and 8 of Article 8 guarantee several subjective rights to persons, including the right to request:

(i) the entry into the register of annotations or adequate integrations, which become part of the document to which they refer;
(ii) the extraction and transmission of data contained in the register (provided that certain limits set out in Article 8, paragraph 7, are respected);

950. General Decree 389/2018 of the Italian Conference of Bishops of 24 May 2018 'Provisions for the protection of the right to good reputation and privacy' (Author's translation), 52:2, 31.5.2018.
951. First Recital of the General Decree 389/2018 (author's translation).
952. This part of Art. 91, para. 2, GDPR, has been subject to conflicting interpretations in doctrine. In favour of the extraneousness and independence of the supervisory authority from the religious denomination of reference, *see* Venerando Marano, *Chiesa e protezione dei dati personali. Sfide giuridiche e comunicative alla luce del Regolamento Europeo per la protezione dei dati* 30 (J. Pujol ed., EDUSC 2019); *contra*: Manuel Ganarin, *Stato, Chiese e pluralismo confessionale* 28 (2018), https://riviste.unimi.it/index.php/statoechiese/article/view/9912.

(iii) the deletion of data: however, such a request can be deemed inadmissible if it concerns data relating to the celebration of sacraments or if it relates to the status of persons. Acceptance of the request for deletion shall be made in the record and obliges the person in charge of the register not to use the data unless authorized by the Diocesan Ordinary.

§4. Relevant GPDP Decisions

772. Among the measures taken by the GPDP on the protection of data protection rights in the religious sphere, an interesting example can be found in a case concerning religious disaffiliation (so-called *sbattezzo*) and the right to deletion of data.

773. In a relevant case, a baptized member of the Catholic Church had asked the data controller, the parish priest in charge of keeping the archives of the local church, to remove their name from the register of baptized persons. The parish priest could not accede to the request and merely annotated the request for deletion within the baptismal record. After having appealed to the GPDP, the appeal was declared unfounded, and the GPDP considered that it was sufficient to simply note the request for deletion in the register.[953]

The reasons for the refusal were to be found in the historical value of the data, since the church cannot erase the trace of a historical event by considering it as having never taken place.

Another relevant argument which justified the outcome of the decision was the respect for denominational independence of a religious faith, since the registers of baptisms are official registers of the Catholic Church, and the preservation of the data contained herein is fully within the space of autonomy guaranteed to the Catholic Church under Article 7 of the Italian Constitution.

Finally, as a further argument, the GPDP took into account the fact that the retention of the data within the register of baptized persons was merely relevant within the confessional order and that it would not be used further for other purposes.

953. GPDP, *Dati sensibili (convinzioni religiose): richiesta di cancellazione dal registro dei battezzati*, 13.9.1999, doc. web no. 1090502, https://www.garanteprivacy.it/home/docweb/-/docweb-display/docweb/1090502.

Other examples which confirm the approach of the GPDP can be find in other more recent provisions of the GPDP (*see* GPDP, *Provvedimento del 20 settembre 2012*, 20.09.2012, doc. web no. 2099418, https://www.garanteprivacy.it/home/docweb/-/docweb-display/docweb/2099418; GPDP, *Provvedimento del 12 febbraio 2015*, 12.2.2015, doc. web no. 3852927, https://www.garanteprivacy.it/home/docweb/-/docweb-display/docweb/3852927.

Chapter 3. Law Enforcement Agencies (National Transposition of Directive 2018/680)

§1. Introduction: Italian Law Enforcement Agencies

774. The main law enforcement agencies in Italy are the *Arma dei Carabinieri*, part of the national armed forces; the *Polizia di Stato* (State Police), i.e., the civil national police, and the *Guardia di Finanza* (Financial Police, abbreviated as 'GdF'), which is a police force responsible for dealing with financial crimes, smuggling, the illegal drug trade, etc.

The GdF, with its specialized unit, is also responsible for conducting investigations related to data protection regulations at the request of the GPDP.[954]

§2. Overview of the National Transposition of Directive 2018/680: Legislative Decree 51/2018

775. With Legislative Decree 18 May 2018, no. 51 (hereinafter referred to as the 'Decree' in this Chapter), the Italian legislator has provided a complete framework to regulate the data protection rules to be followed during criminal investigations, thereby transposing Directive (EU) 680/2016.[955]

In the below paragraphs, we will provide a general overview of the most important provisions of the Decree.

I. Scope of Application

776. The Decree applies to the fully or partially automated processing of personal data of natural persons and the non-automated processing of personal data of natural persons contained in or intended for a filing system, carried out by the competent authorities for the purpose of the prevention, investigation, detection, and prosecution of crimes, or the execution of criminal sanctions, including the safeguarding against and preventing threats to public safety.[956]

According to its Article 2, the Decree does not apply to the processing of personal data:

954. For an overview of this function of the GdF, *see supra* Part VIII, Ch. 1.
955. Directive (EU) 2016/680 of the European Parliament and of the Council of 27 Apr. 2016 on the protection of natural persons with regard to the processing of personal data by competent authorities for the purposes of the prevention, investigation, detection or prosecution of criminal offences or the execution of criminal penalties, and on the free movement of such data, and repealing Council Framework Decision 2008/977/JHA. OJ L 119, 4.5.2016.
956. Article 1 of the Decree.

(i) carried out in the performance of activities concerning national security or falling within the scope of application of Title V, Chapter 2, of the Treaty on the European Union and for all activities that do not fall within the scope of the law of the European Union;
(ii) carried out by institutions, bodies, offices and agencies of the European Union.

II. General Provisions

777. Article 4 of the Decree provides that the data controller shall, taking into account the purpose of the processing and, insofar as possible, distinguish personal data in relation to the different categories of data subjects provided for by law and shall distinguish data based on facts from those based on evaluations. The distinction in relation to the different categories of data subjects applies, in particular, to the following categories of data subjects: persons under investigation; defendants; persons subjected to investigation or accused in related or connected proceedings; people convicted with final sentence; people offended by the crime; set off civilians; people informed of the facts; testimony.

778. As regards the legal basis for the processing, Article 5 of the Decree provides that the processing needs to be necessary for the performance of a task carried out by a competent authority for the purposes referred to in Article 1, paragraph 2, of the Decree and shall be based on European Union law or on provisions of national law including, in the cases provided for by law, on a national regulation[957] that identifies the personal data and the purposes of the processing. In this respect, it is also provided that personal data processed under the provision of Article 1, paragraph 2, of the Decree cannot be processed for other purposes different from the ones provided by the law.[958]

Under Article 7 of the Decree, the processing of data referred to in Article 9 GDPR (i.e., special categories of personal data) is authorized only if strictly necessary and where adequate safeguards for the rights and freedoms of the data subject are provided or if the processing of such data is specifically mandated by European Union law or on provisions of national law including, in the cases provided for by law, on national regulation. In addition, the processing of such data is also allowed if, without prejudice to the guarantees to the rights and freedoms of the data subjects, it is necessary to safeguard a vital interest of the data subject or of another natural person or if it relates to data made manifestly public by the data subject.

---

957. For the category of 'regulation' under the Italian legal framework, *see* n. 409 *supra*.
958. Paragraph 2 of Art. 5 provides that with DPR, are identified, for processing or categories of processing not occasional referred to in para. 1, the terms, if not already established by provisions of law or regulation, and the means of data retention, the subjects entitled to access it, the access conditions, the methods of consultation, as well as the modalities and conditions for exercising the rights referred to in Arts 9, 10, 11 and 13 of the Decree. However, this provision is not currently enacted, as no DPR has been adopted so far.

779. According to Article 8 of the Decree, decisions based solely on automated processing, including profiling, are prohibited, unless they are authorized by European Union law or by specific provisions of national law, which shall lay down appropriate safeguards. In any case, human intervention shall be guaranteed, and automated decisions may not allow the use of special categories of personal data, unless there are appropriate safeguards in place. Moreover, any profiling aimed at discriminating against natural persons on the basis of the categories of data referred to in Article 9 GDPR is prohibited.

III. Data Subjects' Rights

780. Under Article 8, the data controller shall facilitate the exercise of data subjects' rights and provide any communication related to the processing in a concise, intelligible form and easily accessible, with simple and clear language. The exercise of data subjects' rights shall be, in principle, free of charge, but Article 12, paragraph 5, GDPR, applies.

781. In addition, Article 10 provides that the data controller, also on its website, discloses information regarding the:

(i) Identity and contact information of the controller.
(ii) Contact details of the data protection officer.
(iii) Purpose of the processing and recipients of the personal data.
(iv) The right to lodge a complaint with the GPDP.
(v) The existence of the right to request access to the data, the rectification or erasure of the personal data, and the restriction of the processing of personal data from the data controller.

782. According to Article 11 of the Decree, the data subject has the right to access their personal data which is quite similar in content to Article 15 GDPR, but this right can be limited by a provision of national law or regulation adopted pursuant to Article 5, paragraph 2, of the Decree to the extent and for as long as this constitutes a necessary and proportionate measure, taking into account the fundamental rights and legitimate interests of the natural person. These limits shall be provided only for the purpose of:

(i) prevent jeopardizing the prevention, investigation, detection and prosecution of crimes or the execution of criminal sanctions, as well as the application of preventive measures personal and property and security measures;
(ii) protecting public security;
(iii) protecting national security;
(iv) protecting the rights and freedoms of others.

783. In the case of limitation of rights of data subjects, the data controller shall inform the data subject without any delay and in writing about the refusal of their request and the reason for which the data controller cannot comply. In any case, the data subject may file a complaint with the GDPD.

784. To obtain the rectification, erasure, or limitation of the processing of personal data, the same rules under the provision of Article 116 of the Criminal Procedure Code provided in the case of a request for a copy of court documents shall be followed. In this case, the court shall provide, in accordance with Article 130 of the Criminal Procedure Code, following the same rules provided for the procedure of correction of errors in judgments.

785. According to Article 13 of the Decree, except in the case in which the processing is carried out by the judicial authority, the exercise of the rights of the data subject shall also be assured by the GDPD, following the provision of Article 160 of the Personal Data Protection Code. The data controller shall inform the data subject of this possibility.

IV. General Obligations

786. Articles 15 to 24 of the Decree provide for general obligations, mostly addressed at the data controller, which substantially reflect Articles 24–31 GDPR. Such obligations include the adoption of appropriate measures to comply with the Decree in light of the risk for data subjects (Article 15), the principles of data protection by design and by default (Article 16), the regulation of joint controllership (Article 17), the obligation of entering into a contract or other legal act with data processors (Article 18) and the obligation of the processor and persons working under the authority of the data controller to abide by the latter's instructions (Article 19), the obligation to keep records of processing activities (Article 20, also applicable to the data processor), the general obligation to cooperate with the GPDP (Article 22) and, finally, the obligation to carry out data protection impact assessments and prior consultations with the GPDP in case of high-risk processing (Articles 23–24).

787. In this context, Article 21, titled 'Registration' ('*Registrazione*'), is noteworthy, insofar as it establishes a specific obligation for the data controller to produce logs for the collection, modification, consultation, communication, transfer, interconnection and cancellation of data, performed in automated processing systems. The logs shall be kept for the duration established within the decree referred to in Article 5, paragraph 2, which shall allow to understand the reasons, date and time of the operations carried out and, if possible, to identify the person who performed the operations and the recipients of data. The logs shall be processed for the sole purpose of verifying the lawfulness of processing, for internal control purposes, for guaranteeing the integrity and security of personal data and in the context of criminal proceedings.

V. Data Security

788. According to Article 25 of the Decree, both the data controller and the processor shall put in place all the necessary measures to ensure the protection of personal data processed, taking into account the same elements indicated by Article 32, paragraph 1, GDPR.

Paragraph 2 of Article 25 of the Decree provides a number of controls that the data controller and processor shall put in place as the outcome of a previous risk assessment.

789. In case of occurrence of a data breach, according to Articles 26 and 27 of the Decree, the data controller shall follow the provisions set out in Articles 33 and 34 GDPR in the case of the violation of personal data, except for processing carried out by the judicial authority.

If the personal data breach involves personal data that have been transmitted by or to a data controller of another Member State, the information required by Article 33 GDPR is communicated, without undue delay, to the data controller of that Member State.

Finally, the disclosure of the data breach to affected data subjects pursuant to Article 44 GDPR can be limited in the same cases and for the same reasons provided for the limitation of data subjects' rights under Article 14, paragraph 2, GDPR.

VI. Data Protection Officers

790. Articles 28–30 of the Decree regulate the obligation to appoint data protection officers in terms substantially similar to Articles 37–39 GDPR. The main difference is that, according to the Decree, data protection officer shall be appointed by the data controller without exceptions.

VII. International Data Transfers (Referral)

791. Articles 31–36 govern data transfers to third countries and international organizations. This matter is addressed in this volume within Part VII, Chapter 1, *supra*.

VIII. GPDP Tasks and Powers

792. Pursuant to Article 37 of the Decree, the GPDP is the authority in charge of supervising and enforcing the application of the rules set forth in the Decree in order to protect the fundamental rights and freedoms of natural persons with regard to the processing of personal data and to facilitate the free movement of data within the

European Union. In this respect, paragraph 2 of Article 37 confers to the GPDP the tasks set forth in Article 154 of the Personal Data Protection Code (addressed within this volume in Part VIII, Chapter 3).

In addition, Article 37, paragraph 2, confers to the GPDP the following tasks:

(i) promoting the knowledge of the risks, rules, guarantees and rights of the processing activities;
(ii) promoting the importance of the respect of this Decree between data controllers and processors;
(iii) providing opinions in the case set forth by the law;
(iv) giving information about the data subject's rights on request of the data subject and, if appropriate, cooperating with other Member States supervisory authorities;
(v) handling the complaints filed by the data subject, by a body, organization or association within the meaning of Article 40 of the Decree and carrying out investigations on the subject of the complaint, informing the complainant of the state and the outcome of the investigation within a reasonable deadline, in particular where further investigations or coordination with another supervisory authority are needed;
(vi) supporting data subjects about the filing of complaints;
(vii) ascertaining the legality of the processing activities according to Article 13 of the Decree and informing the data subject within a reasonable period of the outcome of the verification pursuant to paragraph 3 of said Article or the reasons why the investigation was not carried out;
(viii) collaborating with other supervisory authorities, including by means of exchange of information and by mutual assistance, in order to ensure the respect of the Decree;
(ix) monitoring the technological development that may have an impact on data protection, in particular as regards the evolution of information and communication technologies;
(x) providing guidance about the processing activities referred to in Article 24 of the Decree;
(xi) contributing to the activities of the European Data Protection Board.

793. The GPDP is also granted the following powers, pursuant to paragraph 3 of Article 37:

(i) carrying out investigations on the application of the Decree, as well as on the basis of information received from another supervisory authority or from a public authority. The carrying out of investigations is governed by the provisions of the Personal Data Protection Code;
(ii) access to all the information from the data controller or processor, where access is necessary for discharging the GPDP's tasks;
(iii) issuing reprimands about the potential violations of the Decree;
(iv) ordering the data controller or processor to conform their processing activities to the Decree, if necessary, with specific modalities and within a fixed

term, in particular by ordering the rectification or the deletion of personal data or limitation of processing pursuant to Article 12 of the Decree;

(v) imposing a provisional or final limitation of the processing activities, including a ban on the processing;

(vi) promoting confidential reporting concerning the violation of the Decree;

(vii) reporting crimes discovered during its activities;

(viii) issuing an annual report about its activities in accordance with Article 154 of the Personal Data Protection Code.

794. Pursuant to paragraph 5 of Article 37, the activities of the GPDP are free of charge for the data subject or data protection officer. The GPDP shall not rule on applications that are manifestly unfounded or inadmissible in that they repropose, without new elements, requests already rejected.

According to the last paragraph of Article 37, the GPDP is not responsible for monitoring compliance with the norms of the Decree, where the processing is carried out by the judicial authority in the exercise of its judicial functions, as well as in the exercise of judicial functions of the public prosecutor's office.

795. Article 38 provides that the GPDP shall cooperate with the European Commission in order to contribute to the consistent application of EU law on protection of personal data and shall exchange with the supervisory authorities of other Member States relevant information and provide mutual assistance in order to implement and apply this Decree in a consistent manner, and to cooperate effectively with them. Mutual assistance includes requests for information and control measures, such as requests to carry out consultations, inspections, and investigations. The GPDP shall, in this respect, follow the provisions of Article 61 of GDPR.

796. According to Article 39 of the Decree, the data subject may submit a complaint pursuant to Articles 142 and 143 of the Personal Data Protection Code.[959] The GPDP shall inform the data subject about the status or the outcome of the complaint, including the possibility of judicial review.

Pursuant to paragraph 3 of Article 39, in case of alleged violation of his or her rights, the data subject may bring a jurisdictional appeal according to the rules contained in Part III, Title I, Chapter II of the Personal Data Protection Code.[960]

797. According to Article 40 of the Decree, the data subject may confer to a non-profit organization which is subject to Legislative Decree 3 July 2017, no. 117, their power of attorney for the exercise of the rights provided by Article 39 of the Decree.

798. Concerning the compensation for the pecuniary or non-pecuniary damage caused by the processing of personal data in violation of the Decree, Article 41 of the Decree refers to the application of Article 82 of GDPR.[961]

---

959. *See supra* Part VIII, Ch. 4, I.
960. *Ibid.*, para. 3.
961. *See supra* Part VIII, Ch. 5, §2.

799. Finally, Article 42 of the Decree sets forth the relevant pecuniary sanctions in case of non-compliance by data controllers and processors with the provisions of the Decree. In particular, paragraph 1 provides that, unless the relevant action or omission constitutes a crime and excluding the processing carried out in the judicial context, the violation of the provisions of Article 3, paragraph 1, subparagraphs a), b), d), e) and f), Article 4, paragraphs 2 and 3, Article 6, paragraphs 3 and 4, Article 7 and Article 8, of the Decree shall be punished by an administrative penalty between EUR 50,000 to EUR 150,000.

The same administrative penalty shall apply to the transfer of personal data to a third country or organization or international organization in the absence of the adequacy decision of the European Commission, except as provided in Articles 33 and 34 of the Decree.

Paragraph 2 of Article 43 provides that unless the action or omission constitutes a crime, and with the exclusion of processing carried out in a judicial context, the violations of the provisions of Article 14, paragraph 2, Article 17, paragraph 2, Article 18, paragraphs 1, 2, 3 and 4, Article 19, Article 20, Article 21, to Article 22, Article 23, Article 24, paragraphs 1 and 4, Article 26, Article 27, Article 28, paragraphs 1 and 4, Article 29, paragraph 2 of the Decree shall be punished by an administrative penalty between EUR 20,000 to EUR 80,000.

In determining the administrative penalty to be applied, the GPDP shall take into account the criteria set forth in Article 83 GDPR. The procedure for the application of sanctions is regulated by Article 166 of the Personal Data Protection Code. The provision of Article 165 of the Personal Data Protection Code is also applicable.[962]

IX. Criminal Sanctions

800. According to Article 43, paragraph 1, of the Decree, unless the action constitutes a more serious crime, whoever, in order to gain profit for himself or others or to cause harm to others, processes personal data in violation of the provisions on the lawfulness of the processing activity provided by the Decree, shall be punished, if actual harm results from his or her action, with imprisonment from six months to one year and six months or, if the action involves communication or dissemination of data, with imprisonment from six months to two years.

Paragraph 2 provides that, unless the act constitutes a more serious crime, whoever, in order to gain profit for himself or others or to cause harm to others, processes personal data in violation of the provisions on the processing of special category of personal data (Article 7 of the Decree) or the prohibition of profiling (Article 8 of the Decree), shall be punished, if actual harm results from the act, by imprisonment from one to three years.

801. Failure to collaborate or put into place the GPDP orders is also criminally punishable, where such failure is serious and voluntary.

962. *See supra* Part VIII, Ch. 6.

In particular, Article 44 of the Decree provides that unless the fact constitutes a more serious crime, anyone, in a proceeding before the GPDP regarding the processing of data referred to in Article 1, paragraph 2, of the Decree or in the course of investigations concerning the same data, falsely declares or certifies facts or circumstances or produces false documents, is punished with the imprisonment from six months to three years.

Moreover, according to Article 45 of the Decree, anyone who, being legally required to do so, fails to comply with the measures adopted by the GPDP pursuant to Article 143, paragraph 1, letter c), of the Personal Data Protection Code, in a proceeding concerning the processing of data referred to the Article 1, paragraph 2, of the Decree, shall be punished by imprisonment from three months to two years.

802. Pursuant to Article 46 of the Decree, the conviction for any of the crimes provided by the Decree shall import the publication of the sentence in accordance with Article 36, paragraphs 2 and 3, of the Criminal Code.

X. Processing by Police Forces

803. Finally, Articles 47 and 48 of the Decree lay down some specific provisions addressing the processing activities carried out by police forces.

804. In particular, Article 47 provides that in cases where the public security authorities or police forces may acquire, in accordance with the current provisions of the law, data, information, acts and documents from other subjects, the acquisition may also be carried out by means of telematic technologies. To this end, the bodies or offices concerned may enter into agreements aimed at facilitating consultation by the same bodies or offices, through electronic communication networks, of public registers, lists, files and databases, in compliance with the relevant provisions and principles of Articles 3 to 8 of the Decree. The model conventions shall be adopted by the Ministry of the Interior, based on the opinion of the GPDP, and shall establish the modalities of connections and accesses also in order to ensure selective access only to the data necessary for the pursuit of the purposes referred to in Article 1, paragraph 2, of the Decree.

The personal data processed by the police forces for the purposes of Article 1, paragraph 2, of the Decree shall be retained separately from other data processed for administrative purposes.

Without prejudice to Articles 2 to 7 of the Decree, the Data Processing Centre of the Department of Public Security (‘*Centro elaborazione dati del Dipartimento della pubblica sicurezza*’) ensures the periodic updating, proportionality, relevance and non-excessiveness of the personal data, also processed through authorized queries of criminal records and the records of pending charges of the Ministry of Justice (regulated by D.P.R. 14 November 2002, no. 313) and the other relevant databases necessary for the purposes of Article 1 of the Decree. The bodies and offices of the police force shall, in any case, periodically verify the conformity with

Articles 2 to 7 of the Decree of the data processing activities they carry out, thereby proceeding as appropriate to update or correct the data by means of corrections and annotations to the relevant documents.

805. Concerning the safeguards for data subjects, Article 48 of the Decree refers to Article 10 of the Law 1 April 1981, no. 121, according to which the GPDP has the power to check the compliance of processing activities carried out through the Centre of the Department of Public Security. It is also provided that the data subject can ask the Centre of the Department of Public Security to confirm the existence of the processing of personal data and their communication, and if they deem the processing to be unlawful, asking the erasure or the anonymization of the data. The decision shall be taken within thirty days from the request, except in the case in which the decision may compromise public security. In this latter case, the GPDP shall be informed.

Chapter 4. National Security Services

§1. The Italian Security Intelligence System

806. The Italian Security Intelligence System used as a collective name to identify the different authorities responsible for intelligence policies and operations, includes the following bodies: President of the Council of Ministers, Undersecretary to the Prime Minister for the Intelligence (if appointed), Interministerial Committee for the Security of the Republic (*Comitato Interministeriale per la Sicurezza della Repubblica* – CISR), Security Intelligence Department (*Dipartimento delle informazioni per la sicurezza* – DIS), External Intelligence and Security Agency (*Agenzia informazioni e sicurezza esterna* – AISE), Internal Intelligence and Security Agency (*Agenzia informazioni e sicurezza interna* – AISI). The competences of the above-mentioned authorities are regulated by Law 3 August 2007, no. 124, which has reformed the Italian Intelligence System for Security (previously regulated by Law 24 October 1977, no. 801) and introduced new provisions on State secrets.

807. The President of the Council of Ministers holds the overall political responsibilities for the intelligence activities conducted in the interest and defence of the Italian Republic. Some of their functions can be delegated to a Delegated Authority, whose role can be entrusted either to an Undersecretary of State or to a Minister without portfolio. The CISR is in charge of defining the goals of intelligence policies and, in particular, of setting intelligence requirements and allocating financial resources among the different competent authorities.

The President of the Council of Ministers and the Delegated Authority exercise their functions through the DIS, which is in charge of ensuring a unified approach to intelligence activities by coordinating intelligence operations, ensuring the exchange of information between the various competent authorities, and overseeing the activities performed by AISE and AISI (among other functions). The AISE and the AISI have similar competencies but with a different territorial scope: the AISE is responsible for safeguarding national security against threats originating abroad, while the AISI is responsible for safeguarding national security from threats originating within Italy's borders.[963]

§2. National Data Protection Rules Applicable to the Italian Security Intelligence System

808. Even if the GDPR does not apply to activities concerning national security (since such activities fall outside European Union Law),[964] Article 58 of the Personal Data Protection Code includes some specific provisions pertaining to the

963. Information on the structure and the organization of the Italian Security Intelligence System is available on the official website of the Security Intelligence Service, https://www.sicurezzanazionale.gov.it/sisr.nsf/english/about-us.html.
964. Cf. Art. 2, para. 2, lett. a), and Recital 16 GDPR.

processing of personal data for purposes of national security and defence (in continuity with the provisions set out in Personal Data Protection Code, before the direct applicability of the GDPR).

The Italian legislator has therefore chosen to set out specific provisions to regulate the activities concerning national security as a means to strike a balance between the right to protection of personal data on the one hand and the need to ensure national security and defence on the other.[965] Precisely, Article 58(1) of the Personal Data Protection Code provides that the processing of personal data that is carried out by the DIS, the AISE, and the AISI pursuant to Article 26 of Law 3 August 2007, no. 124 (under which the gathering and the processing of data or information shall be directed solely at pursuing the Security Intelligence System's institutional goals), and to other laws or regulations/provisions and the processing that concerns data placed under state secrecy rules shall be regulated in accordance with Article 160, paragraph 4, of the Personal Data Protection Code and with Articles 2, 3, 8, 15, 16, 18, 25, 37, 41, 42, and 43 of Legislative Decree 18 May 2018, no. 51 (where compatible), which transposes Directive (EU) 2016/680 into the Italian legal framework.[966]

809. Article 58, paragraph 1, therefore, provides that the DIS, AISE, AISI and other authorities that carry out data processing activities under state secrecy rules are subject to the specific regime set out under Article 160 of the Personal Data Protection Code in the event of inquiries conducted by the GPDP.

Moreover, Article 58, paragraph 1, extends the applicability of some of the provisions set out under Directive (EU) 2016/680 (as transposed into the Italian legal framework by means of D.Lgs. 51/2018) to the DIS, AISE and AISI, and other authorities subject to state secrecy rules. As a result, these bodies are subject to the same data protection provisions which apply to the authorities in charge of the investigation and prosecution of criminal offences, with reference to the general principles which shall govern the processing activities in question (e.g., lawfulness, purpose limitation, minimization), automated decision-making, the principle of data protection by design and by default, the need to implement technical and organizational measures to ensure a level of security of personal data appropriate to the risk, and other obligations specifically prescribed when engaging third parties acting (as processor) on behalf of the entity acting as controller.

Moreover, the DIS, AISE, AISI and other authorities subject to state secrecy rules are also subject to the sanctions regime set out under D.Lgs. 51/2018 (instead of the sanctions regime which results from Article 83 GDPR in combination with Article 166 of the Personal Data Protection Code), under which violations of the said legislative decree may either lead to administrative fines or amount to a criminal offence punished by imprisonment.

810. Article 58, paragraph 2, of the Personal Data Protection Code, further provides that the provisions set out under Article 58, paragraph 1, also apply to the

965. Federica Resta, *Codice della Privacy e Data Protection* 1207–1208 (Roberto D' Orazio, Giusella Dolores Finocchiaro, Oreste Pollicino & Giorgio Resta eds, Giuffrè Francis Lefebvre 2021).
966. For a general overview of the D.Lgs. 51/2018, *see supra* Part X, Ch. 3.

'processing that is carried out by public bodies for purposes of defence or State security in pursuance of provisions set out in laws, regulations or administrative instruments of a general nature that envisage' such processing of personal data, with the addition that such public bodies will also be subject to Articles 23 and 24 of D.Lgs. 51/2018. In other words, all other public bodies – not subject to state secrecy – that carry out processing activities for purposes of defence or state security (in compliance with the law or other regulations and/or administrative instruments) are also subject to the following obligations:

(i) the obligation to carry out a data protection impact assessment where the processing activity in question presents a high risk to the rights and freedoms of natural persons (pursuant to Article 23 of D.Lgs. 51/2018);
(ii) the obligation to consult with the GPDP (pursuant to Article 24 of D.Lgs. 51/2018) where a data protection impact assessment indicates that the processing would result in a high risk in the absence of measures taken by the controller to mitigate the risk or where the type of processing involves a high risk to the rights and freedoms of data subjects, in particular, where using new technologies, mechanisms or procedures, or where genetic and biometric data are involved (pursuant to Article 24 of D.Lgs. 51/2018).

811. Pursuant to Article 58, paragraph 3, of the Personal Data Protection Code, detailed rules for the application of the dispositions provided under Article 58, paragraphs 1 and 2, shall be laid out by means of one or multiple regulations[967] with regard to the types of data, data subjects, processing activities and persons authorized to process the personal data under the authority of the controller or processor. In particular, the regulations applying to the subject matters under Article 58(1) shall be adopted in accordance with Article 43 of L. 124/2007 (meaning by way of one or more Decrees issued by the President of the Council of Ministers) while the regulations applying to the subject matters under Article 58, paragraph 3, shall be adopted by way of a D.P.C.M. in accordance with Article 17, paragraph 3, of Law 23 August 1988, no. 400 (which regulates the Government activity and organization of the Presidency of the Council of Ministers) upon a proposal submitted by the competent Ministers.

812. Lastly, Article 58, paragraph 4, provides that the measures for the implementation of the Personal Data Protection Code in relation to the exercise of defence and national security functions by the armed forces shall be set out in one or more regulations adopted by a D.P.R. upon a proposal submitted by the Minister of Defence.

967. For the category of 'regulation' under the Italian legal framework, *see supra* n. 409.

Chapter 5. Other Specific Regimes (e.g., Civil Protection, etc.)

§1. Criminal Provisions as Safeguards of Confidentiality

813. There are some crimes punished under the Italian Criminal Code that protect individuals in cases where their privacy is violated. Such crimes include not only those punished under the Personal Data Protection Code[968] but also under the Criminal Code. Such crimes are computer crimes (punished under the Articles 615-*bis,* 615-*ter*, 615-*quater*, 617-*quater*, 617-*quinquies*, 635-*bis*, 635-*ter*, 635-*quater*, 635-*quinquies*, 491-*bis*, 640-*quinquies* of the Criminal Code). These provisions protect individuals in cases of the violation of their computer domicile. Such crimes concern the use of informatic instruments and violations of the private space of individuals.

814. The crimes referred to above are also relevant for the administrative liability of entities provided by Legislative Decree 8 June 2001, no. 231. In particular, according to the Decree, the legal entity can be criminally punished if it has committed one of the crimes included in this Decree for the benefit of the legal entity itself, where the crime is committed by a person belonging to the top management of the company.

Among the crimes which are relevant under D.Lgs. 231/2001, there are also the computer crimes mentioned above. The crime punished under Article 615-*bis,* so-called abusive access to IT system, deserves a special mention. In particular, this provision punishes access to an IT system in violation of the security measures put into force to protect the system. According to the case law of the Supreme Court of Cassation,[969] this crime protects the confidentiality of the information contained in the system, where access is forbidden because the information should remain secret. This is, however, dependent on the type of information which is registered in the system.

For that reason, the Supreme Court of Cassation has also punished individuals who have accessed the system violating his authorization profiles and for reasons other than those for which the data controller gave access.[970] In order to ascertain when access is unlawful, therefore, both the concept of *abusive*, which must characterize the access, and the presence of security measures assume importance.

Abusive, in particular, similar to what happens with respect to the protection of a private domicile, means an unauthorized introduction, that is, a permanence against the will of the holder of the *ius escludendi alios* ('right to exclude others'). Abusive introduction thus consists of 'access to the knowledge of the contents of the computer or telematic system concretely considered: in fact, entry into the same is preparatory to the cognition of data and information found in the memory of a computer or transmissible by telematic equipment'.[971]

---

968. *See supra* Part VIII, Ch. 5, §1.
969. *See* Supreme Court of Cassation, no. 26606/2019, crim. sect.
970. *See* Supreme Court of Cassation, no. 8541/2019, crim. sect.
971. *See* Luigi Cuomo & Bernardino Izzi, *Misure di sicurezza e accesso abusivo ad un sistema informatico o telematico*, 3 Cassazione Penale 1018 (2002). Author's translation.

815. The occurrence of the crime in question is irrespective of the purposes that motivate the agent,[972] so much so that the agent may act to acquire data or information or manipulate the data in the electronic archive in order to obtain an advantage or to simply carry out a destructive action or even break into it for 'recreational' purposes. The conduct, in such cases, in addition to being relevant under Article 615-*ter* of the Criminal Code, may constitute additional concurrent offences, such as those provided for in Article 167 of the Personal Data Protection Code,[973] and also result in a personal data breach under Articles 33 and 34 GDPR.

The United Sections of the Supreme Court of Cassation have affirmed an important principle of law whereby a person who, despite being authorized, accesses or remains in a protected computer system by violating the conditions and limits resulting from the set of rules established by the owner of the system to objectively delimit access, while remaining irrelevant, for the purposes of the existence of the crime, the purposes and aims that subjectively motivated the entry into the system.[974] In the case of an authorized person, the objective fact of accessing information which is retained in the computer system in violation of the authorization profiles for which access is permitted is problematic. In other words, carrying out operations which are different from those to which the authorized person is permitted access results in a violation of legitimate access. It should be noted that the purposes that motivated such access and the objectives that are pursued in doing so are irrelevant.[975]

In the opposite sense, the Supreme Court of Cassation has ruled[976] that for the purposes of the crime in question, the so-called misuse of power is also relevant, where the offender carries out operations of an 'ontologically different' nature from those for which the individual is entrusted and in relation to which the access was allowed to him.

The Supreme Court of Cassation ruled that abusive access to a computer system includes:

> [T]he conduct of the employee who, in view of the termination of the employment relationship, takes steps to copy large amounts of data and then brings them outside the Company and uses them for purposes other than those permitted. Specifically, the employee preparing to leave the workplace to go to another competing company, taking advantage of still being authorized to access the company's customer data, copied said data onto removable media and took it outside in contravention of internal organizational policies. This was in addition to the further evidence that the company was being grossly misappropriated for the benefit of the new company at which the former employee was hired.[977]

972. *See* Supreme Court of Cassation, no. 44390/2014, crim. sect.
973. *See supra* Part VIII, Ch. 5, §1.
974. *See* Supreme Court of Cassation, no. 4694/2011, unit. crim. sect.; most recently, in the same vein, Supreme Court of Cassation, no. 254911/2013.
975. *See* Supreme Court of Cassation, no. 10083/2015, crim. sect.
976. *See* Supreme Court of Cassation, no. 4121/2017, unit. crim. sect.
977. *See* Supreme Court of Cassation, no. 26625/2019, unit. crim. sect. Author's translation.

816. The ruling above demonstrates that the crime in question also takes place when the former employee is still in possession of the credentials to access company systems they had access to in the exercise of their official duties even, where such access has not been disabled. When such an insider threat occurs, the data protection implications may also result in liability of the entity (as data controller or processor) if not properly handled. Such conduct, in fact, may constitute a personal data breach under Article 33 GDPR and possibly a violation of Article 32 GDPR in terms of inadequate security measures.

The receiving entity/company, in such a case, would then have unlawfully misappropriated data provided by the offender and could be held liable for the unlawful processing of such personal data.

Finally, it should be noted that the crime in question could also result in the liability of the entity, as data controller, in the event that a senior person of the company makes a request for their subordinate to enter a database they are not authorized to access, requesting that activities that would benefit the entity be carried out. For example, this could be the case for the purpose of customer profiling (in the absence of a suitable legal basis legitimizing the processing under consideration) with the aim of developing new marketing strategies.

§2. The Italian Regulation of Whistleblowing

817. In April 2019, the European Parliament approved Directive (EU) 2019/1937 (hereinafter referred to as the 'Directive') concerning the Whistleblowing Reporting System (hereinafter referred to as 'whistleblowing') which should have been transposed by EU Member States before December 2021.

818. Italy has transposed the Directive[978] with Law 10 March 2023, no. 2430, almost two years after the end of the deadline.[979] In particular, this law extends the protection for persons (in private and public companies) who report illicit actions committed within the company which were discovered during their employment, going beyond provisions in this sense.

Companies that have employed more than 50 employees in the past year should implement a reporting system by the end of 2023. If the company has more than 250 employees, the deadline is July 2023. In some cases, companies with fewer than 50 employees will also have to comply with the new provisions (e.g., in the case of the company that has adopted the Organization, Management and Control Model required by Decree Legislative no. 231/2001).

The new provisions give wide protection to whistle-blowers. In fact, the older provisions protected such individuals only if the report was made by the employee

978. *See* the Opinion of the GPDP concerning the Legislative Decree Scheme, 11.1.2023, at https://www.garanteprivacy.it/home/docweb/-/docweb-display/docweb/9844945.

979. The European Commission decided to refer 8 Member States to the Court of Justice of the European Union (among them, Italy) for failure to transpose and notify the national measures transposing the directive on the protection of persons who report breaches of Union law into their legal framework (Directive (EU) 2019/1937) (*see* https://ec.europa.eu/commission/presscorner/detail/EN/IP_23_703).

and only if the illicit was a violation of the ethics code adopted by the company or its Organization, Management and Control Model.

Under the new law, however, everyone who has an employment relationship with the company can report wrongdoings they have discovered during their work, meaning that trainees, staff, stakeholders can also freelance or VAT employees may report issues.

To comply with the new law, companies should create a reporting system that could include written or oral channels and also appoint a specific office, internal or external to the company, or a single person who should receive the reports. It is also provided that a specific facilitator could assist the whistle-blower during the entire procedure.

In addition, it also provides that under certain circumstances, the whistle-blower may report the illicit activity to the 'public' channel provided by the National Anti-corruption Authority. The aforementioned Authority is also in charge of imposing sanctions on companies which fail to create an efficient reporting system. In addition, the law also introduces an express prohibition of retaliatory actions against the reporting employee and sanctions in the case of violation of these provisions.

The reporting system must be implemented by applying the necessary security measures to ensure the confidentiality of reports. The new law does not provide anything about the admissibility of anonymous reporting.

819. The reports must be followed up within a reasonable period of time, which is, in any case, specified as a maximum of three months. The reporting should be taken into consideration within seven days after receipt of the reports. All the documentation collected to analyse the report should be kept for a maximum of five years.

Privacy rights are subjected to the limitations of Article 2-*undecies*, paragraph 1, lett. f), of the Personal Data Protection Code, which restricts the possibility of exercising data subjects' rights in the context of whistleblowing: *see*, in this volume, Part IV, Chapter 8, §1, I, F.

I. GPDP Decisions on Whistleblowing

820. The GPDP fined the Airport of Bologna[980] EUR 40,000 because the whistleblowing system was not in line with the GDPR. Also, the platform provider, as a data processor, was fined EUR 20,000. In particular, according to the GPDP, even if the processing carried out by parties falls under the provisions of Article 6, paragraph 1, letter c), GDPR, this does not exempt the companies from complying with the adoption of appropriate security measures to ensure that no unauthorized or unlawful processing is carried out.

From the investigation carried out with respect to the application in use by the Airport of Bologna for the facilitation of whistleblowing reports, the GPDP found that the Airport did not implement security measures which were appropriate to the

980. GPDP, *Ordinanza ingiunzione nei confronti di Aeroporto Guglielmo Marconi di Bologna S.p.a.*, 10.6.2021, doc. web no. 9685922.

risk posed to data subjects and, furthermore, that the principle of data protection by design under Article 25 GDPR had not been respected. This was because the platform did not use a secure network protocol (such as the 'https' protocol), nor did it encrypt the reporter's identifying information, the information reported, or any attached documentation.

A further critical issue highlighted by the GPDP was found in the tracking, through the logs generated by the firewalls, of the access made to the platform by employees who connected to the whistleblowing application through the company network, thus nullifying the protective measures put in place in order to protect the confidentiality of the identity of the reporting party, also because of the limited number of reports that had been submitted.

821. The GPDP more recently returned to the issue of whistleblowing in the context of two new decisions, confirming that both public and private entities are required to observe the maximum care in setting up and managing whistleblowing systems, guaranteeing the highest confidentiality of employees and other persons reporting illegal behaviours.

Indeed, on 7 April 2022, the GPDP published two decisions concerning violations of the legislation on personal data protection with a specific focus on whistleblowing and imposed administrative sanctions of EUR 40,000 both on the Azienda ospedaliera di Perugia (a hospital located in Perugia, Italy)[981] and its data processor, ISWEB S.p.A.[982] The main aspects highlighted by the GPDP in the aforementioned decisions are once again found in the need to preserve the confidentiality of whistle-blowers, which should be guaranteed in all stages of processing.

§3. The Italian Regulation of Wiretapping

822. The Italian regulation of wiretapping is found in the Code of Criminal Procedure and, in particular, in Articles 266–271.[983]

981. *See* GPDP, *Ordinanza ingiunzione nei confronti di Azienda ospedaliera di Perugia*, 7.4.2022, doc. web no. 9768363, https://www.garanteprivacy.it/web/guest/home/docweb/-/docweb-display/docweb/9768363.

982. *See* GPDP, *Ordinanza ingiunzione nei confronti di ISWEB S.p.A.*, 7.4.2022, doc. web no. 9768387, https://www.garanteprivacy.it/web/guest/home/docweb/-/docweb-display/docweb/9768387.

983. It should be noted that wiretapping, which includes the interception of the content of a communication and is regulated by the Code of Criminal Procedure (as shall be seen *infra*), is different than the acquisition of traffic data for purposes of prosecution of crimes, which includes the acquisition of communication meta-data with the express exclusion of their content and is regulated primarily by Art. 132 of the Personal Data Protection Code (as seen in this volume within Part II, Ch. 3, §4.IV).

It is worth recalling that the matter of wiretapping is not in the scope of the GDPR, pursuant to its Article 2, paragraph 2, letter d),[984] but is instead regulated under the framework provided by Directive (EU) 2016/680 and D.Lgs. 51/2018.[985]

823. Wiretapping can only take place after a specific authorization from a judge for preliminary investigation after the public prosecutor makes a request and only in the case that doing so is absolutely necessary for the purposes of an investigation, where there is a serious indication of a crime between those listed in Article 266 of the Code of Criminal Procedure having been committed.

824. The legislation provides for a maximum period for the duration of wiretapping operations of fifteen days, with three possible subsequent extensions up to a maximum limit of seventy-five days, if the conditions for ordering the wiretapping remain in place. After this period has expired, the prosecutor is given the power to request extensions not exceeding a period of fifteen days, if they may permit the acquisition of elements fundamental to the investigation of the crime for which the investigation is being conducted.

825. In 2013, the GPDP set out 'measures and arrangements to be implemented by public prosecutor's offices, in order to enhance the security of any personal data they collect and use as part of wiretapping.'[986]

The 2013 Decision of the GPDP followed a fact-finding survey carried out by the GPDP on a sample of medium-sized public prosecutor's offices in Italy (located in Bologna, Catanzaro, Perugia, Potenza, Venice). The survey was aimed to assess the technological and organizational measures that were applied by those judicial offices when carrying out telephone wiretapping or the interception of Internet and electronic communications. Security measures had already been imposed on the electronic communications service providers that forward intercepted data to the judicial authorities requesting such data. The findings of the survey showed a patchwork of situations, which made it necessary to step in so as to enhance the security of both data and data management systems by applying the relevant measures to all public prosecutor's offices. In this manner, data protection measures would also be harmonized in light of the continuously evolving electronic communications technologies as well as the possible risks arising from the use of IT tools.

Within the Decision, the GPDP prescribed a number of security measures to be applied by the prosecutor's office:[987]

---

984. 'This Regulation does not apply to the processing of personal data: ... by competent authorities for the purposes of the prevention, investigation, detection or prosecution of criminal offences or the execution of criminal penalties, including the safeguarding against and the prevention of threats to public security.'

985. *See supra*, Part X, Ch. 3.

986. *See* GPDP, *Interception of Communications by Judicial Authorities: Enhanced Security Measures To Be Implemented*, 24.7.2013, doc. web no. 2624069, https://www.garanteprivacy.it/home/docweb/-/docweb-display/docweb/2624069.

987. All the following prescription are taken from the decision https://www.garanteprivacy.it/home/docweb/-/docweb-display/docweb/2624069, English version.

(i) Access to the listening room is permitted only to persons who have a badge associated with a numerical code (only known to the individual); alternatively, biometric devices must be used for access control.
(ii) All accesses must be logged. The technical staff in charge of maintenance or technical interventions must be authorized beforehand by the individual public prosecutor's office.
(iii) Such technical staff is only allowed to access the data, information and records that are absolutely necessary for their maintenance activities. CCTV cameras must be in operation.
(iv) The systems and servers used for interception activities may only be accessed by operators (including system administrators) from dedicated workstations on the basis of strong authentication procedures. Such workstations must be connected to firewall-protected networks.
(v) All the operations performed as part of interception activities – such as listening, browsing, recording, duplicating, and storing information, making transcripts of intercepted communications, system maintenance, and destroying records and media – must be logged via IT techniques that can ensure the non-alterability of such logs.
(vi) Mastering and duplication of intercepted contents may only be performed where indispensable by duly authorized staff. Records copied to removable media (e.g., CD-ROMs) will have to be protected via encryption. Containers or envelopes used to carry such media may not bear any information that would allow unauthorized third parties to infer or deduce the scope of the interception.
(vii) Only judicial police staff may be relied upon to deliver media and paper records (including transcripts) to judicial authorities.
(viii) Soundtracks, any other type of collected information, and backup copies must be stored in an encrypted format. Data extraction may only be performed by way of cryptographic procedures.
(ix) All data must be exchanged between judicial authorities and Internet service providers via secure network protocols in encrypted format. The intercepted electronic communications – IP-address flows, e-mails – must be transmitted from the interception access point on the provider's network to the receiver equipment at a Telecommunications Interception Centre (CIT) in encrypted format as well.
(x) As regards the so-called roaming of interceptions – i.e., the re-routing of intercepted communication flows from the CITs at public prosecutor's offices to the judicial police offices tasked with such interceptions – the physical and IT security measures to be deployed on the premises used for listening to and recording such flows must be the same as those applying to CITs.
(xi) The links between public prosecutor's offices and the relevant police offices will consist of dedicated 'point-to-point' connections or otherwise be based on secure networks (e.g., VPNs).

826. On 26 January 2018, the reform of wiretapping regulations implemented by Legislative Decree 29 December 2017, no. 216, came into effect. The main novelties of the reformed regulation include:[988]

(i) The introduction of a new crime punished under Article 617-*septies* of the Criminal Code, i.e., the 'dissemination of fraudulent filming and recording of communications'. The provision punishes, with imprisonment of up to four years, anyone who, in order to cause damage to the reputation or image of others, disseminates fraudulently made audio or video footage by any means of private meetings or recordings; also fraudulent conversations, including telephone or telematic conversations, carried out in their presence. Punishability is excluded if the dissemination of the filming or recordings results directly and immediately from their use in administrative or judicial proceedings or for the exercise of the right of defence or the right to report the news. The crime is punishable on complaint by the offended person.

(ii) Greater protection of confidentiality in communications between defence counsel and the defendant. The prohibition, already provided for, of direct wiretapping activities against the defence counsel, with the consequent unusability of the related acquisitions, is, in fact, broadened, providing that any involvement, even occasional, of the defence counsel in the legitimately carried out listening activity cannot lead to the minutes of the related communications or conversations.

(iii) The introduction of the prohibition of transcripts and transcript summaries of communications or conversations deemed irrelevant to the investigation, both in terms of their subject matter and the subjects involved, as well as those involving personal data defined as sensitive by law, always if they were not deemed relevant for the purposes of evidence collection. The prosecutor has the power to order, by reasoned decree, that communications and conversations be transcribed in the record when deemed relevant to the facts being tried and also necessary for the same purpose, if they involve sensitive personal data (*see* Article 268, paragraph 2-bis, of the Code of Criminal Procedure).

(iv) A new regulation of the filing of documents regarding wiretaps and the selection of the material collected, with the introduction of a two-stage procedure. This procedure envisages first the filing of conversations and communications, as well as related documents, and only then the acquisition of those that are relevant and usable. Those ones which are irrelevant and unusable are deleted. In addition, the prosecutor is identified as the guarantor of the confidentiality of the documentation, since the prosecutor is responsible for the custody, in the context of a special confidential archive, of the irrelevant and

988. *See also* the GPDP Opinion on the (at the time) draft legislative scheme: GPDP, *Parere sullo schema di decreto del Ministro della giustizia recante disposizioni di attuazione per le intercettazioni mediante inserimento di captatore informatico e per l'accesso all'archivio informatico a norma dell'articolo 7, commi 1 e 3, del decreto legislativo 29 dicembre 2017*, n. 216, 12.4.2018, doc. web no. 8987309, https://www.garanteprivacy.it/home/docweb/-/docweb-display/docweb/8987309. For an in-depth study, *see* Paolo Gentilucci, La nuova disciplina della intercettazioni telefoniche, www.diritto.it, 13.10.2021.

unusable material, with the right to listen and examine, but not to copy, by the defence attorneys and the judge, until the moment of the conclusion of the acquisition procedure. Consequently, the procedure aimed at selecting the material collected by the prosecutor is redefined, and as provided for in the delegation of powers, a differentiated acquisition mechanism is provided for cases where the relevant wiretap material has already been used for the issuance of a precautionary measure. Thus, the previous model centred on the so-called excerpted hearing, characterized by the fact that all wiretapping material was included in the preliminary investigation file from the outset instead of being placed in a confidential archive, with the consequence that it had to be fully examined in order to eliminate content which was excessive and unusable. This was done in order to exclude any reference to persons only occasionally involved in the listening activity and, in general, the interception of material not relevant for the purposes of justice, with a view to preventing the undue disclosure of facts and references to persons unrelated to the matter under investigation. It should be noted, however, that this rule has not always been respected in practice.

(v) A new regulation on 'trojan horses', i.e., the interception of communications or conversations by placing captors in portable electronic devices. Specifically, it is stipulated that such devices cannot be kept active without limitation of time or space but shall be activated remotely as provided by the prosecutor in their investigation programme and, among other things, shall be deactivated if the interception takes place in a household environment, unless there is evidence that the criminal activity under investigation is taking place there, or that the investigation itself concerns most serious crimes, including mafia and terrorism, referred to in Article 51, paragraphs 3-*bis* and 3-*quater*, of the Code of Criminal Procedure.

(vi) Simplification of conditions for the use of wiretapping of telephone and telematic conversations and communications in proceedings for the most serious crimes of public officials against public administration through the provision of less restrictive conditions for their authorization.

(vii) Raising the time limit given to the defence to examine the intercepted material once it has been filed for five to ten days also provides for an extension of the time limit depending on the quantity of the investigative material collected and its complexity.

(viii) Anticipation of the issuance of copies of summary transcriptions (those made by the judicial police in the course of operations) once their acquisition has been ordered by the judge with almost definitive elimination, except for recovery, at the preliminary hearing or at the trial, of material that was at first considered irrelevant and that is later evaluated differently, also because of subsequent elements.

827. Subsequently, by way of Law Decree 30 December 2019, no. 161, converted by Law 28 February 2020, no. 7, the use of Trojan horses in wiretapping for investigating crimes against the public administration was also extended to crimes committed by public service officers (previously, the use was provided only for those committed by public officials). Only programmes complying with the technical requirements established by the Decree of the Ministry of Justice may be used for this purpose. The record of operations must indicate the type of programme used and, if possible, the places where communications or conversations take place.

828. Wiretapped communications shall be transferred exclusively to a digital archive. During the transfer of data, constant integrity controls should be carried out to ensure that what is intercepted, recorded, and transmitted fully corresponds to reality. If the simultaneous transfer of intercepted data is not possible, the record of operations shall note the reasons preventing this and the chronological succession of the intercepted events and intercepted conversations. Upon completion of the operations, the programme shall be deactivated in a manner that makes it unsuitable for further use.

829. According to Article 269 of the Code of Criminal Procedure, the minutes and recordings must be immediately transmitted to the prosecutor for storage in the digital archive, where they are to be deposited within five days after the conclusion of the operations, together with the decrees that ordered, authorized, validated or extended the wiretap. They must remain there for the period of time established by the prosecutor, unless the judge recognizes that an extension is necessary; if serious prejudice to the investigation may result from the deposit, the judge authorizes the prosecutor to delay such deposit to a time no later than the closure of the preliminary investigation.

830. According to Article 293, paragraph 3, of the Code of Criminal Procedure, the defendant's counsel should immediately be given notice that, within the time limit set by the prosecutor, they are entitled to examine the records and listen to the recordings.

831. As for the excerpting of prohibited wiretaps, once the time limit set by the prosecutor has expired, the judge must order the acquisition of the conversations or streams of computer or telematic communications indicated by the parties which appear to be relevant. At the same time, the judge must also excerpt ex officio the recordings and minutes whose use was prohibited and those that concerned special categories of personal data under Article 9 GDPR, provided that their relevance was not demonstrated. The prosecutor and defence counsel are entitled to participate in the excerpting and must be notified at least twenty-four hours in advance.

832. The legislation under consideration also deals with the transcription of recordings and the rights of the defence and states that the judge, including in the formation of the trial file for the hearing, shall order the verbatim transcription of recordings or the printing in intelligible form of the information contained in the streams of computer or telematic communications to be acquired; the forms, methods and safeguards are those provided by the Code of Procedure for the conduct of expert opinions.

The transcripts or printouts are to be placed in the case file for the hearing. Defence attorneys may extract copies of transcripts and have the recording transposed to suitable media; for the interception of computer or telematic communication streams, defence attorneys may request copies on suitable media of the intercepted streams or copies of the printout.

833. With reference to the digital archive of wiretaps and methods of access, the systems of record-keeping change: the confidential archive at the prosecutor's office is to be replaced by a special digital archive, managed and kept under the direction and supervision of the prosecutor's office.

I. The Wiretapping Prevention Carried out by Intelligence Services

834. The prevention of wiretapping carried out by National Intelligence Services was introduced in Italy for the first time with Article 4, of Legislative Decree 27 July 2005, no. 144, now amended by Law 29 December 2022, no. 197. This type of wiretapping prevention is carried out by the Intelligence service, *ante delictum* and is absolutely unusable in criminal proceedings. It is aimed at gathering information which is useful for the prevention of serious crimes and not for the acquisition of elements aimed at ascertaining responsibility for individual criminal acts. In essence, this activity can be understood as the tapping of conversations or communications (telephone, environmental, home or telematic) and monitoring activities on communications, which can be carried out even in the absence of criminal proceedings, regardless of the existence of a *notitia criminis* and of the objective of gathering evidence that can be used in court.

According to Article 4, paragraph 1, of D.Lgs. no. 144/2005, the Intelligence Services could wiretap communications or conversations, including by telematic means, as well as the interception of communications or conversations between persons present, even if these take place in the places indicated in Article 614 of the Criminal Code. The Intelligence Services could act only after obtaining an authorization decree by the General Prosecutor in Rome and only if those wiretaps are necessary for the purposes prosecuted by the Intelligence Services.

§4. Cyberbullying

835. Prior to 2017, there were no specific provisions against acts of cyberbullying in the Italian legal system, and the protection of the victim was left only to the non-specific civil and criminal law provisions. With L. 71/2017, the Italian legislator introduced new provisions aimed at protecting the victims of cyberbullying.

836. The term 'cyberbullying' refers to any form of pressure, aggression, harassment, blackmail, insult, denigration, defamation, identity theft, alteration, unlawful acquisition, manipulation, and unlawful processing of personal data carried out by electronic means to the detriment of minors, as well as the dissemination of online content concerning one or more members of a minor's family with the aim of isolating, attacking, or ridiculing them.[989]

837. According to Article 2 of L. 71/2017, minors over the age of fourteen, as well as parents or persons exercising parental authority over the minor who has been subjected to any of the acts referred to in Article 1, paragraph 2, of L. 71/2017, may file a complaint with the data controller or publisher of the website or social media for the obscuration, removal or blocking of any other personal data of the minor disseminated on the Internet, subject to the preservation of the original data. This is the case even if the conduct referred to in Article 1, paragraph 2, to be expressly identified by means of the relevant URL (Uniform resource locator), has not committed the crime provided for in Article 167 of the Personal Data Protection Code or by other criminal provisions.[990]

838. According to Article 7 of L. 71/2017, until a lawsuit is filed or a complaint is lodged for any of the offences referred to in Articles 594, 595, and 612 of the Criminal Code and Article 167 of the Personal Data Protection Code, committed, by means of the internet, by minors over the age of 14 years against another minor, the warning procedure referred to in Article 8, paragraphs 1 and 2, of Decree-Law 23 February 2009, no. 11, converted with amendments by Law 23 April 2009, no. 38, is applicable. For the purpose of the warning, the territorially competent police commissioner (*questore*) shall summon the minor, together with at least one parent or other person exercising parental authority, for an official reprimand. In case the offender reiterates the conduct, the official reprimand has the effect of increasing the punishment for the offender, in case the crime set forth in Article 612-*bis* of the Criminal Code (stalking) is ascertained, and to make such crime punishable ex officio.

---

989. *See* the GPDP factsheet at the following URL: https://www.garanteprivacy.it/documents/10160/0/Infografica+-+Legge+n+71+2017+sul+cyberbullismo.pdf/ac01f3f3-7104-40dd-b688-d7fab3eb0091?version=3.0. *See also* Art. 1, para. 2, of L. 71/2017.

990. Article 167 of the Personal Data Protection Code and other criminal provisions related to illicit data processing are examined *supra* in Part VIII, Ch. 5, §1.

Selected Bibliography

Alessia Cozzi et al., *Comparative study on the implementation of the ECHR at the national level*, Council of Europe (2016), https://rm.coe.int/16806fbc14.

Enrico Pelino, *Il Regolamento Privacy Europeo* (Luca Bolognini, Enrico Pelino & Camilla Bistrolfi eds, Giuffrè Francis Lefebvre, 2016).

Giulio Bacosi, *Accesso e Privacy: prima e dopo la riforma della l. 241/90: l'emblematico caso INAIL. Spunti su un fantomatico 'diritto' e su un esercizio negletto*, 2 Diritto Procedura Amministrativa 360, (2007).

Gianclaudio Malgieri, *Automated decision-making in the EU Member States: The right to explanation and other 'suitable safeguards' in the national legislations*, 35 Computer Law & Security Review 1 (2019).

Laura Greco, *Il nuovo Rregolamento Europeo sulla privacy e sulla protezione dei dati personali* (Giusella Finocchiaro ed., Zanichelli editore 2017).

Licia Califano, *Trasparenza e privacy nell'evoluzione dell'ordinamento costituzionale*, 31 Giornale di Storia Costituzionale 77 (2016).

Luca Bolognini & Enrico Pelino, *Codice della disciplina Privacy* (Giuffrè Francis Lefebvre, 2019).

Luca Bolognini & Enrico Pelino, *Codice Privacy: tutte le novità del D.lgs. 101/2018* (Giuffré Francis Lefebvre, 2019).

Luana Patti, *Privacy e Libero Mercato Digitale: Convergenza tra Regolazioni e Tutele Individuali nell'Economia Data-Driven* (Luca Bolognini ed., 2021).

Mario Einaudi, *The Constitution of the Italian Republic*, 42 American Political Science Review no. 4 (1948).

Mariafrancesca Cocuccio, *Dimensione 'patrimoniale' del dato personale e tutele risarcitorie*, 1 Diritto di Famiglia e delle Persone 230, (2022).

Michael A. Livingston, Pier Giuseppe Monateri & Francesco Parisi, *The Italian Legal System: An Introduction*, (2nd ed. Stanford Law Books 2015).

Nadia Zorzi Galgano et al., *Persona e Mercato dei Dati. Riflessioni sul GDPR* (1st ed. 2019).

Paolo Balboni, *Video Surveillance and Related Privacy and Data Protection Issues: The Italian Experience* (Sjaak Nouwt, Berend R. de Vries, & Corien Prins (eds.), Reasonable Expectation of Privacy? Eleven Country Reports on Camera Surveillance and Workplace Privacy, T.M.C. Asser Press, The Hague).

Paolo Grossi, *L'invenzione del diritto* (2017).

Paolo Tonini, *Manuale Breve di diritto processuale penale* (Giuffrè Francis Lefebvre, 2022).

Selected Bibliography

Roberto Bin & Giovanni Pitruzzella, *Diritto Costituzionale* (Giappichelli Editore 20th ed. 2019).

Samuel D. Warren & Louis D. Brandeis, *The Right to Privacy*, 4 Harvard Law Review 193, (1890).

Index

The numbers here refer to paragraph numbers.